BH759B
Berkman, Ted.
Lady and the law : Holtzmann
A   ocm01818479

19019200025 6252

 W9-CLB-815

BH759B

Berkman.

The lady and the law.

#AA|

A

June 1976

NO LONGER PROPERTY
OF EASTON AREA
PUBLIC LIBRARY

Books by Ted Berkman

Cast a Giant Shadow
Sabra
To Seize the Passing Dream
The Lady and the Law

SCREENPLAYS

The Squeaker
The Green Cockatoo
Fear Strikes Out

The Lady and the Law

LORSTAN

Fanny Holtzmann

The Lady and the Law

The Remarkable Life
of
Fanny Holtzmann

by Ted Berkman

Little, Brown and Company · Boston · Toronto

EASTON PUBLIC LIBRARY
EASTON PA

BH759B

COPYRIGHT © 1976 by Edward O. Berkman
ALL RIGHTS RESERVED. NO PART OF THIS BOOK MAY BE REPRODUCED
IN ANY FORM OR BY ANY ELECTRONIC OR MECHANICAL MEANS IN-
CLUDING INFORMATION STORAGE AND RETRIEVAL SYSTEMS WITHOUT
PERMISSION IN WRITING FROM THE PUBLISHER, EXCEPT BY A
REVIEWER WHO MAY QUOTE BRIEF PASSAGES IN A REVIEW.

FIRST EDITION
T03/76

The author is grateful to the New York *Times* for excerpts from the article "Notes from the Frenzied Saga of
Gertie," by Moss Hart, as published in its March 2, 1941
issue. Copyright 1941 by The New York Times Company.

Unless otherwise noted, the photographs are from private
collections of the Holtzmann family.

Library of Congress Cataloging in Publication Data
Berkman, Ted.
    The lady and the law.
    Includes index.
    1. Holtzmann, Fanny E.,   1903-   I. Title.
KF373.H616.B4   340'.092'4 [B]   75-33891
    ISBN 0-316-09175-8

Designed by D. Christine Benders
Published simultaneously in Canada
by Little, Brown & Company (Canada) Limited
PRINTED IN THE UNITED STATES OF AMERICA

MAY 0 6 1976

To the memory of
David Marshall Holtzmann

Prologue

SHE WAS an elfin creature, with huge innocent eyes, who stilled the roar of the MGM lion. In her prime, tales of her legal wizardry were whispered from her native Brooklyn to the chancelleries of the Orient. Noel Coward and Eleanor Roosevelt and George Bernard Shaw were her friends; Joseph P. Kennedy her bitter enemy.

She presented many and contradictory images. A sketch by the duchess of Rutland portrayed her as a vision of curly-haired, fawn-eyed defenselessness; to the playwright Moss Hart she was "as helpless as the Bethlehem Steel Company." Louis B. Mayer pronounced her "a female Solomon"; others claimed to detect a closer kinship to Machiavelli.

Interviewers divined the heady romantic aura of a Levantine Dorothy Lamour, although a French journalist opted for Joan Crawford, and a Briton, surveying her from the rear, was reminded of Janet Gaynor. Her sisters, appalled by Fanny's susceptibility to "bargains," branded her "irresponsible"; but the greatest English statesman of the twentieth century, along with his country's leading literary figure, welcomed her counsel.

Fanny Holtzmann won the respect of Justice Felix Frankfurter, and the affectionate envy of his great predecessor, Benjamin Cardozo. She was on the set when Garbo's Hollywood career was launched, and with the Churchills at Chartwell for the intimate family celebration of Sir Winston's eightieth birthday. When the United Nations assembled at San Francisco to create a charter, her saucy, feathered hat bobbed among the diplomatic derbies. She was instrumental in the prewar struggle to extricate Jews from Europe, and later in the creation of the state of Israel.

A night-school lawyer, Fanny for years flitted in the background between New York, London and Hollywood, a mysterious figure famous only among the famous. Then came her "impossible" victory over MGM in the *Rasputin* libel case, a triumph so spectacular it could not be kept out of the headlines. The trial, in which she represented members of the Russian royal family, was a financial disaster for the film company and a landmark in legal history.

The New Yorker profiled Fanny and publishers begged for her full story. She shook them off. Like the "super-lawyers" of the nation's capital, the "Greta Garbo of the Bar" operated most effectively in the shadows, behind the scenes.

Out of inborn idealism and deep personal need, she gloried in *mitzvoth* — the good deeds prescribed by the Talmudic sages. Her mentor in this and other virtues was a gingery, whimsical grandfather, the solace of her youth. From him she acquired integrity, unshakable persistence, and a flexible, imaginative approach to the law. Her sense of loyalty and dry wit were her own.

Faults too were Fanny's, and cut to the same generous measure. She could move in on a situation without invitation and reverse an attitude without warning; embellish a story beyond recognition and continue it beyond the point of endurance. Although generally indifferent to the past, and quick to forgive, she was capable in a few instances of nursing an ancient grievance to the end of time. Her rages, if brief, were awesome; behind her soft femininity was a determination which, driving toward an objective, often gathered up the intensity of a hurricane.

And she was crashingly unlucky in love. The course of carving a lonely path upward in a man's world left some corners of her personality, neglected in the early years, almost untouched. Among the jaded sophisticates of the Coward-Maugham set she remained a naive romantic, a Sleeping Beauty awaiting the release of her dream prince's kiss.

Real princes there were in her life, even a king-in-exile who squired her proudly to London openings. And no shortage of other attentions — from a magnetic film director, a wealthy publisher, a swashbuckling war correspondent — topped off by a mischievous "proposal" to "Fairest Fanny" from ninety-year-old George Bernard Shaw. But the trousseau bought at the time of an early engagement remained in a trunk, and the domestic life she yearned for never came within her grasp.

For too many years, Fanny was all dressed up with a love that had no place to go. Much of it she bestowed on the sprawling family that was at once her burden and her salvation; sometimes in her missionary zeal she thrust upon her targets more than they could absorb. Far more often, her overflowing affection and boundless energy were channeled to constructive ends: rescuing British war orphans and stranded Hong Kong refugees, financing medical research, bringing canvases to flaming life, guiding men and women of genius through the morass of the "practical" world.

How do I know all this? Partly from many hours of research: taped interviews with Fanny and various associates, examination of her voluminous files and correspondence, careful counterchecking against other sources, public and private.

And something more. Fanny and I grew up in closely parallel households; her eldest sister and virtual guardian was my mother. Over a span of five decades, my life and Fanny's have criss-crossed sporadically. At first I saw her through the distorted prism of youth, as a legendary creature soaring above the lotus pools of Hollywood. For a time afterward, swept up in her fiery orbit, I resented the hypnotic power of her personality and had to fight my way free. At long last I perceived the interlocked tenderness and turbulence, fury and humor and compassion that make Fanny Holtzmann unique. Finally I came to see her whole.

Book One

Chapter 1

*T*HE GREEN LINE BUS, ninety minutes out of London, swung off the Hampton Court road at Windsor, rumbled down High Street, and screeched to a halt on the wet pavement before the Town Hall. Fifty yards to the east, scarcely an arrow's flight away, rose the ancient gray battlements of Windsor Castle. The front door of the bus wheezed open, and a lone passenger stepped out into the faint morning drizzle of an English autumn.

The visitor was female and small. Long braids of tightly woven black hair ran tiaralike around her head, a gesture toward mature appearance that only emphasized the youthfulness of her pleasant, fresh-complexioned face. She was dressed against the damp in a knitted woolen pullover and skirt. The heels of her shoes were discreetly low; her neckline as discreetly high, and half hidden by a string of pearls.

She gazed around absently, gloved hand fluttering in a movement of mild confusion. She might, on that peaceable morning in the early 1930's, have been a tour-bound teacher from Ohio — except for her eyes. Gleaming brown, liquid and intense, they were charged with restless energy.

A tall slim man hastened from the ancient portico of the Town Hall across the cobbled road. "Miss Fanny Holtzmann?" He had the quiet, remote good looks of the Russian Romanoffs and an Oxford-tinged accent to match.

The woman smiled. "You must be Prince Andrei." Her voice was low, self-assured.

"Yes. My mother is waiting in the house." He waved vaguely southward. "Shall we take a carriage?"

"How far is it to Frogmore?"

"A trifle over a mile."

"One doesn't like to keep a grand duchess waiting. But it would be nice to stretch my legs after that bus ride. We could walk and still be there in time for lunch."

The prince nodded, looking positively relieved. He had not expected such consideration for the reduced fortunes of the Romanoffs. The Grand Duchess Xenia, a sister of Czar Nicholas II, had brought up her children in gold-encrusted palaces; now, uprooted and dependent on the charity of the British Crown, they counted their expenditures in coppers.

Fanny knew that — and a few other things. She had been summoned to Frogmore on the strength of her reputation as a backstage power in Hollywood because the grand duchess faced a new problem: an American film company had made a movie reportedly impugning the chastity of her daughter, the Princess Youssoupoff. Fanny was to absorb the details over a leisurely lunch.

The menu for the day included an item even more promising: a private meeting with King George V of England, not for social purposes but because of the close family connections linking the various royal houses of Europe, and especially those of England and Russia.

After the slaughter of Czar Nicholas II and his family by the Bolsheviks in 1918, King George, as first cousin of the czar, assumed responsibility for protecting the interests of Nicholas's sister Xenia and the remaining Romanoffs.

The king welcomed his role as adviser. As the ruler of Great Britain and its dominions, he was called upon for his official royal seal of approval a thousand times a year — but for his personal opinion, almost never. He had the paper-tiger authority of a constitutional monarch. By contrast, with Xenia and her family he was the senior cousin, trustee for the estate of her mother, the Dowager Empress Marie, and the benefactor without whom no move could be made. Unless Fanny could pass inspection by the reigning Windsor, she could never represent a Romanoff.

The lanky prince and his diminutive charge walked through the magnificent castle grounds. Just below the private apartments of the sovereign, the prince turned right onto the Long Walk, a broad elm-lined path paved with fine gravel, stretching several miles southward through the heart of Great Windsor Park. After ten minutes of silent trudging, he and Fanny took a road branching left toward Frogmore House.

Suddenly they confronted an enchanting vista. Framed within a sweeping, tree-shaded driveway was a garden paradise of giant oaks and willows, purple rhododendrons and meandering waterways. Beyond the garden stood Frogmore House, a handsome three-story structure fronted by imposing glazed-wood colonnades.

Fanny's eyes roamed over the scene. "This area, I take it, is off limits to most visitors."

The prince smiled. "I believe you are the first American ever to set foot here." Frogmore, he explained, was acquired originally by Henry VIII, and later converted to an ultraprivate royal retreat where members of the ruling house could escape the routine of court duties and the eyes of the curious.

Frogmore had seen a great deal of history: Nell Gwyn gamboling over the lush lawn, Victoria and Albert buried in their vast Romano-German mausoleum, and Nicholas II on a visit in 1894 to his royal cousin. In the midst of the grandeur, Fanny wondered if its sceptered proprietors had ever entertained a dropout from Girls' High School in Brooklyn.

Lunch went quite smoothly, under dazzling chandeliers hanging down from a lofty, gilt-bordered ceiling. If Frogmore was not as coldly sumptuous as the cavernous halls of Windsor, it was still very much a royal residence. The rug on the floor was thick and Persian; the heavy red draperies clustered at the windows reinforced the silence of the ancestral portraits on the walls.

The grand duchess herself melted without effort into this setting. At fifty-eight, she bore traces of a glacial beauty. A small, thin-lipped woman, she wore her hair in a tight bun and met the world with a wary, dignified eye. She carried herself absolutely erect, like a sergeant major on parade.

Fanny was not intimidated. For nine years, since her first trip to England in 1924, she had been welcomed on what inveterate weekenders called the "castle circuit." She had long ago discovered, and reported back to her mother, that the stiffness of the aristocracy usually masked an unbearable shyness ("They grow up in such isolation — nothing but cousins and nannies!").

There were some ladies-in-waiting and small-fry Romanoffs at the table. Fanny promptly engaged the grand duchess's eight-year-old grandson, Mikhail, in a discussion of toy sailboats, drawing on her experience with her own nephews in the Central Park lagoon. Cautious smiles came out of hiding, and in a few minutes the table was alive with conversation.

The grand duchess was the last to yield. There was a brief skirmish about the forms of address to be employed. "How do I address you, Miss Holtzmann? After all, you are a distinguished barrister."

"No, I'm not. I'm an American lawyer. Call me Fanny. But what is the proper salutation for you? I don't suppose it would be 'Mrs. Romanoff'?"

The czar's sister allowed a flicker of amusement to cross her face, and gave up. "Call me Xenia." Later Fanny learned this was a privilege shared only by King George and a handful of others.

After lunch, there was the obligatory tour of the mansion.

Finally, the American guest and assorted Romanoffs settled in the spacious family drawing room, huddled in shawls around the fireplace, as far as possible from the magnificent but drafty bay windows. Here the grand duchess sketched the broad outlines of the Rasputin affair, which culminated in the admitted murder of the wily mystic by her son-in-law, Prince Youssoupoff. Fanny listened attentively, caught up in the intrigues and splendors of imperial St. Petersburg: "It was like having a picture book come to life."

But everybody understood they were only marking time, waiting upon tea and the visitors from Windsor . . .

If the prospect of a chat with a king was appealing to Fanny, she knew from experience that the anticipation would not be less keen on the other side. Above her head danced the nimbus of Hollywood: exotic, mysterious, unattainable as the moon and far more intoxicating. American films were at their zenith in the thirties, a mobile popular theater soothing the sorrows and nurturing the dreams of millions. She was a personage of that august realm, mingling on at least equal terms with Garbo, Goldwyn, Chaplin.

In England, the impact of Hollywood movies transcended class lines. Obviously, the shadows flickering across the screen brought princes into the fantasy-focus of shopgirls. Conversely, they introduced sheltered lordlings to the struggles of ordinary humanity. The British upper classes, traditionally enamored of theater people, embraced not only the new medium but its celebrities. Since the days of Shakespeare, baronets had sought relief from the tedium of each other's company in wicked "players." Now they had a new set of idols. If John Gilbert and Norma Shearer were household gods in Belgravia, how much higher on Olympus was the dainty young lawyer who had arranged the divorce of the first, and conspired to promote the courtship of the second?

Promptly at four the royal party arrived; King George, an old naval hand, observed quarter-deck punctuality. Fanny recognized at once the grave, heavily bearded visage that adorned every English coin from the lowly farthing to the five-pound gold piece. But the king in person seemed less imposing: a frail, smallish man in his late sixties with an open, inquiring and friendly countenance. In his gray lounge suit and high collar, he might, Fanny thought, have stepped out from behind a teller's cage at Barclay's Bank.

The queen walked a step behind the king, trailed by a retinue of male and female attendants. The former Princess Mary of Teck (a German province) was as diffident in manner as her husband, but more redoubtable in appearance. Her ample hourglass figure was encased in a long voluminous black skirt and a neck-high blouse covered with folds of blue and mauve brocade; a toque sat atop her gray head. Fanny could not repress the irreverent thought: "She looks like a good, respectable *Hausmädchen* on her Thursday evening off!"

The grand duchess made the presentations. "Geordie"— her nickname for the king since the stumbling enunciation of nursery days —"this is Miss Holtzmann."

Fanny inclined her head slightly: "How do you do, sir . . . ma'am." Passionately American, she would not permit herself any more humble salutation ("My parents ran away from the monarchies of Europe; I was still reeling from my discovery of democracy in high-school textbooks").

The king settled into an armchair opposite the visitor from overseas and stared. His candid blue eyes reflected mild surprise. "So you are Fanny Holtzmann!"

"Yes, sir. Did you expect something else?"

The royal lips, barely visible under the thick shrubbery of moustache and beard, parted; but no sound came forth. The king was notoriously nervous in the presence of people he considered clever. Finally he spoke: "Are you a barrister or a solicitor?" Under the English legal system, only barristers could try cases in the higher courts.

"I'm a lawyer." Fanny outlined the American legal structure, with its separate branches of state and federal tribunals and their respective appeals courts. She herself, she noted, had been admitted to the bar in California as well as in New York.

The grand duchess leaned toward her cousin. "Fanny," she announced impressively, "has appeared before the United States Supreme Court."

"Really?" The king looked at the grand duchess, then back at Fanny. "But you seem so — forgive me — so very young!"

"One need never apologize for telling a woman she looks young."

George smiled, relaxing visibly. Although he had no pretensions to intellectuality ("I'm a very ordinary fellow," he once confided cheerfully to the Archbishop of Canterbury), he was a thorough, methodical questioner. Were there many women barristers in America, he inquired? Where did they study? And for how many years?

Queen Mary touched her husband's arm. "You're not giving her a chance to answer, Majesty."

"Oh, Fanny doesn't mind . . ." He turned in quick apology. "I didn't mean to be presumptuous, Miss Holtzmann."

"That's all right. All my friends call me Fanny."

King George hesitated. A stickler for proprieties, he decided to compromise on "Miss Fanny." "Tell me, Miss Fanny, where did you study?"

"At Fordham University — the downtown branch, in the heart of the financial district. Our 'campus' was on the twenty-eighth floor."

"But where did you take your dinners?"

"At the Liggett's Drug Store downstairs." Drug stores in New York, Fanny explained, sold sandwiches, books, games; everything in America was geared to accommodating the needs of the upward-striving masses.

And they in turn had built the country. Its giant skyscrapers, like its great factories and wilderness-piercing roads, were the product of immigrant labor: people of many lands uniting in a common effort. "You see, sir, your people — the English — were our aristocrats. They threw open their gates to Europe. Italian newcomers built our railroads. Polish country people settled our farmlands. A Jewish storekeeper named Meyer Guggenheim befriended the copper miners, and became a millionaire. That's American democracy, where anybody can become anything!"

7

Fanny's capsule history, whatever its inadequacies, held her audience enthralled. Finally the king broke the silence. "Why is it nobody ever talks to me of these things? I assure you American diplomats are never so interesting."

Fanny understood his complaint. Ambassadors from Washington always appeared at court in rented cutaways and striped pants. Straining to submerge their gauche New World accents, they stuck to safe subjects like the weather and wound up sounding more British — and duller — than the palace guard.

The king was enjoying his indignation. "How is it they show me films of American jazz and short skirts and bobbed hair — but never anything really informative?"

The queen, startlingly, spoke up. "I suspect it's your beard, Majesty, that frightens away Americans and everyone else."

"But it doesn't frighten Miss Fanny here — does it?" The king tilted his luxuriant Vandyke challengingly in Fanny's direction.

"Certainly not," she said. "I grew up among beards. All my grandfather's cronies, the wise men of the synagogue, had them.'

George looked at Mary in quiet triumph. They were like a homey couple bickering on a radio soap opera, Fanny reflected. Or her own parents.

Instinct told her it was time for a change of subject. "Of course, I speak about America only from my own experience . . . what I picked up crossing the country so often from New York to Hollywood."

The magic word had been spoken. From the hush that fell over the company, it was clear that everything up to now had been prelude. Fanny was not surprised. After all, what did the royal family read? The *New Statesman and Nation*? The *Manchester Guardian*? No. They read the penny papers: Beaverbrook's *Express*, Northcliffe's *Daily Mirror*, the tabloid *Sketch* and *Inquirer*. And she had been on the front pages of all of them since the early 1920's.

It was Queen Mary, more tolerant of new fashions than her husband but normally submerged in wifely obedience, who could not resist the first question: "Did you ever actually *see* Mary Pickford?"

"Of course. I've dined with her a number of times."

"And Mr. Charles Chaplin?"

"He's one of Mary's business colleagues. A delightful, very cultivated man. He's a British subject, you know. Like so many of us, he had to leave home to find acceptance."

Shyly but resolutely the queen plunged ahead. "What about John Gilbert?"

"I represented his wife, Ina Claire, in their divorce — and then John became one of my clients."

"Just what is he like, Miss Holtzmann?"

At this point, as far as Fanny could tell, the royal attendants and ladies-in-waiting stopped breathing. The Delphic oracle itself, about to pronounce judgment on the fate of empires, could not have commanded more attention. But then, what did the Delphic oracle know about John Gilbert, the great screen lover of the twenties? Gilbert's black curly hair and crisp moustache; his swashbuckling costumes as Viennese grenadier, gallant doughboy and intrepid naval commander; his role in *Flesh and the Devil* in which he made torrid love to the enigmatic Garbo — all had melted stonier hearts than that of the sentimental queen from the romantic Wagnerian fatherland.

Fanny chose her words carefully: "Mr. Gilbert is very charming."

That wasn't enough for Queen Mary. "Did you see him up close?"

"Close enough," Fanny was tempted to reply, "to be nearly bowled over by his breath." But she resisted the temptation; even crowned heads were entitled to their illusions.

"We met privately many times," Fanny said. "I wouldn't describe John as the most scintillating of conversationalists. But then, few film people are."

That brought the king's ears up. "What do they talk about?"

"The same things other people do. Their bosses, their complaints — the wonderful new makeup man and the terrible new script."

Did the stars mix with each other socially, the queen wanted to know.

"Oh, no — each studio is a little world unto itself. The MGM people, for instance, all stay within the circle of Mr. Mayer, Louis B. Mayer."

"Rather like ancient dukedoms," suggested the king.

"Are they all enormously wealthy?"

"If they are, they work hard for it." Personally, she added, she found the mechanics of film production enervating. "But when it comes to influencing public opinion — there's nothing like celluloid. Noel Coward's *Cavalcade*, which I happened to bring to Hollywood, changed the worldwide image of Britain."

The king nodded, looking a bit at sea. He was rescued by the arrival of butlers bearing tea trays. Although not served in tall Russian glasses, the tea was flavored with lemon slices, the way Fanny recalled her father's drinking it at home. The accompanying refreshments, too, were familiar: yeast cake, cold cherries, jam, Russian coffee cake with raisins and spices. Fanny reached for a generous slice of coffee cake.

"I say," cried the king admiringly, "you *are* venturesome — eating these rich foreign sweets!"

"You should have seen her at lunch, Geordie," the grand duchess told him. "Enjoying the borscht and *kasha* [buckwheat groats] as if she'd been brought up on it." Fanny did not bother to point out that she had.

King George shook his head. "I never could stand kasha. I remember as a child, when we went to Xenia's — our mothers were sisters, you know — we brought along our own food."

Suddenly the atmosphere was animated, relaxed, as if everyone was glad that the interviewing was over. "I always take along my own food when I'm traveling," offered the queen. "It's such an ordeal to eat what you're not accustomed to."

Fanny nodded. "I can appreciate your point, ma'am. My own family comes from your part of the world. Holtzmann means woodman, of course, in German."

"German bread I miss, especially."

"Still"— Fanny smiled at the grand duchess —"the chef here at Frogmore is excellent. I haven't had such a good meal since I left home."

"Ah"— King George waved his hand in a small deprecatory gesture — "you're a cosmopolitan, Miss Fanny. You would fit in anywhere."

One of the ladies-in-waiting murmured something to the queen, who turned to her husband. "The afternoon is wearing on, Majesty."

"Well, let it, let it."

"But Majesty"— Fanny was reminded of the way physicians' wives in Brooklyn always addressed their husbands as "Doctor"—"don't you think you ought to rest?"

"I can rest this evening," the sovereign grumbled. But he got to his feet. His parting words were an invitation to Fanny to visit Windsor Castle: "We'll give you a good cup of *English* tea."

The grand duchess looked after her cousin with evident satisfaction. Clearly "Geordie" would not stand in the way. "You must stay with us overnight, Fanny. We shall have to make plans."

"Next time, perhaps. I have an appointment in town." The appointment was a hasty invention, inspired by Fanny's recollection of her comfortable bathroom at the Savoy Hotel. Deplorable plumbing was almost a badge of aristocracy — the higher the rank, the more primitive the facilities — and Frogmore was a full-fledged royal residence. It had exactly one toilet, fitted out in a manner that suggested a stubborn devotion to the sixteenth century.

Besides, she warned Xenia, the *Rasputin* case would not be settled overnight. Given MGM's tremendous resources in money and manpower, it was likely to be a long, complex affair, beset with problems and disappointments.

The grand duchess was undismayed. "It is quite strange, but since your arrival I have felt perfect confidence." She walked with Fanny to the waiting hansom. "My dear, I foresee a great victory."

Fanny, brown eyes glinting in the early twilight, gazed at her intently. "From your mouth," she sighed, "into God's ears."

The grand duchess drew back, astonished and amused. "What a pungent expression, Fanny! Where on earth did you get it?"

"Where I got practically everything. From my grandfather."

Chapter 2

*I*N A WAY, it was true. Everything for Fanny began with Zaida. He it was who softened her sorrows, encouraged her dreams, and through his unquenchable good humor eased the nightmare of her childhood.

Zaida was a picturesque patriarch snatched in old age out of the East European ghetto. He was brought to America in his seventies as a gesture of atonement by a guilt-ridden daughter, Fanny's mother. It was expected that he would live out his remaining few years in pious meditation and then slip into oblivion.

Instead, the New World gave Zaida a new life. He became the revered sage of the Brownsville community in Brooklyn, sought after as the dispenser of holy benedictions, arbiter of business disputes, presiding *macher* (dignitary) at graduation ceremonies and campaign rallies. He lived to the age of ninety-six, and his funeral procession was interminable: every few blocks it was joined by a new corps of mourners from one of the numerous Talmud Torahs (Hebrew schools) he had founded.

Most importantly, he was indispensable to Fanny — as she was to him. Their firm alliance was the mainstay of their lives.

Fanny's mother and father, Henry and Theresa Holtzmann, had come to the United States in the late 1880's after an impetuous courtship that mildly scandalized their neighbors in the eastern reaches of the Austro-Hungarian Empire. Theresa, the reigning local beauty, had been engaged to Henry's best friend until she met Henry, a dimpled young scholar overflowing with verses from Heine, Schiller and his own pen.

It was a wildly impractical match. Theresa was the first of seven children to survive, and had been spoiled to proportion: lacy bonnets to dramatize her golden hair and violet eyes, custom-made gowns to set off her voluptuous figure, a *gymnasium* education in Vienna (equivalent to junior college in America) that in her day was rare for women and almost unheard of for Jewesses. Queenly privilege — not responsibility — was her heritage. As for Henry, he was a professional dreamer, a wandering philosopher-journalist absorbed in the worship of beauty and the riddles of the universe. From boyhood he had been trained in Hebrew studies. Unhappy when, after his father's early death, his mother remarried, he had moved into his grandfather's home and buried himself in books, teaching himself English and German. He was as ill equipped to support a family as Theresa was to rear one.

Two years later they set out together, gentle round-faced poet and imperious teen-age bride, for America, where the children of oppressed minorities could throw off the shackles of the ghetto and grow in the sunlight.

It turned out to be not quite that simple. Henry and Theresa were mere specks in the human tide flooding across the Atlantic, nearly a million persons a year, from Eastern and Southeastern Europe. They settled on the lower East Side of Manhattan.

Henry, untrained in industry but too proud to let his wife work, took what he could get. It wasn't much. During their first winter in New York, they prayed for snow. A heavy snowfall could mean a whole dollar's pay for a day of shoveling — if one were in line early enough. To make sure that he was, Henry rose at three in the morning and walked alone in the darkness down to City Hall.

Gradually, he made friends who provided an occasional writing or teaching chore: for the Yiddish daily *Tageblatt*, Lillian Wald's newly founded Henry Street Settlement, the Educational Alliance on East Broadway. At Shenkman's Restaurant, a newspaperman's hangout nearby, he became friendly with Jacob Riis, then a crusading columnist for the *Evening Sun*, and was able to pick up a few dollars now and then for story tips.

But all this yielded only a sporadic income, and by now the Holtzmanns were a family. Bertha had been born, then Edward, known as Eddie. An older boy, Jacob, had been left behind in Europe and was still being cared for by Theresa's parents; a fourth child was on the way.

Desperate, Henry enrolled as an apprentice in the hatter's trade, where a man who survived the sulfurous fumes might ultimately earn thirty-five dollars a week. On his second morning, lunging after a slippery felt, he thrust his arm up to the elbow in a boiling vat; he was hospitalized with third-degree burns — then fired.

Salvation came through Lillian Wald, who needed a full-time helper to instruct immigrants in English and cushion them to the shocks of an unfamiliar environment.

His new job — and a rare burst of boldness — brought Fanny's father to the attention of Theodore Roosevelt. The settlement was concerned with improving living conditions on the lower East Side. So when energetic young Teddy, fresh from reformist triumphs in the United States Civil Service Commission, took over as the police commissioner of

New York City in 1895, Henry asked his friend Jacob Riis to arrange an introduction.

TR — for whom the present writer is nicknamed — took an immediate fancy to the erudite Henry. The future president had been educated largely in Germany, and was struck by Henry's knowledge of German literature. Thus encouraged, Henry took the commissioner on a tour of the tenements, pointing out substandard facilities and in particular the hazards created by basement bakeries. Roosevelt promised intervention by City Hall — and delivered it.

On quite another level, Henry opened up Jewish intellectual life to the eyes of the fascinated police commissioner. During his tenement visits, Roosevelt had remarked on the music and warmth that brightened the most modest immigrant households. Now Henry presented to him the creative elite of the district: publishers, composers, and the poet Naftali Imber, who wrote the words to *Hatikvah*, the Jewish national anthem. Often, after midnight, Roosevelt and Henry joined the freewheeling debaters gathered over coffee at Shenkman's. The commissioner came to Henry's home to pat little Bertha on the head; Henry made the first of many visits to Roosevelt's rambling mansion on Sagamore Hill.

They were friends, the burly, walrus-moustached ex-rancher and the gentle scholar. They would remain friends through the historic decade and a half to come, with important consequences for all of the Holtzmann family, not least among them Fanny.

It was through Roosevelt's friend Willard Curtis that Henry made his move to Brooklyn. A fanatic nature lover, he had been increasingly uncomfortable in the treeless concrete of the East Side.

Curtis whisked Henry by private carriage across the Brooklyn Bridge and deep into East New York. Henry was enchanted by the rolling fields, barely sprinkled with large estates. Before the day was over, he decided that he would not only settle his own family in Brooklyn, but would encourage a mass exodus to these greener pastures.

He had no trouble enlisting recruits. Rents in Brooklyn averaged three dollars a month per room — a fraction of the rate in the congested, vermin-spawning lower East Side. At the offices of the Hebrew Sheltering and Immigrant Aid Society (the future HIAS), he diverted hundreds of anxious newcomers eastward. Most headed for Brownsville, a triangle bounded by Atlantic, Williams and East New York avenues; it had been carved out of two farm properties in 1859 by a Connecticut real estate entrepreneur and originally named "Brown's Village."

Henry himself opted for Eastern Parkway, a few blocks to the northwest. This was the Champs-Elysées of Brooklyn, a wide boulevard lined with giant elms, already the preferred street of the immigrant professional class: doctors, lawyers, educators. He chose a generously designed, three-story brown brick house near Saratoga Avenue, with privet hedges sheltering the entrance, and an ample garden in the rear overlooked by a cluster of porches. Although for the next twenty years he would be half drowned in mortgage payments, he never regretted the decision.

When Henry moved in, the values of the Old World still prevailed. The family, large and closely knit, was the core of existence. Scarcely less cohesive — almost an extension of the home — was the wider community. What happened to a neighbor was everybody's business. If this involved some sacrifice of privacy, it also meant that nobody was ever abandoned; the better-off took responsibility for the poor.

Henry had qualified as a notary public on the East Side. Now, with the confidence born of his experience with various immigrant-aid institutions there, he hung out two shingles: "Henry Holtzmann — Notary Public — Legal Papers Drawn," and "The Henry Holtzmann Tutoring School." Meantime he hustled over to the nearest public school and was rewarded with an appointment as a substitute teacher, conducting night classes.

Of greater significance for the family's future, he was hired by the Hebrew Educational Society to prepare immigrants for citizenship. He went at the task energetically, beating the drum not only for democracy ("Forget about Karl Marx and destruction. Here, if you study you can become anything. And what Jew doesn't know how to study?"), but for the particular brand of Republican liberalism espoused by his friend Theodore Roosevelt.

Tammany politicians complained that Henry was subverting the innocent — not to mention draining off possible Democratic votes. The matter was appealed to Albany, where the resident governor — that same Theodore Roosevelt — ruled that Henry was "simply educating new Americans about the party system."

Henry was quietly acquiring influence, if not capital. He was elected secretary of his local lodge, the Young Friends. Thanks to his contacts at Borough Hall, in the school system, and in real estate circles, he knew the man to see if a storekeeper needed a license or an immigrant was having trouble with his citizenship papers.

Meanwhile, like his neighbors, he put his heart into his home. He acquired a piano, the first of three (each was carted off for nonpayment of installments, only to be replaced by another, more elegant one), and set aside quarters on the ground floor as the family music room, where the girls could practice piano and the boys slash away on squeaky violins. Directly above, a large library of English-language classics reinforced the themes of culture and self-improvement. The Holtzmann house, whatever the strains and improvisations imposed by economics, was a comfortable place to live in, with a hammock swinging gently on the lower porch and gaily painted rocking chairs overhead. Flowers, a vegetable patch and ultimately a summerhouse filled the garden.

On Friday nights, "Papa Henry" welcomed the Sabbath, singing loud and clear, as "Mama" blessed the candles. In general, however, the

Holtzmanns were less concerned with the rituals of their religion than with its ethical teachings. Fanny grew up in a setting where Judaism was essentially a philosophical system, a guide to daily behavior. Secondarily, the Jews were a tribe, indissolubly bound together not only by the Torah but by centuries of persecution. One could enjoy friends and colleagues outside the faith — among Henry's own closest cronies was Father Pacelli of the Canarsie parish — but one did not marry a Gentile lest the tenuous stream of continuity be diluted and finally washed away. That was an unspoken covenant with the past and the future.

Part of Henry's credo, from early youth, was Zionism. Although his own family was now settled in the New World, he did not slacken in his conviction that a Jewish homeland was a necessity, if only to receive the millions still under the whip in czarist Russia. He became the first president in Brooklyn of Hoveve Zion, and the correspondent in America for Theodor Herzl's Viennese newspaper, *Die Deutsche Welt*.

If Henry, smiling benignly under a neat blond moustache, provided the moral tone for the menage, it was Theresa who supplied its earthly underpinnings. She was preeminently a realist: practical, sharply perceptive. Theresa drew intuitive judgments from the way people looked, rather than what they said. She always had a dollar or two hidden away for emergencies, and she knew exactly how much tea Henry could consume without inviting insomnia.

She also knew which were the prettiest girls among his pupils, and ever the prima donna, accused him of gallantries not in the curriculum. Henry, nettled, replied in kind. Their mutual jealousy was to enliven more than half a century of marriage.

Such was the household in which Fanny Holtzmann arrived at the turn of the century, the first of Henry and Theresa's children to be born in Brooklyn. Her appearance was more of an interruption, to be patiently endured, than a cause for celebration. It could not have been more ill timed. Henry's fortunes, chronically erratic, were in a downward phase. Theresa was carrying the burden of two sick children. Eddie, born in 1891, had undergone a siege of measles at the age of four, and from then on never knew a healthy day. He fell victim to so-called "hip disease," which would later be diagnosed as polio. Twice a week, throughout the rest of the decade, Theresa hoisted the child, encased in a sixty-pound plaster cast, onto her back and climbed the steep steps of the elevated train line for the long trip from Brownsville to St. Luke's Hospital in uptown Manhattan.

The second Holtzmann girl, Clara, entered the world so tiny and feeble she was not expected to survive. Henry had been laid off at the hat factory, and not yet rescued by Lillian Wald. Theresa, too prideful to go on the dole, placed the child in a New Jersey home for infants. When she came to call for Clara months later, she was greeted by a gloomy shake of the head: "Clara Holtzmann is dead."

Theresa pushed her way through to the nursery, where she found Clara immobile on a rocking horse, anemic but alive. At the age of two, Clara was barely beginning to speak, susceptible to every passing ailment — and, with her pale delicate complexion, inevitably installed as her father's "Princess."

When Fanny joined the brood a couple of years later, there was simply no emotional niche open for her. She became the charge of thirteen-year-old Bertha, already loaded down with schoolwork, shopping chores, and dressing Eddie's wounds. Fanny was placed in a makeshift crib — actually the boxlike cover of a sewing machine — and left to herself. Whenever the overworked Bertha remembered, Fanny got a scrubbing and a meal.

Somehow emerging from infancy plump and rosy-cheeked, she was a remarkably placid child, uncomplaining when disregarded, glowing with happiness when shown the slightest attention. But when she sat alone in some out-of-the-way nook, a dark-haired, gypsy-eyed Cinderella, her hand went automatically to her mouth. And often she lay awake at night, gaze fixed anxiously on the ceiling. Curiously, her earliest happy memory was of a severe case of measles at five — because the handsome mustachioed family physician, Dr. Israel Kaufman, was in constant attendance.

By the time Fanny was ready for school, there were two more little sisters — Selema and Stella — and also her big brother Jacob ("Jack"), brought over belatedly from Europe. Of the family's seven students enrolled in grade school, only one was an unmitigated disaster: Fanny.

Her special enemy was long division (thirty years later, she was still unable to compute for reporters the payments owed by MGM for the *Rasputin* judgment). Poor in geography, only faintly redeemed by an aptitude for English, she was invariably the class dunce, consigned to permanent occupation of the last row, last seat. Strangely enough, Fanny did not seem to mind her exile. She sat quietly in her corner of shame, eyes glued as if in a trance on the textbook before her. Between its covers, however, there was usually a novel from Henry Holtzmann's library: George Eliot, Thackeray, Victor Hugo, Dickens, Sir Walter Scott. Mass instruction, the litany of classroom recital, bored her; in the world of private imagination she was happy.

Her only terror came at the end of the month, when the official report card inexorably recorded her disgrace. The best she could hope for was C-C-C — in effort, proficiency and conduct. The close of each term saw Fanny in a desperate push to get over the top, but she could never be sure of promotion until the final week. Often there was a frantic face-saving conference between Theresa and the teacher before the delinquent pulled through, sometimes by way of a special examination in September.

Nor was her incompetence confined to studies. Clara, Stella and Selema were appearing together in community dance recitals. Bertha had been declaiming poetry in German for years, and returning a profit to the family for her piano lessons (she paid fifty cents an hour, and promptly relayed the instruction to the neighbors' children at twenty-five cents a head). Only Fanny could not memorize a quatrain, keep track of a rhythm, coordinate her arm and leg movements.

At nine, she was thrown out of the children's dance line at school. To spare her from total humiliation, she was given a poem to recite — and developed a sore throat. When a playmate had a birthday party, Fanny spilled her milk over the tablecloth. She was sent home weeping, the playmate's complaint ringing in her ears: "You can always count on Fanny to spoil a party."

By this time, the financial pressures on Henry were easing. His teaching income was being supplemented by an occasional commission in real estate; his eldest children were beginning to bring home money. Keenly conscious of his status as a community leader, Henry didn't save anything; he simply lived better. The Holtzmanns were first to have electricity installed, first with a grand piano, an automobile, a telephone (the neighbors proudly printed up calling cards — listing Henry's number). Theresa hired an immigrant girl to help with the children and displayed her magnolia shrubs at the borough garden show.

The more the other girls flourished under these conditions, the more Fanny lagged. To her father's immense chagrin, she capped her academic failures by being dismissed even from Sunday School at the Hebrew Educational Society.

Clara, by contrast, lived in an exalted special world. At the top of her class in spelling, archery and ballet, she had her dresses custom-made and took private piano lessons from the famous Professor Ostermeyer. Stella, a saucy, golden blonde, made the most of a formidable musical talent to elbow her way into the limelight; before reaching her teens, she had a job in the local movie house improvising keyboard accompaniments to the adventures of Chaplin and Mary Pickford. Slim, fair-haired Selema got what she wanted by pleading headaches or homework. Bertha bustled about importantly, secure in her role of deputy mother.

Only Fanny was defenseless and alone, the inept goose of a brilliant household. To her fell the old clothes and odd jobs that nobody else wanted. Someone hung a Yiddish colloquialism on the most obliging of Henry Holtzmann's daughters: *"Alleh lecher farshtopped mehn mit Fanny"* — Every leftover chore is piled onto Fanny."

Fanny found comfort for a time in her eldest brother, Jack. Since his arrival in America at the age of nine, a shy, gawky child without a word of English, Jack had made phenomenal progress. Under his father's tutelage, he blazed through the elementary grades and high school in a few years, and passed his state Regents' exams. College was not then a prerequisite to law school. Two years later, after getting his law degree, he was established as the partner of Congressman Charles B. Law, and had successfully defended a man on trial for murder. Already his exploits had won the attention of Theodore Roosevelt, then in his first elected term as President, and brought him an invitation to lunch at the White House.

Fanny was fascinated by Jack's rapid rise. The practice of law had always been part of the atmosphere around the Holtzmann house: for as far back as anyone could remember, typewriters had been clacking away in the parlor at contracts, citizenship applications, leases.

School, conversely, was more than ever disenchanting. Sometimes Fanny, arriving bleary-eyed and late after reading past midnight, found it hardly worth the trouble to sit through a day of classes, so she wandered off downtown instead. These odysseys tended to wind up in municipal court, where Jack usually had a case on the calendar.

The dramas unfolding there — family quarrels, dispossess actions, insurance claims — were infinitely more interesting to Fanny than square-root tables. And she was thrilled by her big brother's mastery of courtroom technique, the brisk intuitive mind, so much like Theresa's, that thrust to the heart of a problem. Jack was slim, carefully tailored, distinguished-looking, the perfect father-substitute for a neglected, worshipful preadolescent. Fanny began volunteering her services for running messages and performing minor clerical tasks.

Jack welcomed the assistance. He loved to sleep late, and it was convenient to have someone who would report gravely to the judge that Mr. Holtzmann was tied up on an important matter. In return, he introduced the little girl to legal procedures, tolerated her presence at his elbow when he was conducting a title search, and let her riffle through his copies of the *Law Journal*.

But he by no means reciprocated her idolization. Bent on affirming his ascendancy among the children, eager for the applause of a mother preoccupied with more pressing concerns, he had appointed himself guardian of the family's lofty academic standards. Fanny's defections as a student were punished with harsh efficiency.

Wounded and bewildered, Fanny retreated into herself. At this juncture, fate sent her Zaida.

The family had been in Brooklyn for a decade. The second Holtzmann son, Eddie, had been outstripping his classmates at school despite the pain and interruptions of frequent surgery. On the verge of his scheduled entry into Cornell as a scholarship student, he died following surgery, the victim of an anesthesia failure.

Theresa was inconsolable. She refused to hear medical explanations. Eddie's death, she insisted, was the retribution visited upon a wicked daughter: she had broken off with her elderly father in Europe after a series of disputes that had begun with her marriage. Subsequently, her mother died.

After several weeks of solitary brooding, Theresa announced suddenly that she was going back to join the widower. "I am his only child. I must comfort his remaining days. Otherwise God will take away all of our family, one by one."

It was obvious to Henry that she meant it. He had to do something to head her off. Perhaps his political contacts would help; his friend Theodore Roosevelt had been in office as president since 1901.

He took a train for Washington and met with White House secretary William Loeb, whose son would become publisher of the controversial Manchester (N.H.) *Union Leader*. Five minutes after Henry had outlined his problem, Loeb was on the telephone to Elihu Root, the secretary of state. Two hours later an urgent cable was en route to the American minister in Vienna, instructing him to make immediate arrangements for the transfer of Henry Holtzmann's father-in-law, Rabbi Hirsch Bornfeld, from the tiny village of Rohatyn to New York.

The arrival in Rohatyn of frock-coated foreigners in a smart carriage, inquiring after Hirsch Bornfeld, brought all business to a halt. The population poured into the street, everybody talking at once. "Rabbi Hirsch" was a well-known figure in town, something between a celebrity and a character. Nephew and protégé of the childless Itzik Bornfeld, who had been steward for the estate of the local *Graf*, Hirsch was himself the first Jewish postmaster of the district. He held a certificate in Talmudic studies. He was also a considerable wheeler-dealer and a flamboyant storyteller.

When the strangers disappeared into the burgomaster's office, speculation split along predictable lines. A little boy reported mention of a trip to America, but this was dismissed as childish fantasy. A small pro-Bornfeld faction predicted new honors for their learned and ebullient champion. The majority view was less flattering: "The law has caught up with Rabbi Hirsch. He must have told one story too many about his adventures in Constantinople and Trieste." The cantor of the synagogue, a notorious gloom-spreader, saw the ruin of the village: "Oy, that rascal! He's got mixed up in some international plot, and we Jews will all suffer for it."

The subject of these conjectures, meanwhile, was strolling calmly home from *shul* (synagogue), a tall, spare man whose small-boned patrician features were half-hidden behind a cascading white beard. His shoulders were slightly bent, but his firm step and the piercing glance of his light-blue eyes belied his seventy-seven years.

Rounding the corner, the old man found himself confronted by a group of town officials. An excited aide to the burgomaster spluttered forth the news: a summons to Hirsch from across the seas — instructions from the president of the United States — two official emissaries in a black carriage — a steamship waiting —

It did not take the old man long to unravel the message — or to accept this extraordinary treatment as his due. The bent shoulders snapped back, a triumphant gleam came into the keen blue eyes. "Fetch my *shab-*

bath clothes from the house," he commanded an onlooker. "And my toilet articles. I already have my prayer book."

A battered suitcase materialized from a neighbor. Passenger and baggage were swallowed up by the carriage, and Hirsch Bornfeld departed forever from Rohatyn, leaving behind a trail of dust and a swarm of rumors that would not be put to rest for twenty-five years.

The ministry in Vienna had booked a top-deck cabin for their VIP aboard the sumptuous *Kaiser Wilhelm Grosse,* poised at Hamburg for a crack at the transatlantic crossing record (for the next two years, Henry Holtzmann would be making payments on his father-in-law's luxurious passage). At the request of the ministry, sailing was delayed for more than an hour while their Important Personage was being rushed from Vienna to the dock, thereby conferring upon Herr Bornfeld an instant prestige which he did not relinquish throughout the voyage — or thereafter.

Invited to the captain's table on the first night out, the old man cut an impressive figure in his long black robe and lustrous white beard. Hirsch's intricately designed, multicolored skullcap was of papal splendor. When he pronounced a benediction before the meal, rolling his tongue with sonorous authority over the strange Hebrew phrases, the celebrities around the table were awed and enchanted.

Because the menu in first class did not conform to orthodox dietary laws, special kosher food for "the Rabbi" was ordered from the steerage kitchen, which was providing meals for the thousands of Jewish immigrants below deck. The immigrants, learning that there was a Chasidic Holy Man aboard, petitioned the captain to send their distinguished coreligionist below. Once a day, Hirsch made a ceremonial descent by iron staircase to conduct services.

Among the passengers were several stars of the Metropolitan Opera Company, including Enrico Caruso and the renowned lyric coloratura Marcella Sembrich. Mme. Sembrich, like Hirsch, had been born in Galicia. She walked the deck with the Holy Man, took comfort from his blessing, and before the end of the voyage invited him to be her guest at the next performance of *Lucia di Lammermoor,* for which she had created the title role at the Metropolitan. (Hirsch later claimed that he had responded with a counterinvitation for her to catch him at the altar in Brooklyn.)

The *Wilhelm Grosse did* break the crossing record, with much attendant publicity. Among the reporters and officials going down to quarantine to meet her by coast guard cutter were Henry Holtzmann and Jack, who half-expected to find old Hirsch laid out on a stretcher, green with seasickness. His cabin was deserted. Long-faced, Jack suggested they try the infirmary.

News photographers, meanwhile, were clambering over the deck, snapping pictures at the rail of J. P. Morgan, Caruso, Mme. Sembrich — and, by unanimous instinct, the fine-looking white-haired patriarch, vaguely resembling the poet John Greenleaf Whittier, who mingled freely with the captain's party.

In years to come, Hirsch Bornfeld's trip would be embedded in Brooklyn folklore, including his own summation of how he came to America: "I simply rolled up my trousers and waded across the ocean."

If Hirsch's arrival gladdened the hearts of the ship news photographers, it was regarded with less enthusiasm by his daughter. Theresa had been told only that "a surprise" was on the way, with hints that it was someone from the old country. She was furious that Henry had made such a serious move without consulting her. It was one thing to indulge in sentimental yearning for a presumably helpless old man; it was another to be confronted every day by a vigorous patriarch of the same imperious stamp as herself.

Her family might welcome the newcomer as "Zaida," the traditional Yiddish endearment for elderly grandfather; to Theresa he was "a meddlesome old busybody" who checked out every plate of china to see if it was *milchedig* or *flayshedig* (for dairy or meat dishes), stuck his beard into her oven, and interfered with the disciplining of her children.

To get Zaida out of her kitchen, she set up private quarters for him in the basement: a bedroom-parlor in what had been the laundry and sewing room, and a kitchen in the back facing the garden, where he could observe his own dietary laws. This too had its difficulties. Zaida was a gregarious man. The friends who came to share a smoke with him invariably took the short route from the gate, which led directly across Theresa's precious flower bed. Zaida and his daughter were in a state of undeclared war.

His grandchildren, for the most part, were not long in picking up their mother's cue; they considered Zaida old-fashioned, eccentric, dimly disreputable. Of all the household, Fanny alone cast a tolerant eye on him. The other children had their own sources of emotional sustenance; even the two youngest of Theresa's brood, Rita and three-year-old David, enjoyed the special attentions of babyhood. Only Fanny was a fifth wheel who didn't fit anywhere. Zaida too was an outcast; theirs was a natural alliance.

It started with Fanny taking over in Zaida's kitchen, to prepare the heavy meats and gravies of Central Europe. By the age of ten, she had filled in so often in the kitchen that with guidance she could assemble an eight-course meal. Zaida was delighted by the windfall; Fanny was equally pleased at having someone to take care of. Zaida provided an outlet for the maternal yearnings of a little girl who had never had a doll of her own.

Soon she was combing the old man's hair, trimming his elegant beard, fetching tea for his larder and tobacco for his pipe. Zaida in turn told her tales of the old country: the great castles he had visited, the marvelous exploits of his Uncle Itzik who, from Zaida's account, practically ran the Austro-Hungarian Empire — with, of course, a dexterous assist here and there from his clever nephew. Tapping his temple with his forefinger, he murmured, "What this head has figured out!"

Fanny drank it all in hungrily. Here was someone who had lived in the world, whose horizons were not bounded by schoolrooms and diapers; who, because he had a sense of many yesterdays, could put in perspective the petty tribulations of today. He listened, sheltered, comforted her in a way that her parents could not. As for Zaida, he had lost all but one of his own children; there was ample room in his heart for this adoring granddaughter with her quick intelligence and huge, serious brown eyes.

Gradually, a tacit contract between them evolved: she would look after his physical needs; he would superintend her social and spiritual development.

His initial service was on an earthier level. Fanny was still bringing home the worst grades in the family. To spare her the monthly ordeal of confrontation by Jack and her father, Zaida picked up her report card and scribbled in the name of his son-in-law. He got away with it twice before the maneuver was discovered. The ensuing cries of "Forger!" confirmed their lowly estate but cemented the partnership.

With a physical base established, Zaida felt the need to expand his activities. He was, after all, not even eighty years old (to skeptics who challenged this figure he snapped "Were you at my *briss* [circumcision]?"); he had his Chasidic rabbinical certificate, his reputation as a newspaper celebrity — and above all, his *chutzpa.**

He started neighborhood *yeshivas* — Talmudic study centers — and simultaneously announced his availability for weddings, Bar Mitzvas, graduations and other ceremonial occasions. Since none of the local rabbis could match his baronial manner, his services were highly prized. It was Fanny's cherished responsibility to fit Zaida out every morning in his secondhand "working clothes": Prince Albert coat, black pants and towering stovepipe.

Rabbi Hirsch was also much in demand among the neighborhood widows, who vied for the honor of having him pronounce the premeal *Kiddush* at their Sabbath tables. Zaida went impartially from one to the next, covering the circuit like a district judge. Several of the older ladies, it was said, would have welcomed a more permanent arrangement, but Zaida saw no point in spoiling a good thing: "I get my fresh-baked *challa* [fine white bread] from Mrs. Weinstein, a good schnapps at Mrs. Gordon's — why should I give that up for one woman?" Besides, he had plans — and a busy man needed his freedom.

The plans were for politics. In the immigrant community, synagogue affairs were intertwined with party alignments. Newcomers needed

* "Brazen assurance" comes close to conveying the meaning. Leo Rosten offers as the "classic" definition "that quality enshrined in a man who, having killed his mother and father, throws himself on the mercy of the court because he is an orphan" (*The Joys of Yiddish*, p. 92).

guidance. It was a short step from the prayer altar to the voting booth — and the former postmaster had politicking in his blood. Zaida brushed up his English at night school, signed a registration card, and stepped forth as the newest activist for the GOP. He liked the "change-but-don't-destroy" liberalism of Teddy Roosevelt's party. It also happened to be the group that held power in Brownsville, where his son-in-law had a firm foothold.

When newcomers at one of his *yeshivas* had problems getting settled, Zaida steered them to Henry Holtzmann's classes in Americanization. They generally emerged as registered Republicans. At Rabbi Hirsch's Sabbath services, congregants noted that the call to *aliyah* — the honor of reading a portion of the Law at the altar — never seemed to fall to Democrats.

As his "constituency" grew, Zaida encouraged them to visit him at home. There, if necessary, he condescended to discuss their business in Yiddish. He much preferred his "aristocratic" German; but he was an adaptable man who could shift tongues in midsentence. Ten-year-old Fanny, unofficial hostess at these gatherings, listened absorbedly as her grandfather flipped the dials of his mind from English to the colloquial Yiddish to Biblical Hebrew. Unconsciously she absorbed a technique that would serve her well in days to come. Meanwhile, she received the visitors who threaded their way through Theresa's garden, made them comfortable in rocking chairs borrowed from upstairs, and kept their glasses filled with tea, which they filtered through a sugar cube held between the teeth.

Inevitably, Zaida's proximity to his daughter's garden provoked a crisis. One September morning Theresa came downstairs to put the final touches on her prize dahlias, scheduled for entry the following week in the Botanical Garden flower show. She found two followers of Rabbi Hirsch lustily hammering stakes into the ground. They were building a hut for the harvest holiday of Succoth — over the remains of her trampled dahlias. Theresa shrieked and fainted.

Zaida, not to be outdone in histrionics, took to his bed and sent Fanny out to inform the community that his family's heartlessness had brought him to the point of death. Tongues clucked in sympathy. Zaida, munching sponge cake in his room, had won at least a standoff.

By now, the old man and his granddaughter were inseparable. They made a frequent, if unlikely, twosome at the theater. Spare tickets were generally floating around the house: for the Brooklyn Academy of Music, where Henry held a subscription; for the Yiddish Theater on the lower East Side, which he disliked but as a civic leader felt obliged to support; for various entertainments on Broadway where admirers of Bertha had contacts. There were also movie passes on Sunday from the Schenck brothers, future moguls of MGM, who lived a few doors away and owned the Liberty Theater nearby.

Zaida's tastes were catholic — he liked any show that was free, and was equally pleased at the prospect of a ballet or an Indian shootout. They saw a Yiddish *King Lear*, in which Zaida was delighted by Boris Thomashefsky's performance but less impressed with the plot. "It's all in the Book of Job," he told Fanny. "I can pick up my Bible and read about all the *tsouris* [suffering] I want."

One fall day, during a post matinée stroll in Central Park, Zaida was ladling out "memories" of his glorious past. In accordance with his credo —"Never tell a lie, but don't be modest about admitting you know somebody"— he was discoursing on the close bonds between himself, Uncle Itzik and the emperor Franz Josef, and on the huge mansion he had occupied in Rohatyn. "Oh, it was big, very very big."

"*How* big?" demanded Fanny.

They were approaching the Metropolitan Museum. She pointed: "As big as *that*?"

Zaida scarcely blinked an eye. "Bigger."

The sheer enormity of his conceits was endearing. It would be three decades before Fanny would again encounter, in her bristling dialogues with George Bernard Shaw, anything like it.

A special treat for Fanny was to accompany Zaida on his Sunday-morning safari along Belmont Avenue. This was a noisy, crowded thoroughfare lined with shopping stalls and pushcarts. The ostensible purpose of the weekly expeditions was to round up food and sundries for the household; Fanny and Sura, the family cook, carried roomy shopping bags. But the real object was for Zaida to patrol his political domain, throwing in a good word among the immigrant tradesmen for the GOP and the family: "You didn't become a citizen yet? Go see my son-in-law. Don't worry, you become a good Republican, the party will look after you!"

Although Sura chose the vegetables, it was Zaida who held the purse strings. Confronted with a tradesman of dubious political leanings, Zaida would allow Sura to commence the bargaining:

"How much for the head of lettuce?"

"Well, it's my last one, I'll make you a bargain: six cents."

"I'll give you three."

"Three! Not to my own mother!"

"Ah, you never had a mother."

Fanny watched; this was better than a Broadway show.

At the moment of total impasse, as the insults were pyramiding, Zaida would step in magnanimously: "Enough, Moshe, we'll pay your price." The relieved merchant was his friend for life, already nodding at the homily that was on the way: "Take advantage, Moshe, send your children to school, they should have the education you didn't get. And join the right party, that will look after you."

The bargaining fever that Fanny picked up on Belmont Avenue and

Fanny in the garden at Eastern Parkway with her adored Zaida

the insights into human motivation gained there were a permanent part of her education.

But Zaida exercised his most important influence on Fanny in less tangible areas: ethics, justice, the relationship of man to God and to his neighbor. Underneath, Zaida the showman was a philosopher-mystic; and it was to Fanny alone that the old man revealed this precious core.

Zaida was, after all, a trained scholar, steeped in the writings and the rich oral tradition of his people. For the Jews of Eastern Europe, as elsewhere in the Diaspora, this tradition had been the binding force in survival. Oppressed by Crusader, landowner and Cossack, the Jews had turned inward, finding strength and consolation in their special compact with the Lord. It was for breaking that compact that the early Jews, according to the sages, had been punished with exile; the return to religion therefore had a fanatical intensity. Every aspect of living had its own protective prayer; every man and woman a direct, personal pipeline to the Lord (hence, the murmured supplication that the Grand Duchess Xenia found so striking: "From your mouth into God's ears").

It was this inner life that made all ills supportable. As a further defense, Jewry developed a wry humor. If an unarmed peddler could not topple a mailed warrior from a horse, at least he could make a joke about it. What Zaida passed along to Fanny was the distilled rueful

25

Jack Holtzmann:
teen-aged lawyer,
family idol and
a protégé of
Teddy Roosevelt's

wisdom of centuries. In medieval Spain, Rabbi Abraham Ibn Ezra began a set of verses: "If I were selling candles, the sun would never set." Seven hundred years later in Galicia the rabbi's self-mocking lament had been paraphrased to: "When it rains soup, I'm there with a fork."

Maxims and injunctions were scattered through Zaida's conversation. "If you want nothing — go to your relatives, and enjoy them. If you want advice, go to your friends; they love telling you what to do, it makes them feel important. But if you want to do business or borrow money — go to strangers." And: "Never judge a fellowman by a single action; try to see his whole record. Every man has something good in his past; contemplate that."

Zaida's source book was the Talmud, that cornucopia of moral and philosophical values created by the early interpreters of Jewish oral law. The Talmud, like the Old Testament from which it was derived, extolled action above words. Hence *mitzvoth* — good deeds — loomed large in the unspoken understanding between man and his Maker that powered the heartbeat of Jewish life.

Zaida's special territory for *mitzvoth* was the municipal court, where dispossess cases among the immigrants came up with discouraging regularity. Impressively rigged out in his rabbinical Prince Albert and formal trousers, Zaida would request the floor, then deliver an eloquent appeal for mercy on behalf of the wretched defendant. If a landlord insisted on some token payment in exchange for putting off eviction, Zaida had no compunctions about drumming up a collection among spectators, policemen and court attendants. Once he even extracted ten dollars from a dazed judge.

To Fanny, who never missed one of these appearances, Zaida was careful to point out that the good deed had to come from the heart, spontaneously. It was not a question of bribing the Lord; that was unthinkable. One did the right thing simply because it was right.

But, freely offered, the good deed brought unexpected dividends. "God

26

has the greatest of bookkeeping systems. His angels keep track of every action you take, every thought in your head, awake or asleep. Nothing — good or bad — can be hidden from them.

"The more you give, the more the Lord will replenish your resources. And when your time comes to need help, you will have a fine credit rating; you will not be abandoned."

The little girl believed him. That belief stood behind Fanny's future resistance to disaster and her amazing resilience. Again and again, faced with a shattered dream, she would repeat to herself Zaida's words:

"God is with you. Right now you may be disappointed, hurt, even crushed — but you can be sure He had his reasons for what happened. You're like a traveler who comes to a rough, rocky section of road: climb over the stones, or circle around them — but keep going. If you trust in Him, everything will be all right in the end."

Zaida didn't merely keep an eye on the overworked magistrates of the municipal court; he ran a little judicial system of his own. The rabbinical *Bes Din* (House of Judgment) dates back more than three thousand years and is mentioned in the Old Testament; for centuries it settled all legal matters in autonomous Jewish communities.

Zaida's courtroom was his kitchen. The disputants were mostly small businessmen of his congregation. Complainant and defendant sat flanking "Rabbi Hirsch" at the long table, while Fanny hovered in the background, brewing tea and soaking up impressions.

A typical case brought together one Eli Stein and his friend Chaim, who had stumbled onto a profitable real estate deal while visiting Eli's house. Eli felt he was entitled to a percentage; he was ready to pursue the issue in municipal court.

Zaida heard out each side carefully, then made his analysis. As for Eli going to court: "What does a *goyish* judge, raised in Boston, know how things are between you and Chaim?"

He turned to Chaim. "The details of who made the introduction are not important. If you had not been invited to Eli's to play pinochle that night, would you have sold the property? No. So there is an obligation, a debt of conscience."

Chaim, he ruled, should pay Eli half of the two hundred dollars claimed by his friend. As for the other hundred: "Well, we need a new window for the *shul*. It will be put up in both your names. Everybody saves money on legal fees — and at the same time gets his name inscribed in Heaven! Now shake hands. And hurry up, Fanny, bring the gentlemen some tea!"

Fanny brought the tea, and absorbed the point. The task of law was to solve problems, harmonize differences — not aggravate them.

Again and again Fanny saw litigants arrive red-faced and unsmiling, only to depart later arm in arm, a quotation from King Solomon ringing in their ears. The secret, Zaida confided, was to single out the area most precious to each side. With that determined, compromise was always possible on other points. Reasonable men could settle their differences without coming to blows or going to court. Every problem had its answer, every rule its exception. Falsehood, however, was out of bounds; even the so-called white lie, Zaida emphasized, was impermissible. "You must use only the ingredients of truth. Judiciously interpreted, there are always enough facts on both sides so that each party gets what he wants."

In later years, Fanny would imbibe the wisdom of great law professors and even Supreme Court justices; but none of their counsel would leave a more enduring imprint than Zaida's handling of the renegade Meyer, who had retained a mere secular lawyer.

"I am ashamed of you," the old man stormed. "You turn for advice to a man whose knowledge of the *real* law, the Torah, ended with his Bar Mitzva studies at the age of thirteen.

"What does it amount to, this American law, compared with the wisdom of the sages? How old is it? In the eyes of history, just a baby!

"Furthermore, you have more than forty states in this country, and no two with the same laws. If you get into a quarrel on the Hoboken Ferry, by the time you land in New Jersey you're being judged under a new set of statutes. What kind of law can it be that loses its meaning in the very next state?

"Torah law is basic, universal, the same for all places and all times. You think you have a 'Supreme Court' here? The true Supreme Court presides"— index finger heavenward —"only up there!"

In 1912, Theodore Roosevelt made a dramatic repudiation of his hand-picked Republican successor in the presidency, William Howard Taft, who had allied himself with the conservative wing of the party. Roosevelt reentered the political arena. He dominated the presidential primaries, but was maneuvered out of the nomination in the Taft-controlled convention. Furious, the former Rough Rider decided to launch a third party, the Progressive.

New York was a pivotal state. The heaviest voting was in the metropolitan area, where the newly settled immigrant districts could be decisive. Brownsville, in the Twenty-sixth Ward, had grown in the past decade from a community of a dozen blocks and 20,000 people to 420 blocks with a population of 176,000, many of them recently registered Republicans.

Henry Holtzmann's support was suddenly important. As the resident scholar in a culture-conscious but still largely illiterate community, he could swing a great many votes to the insurgents — or preserve them for Taft.

Henry knew where his sympathies lay — and also his ambitions for his eldest son. He had been grooming twenty-five-year-old Jack for office: shielding him from contact with East Europeans mired in the past, bringing him out to Oyster Bay to mingle with the 100 percent American

Roosevelt boys. Under his guidance, Jack had become leader of the local Republican Club. The next step up would be election to Congress.

The Bull Moosers had no objection. TR thought highly of young Holtzmann; and as a delegate to the recent Republican convention, Jack had stood loyally with the Roosevelt forces despite fulsome overtures from the Taft people. Jack was not only nominated for Congress, but designated the New York State secretary of the Progressive Party, in close daily contact with the former president.

The entire household on Eastern Parkway was swept along in the wake of the dazzling elder brother. Efficient Bertha raced up to Albany to file the formal papers of incorporation for the new party. Her marriage, scheduled for September 2, was put off until spring ("Love Waits on Politics," gushed the New York *American*). Henry took out another mortgage, Theresa baked cakes for rallies, Clara gave up plans to enroll in the Savage School for Physical Education.

But by far the most ardent campaigner for Jack was Fanny. Forgotten were the rebukes and humiliations, the painful dismissals. Jack was once again her adored big brother: articulate, audacious, imaginative far beyond any of his contemporaries. Fanny was the first one up in the morning to deliver circulars, mail letters, buttonhole neighbors; after school, she rushed to proselytize by telephone (who could tell that the low-voiced "Miss Holtzmann" was only a precocious adolescent?).

Spare moments she lent to Zaida. The old man had exuberantly appointed himself Jack's campaign manager for the elder-citizen vote. In top hat and long coat, he rode down to Wall Street by subway to seek funds from George W. Perkins, a partner in the Morgan banking house who was treasurer of the Bull Moose Party. His first allocation went for expensive ads in the Yiddish press where, as Fanny observed half a century later, "one in twenty-five readers had the vote."

But Zaida knew his "constituency." To the ultra-orthodox Chasidim from Galicia, he pointed out that Roosevelt's concern for forests upheld the teachings of the Talmud; to the politically idealistic Russians he cited the prolabor stand of the Bull Moosers. And to everybody he made it plain that only those wise enough to get aboard the Roosevelt-Holtzmann bandwagon would be considered worthy of honors at *shul*.

It was a tumultuous campaign. Roosevelt came in person to the Brownsville ghetto, riding through the streets with Jack in a big touring car. Zaida, accompanied by the towering Hamilton Fish, led his bearded followers in a noisy parade (to the tune of "Onward, Christian Soldiers"). At an election eve rally, the old man was mistaken for Oscar S. Straus, who had been secretary of commerce and labor in Roosevelt's second administration. Zaida acknowledged the applause by doffing his silk hat and stroking his *Kaiserbart*.

The congressional contest was essentially between Jack and his Democratic opponent, Herman Metz, who was running on Woodrow Wilson's militant liberal platform of not merely regulating the trusts, à la Roosevelt, but completely dissolving them. The third entrant, the big-money Taft candidate, had no backing in immigrant Brownsville.

As the tallying began, Jack moved into a commanding lead. But by next morning, a "final" tabulation recorded Metz as the victor by 192 votes. A recount was demanded, there were charges of irregularities — but Metz went to Congress.

Roosevelt was outpolled by Woodrow Wilson, overwhelmingly in the electoral vote and by a 42 to 27 percent margin in the popular figures. Together, Roosevelt and Taft collected more votes than Wilson; but their split let the Democrats in.

Fanny's big brother, although defeated, emerged as a force in national politics. But he never again ran for public office, and in a sense remained a disappointment to his earliest admirers: he became merely wealthy, a Regent of New York State, president in 1952 of the national Electoral College, and head of a prestigious Wall Street law firm. His devotees of the TR days — Fanny prominently among them — had felt he was destined for at least the United States Supreme Court.

Fanny was still the family disgrace at P.S. 84. After two more years of complaints, suspensions and end-of-term cliffhanging, she finally graduated and moved on to the ascetic confines of Girls' High School. Girls' was as famous for its academic eminence as it was notorious for its rigidity.

Fanny lasted until the second semester of her junior year. The placidity of her childhood had been rubbed away by the tensions of home and classroom; repeatedly disciplined by a mathematics instructor, she let fly with a newly emerging emotionality. There was a stormy confrontation. By "mutual agreement" — a sop to Henry Holtzmann's prominence — she became an ex-student.

Only the ambience of the law satisfied her. But she lacked the training to be a legal secretary, and most business courses were expensive as well as time-consuming. A friend told her about the Pernin School, in the *World* building on Park Row, where a new shorthand system was being imparted in thirty days. Fanny signed up and got her diploma.

She borrowed a dress and high-heeled shoes from Bertha, and took the subway down to the Singer Building at 149 Broadway, the city's first skyscraper (it had forty-seven stories), where a lawyer gave her a week's trial as office assistant at eight dollars a week. On Saturday morning she received a special delivery letter suggesting she postpone a working career until she was older.

She was humiliated to the core, doubly so because she knew her employer had made every effort to be tolerant of her deficiencies. Her shorthand and typing were simply intolerable. Once again, in the business world as at school, she was a failure. Fanny flung the letter aside, dashed down the steps of the subway, and spent the afternoon in Manhattan sitting beside Robert Fulton's grave in Trinity churchyard, weeping.

When she returned, her mother was waiting. "You didn't finish that lawyer's letter," said Theresa. "Look at the last sentence: he says you have great natural intelligence, and would probably do better as a lawyer than as a secretary. Why don't you go have a talk with Cecilia?"

A few doors away on Eastern Parkway, in intimate daily contact with the Holtzmanns, lived Theresa's close friend Cecilia, a gifted attorney who shared her husband's busy practice. Cecilia, mother of the philanthropist-to-be George T. Delacorte, had always made a point of encouraging Fanny. She was no less sympathetic now. "You do indeed have every ingredient essential to a legal career," she told the young girl. "The first thing you must do is take more practice in dictation at Pernin, so you can get a daytime job while you study at night." At the East New York Preparatory School, Cecilia went on, Fanny could obtain the necessary "counts" or Regents' credits required for entry into law school.

Listening, rapt, Fanny took heart. Instead of haunting the fringes of the law, hoping by her devotion to earn a glimpse of its magic, she would become an attorney herself! She would show them all — teachers, classmates, and especially her beloved nemesis, Jack — that she could be anything anyone else could, and more.

The era and the setting were propitious. Since the first appearance of a female attorney in Iowa at the end of the Civil War, resistance to the notion of a lawyer in skirts, although still considerable, had gradually been diminishing; the American Bar Association was on the verge of admitting its first woman member. The Bull Moose emphasis on minority rights had also embraced an expanded role for women.

In Brownsville, every household focused on the limitless opportunities of the New World. Above all, there was the quiet influence of Henry Holtzmann on his daughters. A man who every night upon retiring inquired of himself, "What did I learn today?" was not likely to hold static views on the role of women. And Henry didn't. Not only did he oppose the practice of segregating women in the synagogue, but he was an early advocate of the Bas Mitzva, which accords equal treatment to females in the confirmation ceremony.

Henry held up as a model to his own daughters the poetess-prophet Deborah, a "judge over Israel," who for forty years helped her people resist the pagan Canaanite tide. He foresaw the day when Deborah's successors would sit on the bench in the redeemed Jewish homeland and in America, tempering justice with mercy, logic with humanity.

Between Fanny and her goal stood a formidable obstacle: the forty-eight units of Regents' examination credits required for entry into law school.

On Pitkin Avenue, a half-hour's trolley ride away, was the East New

York Preparatory School. Saying nothing to her family, Fanny made an appointment to see Lucy Schneeberg, the principal. She found herself seated before a slender woman of twenty-five, with the long sensitive face of an El Greco saint: irregular of feature, but so illuminated with compassion as to be beautiful. Fanny felt at home. Within moments she was weeping in a kind of relief, pouring out her anguish and her hopes.

Lucy got up from her desk and put her arms around Fanny until the tears subsided. Fifty years later, Lucy recalled the scene: "I knew from the moment the child started talking that she was someone unusual. She was determined to prove herself; and underneath all the ranting, the *mishegoss* [craziness] about Jack and Clara, you could sense that she was going to arrive wherever she wanted to get. There was a compelling power of personality, an intensity in her eyes. Fanny was like some rare tropical flower that could not grow under ordinary conditions, but that with proper nourishment would reward one's efforts a hundredfold."

Once again, as with Zaida, Fanny had found the indispensable friend at the critical moment.

Zaida, of course, took the news genially. This was a different land; if his beloved *faygeleh* [little bird] wanted to branch out from kitchen and parlor, why not? "You will be not only a lawyer," he predicted, "but a judge."

Henry, too, was pleased if privately dubious. Theresa merely eyed her daughter reflectively. The attitude of Fanny's sisters was summed up in a shrug of dismissal. Only Jack was openly jeering: it was ludicrous that the family dropout should go after the highest of prizes; women were for marriage and children. Nonetheless, he agreed to avail himself of Fanny's services; capable clerks were hard to find.

A grueling year followed: office all day, classes at night, schoolbooks in between. The Holtzmann girls lived two to a room; Fanny's study hours, running into the early morning, made her an unpopular roommate. Often, rather than risk provoking an angry protest, she took textbooks and bedding into the library and slept on the sofa there.

But in a large household of outspoken individualists, clashes could not always be avoided. Sparks (and on occasion larger objects) flew. However, the spilling over and spontaneous airing of grievances created the freedom to move on. Fanny's turbulent family was the stone on which her resilience and tenacity were honed.

Her social life was a vacuum, the Spartan regime a convenient shield against unwelcome encounters. Beside graceful Clara and smartly coiffed Bertha, Fanny felt awkward, insignificant. When a beau of Stella's complimented her on her fresh, glowing complexion, she fled in humiliation, convinced she was being ridiculed.

She had no instinct for sexual banter. Men were a mysterious wickedness to be kept at bay: "If a fellow got fresh, you slapped him." On the few occasions when her sisters offered to provide a date, she pretended to be "too busy," or "above such nonsense," postponing an unsettling confrontation.

It was safer to create her own little world: Rita and David, to whom she spun fairy tales in Prospect Park; her sister Bertha, whose scholarly husband, Sam Berkman, helped her with algebra and chemistry; Lucy Schneeberg, available at home on Sundays for a few precious hours of tutoring.

After eighteen months, with nearly half her Regents' credits completed, the fragile link with Jack was abruptly severed. Arriving for work one hot June morning, she found Jack standing over her desk, ridiculing for the benefit of the office staff a minor typing error: "Look what thinks she's going to be a lawyer!"

Fanny scooped up her books and swept to the door. "You're wrong about that, Mr. Genius! I'll *be* a lawyer — and I'll do it on my own!"

She threw herself furiously into her remaining studies.

The dedication — and Lucy's patient support — paid off. With the grade of 100 in chemistry, and strong showings in English composition and history, Fanny was admitted to Fordham Law School as a night student.

When registering, she paused for a moment over her name. "Fanny" had made her wince since childhood. But while the Doras of the schoolyard had become Dorothys, she had stuck to her name simply because it was hers. Now she made a double bow, toward euphony and her parents' friend Ellen O'Grady, the first woman deputy commissioner of the Police Department. She gave herself the middle initial "E."

Her law classes would be held in the Woolworth Building downtown. It would be a great advantage, Fanny reasoned, if she could get a job in the same neighborhood or even in the building itself. In August she went to the Underwood Typewriter Company, which ran a free employment service. There she was informed that the law firm of Keppler and Hochman, in the Woolworth Building, had an opening. In fact, the opening was described as "chronic," because of the erratic hours and unconventional work habits of the two young partners. They were said to be looking for someone "unusual." That, Fanny decided, was a qualification she could meet. She went down to the Woolworth Building for an interview.

The partners were not prepossessing. Tobias Keppler had a bad rolling eye and a nervous habit of scratching at the seat of his pants while he talked. Joseph Hochman's physiognomy carried startling references to the animal kingdom: he was buck-toothed and parrot-beaked, with flapping elephant ears. However, Hochman had a kindly air, coupled with an encyclopedic grasp of legal literature; and Keppler, if one could override the visual distractions and focus on what he was saying, clearly possessed a fertile, original mind.

That, Hochman explained, was part of the firm's problem. They were spinning off in too many directions, and needed someone to unscramble the resulting chaos. "For us, shorthand is secondary."

No sweeter words could have fallen on Fanny's ears. Her shorthand, an amalgam of several systems, was at best serviceable; but she knew her way around the legal scene. Quickly she rattled off her experience. Hochman nodded, and went in to see his partner. When he came back, he was smiling. Fanny scarcely heard the details — a respectable salary of twelve dollars a week. She was "with the law firm of Keppler and Hochman"— a casual phrase that over the next few years Fanny would stretch to astonishing dimensions.

Chapter 3

WHAT FANNY'S "campus" lacked in greenery, it made up in convenience. The Fordham School of Law was located on the twenty-eighth floor of the Woolworth Building, a scant 250 feet up from the offices of Keppler and Hochman on the seventh. At 5 P.M., having put in a solid workday, Fanny would make a dash for the elevator. She attended classes all evening, with a brief break for a sandwich, and was home in Brooklyn by midnight.

It was a schedule with few loopholes, so she learned to study in transit. By taking the long, slow trolley ride all the way into Manhattan, she could assure herself of an uninterrupted hour with her lawbooks. The return ride by late-night subway was even better, with the roar of the trains providing a curtain behind which each passenger could retreat into privacy.

Fanny's office chores sometimes took her to other parts of town — never without a textbook or notebook in hand. Like a sailor attuned to the roll of the deck, she became conditioned to the sway of large moving vehicles, so much so that for the rest of her life, whenever faced in New York with a task requiring total concentration, she would pick up pad and pencil and board a bus for distant Fort Tryon Park, or take a subway to the end of the line at South Ferry.

Fordham Law, despite limited material resources, was staffed largely with no-nonsense Ivy League professors. Fanny's classmates were a serious-minded lot, for the most part middle-aged, middle-class and male. At enrollment time there were three females. By midterm there were two, and before the end of the year Fanny reigned alone.

She was maturing physically now, blossoming in a way that many men found striking. Her figure was filling out. With her rosy cheeks, great flashing eyes, and glossy black hair braided in the fashion set by the

35

opera star Alma Gluck, she could awaken visions of the Mediterranean *femme fatale.* The front seat in the classroom was reserved for her. She was named head of the Freshman Prom Committee. Her classmates vied for the honor of escorting her to the subway.

And yet she remained almost pathetically innocent. In three years at law school she had exactly one date: an invitation to the Freshman Prom from Walter McIntyre, who was headed for the priesthood. Other fellow students joined her occasionally for study sessions or after-class coffee, but their suggestions of a Sunday walk or movie were never taken up.

Instead, she continued to release the yearnings of an affectionate nature at home. Her first week's salary bought a blue serge Bar Mitzva suit for young David. She took Zaida to see St. John Ervine's latest play and, emulating Bertha, began bringing home pound boxes of Loft candy.

Nor did she confine her favors to relatives. The Tunick family had first come to her notice more than a year earlier in municipal court, where she was filing a motion on behalf of her brother Jack, and they were defendants in a dispossess case. Fanny saw before the bench a pregnant woman of about thirty, with several teeth missing and a small boy clinging to her hand.

The woman told the court she had eight other children at home; her tubercular husband had left the brood, arguing "you'll be better off without me." As for defense against the sheriff's writ, or means of payment — she had none.

Automatically, the magistrate ordered a judgment entered against her.

Fanny leaped up from her seat at the court clerk's desk. "If Your Honor please — this woman *can't* be thrown out on the sidewalk! What will happen to her children? The court must have a heart!"

The judge peered down at the pigtailed interloper. "Are you an attorney?"

"I'm going to be one. But I'm a human being!" Her eyes swept around the courtroom. "I can't believe the officers and citizens of this court will turn their backs on an unfortunate woman who has committed no wrong, whose only sin is poverty!"

It was a plea worthy of Zaida. A hasty conference was assembled before the bench, and a collection was taken up to stave off the eviction. Thus Fanny inherited the Tunicks.

The little boy, Willie, became her special responsibility. She financed his secretarial training, gave him carfare, loaned him David's Bar Mitzva suit to answer a job application. From the day she started work at Keppler and Hochman, one-fourth of her salary went to the Tunicks every week. That meant serving summonses on Saturday to supplement her income. But, as her mentor Lucy Schneeberg pointed out, "Money per se never meant anything to Fanny. It was recognition she wanted."

Within weeks after starting her new job, Fanny was able to make a valuable contribution to Keppler and Hochman. The firm was representing the popular vaudeville singing team, Gallagher and Shean, in a claim against the Shuberts, who because they had the pair under contract for a Broadway musical show were trying to enjoin them from working in vaudeville for B. F. Keith. Fanny suggested that the case be pressed as an example of peonage, in that performers with a limited earning period were being barred from using their talents; and the appellate division of the New York State Supreme Court agreed.

The partners were impressed. Clearly they would be receptive to further ideas, and Fanny lost no time coming up with one. Rummaging through the "inactive" files in the office storeroom, she ran across a sheaf of uncollected bills owed to an uptown client of the firm, the *Morning Telegraph*. The bills were for various ads taken by character actors, tap dancers, choreographers and other denizens of show business, usually for the purpose of announcing that the advertisers were "at liberty"; obviously the unemployed status they were trumpeting had mitigated against payment for the ads.

But by now, Fanny reasoned, some of these people must have achieved solvency, if not fame. Why not collect? She put the question to Keppler:

"Actors, saxophone players — they're all a bunch of lunatics. Let them in the door, they'll be juggling oranges all over my desk. Besides, we don't have the space here to follow through."

Then maybe what Keppler and Hochman needed, Fanny suggested, was a branch office in midtown. Theater people were notoriously weak at managing finances: "We can either put them into bankruptcy, or straighten them out!"

And there was something else — she'd been reading about it in the *Times* just the other day — movie companies were beginning to set up offices in the Broadway area. "That means big stars, big contracts. There's going to be a lot of work in copyrights coming up, with very few law firms equipped to handle it!"

"We're a downtown firm. We don't have contacts up there."

"You have the *Morning Telegraph* — and they know everybody."

Keppler scratched furiously at the shiny pants of his suit. "Where will I get the money?"

"For fifty dollars you don't have to rob a bank."

"Fifty dollars?"

"Give me that for a month's rent, and eight dollars a week for a secretary. What can you lose?"

"I can lose eighty-two dollars," Keppler grumbled. But he was reaching for his checkbook.

With office buildings scarce in the Times Square area, space was at a premium. In prowling past the Astor Theatre Building on Broadway at Forty-fifth Street, Fanny struck up an acquaintance with the grizzled superintendent, Frank Blaney, who doubled as janitor for all the Shubert houses. Yes, Blaney had a place available on the third floor. "Never had no lawyers in there, but if you can pay the rent, reckon it don't matter *what* you do there." He winked genially.

Fanny didn't get the joke, but she got the office. The space assigned to her was a ten-foot-square cubicle with a minuscule waiting room, both partitioned off by translucent glass from the occupant next door, a booking agent. In fact the whole floor, apart from Fanny, was occupied by bookers, all of them tilted back in their chairs, feet planted on their desks, bellowing into telephones.

Blaney had assured her he was putting her on a quiet floor. Relatively speaking, it was true. The real racket came from the rehearsal rooms overhead, where the thumping of tap clogs and the pounding of tinny pianos resounded through the day.

However, she was in the heart of the Great White Way, with a bay window overlooking Times Square. In clear view was the Palace Theatre, and directly across Forty-fifth Street stood the Astor Hotel, where the big names of the Shubert empire gathered for lunch. A few blocks away was the Algonquin, where the new entertainment elite — Pickford, Fairbanks, Barthelmess — mingled with the literati.

Armed with a pad, a secretary, and a list of *Morning Telegraph* debtors, Fanny sat down and wrote a series of charming dunning letters. She acted on the theory that most of the people who owed money to the paper were less malevolent than confused, and simply hemmed in by too many pressures; the burden of her message was that they might want to drop in for a friendly chat with F. Holtzmann, midtown manager for Keppler and Hochman. "Artists face special problems," she wrote. "But a sympathetic discussion is half the battle. I'm sure we can work things out together."

The collection letters dispatched, Fanny turned to the handful of other folders she had plucked out of the "inactive" file for transfer uptown: Young vs. Hollywood . . . Oh, yes — that was some actor making a claim against a theater entrepreneur in connection with an old loan. *Very* old, she suspected; the whole thing might not have survived the statute of limitations.

It was worth a nickel to find out. Scrawled in pencil next to the name of the plaintiff, James Young, was a faintly legible address: "Ansonia Hotel, New York." Fanny dug out the number and picked up her telephone.

Young had not been living at the Ansonia for several years. He stayed regularly at the Algonquin in midtown; but as it happened, he had moved out of his suite there the night before after a tiff with the manager, Frank Case, and had taken temporary quarters at his old residence some thirty blocks uptown. As it also happened, he came through the door, bent on a predinner bath, just as the phone started ringing.

Young, a prominent Shakespearean actor who had been involved in early film-making at the Vitagraph Company of America, had of course never heard of Fanny Holtzmann; nor did his ancient case against Edwin Hollywood stir more than the haziest of memories. But he was intrigued by the cool, poised voice at the other end of the phone. He invited Fanny to lunch the next day at the Astor Hotel.

Fanny arrived a discreet five minutes late, and was ushered to Young's table with some ceremony by the headwaiter. She found herself confronting a ruddy, vigorous-looking man in his middle forties, with the well-defined facial bone structure and resonant baritone appropriate to a seasoned matinée idol. Young, for his part, was astonished to see a very young girl dressed in a plain white blouse and a navy-blue jumper. With her low-heeled shoes and chastely braided hair, she might have been on her way to classes at a ladies' seminary.

Fanny's modest appearance was calculated. "As an embryonic attorney, I was in a privileged position — but also a very exposed one. I decided to maintain a low profile: not winsomely fluffy, but not excessively mannish, either, like the aggressive suffragettes in their tailored vests that Papa Henry complained about. Either extreme of dress would remind people of my femaleness, and get in the way of being treated as a serious professional person." Lipstick and rouge seemed superfluous: "My cheeks were red anyway, from all the walking I did."

She sat down gravely. A glass of wine? No, thanks — she "never drank before evening." (Or after, either, Young correctly surmised; but he said nothing.) He was baffled, amused. Why the telephone call out of the blue?

"A perfectly normal procedure, Mr. Young. I've recently become associated with Keppler and Hochman. It's the business of a law office to keep up with its clients, to pursue their claims and their interests. And, no matter how much time passes, to follow through on matters and keep searching out the truth."

"You have nice eyes for it," ventured her host.

"Law is not a matter of dry technicalities," Fanny went on. "It deals in human relationships. Take your own field, the theater. How much can a contract ever guarantee if there is no good will and mutual trust behind it? What is more important: the phrasing of an agreement or the sincerity of the handshake that seals it?"

Young nodded thoughtfully, conscious of the intense glance bearing down on him.

"The way I see it, Mr. Young, a lawyer's job is to *anticipate* difficulties — bring people together, instead of feeding on conflict. I'm sure that as a sensitive man, an artist, you've had your share of heartaches . . ." The great glowing eyes fixed on him, brimming over with concern.

Young was touched. He reacted as would scores of performers and creators after him: with total capitulation. This young girl cared about him, somehow understood; within her slender figure was an incipient earth mother, overflowing with regenerative warmth. He began talking: of his turbulent first marriage to the alluring Clara Kimball Young, who starred in the movie *Anne Boleyn*; of his dispute with Frank Case of the Algonquin, who had "callously" rented Young's regular suite to a mere film star, Mae Murray; finally, of the real problem on his mind. He was "in a bad jam" with the powerful William Randolph Hearst, then operating Cosmopolitan Pictures as an outlet for the talents of his protégée, Marion Davies.

Hearst had hired Young, an experienced man on both sides of the camera, to direct Miss Davies in a new melodrama. Young had assumed that he would be allowed to develop the screenplay with a writer of his own choosing, as was his custom. "Instead, I came to my office two days later and there on my desk was a shooting script!"

Fanny had no idea what a shooting script was; probably, she supposed, something to do with a murder mystery. She shook her head sympathetically.

It wasn't that the script was bad, Young explained; it just wasn't done in his style: "I wouldn't be comfortable with it!" Now, if he could only use his own man — Edmund Goulding. "He's a drunkard and a wild man — but a great scenarist. In fact, when it comes to understanding films, he's a fourteen-carat genius."

"Let me look into it, Mr. Young. But first, let's straighten things out with Frank Case at the Algonquin. It's silly for you to be stuck uptown when all your friends are down here."

Case proved surprisingly amenable. He was as unhappy as Young about the rift. At Fanny's suggestion, he shifted a visiting couple from Chicago to the rear of the hotel and gave their suite overlooking Forty-fourth Street to Young.

The dispute with Hearst would not be managed so easily. To begin with, Fanny had to find out what her "client" was talking about. Before going to classes in the Woolworth Building that evening, she stopped in for a briefing by Joe Hochman, who had writing ambitions and was something of a theater buff.

The director of a movie, Hochman explained, was the man who told the actors "where to go." The scenarist provided the director with a description of the action on paper, variously called a "scenario," "continuity" or "story line." A shooting script had nothing to do with gang warfare but was a fully worked out scenario, with every "shot" or camera "setup" specified, and occasional titles to accompany the silent action.

Fanny made careful notes. She wasn't going to take on William Randolph Hearst without a shooting script of her own.

The big man received her in his offices on the upper reaches of Third Avenue. Fanny felt few tremors on arrival —"after all, I'd seen people like Bainbridge Colby and Hamilton Fish around my house since I was a child" — and fewer when the interview got under way. Hearst, then fifty-six, "took pains to put me at my ease. He was very soft-spoken and humble."

Fanny presented her case directly. She was "with Keppler and Hochman." Their client, Mr. Young, was most eager to join forces with Mr. Hearst, and to direct the gifted Miss Davies; but Mr. Young, like Miss Davies, was an artist, a man of conscience, and he felt that if confined to the present script, he could not do justice to Mr. Hearst's property. What he was seeking was in the common interest: permission to engage the distinguished English scenarist, Mr. Edmund Goulding, to collaborate with him on certain revisions.

"No," said Hearst quietly. "Miss Davies is familiar with the work of the lady who did our script. She does not want anyone else to write for her. Not *anyone*."

"In that case, Mr. Hearst, we have an impasse — an honest disagreement in which nobody is at fault. Mr. Young has no desire to bring a court action. That would be time-consuming and costly on all sides. Yet, if he is going to be forced off an assignment after giving up other work to take it, some compensation is in order. Don't you agree?"

Hearst pursed his lips.

"Compared to the total cost of producing a film, a token payment would be negligible. It would preserve friendly relations for possible future association. As for the alternative — legal action — well, one never knows how a court will rule. And how much."

Hearst thought that one over. "Go in and see my production manager, Mr. Silverstone. You and he can work something out."

Maurice Silverstone, a former assistant district attorney in Brooklyn, was amiable and quick. Within a week Jimmy Young had a check for $25,000, in full settlement. He sent Keppler and Hochman a fee of $2,500.

Fanny claimed no part of this. She even declined a Christmas bonus, telling the startled Hochman: "The best payment I know is a satisfied client." As for the original case that had prompted her telephone call to Jimmy Young, investigation revealed that it had indeed been outdated by the statute of limitations.

Meanwhile, the net spread by her cheerful collection letters was pulling in a motley haul. Show people were accustomed to being badgered by their creditors; offers of help were something else. They descended in gratifying numbers on Fanny's cubbyhole, laying their problems across her desk. They were unemployed; or in bad standing at Actors Equity; worried about their taxes or their stock company contracts or their grandchildren.

Fanny listened, with the patience born of growing up in a household where four generations lived together under one roof. Most of these people, she decided, were in a hopeless tangle with their finances. They would never pay their bills to the *Morning Telegraph* or anyone else unless their accounts were put in order. She set about doing just that.

The show folk were delighted, and as money started trickling in, so were the owners of the *Telegraph*. Fanny was invited up to their offices on the southeast corner of Eighth Avenue and Fiftieth Street, opposite the old Madison Square Garden, to meet their motion picture editor, Louella Parsons. One of Louella's bosses was so impressed with Fanny's practicality that he wanted her named guardian for his children.

The first-year Fordham Law School student beat an alarmed retreat; she was scarcely old enough to be a guardian for herself. On the same principle, she relayed to the downtown office all requests that she draw up contracts for her booking-agent neighbors; she wasn't going to be accused of practicing law without a license.

In May of 1920, she noticed in the list of delinquents forwarded by the *Telegraph* a familiar name: Edmund Goulding. She had sent Goulding a note the previous fall, after settling the Young case, but had had no response to her invitation to drop in. Evidently the writer was still in America; he had taken — but not paid for — a quarter-page ad at Christmas in the *Telegraph*.

Fanny tried again, in her most ingratiating manner. She had heard so many wonderful things about Goulding from Jimmy Young, she wrote, that she welcomed this opportunity to communicate again. The advertising bill itself was of no consequence: "an oversight, I'm sure." But perhaps if he stopped in at her office for a chat she would be able to protect him in the future from such "quite unnecessary irritants."

Still no reply. Then, after several weeks, a brief telephone call. The light, mellow voice and airy British manner were disarming; but Fanny could not make out what, if anything, Goulding wanted to convey. Over the next few months there were more calls, equally charming and equally vague; Goulding would not be pinned down to an appointment.

One noontime, with her secretary at lunch, Fanny was alone in the office. She was munching on a *lox* (smoked salmon) sandwich brought from home, sipping at her thermos of coffee when the door burst open and "in walked this dazzling man."

Edmund Goulding at twenty-nine was dazzling indeed. He had played the title role in a British musical production of Oscar Wilde's *Portrait of Dorian Gray*. He had the cool, chiseled beauty for the part, and also the dissolute charm of Wilde's wastrel. Deep-chested and lithe of movement, he vibrated with what would later be called charisma.

Fanny tucked the remains of her sandwich into the basket, slipped the thermos into a drawer, and straightened up. Mechanically she accepted from her visitor a huge box of Irene Hayes flowers, thoughts tumbling over each other in her mind: Such vivid blue eyes . . . I wonder if he's paid for these flowers [he hadn't; there was a court summons from the florist a month later] . . . Bertha will love them; but how do I get through night school and the subway with two dozen roses?

Goulding had already pulled up a chair and was firing away at a machine-gun clip: he hadn't been around sooner because he was simply swamped with commitments, deadlines, obligations. There was a Broadway opening this evening and a weekend party at Southampton, but unless he could work things out with his tailor . . . On the other hand, his new script wasn't finished, so if he should run into Walter Wanger —

Fanny slowed him down and managed to sort out some specifics. There were bills to be paid, chiefly for back rent at the Algonquin and to an assortment of clothiers. He had fallen behind in sending support money to his mother and sister in London.

Professionally he was performing well, yet faring miserably. On his last assignment he had been called in to make script revisions by Mae Murray and her director-husband, Robert Z. Leonard. His contributions had been not only accepted but highly praised; yet his cash payment had been only $250, and his screen credit nil. By contrast, the original author received $10,000, and could take all the bows for Goulding's ghost work.

It was obvious that Goulding was being subjected to cavalier treatment. It was equally obvious, even without Jimmy Young's encomiums, that the man was a torrent of creativity, waiting only to be channeled. Fanny leaned toward him, her expressive features charged with sympathy and concern. "You're a man of imagination, Mr. Goulding. You shouldn't be troubled with business matters."

Goulding sighed, the beautiful blue eyes clouding. "Who's going to handle them for me?"

"I will . . . if you wish."

The Englishman stared at the girl across the desk: small, determined, as vibrant in her way as he was in his. "I wish," he said.

Fanny's new client had been born in the London suburb of Streatham, to a middle-class mother who had married the local butcher. A talented singer from boyhood, young Edmund had while working as a bellhop at the Savoy Hotel come to the attention of the manager, Robert Gelardi, who opened doors for him in the theater. Goulding had been an overnight sensation as Dorian Gray.

Enlisting in World War I, he was singled out by Lord Northcliffe for liaison with American Intelligence. Afterward another sponsor, Sir William Wiseman of the Foreign Office, urged Goulding to cross the Atlantic and try his hand in the American entertainment world. Introductions from Wiseman ushered him into the Otto Kahn circle of bankers, sportsmen and opera buffs who dominated the New York social scene.

Ebullient, faultlessly tailored, a splendid raconteur and the possessor of a fine tenor voice, the young Englishman was the dream guest of every hostess in town. His improvisational skills at parties were said to be rivaled only by those of Charlie Chaplin.

Into his crowded social calendar Goulding managed to weave a brief appearance in a play, and a few flings at screen writing. But he soon found himself caught in a punishing cycle. It was a thrill for a butcher's son to swap polo ponies on Long Island with the likes of Averell Harriman, but even for a popular guest, life among the millionaires cost money. He could not bring orchids to his dinner hostess, send checks back to England, and keep up with the rent.

Goulding worried. When he worried, he drank. "Busts" of two or three days created more bills to pay.

As a result, his bargaining position was terrible, and the movie studios knew it. He had neither a Screen Writers' Guild to protect him nor craft status as a playwright or literary man; so producers stuck with a bad scenario could engage his nimble pen on their own terms. Afterward, it was easy to salve their consciences by telling each other he was a hopeless drunk.

Once again, Fanny's first port of call was the Algonquin. Frank Case was impressed by her faith in the Englishman's future and the fact that she was going to manage Goulding's affairs; Case knew what she had achieved for Jimmy Young. Goulding could have a two weeks' extension.

With Case in her corner, Fanny found Goulding's other creditors more approachable. To each she spoke of his brilliant prospects and her plans for taking his finances in hand. For a while at least, they were willing to gamble.

Then she set about delivering on her pledge. She consolidated Goulding's assets, arranged a schedule for regular disbursements to England, and put him on a strict personal budget; every cash outlay, from a haircut to membership in a country club, was to be cleared through her. Finally, she superintended a hatchet-burying lunch with Mae Murray and Bob Leonard: "They're going to need you, and you're going to need them. There's no point in clinging to an old grievance; better to start a new page."

Goulding came away from the meeting bubbling over with enthusiasm. "I tossed a few ideas at them, and they're definitely excited. It's extraordinary how different you've made things look to me, in just a matter of days. Tell me, Miss Holtzmann, what do I owe you?"

"Nothing. You're going to be a great writer. But I *would* like you to sign this check for the *Morning Telegraph* bill."

Goulding signed, waved a "Cheerio!," and was gone. Two hours later a messenger arrived from Tiffany's with a small, elegantly wrapped package. It contained a gold fountain pen, inscribed "To the one and only Fanny Holtzmann." It was the first personal gift Fanny had ever received in her life, other than a ten-cent box of nougats on a birthday. She locked the door, sat down at her desk, and cried.

Goulding found other ways to express his appreciation. He took Fanny to the celebrated Round Table at the Algonquin, where he had high standing among the wits and literary lights of the town. Fanny, for whom "lunch at Childs' was a big treat," found herself surrounded by Alexander Woollcott, Dorothy Parker, Robert Benchley, and the columnist Franklin

P. Adams. And not merely surrounded: she was presented with a flourish as "the greatest lawyer in the world — man or woman!"

It was hardly the moment to announce that she was merely a second-year law student. She had never herself pretended to be a member of the bar; that would be inviting disaster. But she recognized that for theater people, exaggeration was a way of life, and the very notion of a girl lawyer exhilarating.

Her reticence, though in self-defense, made a very favorable impression. In a setting where everyone was scrambling for attention, doing verbal backflips to get a line in a column, here was a girl begging *not* to be publicized: "Please, Mr. Woollcott, promise you won't mention my name." Fanny was accorded a unique respect within the cynical circle.

Her sophisticated new milieu benefited not only Fanny's status, but her wardrobe. A girl could hardly be seen around town with Eddie Goulding in hand-me-downs. Fanny's mother took her to Hattie Carnegie, from whom Theresa had been getting clothes since early days on the lower East Side. The little-girl blouses gradually gave way to smart, simple suits; the unsullied skin acquired a faint touch of lipstick.

Some five weeks after tying up with Fanny, Goulding came charging through her door. He had developed a tremendous idea for an original movie, a sweeping epic of the sea with strong characters and built-in production values. What was more, he had told it to Dick Barthelmess, and the actor was entranced. Barthelmess's producers, Charlie Duell and John Boyce-Smith, independents who released through First National, were "dying for it."

"Have you told them the story?"

"Yes, and they'll pay twenty-five hundred dollars for it. But —" Goulding added hastily —"I haven't signed anything."

Well, Fanny thought to herself, that's an improvement.

Charles Holland Duell and his partner were the bluebloods of the film industry. Duell was an attorney, Boyce-Smith a prominent churchman. They did not mix with the Warners or Louis B. Mayer on the West Coast, or Walter Wanger in New York; they had Dick Barthelmess, the Gish sisters, and their community standing. That was enough.

With Goulding's approval, Fanny picked up the telephone and made an appointment to see Duell and Boyce-Smith the next day.

The producers were very dignified, very polite. They listened attentively while Fanny explained that $2,500 was quite out of the question. "You see, writers are like opera singers or ballet dancers who start in the chorus; if they click, their price goes up." It was Goulding's adaptation, she ·pointed out, of the Joseph Hergesheimer short story "Tol'able David" that had earned the Photoplay Gold Medal of 1921 and launched Dick Barthelmess's career. "Mr. Goulding's new story is not necessarily better than his script for *Tol'able David*, on which he worked for a small fee. But his talents are no longer a matter for speculation."

45

"Conceded. Still, that doesn't make him a major writer."

"The next picture will, Mr. Duell. And you have something to gain by being the first to recognize it."

"Well, we'll think it over." Duell walked with Fanny to the door. "And I must say, Mr. Goulding has been wise in his choice of attorneys."

Fanny lowered her eyes. "Keppler and Hochman are a very reputable firm, sir."

Goulding was willing to be guided to solvency — but not via the Automat. He took Fanny to lunch the next day at the Ritz. How high did she think Charlie Duell would go?

"Maybe four thousand, with a separate fee for filling out the script."

"I say, that's marvelous! How did you do it?"

"But I don't think you ought to make a picture deal — not even for five thousand."

"Not make — I don't understand."

"You're always grumbling about book authors, Mr. Goulding: the prices they command, how the movie people kowtow to them. Well, why not write a book yourself? You've got the story."

Goulding's blue eyes blinked anxiously. "A book? Do you think I could?"

"I know you could."

"I'd be a novice. I might need help."

Fanny smiled. "I've never written a book — but I've certainly read enough of them."

"I, ah, sometimes get restless when I'm working. I've even been known to, ah, drop out of sight." It was his first reference — an oblique one — to his drinking problem.

Fanny met his gaze levelly. "I can be patient, Mr. Goulding."

That left the practical question of a time and place for conferring. By day, Fanny's little office was buzzing with nervous actors; at night, she had her law school classes. "But I'm free in the early morning . . . Let's see, there's a Childs' restaurant on Seventh Avenue near Forty-first Street, just outside the subway. We could meet for breakfast every morning at seven-thirty."

"Seven-thirty?" Goulding looked appalled. "Sometimes I don't get to bed before —" He checked himself, and smiled. "Smashing idea. Creativity at the coffeehouse. Shakespeare and Sam Johnson would have approved."

For the next two weeks, Fanny rose in the chill autumn dawn, shivered as she clutched her lawbooks on a drafty subway platform, and emerged forty-five minutes later among the throng disgorged at Times Square. Always Goulding would be waiting at a table near the window, freshly shaven and immaculate. Sometimes his eyes would be bleary and his cheeks a trifle puffy, leading Fanny to suspect that he had been up all

46

night; but there was no trace of liquor on his breath. Like Dorian Gray, he had the faculty of absorbing the consequences of his revels; in thirty years, Fanny was never to see him under the influence of alcohol.

Usually, Goulding had penciled notes before him. He read rapidly, ad-libbing as he went along, impersonating all the characters. As he wove his tale of high passion — the clash of three strong men at sea — Fanny sat absorbed, oblivious to the curious glances from neighboring tables. With an effort, she shifted from the role of admiring audience to critic. Together they thrashed out the broad line of *Fury*, in a kind of amiable, exciting duel.

Law school exams interrupted the collaboration. When Fanny next saw her client again a week later, Goulding was subdued and abashed. By now they were on a first-name basis. "What is it, Eddie? What's wrong?"

"I did something . . . you're going to be angry. I don't know what came over me."

In her absence, Goulding had become panicky about money and gone back to John Boyce-Smith about *Fury*. The producer had been "very decent, really," and the upshot was that Goulding had contracted to take $10,000 for a complete shooting script. "I stayed up all night writing and turned it in to his secretary for typing the next day."

Fanny hid her disappointment. It was too late to backtrack on the deal; once Goulding had committed himself, he was obliged to deliver a script or be blacklisted. Besides, he was clearly already awash with remorse.

"That wasn't such a bad move," she told him. "We can still go ahead with the book version, and make a tie-in with the film company to promote it."

Goulding brightened. "I knew you'd think of something. And I did get in a useful little touch when I was on my own. I talked about the book with Brandt and Brandt. They're the biggest literary agents in town. They're definitely interested in seeing a manuscript."

This time, Fanny kept a tight rein on her elusive charge. Before Goulding's contrition could wear off, she got him started on his draft. Thereafter, he was obliged every morning to bring in to their table at Childs' a specific quota of handwritten pages.

His opening drafts were untrained, almost crude; but there was a freshness of imagery that reminded Fanny of Jack London: "It's good, Eddie! It has the tang and breath of salt air." So intense was her involvement that Goulding would have been ashamed not to hold up his end of the bargain.

Inevitably, however, the morning came when no Goulding appeared. A call to Ruby Busch, the motherly telephone operator at the Algonquin, confirmed Fanny's fears: "He's sleeping it off, Miss Holtzmann. A tremendous toot last night."

Instinct told Fanny not to rebuke her "drunken genius"; Goulding generated his own guilt. Instead, when he returned to circulation two days later, she left him behind in his hotel room and departed with the key. "There you stay until you finish the chapter," she told him from the house phone in the lobby. "I'll be back at the end of the day. If the chapter is ready, you can have the evening off."

Like a dutiful child, he complied. Fanny rewarded him by approving a twenty-four-hour furlough from all literary labors.

It was an extraordinary relationship. Fanny was sister-mother-nanny to Goulding, with overtones of the inspirational Madonna purifying the life of a roué. He treated her with reverence, not only sheltering her from contact with the chorines of his nocturnal prowls, but refusing to let anyone swear in her presence. When she reached teasingly for a cigarette one day, he snatched it from her hand.

Fanny, for her part, found Goulding the perfect foil to her ambitions. She had few connections but was strong on imagination and planning; he was brilliant, undisciplined, with a precarious foothold in the burgeoning film industry. In the view of Lucy Schneeberg, "he was a fantasy to her, something she could shape and lead. By putting across his career, she would prove herself."

When Goulding had several chapters finished, Fanny arranged to see Duell and Boyce-Smith at lunch. "Eddie is doing *Fury* as a book," she told them. "That means you'll have a presold picture property, worth as much as anything of Hergesheimer's. And if you synchronize the promotion campaigns, you'll have a gold mine. The book can be put on sale in every theater lobby across the country, backed up by huge newspaper ads in which the publisher plugs the picture!"

The partners leaned forward. Joint promotions were at that time an unfamiliar notion, but the two were shrewd businessmen, alert to possibilities. "Does Goulding have a publisher?" asked Duell.

"That won't be any problem. Brandt and Brandt are handling the book. But if we could go to the publishers with an order already in hand from the picture company, they would have an incentive to put up a matching figure for advertising, which in turn would snowball into more tickets at the box office. One hand feeds the other."

"How much are you thinking of from us?"

"Oh, it wouldn't come to much. Maybe enough to cover the costs of a first printing. Look at it this way, Mr. Duell. You're planning a major production for *Fury*, are you not? I'm speaking in budget terms."

"Well, yes. There are quite a few elaborate exteriors. Action scenes at sea."

"And special effects also, if I am not mistaken." Fanny didn't quite know what the phrase meant — she had picked it up from Goulding — but it had an expensive ring.

"Quite true," said Boyce-Smith.

"By comparison, gentlemen, printing costs are relatively trivial. For an investment you won't even notice, you can double your return on the picture."

Fanny's first flight: back from her Atlantic City rescue mission in 1922 with the errant genius Eddie Goulding. The lady in the center was taken along as a chaperone at Goulding's insistence

Duell pondered a moment. "As I said before, Miss Holtzmann," he observed drily, "Mr. Goulding has a very capable attorney."

"I think we should go along with it, Charlie," said Boyce-Smith. He took out a cigar. "Does tobacco bother you, Miss Holtzmann?"

"Not at all, sir. My grandfather uses it incessantly. Of course, I don't smoke or drink myself."

The churchman looked even more pleased than his partner.

Things were going well — too well. In the spring of 1922, a call to Goulding's room at the Algonquin elicited the information from Ruby Busch that he was "off on a bust." Eddie had gone off to the Traymore Hotel in Atlantic City with Tallulah Bankhead and Estelle Winwood; Frank Case, who liked to keep an eye on his more wayward guests, was "having a fit."

Fanny had visions of everything — client, book, plans — dissolving into an alcoholic morass. Clearly, strong measures were called for. She called Lucy Schneeberg, her perennial source of reinforcement; Lucy agreed she should head for Atlantic City herself.

A convenient excuse was at hand: the Commercial Law League, which specialized in collection cases, was holding a convention at the New Jersey resort. Fanny made a reservation to join the delegates at the Ambassador Hotel. With her usual penchant for sharing, she took along her big sister Bertha and Bertha's baby daughter, Helen; they could enjoy the beach while she grappled with Goulding's caprices.

On arrival the following noon, she left word at Goulding's hotel that she was in town for the convention. Two hours later he turned up on the beach, sober: "Forgive me for running off that way, Fanny. I must be the wickedest, and certainly the most foolish client any lawyer ever had to contend with."

"What's there to forgive?" Fanny shrugged. "You needed a release from tension."

Eddie urged Fanny to stay at the resort a few days, promising he would resume his writing.

As Fanny hesitated, a small open airplane — one of the early strut-designed "Jennies"— roared overhead. Fanny looked up, following the flight with disbelieving fascination. Goulding threw in his clincher: "I'm flying back to New York in that plane. Stay the weekend, and you can fly back with me."

Why not, Fanny decided? She'd been under a bit of tension herself.

Goulding had buckled down hard at the beach to complete his manuscript. Fanny, thrilled with anticipation, submitted it to Brandt and Brandt — and ran into a shock.

"Completely unpublishable," was the agency's verdict. "The man's lack of education sticks out on every page. We couldn't possibly offer it under our letterhead."

Fanny was crushed — momentarily. Could she have been so totally wrong? Was Goulding really a bumbling amateur?

She refused to believe it. Why was an agency's judgment, or an editor's, better than her own? She brooded on the matter all through the long subway ride home . . .

On the table beside her bed was a book, a recent birthday gift from her sister Bertha. Glancing at the jacket, she saw it was published by Dodd, Mead and Company.

Well, why not?

The next day Fanny donned her most circumspect outfit: long black skirt, long-sleeved blouse, flat heels. She tied up her hair in prissy school-marm braids, and for good measure put on a pair of uncorrected glasses. They made her look older, and were an effective prop for waving at people.

Then she descended on the publisher's office: "I am Miss Holtzmann, from the law firm of Keppler and Hochman, and I would like to see Mr. Dodd."

The chairman was a slight, elderly man with a pince-nez and impeccable manners. He blinked as Fanny outlined the rare opportunity being offered to his firm: "Our client is one of the outstanding authors of the English-speaking world. Just recently he won a national prize here for his screen adaptation of the Joseph Hergesheimer story 'Tol'able David.'

"This manuscript"— she dropped it on Dodd's desk —"has already been purchased for the films, as a starring picture for Richard Barthelmess. That's why we picked Dodd, Mead to publish it. The producer of the film, Mr. Charles Holland Duell, insists that the book must have nothing less than the very best imprint!"

"Thank you. But, ah —"

Fanny flourished her glasses, and Dodd retreated. "The few people who have been privileged to see this manuscript all agree: our author is being compared to Jack London, Joseph Conrad. But I'm not asking you to take the book on hearsay: read it. Judge its merits for yourself."

Dodd rang a bell on his desk. A tiny woman bustled in. "Hazel, I'd like a report on this right away."

Hazel was no more impressed than Brandt and Brandt. "It's very rough, sir. It would take weeks of polishing, and we still might not have anything. I'm sorry, Miss Holtzmann."

But Fanny was not to be put off. "That," she stormed, "is precisely what is wrong with the publishing business, Mr. Dodd! You cling to your stick-in-the-mud attitudes, instead of keeping up with the times! Here I'm introducing you to a new public, through a producer who will sell your book in hundreds of theaters all over America and England. You have a guaranteed market. What have you got to lose?"

"How do we know they'll do it?"

"I'll get you an order in writing. What figure do I tell them?"

"Ten thousand books would do it."

Fanny rushed back to the Woolworth Building and sat down with Joe Hochman to drew up the necessary papers. Duell promptly signed. And with the printing costs covered, Dodd, Mead decided to forgo editorial tinkering. "Maybe," commented Hazel, "the style will be considered original."

It was: by the critics, who pronounced Goulding an "English Jim Tully," and by the reading public, who responded to the author's raw, often striking imagery. When the movie was completed, an eager audience would be waiting.

First to feel the effects of Eddie's revised status was Mae Murray. She and Bob Leonard had last hired Goulding for $250. Now, seeking to buy his original screen story *Fascination*, they offered $1,000. Fanny waved them aside: "Terribly sorry, Bob. We have another star interested. But Eddie isn't going to pick up a pencil for less than ten thousand. At that figure, he thinks you ought to have first opportunity. Remember, a Goulding script means story plus full continuity. You don't need any other writer."

Leonard remembered. He put up the $10,000.

Fanny's stock shot up with Goulding's. The first copy of *Fury* was inscribed by the author "naturally to the person responsible for its existence"; the second went to Henry and Theresa Holtzmann, whose

EASTON PA

brilliant daughter's astute and clever handling of this book — in its early and unattractive stages — made its publication possible."

Although Goulding's legal fees had to be made out to Keppler and Hochman, he kept up a stream of gifts to the little office in the Astor Theatre Building: flowers, end tables, a silver desk set.

And he made sure that everybody on Broadway heard about her: "not only my business coups, but what he portrayed as my saintliness. I was different, according to Goulding: incorruptible, untouchable. It's a good thing I couldn't stand the taste of whiskey. If I had taken one drink, smoked one cigarette, I'd have destroyed the illusion."

The fact that a notorious libertine like Goulding treated Fanny as if she were Joan of Arc put a further sheen on her reputation. The Algonquin crowd came running. "If anybody had a problem — and who didn't, it was like a boarding house"— Goulding sent him or her to "my lawyer," who from his description combined the best qualities of psychiatrist, manager and intimate friend.

Fanny was cautious in her advice, managing to provide guidance without exceeding her legal authority: "Of course, I'm not speaking as your attorney. But if I found myself in that situation, here's what I would do. . . . My grandfather used to say, 'Never kill a mosquito with a sixteen-inch gun.' " Her comments, shrewd and to the point, did nothing to diminish her standing.

Fanny's circle expanded. Clifton Webb, then a young dancing star, became a devoted follower; he brought along Noel Coward, who was captivating New York in his own early play *The Vortex*, and Ivor Novello, the leading light of the London musical theater. A major British acquisition was Goulding's friend and Coward's producer, Charles B. Cochran, a West End impresario who faced a delicate negotiation in international law.

Fanny's spreading prestige was becoming an embarrassment. People wanted suits filed, claims settled, contracts drawn up. Checks for five-figure sums were being flourished by Clifton Webb and Charles Cochran. Everybody insisted on engaging Fanny in person — and she had not yet been admitted to the bar. Steadfastly, she put the besiegers off.

There was a clear sequence to be traversed: graduation from law school, passing the state bar examinations, clearance by the Character Committee, and setting up practice in a dignified atmosphere.

Graduation for Fanny veered between low farce and nightmare. Charles Holland Duell had chosen the very day of the ceremonies for a business lunch that would launch his "Inspiration Pictures." For his first venture, he wanted Goulding to write *The White Sister*, to star Lillian Gish along with an English actor, Ronald Colman, who would be making his debut before American audiences. Dick Barthelmess and Mae Murray had been invited to the meeting for window dressing; Fanny could hardly stay away on grounds of school graduation.

She did manage to break loose from lunch, after closing a deal for

Goulding at $10,000, at a little past two o'clock. The graduation was to start at three. Too late for her gown-fitting, she hurried to the Forty-second Street station of the Third Avenue El, boarded an uptown train, and asked to be let off at "the University."

She was — at New York University.

The explanation was simple: "My classes were all downtown in the Woolworth Building. I'd never been to the *real* Fordham; nobody told me there were two universities in the Bronx!"

Frantic and miserable, Fanny arrived at the Fordham Stadium just as the class parade was ending. In a desperate gesture, she threw on a graduation robe designed for a six-foot classmate and tagged along like a bedraggled circus clown at the end of the line. To cap her frustration, only a handful of relatives and friends had used any of the two dozen invitations sent out so proudly the week before. Most of her sisters had stayed home.

Appreciated or not, Fanny had to pass the bar examinations. Every day she attended the 7 A.M. cramming sessions held by the assistant to the celebrated Harold R. Medina, and for a week before the exams she studied with Horace London, a distinguished attorney who was a family friend. In the final twelve hours of preparation, London went without sleep all night to help Fanny pore over her texts.

She came out of the examinations with the third highest rating in the state.

Particularly because she was a woman, Fanny wanted the reinforcement of a dignified setting. Diagonally across from the Algonquin on Forty-fourth Street was precisely the building she sought — if she could gain admission to it. The Bar Building, owned by the staid and stately Association of the Bar of the City of New York, was just being completed and was already drawing well-known firms from the more traditional downtown area.

Goulding was delighted with the prospect. It had already been agreed, at his suggestion, that he would pay Fanny an annual retainer of $15,000. The Bar Building location was convenient, and a room would be set aside for his use.

Only Jack, approached to intercede for Fanny with the Bar Association, put a damper on the scheme. "Your rent alone would be five thousand a year. How can you count on people like Goulding, fly-by-night actors, to keep their commitments?"

That was before he met Goulding. Reluctantly journeying uptown for lunch at the Algonquin, Jack found himself in a never-never land of famous personalities. People he'd read about — Dorothy Parker, Heywood Broun, Lillian Gish — were on every side, all being very deferential to the little sister he held in such light esteem.

And at the center of the sparkling circle, mesmerizing one and all with his witty mimicry, sat Fanny's number one client.

Girl graduate: shortly after receiving her LL.B. degree from Fordham Law School

Jack had second thoughts. Perhaps, he conceded, it wouldn't be such a bad idea for Fanny to have an office in the nearby Bar Building. But not on her own. "It wouldn't look right," he remarked to Goulding, for a man in Goulding's position to be represented officially by "a little girl." The formal retainer could, if Goulding wished, be with his own well-established Woolworth Building firm of Holtzmann, Mendes and Kreisel; Fanny would be "our uptown office."

Fanny sat open-mouthed; she had not been consulted about any such arrangement. To her dismay, Goulding saw merit in the idea. He would still have the advantage of Fanny's personal guidance. But among his friends, friends like Otto Kahn and Sir William Wiseman, a solid downtown law firm would raise fewer eyebrows.

Fanny could not begin practice, with or without Jack, until she had the approval of the Character Committee, convened under the aegis of the Appellate Division of the New York State Supreme Court. Normally the committee met in Kings County (Brooklyn) three times a year.

Normally was not good enough for Fanny. Big retainers were beckoning over the horizon. Charles B. Cochran was pressing to know when she could sail for England.

Final jurisdiction over admission to practice was held, although rarely exercised, by the state's highest judicial body, the Court of Appeals. Fanny went to Judge Frederick E. Crane in his chambers in Brooklyn and asked for immediate admission, with a waiver of the usual clerkship period.

Crane was nonplused. He admitted later that he thought the author of this strange request was "mentally unsound"; but he told her to make a formal motion, mentioning her expected retainers. He would refer it to the full court, about to convene in Albany.

A few days later, word came back: her application had been denied.

The next morning, Edmund Goulding received a carbon copy of a curt, anonymous letter addressed to the Character Committee of Kings County: "That little Jew-girl who holds herself out to be a lawyer isn't, and never will be!"

Fanny was in despair. Her career was coming to an end almost before it started. She took the letter to Jack, who turned pale. "Let me have that."

Late that night Jack telephoned, his voice choked and distant. He had always been ambivalent about Fanny, part of a larger ambivalence about his life. On one side, Henry Holtzmann's eldest son was a violin-playing dreamer, who in a private moment wept at the sight of a new prison going up "to crush the souls of men not yet born"; on the other he was a driving careerist, fighting down the phantoms of his uncertain youth. He might secretly admire Fanny's courage, but he shrank from a professional association with anyone whose propriety had come under questioning, even anonymously.

Their plans for working together would have to be called off, he told

55

Fanny. He was sorry — it would be a blow to him too — but such an affiliation was out of the question.

Fanny dressed and took a taxi to Jack's house. As she suspected, Jack's wife, Lilian, had been badly shaken by the letter to the Character Committee. Fanny's plans had always impressed Lilian as dubious: why should a nice girl want to compete with men, and come home alone by trolley at midnight? "I can't risk having Jack's name dragged through the mud," she insisted. "He's worked too hard to get where he is."

In vain Fanny pointed out that she too had worked hard; that it was Jack, not she, who had proposed the new arrangement with Goulding; that this abrupt reversal might destroy the client's faith in her. Lilian stood her ground. If Jack defied her, it would be at the risk of his marriage.

Fanny went home. In despair, she turned to the succor of her youth. Zaida listened intently, then said: "You must not give up."

"Where can I go? What can I do? Wait —" An idea had come into her head. "I'll go to Albany myself, petition the whole Court of Appeals. That's the highest tribunal in the state."

Zaida smiled. "There's one higher judge: God. And He will be there for you, I guarantee it. You have been a girl of many *mitzvoth*, and He does not abandon the righteous."

The next morning Fanny boarded the Empire Express, arriving just before court opened at noon. The judges faced a heavy calendar. Not only was Fanny unlisted on it, but as the court clerk, Mr. Armstrong, observed, she had already received a negative judgment. Nonetheless Armstrong was strangely touched by the dark-eyed, fiercely determined girl. "All we can do is wait till the end of the calendar," he told her, "and see if they're willing to sit again for you."

Three judges of the seven-man panel consented to hear her. At nearly seven o'clock, hungry and chilled, Fanny was ushered into the chambers of her first listener, Judge Benjamin Cardozo. She saw a heavy-set, white-thatched man whose stern mien dissolved in a beautiful smile: "There was a luminous look about him, as if a million candles were glowing inside." He spoke in a low, gentle voice, and Fanny felt in the presence of angels.

Without thinking, she poured out her story: the early apprenticeship at municipal court, the long struggle through subway studies and night classes. She laughed over some memories, and wept over others. At the end she produced evidence of the work that was waiting for her, work she felt she had earned: "I ask only for the opportunity to prove myself as an honorable, responsible member of the bar."

From Cardozo she went in turn to each of his colleagues, and repeated her plea. "My only case, Your Honor, is the truth."

Two days later a telegram came down from Albany reversing the previous judgment of the court. Fanny's admission to the bar without clerkship or other preliminaries was ordered.

There remained the formal swearing-in before justices of the Appellate Division. If Fanny waited for the mass admission of the year's new crop of lawyers, she would lose time; also, her name would appear in the comprehensive list published by the New York *Times*, tipping off eagle-eyed members of the Round Table to her elaborate past bluff. She went to Ernest P. Seelman, chairman of the Character Committee. Impressed by her derring-do at Albany, he rounded up five Appellate Division justices sitting in Kings County for the sole purpose of swearing Fanny in.

Afterward, her brother Jack took her to lunch at the nearby Clarendon Hotel, lecturing her on the importance, in her new status, of avoiding distasteful publicity. Fanny was only half listening. Her eyes were on a printing shop across the street, where the machines were stamping out a new business card: "Fanny E. Holtzmann, Counselor-at-Law."

Jack was hesitant about using his old Bull Moose contacts to help Fanny get into the Bar Building. The Bar Association of New York at that time had no women members, was not especially fond of Jews (Jack himself was not a member), and looked more favorably upon a Harvard Law diploma than one obtained at night from Fordham.

But Benjamin Cardozo remembered her favorably. The judge was about to move in as a tenant himself; with him as a shield, Fanny was able to battle her way in alone. The diehards who still resisted were won over by Fanny's appearance before the building's Character Committee: "Gentlemen, women have the vote. Further progress is inevitable. Our common concern should be to attract the best types of women to the law, to set honorable standards. Why admit a woman to the practice of law if you're going to ban her from the Bar Building? A tolerant approach will reflect greater dignity on all of us."

There were thoughtful nods. Fanny pressed her advantage. "One thing I promise you: I will never, never go into the Men's Room."

The nods gave way to chuckles. The argument was over.

Fanny moved into spacious quarters on the ninth floor. She furnished the suite sumptuously, having bought up at a fraction of its original cost the office equipment of a recently deceased corporate attorney. Massively wrought carved oak from Spain — desks, cabinets, sofas — set the tone. With Goulding's assistance, she acquired from a theatrical warehouse a magnificent deep-crimson rug. She found steel prints of courtroom scenes in a secondhand bookstore, polished them up, and strung them out along the library wall.

As her assistant, she hired with typical unorthodoxy her former boss, Joe Hochman. She felt the need for a male associate to handle the not-always-dainty nuances of matrimonial cases. "Hockie," who had just split up with Tobias Keppler, was a meticulous detail man, accustomed to her ways, and no glamour boy apt to charm away her theatrical clients.

Her transition to the Bar Building was eased by Judge Cardozo. In his early fifties and unmarried, Cardozo showed a flattering concern for the little girl from Brooklyn. He welcomed her personally to the building. Two days later, at lunchtime, he telephoned: if she had nothing better scheduled, would she like to come up to his office and share a couple of cheese sandwiches?

Fanny went often in those first weeks. The judge would sit back in a swivel chair, a pencil tucked over his right ear, chatting away at random: about Jewish history, personal philosophy, the law. "Above all," he told her, "stick to your own beliefs, your private values — no matter what people say."

Fanny was gratified by the attention. Cardozo was a man of noble bearing, with a keen gaze and firm square jaw that bespoke calm integrity.

More, Fanny sensed in him a great spiritual depth: "In his piety and dignity, he was a throwback to the rabbinical sages of antiquity." His observations on the law had for her the weight of Mosaic pronouncements. Cardozo stressed what he regarded as the essence of common law: for every wrong, there was a remedy. It did not matter if everything — the statute, the decisions, the body of precedent — was apparently against you; where a case was just and legitimate, a way to press it under law could be found. It was the task and obligation of a conscientious attorney never to give up, to keep trying until one day the breakthrough came.

He suggested that in view of Fanny's interest in films and copyright law, she take a night course at Columbia University in motion picture production. She promptly enrolled. "But your true education," he cautioned, "will come from your clients, your day-to-day experience as a lawyer. In every case, every problem that is brought to you, explore it to the bottom; find out what went wrong. That way, you'll gradually develop an expertise in an entire field. Asking questions is indispensable to this profession. You will be a good lawyer because you have infinite curiosity."

Musing on the great justice fifty years later, long after his appointment to the Supreme Court and his death in the thirties, Fanny commented: "If there was any man in the world I would like to have married, it was Cardozo."

Soon after Fanny's move into the Bar Building there was activity on the Goulding front. His screenplay of *Fascination* was a hit. Script offers rose to $15,000 and then $25,000; from Hollywood, Harry Rapf of MGM hinted at interest in a long-term contract.

"Nothing doing," said Fanny. "What those people really appreciate is success in another medium. You see what a difference *Fury* made. Now I want you to do a play on Broadway."

As usual, Goulding demurred . . . and by lunchtime the next day was spilling over with ideas. He outlined one for Fanny at the Ritz Grill, casting it on the wing, playing all the parts as was his custom. It was a modern drama of a rebellious mother, refusing to be put on the shelf when deserted by her husband at forty.

"Marvelous!," breathed Fanny. "The matinée audiences will eat it up."

Across the room she spied the Selwyn Brothers, Archie and Edgar. They were important producers. Edgar, the younger and gentler of the two, was also a successful playwright. Fanny beckoned him over. "Sit down, Edgar. And listen."

Goulding swung into his play again — with variations, of course. A true artist, he never repeated himself. When he finished. Fanny turned to Selwyn: "What do you say, Edgar? Would you like to collaborate with a new playwright? Between your knowledge of structure and Eddie's feel for dialogue, you can bat out a great play in a matter of weeks!"

Selwyn was intrigued. Before he could change his mind, Fanny steered him back to the Bar Building to sign a letter of agreement.

As Fanny had anticipated, it was a good collaboration. Goulding flung out ideas like a pitching machine in a baseball training camp; Selwyn fielded them deftly, tossed some away, and reworked others. His dialogue meshed nicely with Eddie's. In a month, they had finished a draft of *Dancing Mothers*.

To Fanny's dismay, Goulding announced that he was departing for Rome. This, she knew, was his way with movie scripts; once he had spun out his story, he was impatient with the refinements of polishing. And for this jaunt, he had a good excuse. Charlie Duell's production of *The White Sister* in Italy had run into trouble; Duell himself was in an awkward personal situation with Lillian Gish. The production schedule had to be revised, and only Eddie could make the necessary script changes.

Selwyn was annoyed, but went ahead with plans for the play. A post-Easter tryout in Atlantic City was arranged. In Eddie Goulding's absence, Fanny attended. She wrote to Goulding that Mary Young was excellent as the "Dancing Mother,' and the new blond ingenue, Frances Howard, "simply breathtaking" as the daughter.

Selwyn was less happy with the casting. Nor did he consider the young attorney an adequate substitute for his collaborator. Fanny had a premonition of disaster. She cabled Goulding: "Situation in jeopardy unless hurry back."

Goulding scrambled aboard the next sailing of the *Aquitania*. Fanny went down on the revenue cutter to meet him, and they entrained at once for Atlantic City. Goulding sat through one act of that evening's per-

59

formance, and turned to Selwyn: "You're absolutely right about wanting to replace Frances Howard . . . and you, Fanny, are totally wrong."

"What are you talking about, Eddie? The girl has star quality. She's — she's ethereal!"

"Precisely. With a girl like that making eyes at him, why on earth would the leading man look at her mother?" He put an arm on Selwyn's shoulder. "Get that little girl Helen Hayes."

"Helen Hayes!," protested Fanny. "But she's so drab!"

"Not drab — but not too glamorous either. She's exactly what we want." He turned out to be right. Fanny never forgot the lesson.

And Frances Howard never forgot Fanny's loyalty. Frances didn't get to work for the Selwyns, but she did acquire part of their name. A young film producer named Sam Goldfish teamed up for a time with the Selwyns to form "Goldwyn Productions." When the partnership broke up, Sam decided to keep the name. Frances Howard ultimately became, and has to this day remained, Mrs. Samuel Goldwyn.

The tribulations of *Dancing Mothers* did not end in Atlantic City. With the play booked for a late-summer opening in 1924, Goulding and Selwyn were suddenly confronted with a charge of plagiarism. Clara Lipman Mann, wife of a famous stock-company star, claimed the play had been stolen from her unproduced manuscript "The Lady from Westchester." According to Mrs. Mann, her story had been informally related to Goulding by Nora Bayes, a former Ziegfeld Follies favorite who had figured in a much-discussed romance with the Englishman soon after his arrival in America. Since Miss Bayes, star witness for the plaintiff, had parted company with Goulding some time ago, there were hints of a personal vendetta.

Mrs. Mann had retained formidable counsel. Caruthers Ewing was an imposing and oratorical southerner in his sixties. General counsel to the Atlantic and Pacific Tea Company, frequent adversary of the renowned Max Steuer, Ewing was himself a leading attraction among courtroom audiences. When he pronounced his name, the very roll of the syllables was enough to intimidate most antagonists.

Not Fanny. Thanks to Judge Cardozo, she had been immersing herself in copyright law at Columbia. She had the further reassurance of an extraordinary claque in her corner when the trial opened in the old Federal Court House.

Her status among her fellow tenants in the Bar Building had undergone a considerable change. From the time Mae Murray and Clifton Webb were seen with her in the lobby, curiosity overcame reserve. Venerable heads began poking through the door of Suite 914 in the hope of glimpsing some luminary from the magic world of footlights. The day Fanny arranged tables for her colleagues in the sacrosanct private dining room of the Algonquin, their conversion was complete.

Thus, when Fanny appeared before the bench, she had a high-powered cheering section scattered through the courtroom, urging her on with nods and smiles. At the end of each day's arguments, they swarmed around her with tactical suggestions.

Because Goulding disliked Joe Hochman's elephantine manner, Fanny was trying the case herself. The presiding judge was John C. Knox, thin-faced and austere but always polite and scrupulously objective. Fanny tried to keep in mind a pretrial briefing by Judge Cardozo: "Remember, a judge is a human being. He doesn't know everything; so keep your argument simple, clear, direct.

"And above all, be truthful. The moment you fabricate, you're in trouble. You can *explain* the behavior of your client, its origins and motives — but don't ever misrepresent it."

The climax of the trial came when Nora Bayes took the stand. Fanny's elderly champions thronged the court, relishing the tabloid-headline overtones of the situation: fading Broadway queen clashing with doughty young Portia over handsome rising author. Judge Knox would know how to read between the lines, they assured her. As Judge Cardozo put it, "a judge is a man who lives in the world. Over the years, he develops acute antennae. His own experience tells him when a witness is bending the truth."

By methodical questioning, Fanny was able to torpedo the plaintiff's case on the critical question of access; she established that by the date cited by Miss Bayes as the occasion of her conversation with Goulding, the Selwyn-Goulding manuscript had already been turned in to the typist.

Judge Knox delivered a verdict in favor of Goulding and Selwyn. So did many thousands of theatergoers. *Dancing Mothers* ran for 311 performances and film rights were sold to Paramount Pictures.

Eddie Goulding, with a Broadway smash added to the movie and book triumphs already under his belt, was the "hottest" writer in New York. Now, when calls summoned him to the Hollywood heavens, Fanny sent him spinning into orbit there with a multi-picture contract at MGM. He was on his way to a directorial career that would encompass more than thirty films, and place in his hands the talents and destinies of many of the screen's greatest names: Garbo, Crawford, Swanson, Bette Davis; John Barrymore, Leslie Howard, Tyrone Power.

Parting was not easy. Fanny and Eddie had been more than mutually dependent; in a sense they had created each other.

They embraced fervently — but kissed only on the cheek — as she saw him off on the Twentieth Century Limited from Grand Central Station.

Were Fanny and Eddie Goulding in love? Time provides some intriguing hints, but no absolute answer.

That Goulding was seriously smitten is beyond doubt. He told Fanny's father and her sister Bertha that he would like to settle down, and that as far as he was concerned no other woman could compare with

Fanny. To one of her friends, encountered on Fifth Avenue, he confided the rest of the story: "I'm crazy about Fanny, I'd like to marry her — but I'm afraid of her." Goulding had grown up under the domination of two demanding women, his mother and sister. As a result, he was never comfortable with strong women of "respectable" background. To the world he presented a glittering façade; but he himself was always aware that his polished manners and lilting speech had been acquired secondhand at the Savoy Hotel, not at Oxford.

Nor, finally, could he escape the worry that his tippling would incur Fanny's wrath.

Fanny's situation was even more complex. Indisputably Goulding was a charmer, the cynosure of debutantes and dowagers alike. He was unfailingly attentive, never at a loss for a little gift or a compliment. Fanny was a romantic who had never been courted; Goulding had the accent and the aroma of the misty isles where Ivanhoe clanked his armor. Thrown into constant contact with her gallant knight, her future inextricably linked to his success, sharing the same tensions and suspense, how could a twenty-two-year-old girl with normal instincts *not* have fallen in love, knowingly or otherwise?

And yet there were terrible taboos against allowing her fancies to flow too freely or too far. The *shikker* or drunkard is anathema in Jewish folklore, a man without self-respect or social responsibility. Even more potent was the tribal stricture against marrying outside the faith.

Intensifying the dilemma was the day-to-day presence of the temptation itself, all the more shimmering because it was forbidden. But should Fanny be inclined to waver, to dream of a life devoted to sheltering a Byronic profligate, she faced the haunting question: what then would happen to *her*? "As long as I held myself apart from my clients, kept a kind of castle moat between them and myself, I was worshipped as someone different, untouchable. The moment I became susceptible, vulnerable — in effect, another woman with the usual weaknesses — the magic would be gone. It would be a case of Samson without his hair. Eddie was the focus of my career. If I fell for him, I would lose not only my major client, but the many who followed him."

Perhaps this was a convenient rationale. Fanny was ill prepared to deal with the emotional impact of a tornado like Goulding. It might have been easier to declare herself out of the contest. So, theirs remained an arm's-length romance, with neither raising demands that, instinct warned, the other would be hesitant to meet. Fanny never ceased to be for Goulding an omniscient and sometimes avenging angel; he lingered in her heart as a flawed Greek god, an alcohol-ridden Mercury dropped down from the clouds around Olympus.

And linger he did, for a number of years. In 1927 Fanny's admirer and confidante, the middle-aged duchess of Rutland, was still urging her to "get away your heart from what will never be happy. The first love is strongest in our praising hearts because he was alone." It was the relationship with Goulding that, however oblique and incomplete, awakened Fanny as a woman.

Zaida had been enjoying Fanny's progress. Among her connections, acquired in the interest of "protecting clients from being poisoned," were some of the town's leading bootleggers. Fanny had no penchant for liquor herself, but she let it be known that her grandfather was a connoisseur. To the back-kitchen entrance on Eastern Parkway came mysterious deliveries of plum brandy and rye (scotch, Zaida declared, was too northern a grain, foreign to his palate).

At ninety-five, Zaida went for a dip in the Atlantic at Coney Island; when his trunks were swept away by a wave, he observed cheerfully that he was "no worse off than Adam." But the old man was beginning to slow down, and there was no one at home to look after him. Reluctantly, the family moved him to the nearby Hebrew Home for the Aged.

Even in his sickbed, he clung to his sense of fun. Asked to whom he would bequeath his prayer shawl and holy books, he pointed to his youngest grandson, David, a handsome scamp of eighteen who showed no inclination whatever toward piety. "That," said Zaida, "will ensure their perfect preservation through posterity."

Zaida's most regular visitor, as ever, was Fanny. Writing to the family from out of town, she always enclosed a note to him. As the old man felt his time approaching, he dwelt only on the advantage his demise would confer on his favorite: "For the rest of your life, you have nothing to worry about. I'll be up there in Heaven, making sure you get what you deserve. It isn't everybody who has someone standing guard there to see that God does his duty."

In October 1924, the Home advised the Holtzmanns that Zaida was dying. Fanny rushed to his bedside with Lucy Schneeberg. They found Zaida in a coma, his splendid white beard motionless on the sheet.

"Zaida, this is Fanny! I've brought you a ten-dollar bill for your birthday — look!"

The blue eyes fluttered open. Zaida peered at the single-dollar bill in Fanny's hand. *"Naar op dein bobeh,"* he grunted ("Fool your grandmother"). He raised his eyes to Fanny's face for a long moment: "Go home. I don't want you to see me die. When you think of me, remember the good times we had."

The loss of Zaida and the departure of Eddie Goulding for Hollywood left a gap in Fanny's life — but not for long. The Webbs — Clifton and his ebullient mother, Mabelle — moved in.

Clifton Webb, long before his rise to movie stardom, had established himself as a leading figure of the American musical theater. Tall, slim and limber, with a trim blond moustache under his delicately tilted nose, he was the paradigm of the imperturbable man-about-town and the idol of the palpitating matrons who packed his matinées. Unfortunately, their affection was misplaced. Clifton's heart belonged to mama — as did his career and his checkbook.

It had not been an entirely happy arrangement for Clifton. Although Mabelle was gusty and amusing, she was innocent of Freudian insight. Because her son as an infant had boasted such "gorgeous golden curls," she had festooned him in flowered dresses and hired him out for modeling as a girl; Clifton was seven before he appeared in the theater in pants.

Nor was she better instructed in managing money; Clifton had arrived at international fame without achieving solvency. It was their latest financial calamity that, brought to Goulding's attention in the bar of the Algonquin, led them to Fanny's office.

Clifton had filed no income tax. Mabelle protested that she didn't know actors were *supposed* to. Fanny hastened downtown and explained to the Internal Revenue Service what had happened. The truth was absurd, she conceded — it was hard to believe that *two* grown people could be so irresponsible — but it was the truth nonetheless. There was no intent to evade or deceive; she would guarantee full and prompt payment.

The frank avowal worked; Webb was permitted to file and pay up without penalty or interest. No fee was requested by Fanny at the time, but upon admission to the bar her responsibilities to the Webbs broadened. She reviewed contracts, was consulted on all business moves — and was paid for her services. But, curiously, no written retainer, or even a handshake, ever formalized the agreement. As with Goulding and other longtime clients, "it was more of a personal relationship, almost familial. Nobody was ever tied to me, or I to anybody; people were free to leave. The Webbs had no big problems; my job was to see that they didn't run into any, that they had peace of mind. It was preventive — like a doctor's injections. At the end of the year they sent me a check for whatever sum they wanted."

Mabelle's eccentricities were as engaging as her tinkling laughter. Although a native of Indianapolis, she mingled with the cream of New York society — and kept stirring it briskly. She maintained an up-to-date scorecard on Park Avenue liaisons, and what she didn't know she never hesitated to invent.

Like many extravagant people, she was given to bursts of penny-pinching. One afternoon, in preparation for a particularly lavish party to be given for Katharine Cornell in the Webbs' huge Sutton Place apartment, Mabelle went shopping under the Queensborough Bridge, where a score of vegetable pushcarts were huddled across the street from the neighborhood Rolls-Royces.

As was her custom, Mabelle wandered among the Italian vendors, haggling for a clever buy. As she started off with a bag full of prime tomatoes, the man called her back; she had tucked away a few more specimens than she had paid for, he declared.

Mabelle entered an indignant denial.

Would she permit a recount, then?

Absolutely not — what an insulting idea!

The peddler called a policeman, and the policeman carted off the mink-clad bargain hunter to the police station.

Fanny, summoned by telephone, raced down in a taxi. She found Mabelle threatening to take the matter to her friend the mayor, Jimmy Walker. That suggestion, and a few tactful words from Fanny to the desk sergeant, sufficed to get the lady out on Fanny's recognizance.

The two rode back in silence to Sutton Place where, after slamming the door firmly behind her, Mabelle spread out her haul on the table. "Ha!" she crowed. "Four extra tomatoes I brought home!"

The next day she gave the vendor another dollar and invited him up for a drink; they became firm friends.

Another of Mabelle's cherished coups involved the Alice Foote Mac-Dougall Restaurant in the lobby of the Bar Building, which frequently filled tea orders for Fanny and her clients in the late afternoon. Often the tray delivered to 914 was not picked up until the next afternoon.

That, when Mabelle was among the guests, was too late. The shop used inexpensive but distinctive tea sets; greatly taken with Miss Mac-Dougall's pottery, Mabelle simply took it. Each time a tray disappeared into her taxi, Fanny paid the restaurant a few dollars. That was all the owner would accept: "You send me so many people."

Some of Mabelle's stratagems backfired. Once, angry because Clifton was planning a European vacation without her, she contrived to have their doctor fabricate a harrowing report on her son's physical condition. The impressionable Clifton, who had had a tuberculosis scare in his youth, was so upset by the gloomy diagnosis that he actually did develop alarming chest symptoms. Fanny was obliged to organize an elaborate masquerade in which, posing as Clifton's wife, she smuggled him into a world-famous specialist's office where his fears were allayed.

If Mabelle had her peccadilloes, they were more than offset by her loyalty. Her acquaintance in theatrical and upper-crust social circles was even wider than Eddie Goulding's, and she exercised it tirelessly on Fanny's behalf. Clifton's fellow performers, like Fred and Adele Astaire, were practically dragged into the office. Her approach to Blue Book friends like Mrs. Stuyvesant Fish was less muscular but equally persuasive.

The middle twenties were an era of high prosperity. There was a lot of gold in New York, and an army of ingenious women digging for it; the tabloid *Daily Mirror* reserved page three for its daily quota of millionaires hauled up for accounting by chorus girls. Into this boiling pot, Mabelle dipped zestfully. Fanny, who at the time by her own testimony "scarcely knew how babies were born," was touted by her friend as the world's outstanding authority on paternity cases and marital problems.

Judge Cardozo had urged her to "learn from your clients," and she did, although not necessarily at first in the areas that Cardozo had in mind. For instance, there was the horse-breeding stockbroker on Long Island whose wife was diverting herself with one of the grooms; staying home one day with a fancied headache, the broker discovered he had a real one. Fanny kept the divorce proceedings out of the society columns (and off the sports pages).

Generally, she got along very well with her Social Register clients. They found the little Jewish girl from Brooklyn a refreshing change from the city's "big" lawyers — traditionally white-haired and crusty, redolent of cigar smoke, musty leather armchairs and venerable midtown clubs. Fanny, by contrast, was so lightly feminine that once when she appeared in court on behalf of a British actor being detained at Ellis Island, the judge told her impatiently she'd "better send for Miss Holtzmann." Informed that she *was* Miss Holtzmann, His Honor warned her against "playing jokes with this court." It was not until she pulled credentials from her purse that the judge subsided and the hearing resumed.

Mabelle's friends were impressed also with the keen personal involvement that Fanny brought to every case. This was a lawyer who didn't lock up her desk and turn off her concern at five o'clock. She could throw herself without reservation into the problems of her clients, holding nothing back, staking her fate on theirs.

A postdebutante whose husband had been jailed for a fraudulent stock transaction was overwhelmed with grief; she was threatening to kill not only herself but the couple's six-month-old baby. Fanny went to Washington to seek a pardon from William J. "Wild Bill" Donovan, then a ranking official in the Justice Department.

When Donovan mentioned an appointment before lunch with President Calvin Coolidge, Fanny requested permission to see the chief executive. She presented her story to Coolidge, who commented softly: "Your client should not have done that."

"True," Fanny replied. "And his wife has a right to kill herself if she wishes, Mr. President. But not the *baby!*" And she broke into tears.

Coolidge signed papers releasing the felon in Fanny's custody.

The unconventional presidential encounter was typical of Fanny; she practiced law as if she had invented it. The sketchiness of her formal education actually operated to her advantage. Unburdened by pretense, she felt free to ask direct, penetrating questions; unaware of paralyzing precedent, she could create revolutionary approaches.

In the words of her first secretary, Frances "Fire" Davis, "her imagination worked overtime. There was always something on the burner." She might pencil-draft a letter half the night, dictate revisions the next day — then do the whole thing over from scratch on her own Remington. Once signed, with a flourish and the inevitable middle initial

E, the letter had to be rushed out by special delivery, whether or not its arrival time would make the slightest difference.

The extra stamps were essential to Fanny, part of the theatrical atmosphere on which she thrived. Understatement was not part of the Holtzmann heritage. Zaida had never shrunk from histrionics to make a point, and Theresa was famous for her well-timed "fainting spells."

Fanny's office throbbed with a similar air of high expectancy and cheerful improvisation. In setting fees, she followed the casual pattern established with the Webbs. She never presented a bill: "whatever you think is fair" would be acceptable. If pressed, she might mention what someone else had paid for comparable services. Usually the client, eager to display his or her generosity, would send a check for somewhat more. When that didn't happen, Fanny made no protest: "I figured that my greatest asset was a satisfied client. He'd tell someone else, and that's how the chain would grow."

Late in 1929, Clifton and Mabelle Webb returned from a junket in Europe to a dismal Broadway scene. The October stock-market crash had put the theater, along with everything else, in the doldrums. Vaudeville was dying; radio and the talkies were cutting into box-office receipts. Although the three stars of the successful Howard Dietz–Arthur Schwartz revue *The Little Show* — Clifton, the torch singer Libby Holman and the comedian Fred Allen — were all available, under the circumstances the revue's producers were not interested in putting together a sequel.

But Max Gordon was. Gordon had been a vaudeville advance man, a booking agent, and latterly New York office manager for the Orpheum Circuit. He had a lifelong yearning to be a producer, a $25,000 stake reluctantly supplied by Dr. A. H. Giannini of the Bank of America, and a deep respect for talent. What he didn't have was experience.

He went first to Clifton Webb who, with his agile dancing, operatically trained baritone, and deft clowning was, as an admiring critic said, "his own production." Clifton agreed to talk to his fellow stars if the would-be producer could entice Dietz and Schwartz into his plan. When Dietz said he might go along — provided George S. Kaufman would handle the direction again — Clifton dumped the entire tangle into Fanny's lap.

Fanny was familiar with everybody involved. Howard Dietz, the sketch writer and lyricist, headed the publicity department at Eddie Goulding's studio, MGM. Dietz's composer-partner, Arthur Schwartz, had grown up a few blocks from the Holtzmanns' home on Eastern Parkway. And Fanny knew George Kaufman as a mainstay of the Round Table.

She asked Clifton to bring Schwartz and Dietz to lunch. There she listened to their ideas for the new Webb-Holman-Allen vehicle, to be called *Three's a Crowd*. Everything sounded very promising. The one unknown ingredient, and therefore source of general uneasiness, was Gordon. "Send him to me," Fanny said.

Gordon came to her office: earnest, bespectacled, ribald and cigar-waving but obviously honest. "I like you," Fanny confessed. "And I'd like to let Clifton do a show for you. But your background is in vaude-ville, a dying institution. My first responsibility is to my client. Let me see if I can work something out."

The next day she telephoned Gordon with an audacious proposition. She would give her approval to the project on condition that artistic con-trol was left entirely in the hands of the writers and her client. "All you do is put up the money, provide the theater, pay the bills."

"But — but that's unheard-of!"

"Unheard-of or not, it's the only procedure that makes sense. These people have worked together before, they know each other's strong points and weaknesses; they're a great team. It's not as if I was talking about turning over the reins to amateurs."

Fanny made it clear that it was her way or nothing. Gordon took her way. He was not physically barred from rehearsals, but under the terms of her formula nobody was obliged to pay attention to his com-ments. So he left the aesthetic judgments to the people who were writing, staging and performing the show. It was one of the first instances of creative control by the originators of a production, and one of the most successful. *Three's a Crowd*, sparked by the memorable torch song, "Body and Soul," ran for 272 performances in the midst of a depression.

Fanny's only difficulty came when her father, invited backstage to meet the cast, offered to escort the sultry Libby Holman to an after-theater party at the Webbs'. Theresa, bitterly jealous, scolded Fanny for "leading an innocent man into your sinful world."

Away from home, the laurels were accumulating. H. L. Mencken, the acidulous scoffer at "boobus Americanus," invited Fanny to dinner and took respectful notes on her rocketing career. Judge Lyman Warren, an antifeminist holdout in the Bar Building who had fumed at Fanny's presence and wouldn't even hire a woman secretary, surrendered to the point of entrusting Fanny with his own divorce suit.

And politicians, with an eye on the growing women's vote, were show-ing interest. Elisabeth Marbury, a power in the national Democratic organization, told Fanny that New York State would be ripe for a woman governor in the coming decade; she should consider switching allegiances.

Republicans in Albany went Mrs. Marbury one better with a firm offer of appointment as deputy attorney general, directly under Albert Ottin-ger, the state's highest law-enforcement officer. Republican interest in Fanny had been stimulated in part by her brother Jack's recounting of her successes. Ironically, it was that same brother whose equivocal afterthoughts torpedoed the proposition. According to former Attorney General Nathaniel L. Goldstein, at the time a go-between in the negotiations, Jack had ambitions of his own and persuaded Fanny that "one Holtzmann in politics" was enough.

In New York, Fanny had unmistakably arrived. On the other side of the country, the huge iron gates of the movie studios were swinging open more widely before her. Fanny contemplated them without anxiety. Three thousand miles in the opposite direction she had already conquered an older and in some ways more imposing glamour-realm.

Chapter 4

F<small>ANNY FIRST</small> got to England by way of a cowboy from Texas.

Tex Austin was a big, rangy man — complete with broad sombrero, leather chaps and impenetrable drawl — whose rowdy rodeo was an annual attraction at Madison Square Garden. There it was seen in the early twenties by Eddie Goulding's friend, the impresario Charles B. Cochran, who engaged the entire troupe to cross the Atlantic and appear under his aegis at the Wembley Exhibition.

It was a risky notion. Rodeos were hard-hitting, rough-and-tumble affairs, and the British solicitude for animals was legendary. Cochran would have to tread lightly even to obtain official sanction for such an unorthodox import. His first need was for help in unraveling the legal technicalities involved.

Goulding, of course, recommended Fanny.

Did she know anything, Cochran persisted, about horses, cattle, animal inspection laws?

"My dear Cockie," was the expansive reply, "she knows about *everything*."

In fact, Fanny had never seen a live horse that wasn't pulling a milk wagon: "My riding experience was confined to the Prospect Park merry-go-round."

But she knew how to extract information, from a book or a client. For several evenings she haunted the New York Public Library, reading up on ranches, hoof-and-mouth disease, rodeo competitions and English concepts of sportsmanship. Then she rounded out her education over a lengthy lunch with Cochran and Austin. At first she caught only about every third word of the Texan's languid drawl; soon she discovered that by watching his gestures, "I could decode him."

Contract difficulties were quickly ironed out, and Fanny, now knowledgeable in the ways of animal medicine, made the necessary arrangements for health inspection of the livestock. She saw the troupe off at the dock; they landed in Southampton without a hitch.

A few days later Fanny was munching a cheese sandwich in her office, toying with the idea of investing in a pair of jodhpurs, when devastating news arrived: on the second day of the performance at Wembley a steer had been roped by a cowboy, taken a hard fall, and broken its leg. British animal lovers had risen in furious protest; the newspapers were full of pictures; the Royal Society for the Prevention of Cruelty to Animals was bringing court action to sling the rodeo back to Texas. The end of Cochran's cable was anticlimactic: "Take next boat."

Fanny arrived in London upon a scene of chaos. Cochran's English solicitors, Langton and Passmore, had engaged the famous "silk" or king's counsel Sir Edward Marshall Hall as barrister to plead their case in court. Sir Edward and his colleagues were ready to unleash their eloquence on the rodeo's behalf; but they were stymied by a problem of communication: Tex Austin was unintelligible to his Eton-bred advocates; their high-pitched inflections —"Are they a-talkin' or a-garglin'?" he demanded of Fanny — were equally baffling to him.

Fanny jumped in as interpreter. Austin, she discovered, was enraged at what he considered British hypocrisy regarding the treatment of animals: "Talk about cruelty and fair play — why, they'll turn out a whole lynchin' party for one li'l ole measly fox!"

Fanny did not consider that a productive line to pursue. A British court, put on the defensive about national customs, would not deal kindly with an American interloper. But the big cowboy was ranting on, along lines that struck her as far more promising: "Would I ever be fixin' to hurt one o' my dogies [motherless calves] on purpose, or be mean to a li'l pinto? Why, hosses are my best friends!"

Now there, suggested Fanny, was a theme that the defense could develop: the gallant tradition of America's cowboys, traceable directly to their animal-loving English forebears. She dwelt on the touching images of the Old West that could be evoked: the weary traveler refusing to drink at the stream until his faithful steed has been refreshed; the horse and rider melting together into the sunset; as the moon climbed in the sky, sleeping under the stars a few yards apart. At every turn, a tender regard for the cattle wrangler's four-footed partner.

Sir Edward wiped away a hypothetical tear, and asked Fanny to embody these sentiments in a brief suitable for submission to the court.

She did, drawing freely on her library reading. The rodeo itself, she explained, fitted completely within this affectionate framework. It was a test of skill and courage: no ritual torture by picadors and matadors, but a thrilling and equal competition in which nine-tenths of the bruises were absorbed by the riders. Every precaution was taken to protect horses and steers but, as in rugby and auto racing, accidents were not always preventable.

71

Fanny then met with her associates for a final review before they presented their case in chambers. They should remind the judges, she suggested, that ranching was a *gentleman's* sport. "Theodore Roosevelt, the twenty-sixth president of the United States, was himself a cowboy."

It was an impressive touch. The injury to the steer was ruled an accident, and the rodeo permitted to resume, its receipts substantially boosted by the attendant publicity.

But the news accounts made no mention of Fanny. Still very conscious of her brother Jack's reservations about show people, and his warnings against unseemly notoriety that would "disgrace" the family name, she stayed by scrupulous design in the background.

Her next trip to England was a different story. In the intervening year, many circumstances had changed. Eddie Goulding had been firmly installed on Broadway, and Fanny as firmly in the Bar Building, where her visitors now included emissaries from such potentates as Louis B. Mayer.

Among her warmest supporters in New York was a wartime associate of Goulding's, the eminent English journalist Edward Marshall. Marshall, a bearded pundit comparable in prestige to Walter Lippmann in America, was doubly enthusiastic because he had been initially skeptical about Fanny's powers, and had witnessed personally the transformation in his friend's career.

Marshall operated his own news syndicate. From an office in the New York Times building, he fired off stories, editorials and tips to highly placed publishers and public figures in England. On learning that Fanny was sailing for England, he sent out a buckshot mailing to his friends, advising one and all that a phenomenon was en route: a tiny girl who in her early twenties was already a prominent, respected barrister. He did not stint on her Hollywood connections, tossing in references to luncheon parleys with Mae Murray, Richard Barthelmess and Mary Pickford.

Much later, Fanny discovered there had been a curious sentimental overtone to these unsolicited praises. Marshall, in his middle sixties, had lost a daughter in early womanhood. Fanny, he told Goulding, was "very like my daughter, who resembled her Jewish mother."

Fanny sailed aboard the *Aquitania*, also chosen, as it happened, by a delegation of dignitaries visiting England from the American Bar Association. The first night out, she found herself seated at the captain's table between Justice Pierce Butler of the Supreme Court and former president William Howard Taft. Taft, enormous but kindly, for some reason plunged into an elaborate defense of his role in the Bull Moose breakaway of 1912. Theodore Roosevelt he dismissed as "nothing but a cowboy'; the real villain, in the Taft version of the campaign, was "this egomaniac Wilson" who had smashed the Republican Party and thrown America into war.

Fanny sat in attentive silence. The lone woman attorney on the ship,

Fanny on the deck of the Aquitania, *1924.*
Eddie Goulding is seeing her off

she was ineligible if only by reason of her sex for membership in the Bar Association. Nevertheless by the end of the journey she had been unofficially adopted by the group.

That, and the advance drum-beating by Marshall, were enough to bring the reporters from the London newspapers swooping down on her at Southampton. Judges were no novelty in England; a girl lawyer was, especially if she looked not much older than a teen-ager, wafted a vague, tantalizing aroma of moviedom, and hobnobbed with former president Taft, now chief justice of the United States Supreme Court.

Pencils flashed and cameras clicked. Fanny turned up on a half-dozen front pages and in the color rotogravure section of the *Morning Post*, where she was described as the "youngest attending member of the American Bar Association." Even Jack could not dispute the dignity of that billing — although he could, and did, challenge its accuracy.

By request of Taft and Paul D. Cravath, the distinguished corporation lawyer, she was included in all reception invitations: to Parliament, the British courts, Buckingham Palace. A special luncheon tendered for her by Sir Edward Marshall Hall was crowded with British chief justices. As Fanny saw it, "They were all afraid to miss something. Maybe this prodigy from America had two heads."

Fanny stayed with the Goulding family — his mother, sister and brother — at Kinnerton Studios, their mews dwelling near Hyde Park. Although only a few steps from the bustle of Knightsbridge, it was tucked away in a cobbled courtyard sprinkled with early eighteenth century pubs.

Fanny had barely settled in when the flamboyant Patrick Hastings, then a junior barrister "reading" with Sir Edward Marshall Hall, came

Chorus line drafted for a fiesta aboard.
The fifth cutie from the right is Fanny

around to sip tea and ask questions about the movie world. At that time New York was still the headquarters of film production; Hollywood was a distant backyard where the stars put in a few months of restive exile, returning to the Astor and the Algonquin as soon as the cameras stopped grinding. The British knew that Douglas Fairbanks had come to Fanny's office: "To them I was a Hollywood lawyer, although I hadn't yet been west of New Jersey."

The lustrous image was confirmed by her association with Charles B. Cochran. A bulky, impressive figure in his middle fifties, "Cockie" had produced *The Miracle* in 1911, and been impresario for the French nightclub star Mistinguette and for Houdini before achieving ascendancy in West End musicals. It was he who later brought Fanny such clients as Gertrude Lawrence and Jack Buchanan, and reinforced her ties to Noel Coward.

Childless, the Cochrans treated Fanny like a daughter. They had access to England's inner ruling circle; at their country home they showed off Fanny to MPs, authors, their titled friends. In a social sense, these ministrations were somewhat redundant. Fanny had already been touched by the wand of Nancy Astor.

Lady Astor was *the* hostess of the day: buoyantly outspoken, born in America, one of the beautiful Langhorne sisters of Virginia. She was the first woman in history to be elected to the House of Commons and would acquire further if dubious fame in the late thirties as the mistress of Cliveden, the country place overlooking the Thames near Maidenhead where the supporters of Neville Chamberlain would gather to defend "peace in our time."

Lady Astor made no bones about why she had chosen to honor Fanny with a party rather than the wives of the visiting American jurists. "My dear, you're all over the newspapers. You're even crowding *me* out of the headlines. Besides"— she gave Fanny a little hug —"you've no idea how proud I am that you're a woman — and an American."

Each guest, soon after arriving at the Astor town house in Mayfair, was handed a small badge describing his or her position in society, government or business. Fanny, instead of pinning the badge on her shoulder, tucked it away as a souvenir for her family. Lady Astor caught the move from the other side of the room and shouted her disapproval.

"I'm sorry, your ladyship," Fanny shot back, "but I want to be accepted socially for myself — not because I'm mentioned in the Court Circular. Name tags are for prisoners."

The spitfire of the salons blinked, then broke into a wide smile: "That's what I like about you, Fanny. Nobody ever had the gumption to tell me that before."

When the tabloid cameramen scurried in, Lady Astor directed them repeatedly to "our little American attorney," despite Fanny's protests that her hat had gone askew and "my sister Clara will never forgive me."

Thenceforth the Virginia patrician and the girl from Brownsville remained on good terms, although politically far apart. Usually they met during teatime at Parliament where, twenty years later, Nancy still delighted in presenting Fanny with a flourish as "the youngest lawyer at the American bar."

After her debut at Lady Astor's, Fanny became a collector's item in the small, aristocratic world of Belgravia. Many were eager not only to put their ancestral castles at Fanny's disposal, but to place their affairs in her hands.

Fanny had a shrewd understanding of her appeal to the nobility. Brought up in isolation, never really trained to shift for themselves, they had an essential helplessness, a childlike dependence, akin to that of actors. As she often observed when some high-titled client committed a particularly ghastly blunder, "What can you expect from royalty?" Just as the people of Broadway and Hollywood responded to her sensitive concern, the lords and ladies basked in her cheery confidence, her titillating connections.

She enjoyed her new friends. Once past the agony of adolescence, Fanny had become an easy mixer, striking up conversations with taxi drivers, shoeshine boys and salesgirls; she saw no point in being snobbish about stuttering earls. Carted off for a weekend in some baronial manor, Fanny was relaxed and spontaneous. Humanity at large was for her an extension of the intimate, spirited household in which she grew up.

Within that household, she might frequently have felt abashed, as the least privileged of its members; but away from home it was her unassailable shield: "I was comfortable in any company because I knew who I was and where I came from, and had no yearning to be anything else. My parents had never had material wealth, but they had given their children what money couldn't buy: culture, dignity, self-respect. I could never feel uprooted because wherever I went I took along my special square of soil — my sense of family."

In accordance with what would become a lifelong principle — to begin at the top — Fanny started her exploration of British society with a brace of duchesses. The two great ladies had nothing in common except Fanny. The duchess of Atholl was an earnest humanitarian — plain-faced, buxom and motherly — who radiated kindly concern and dedicated her days to social reform. In years to come she would be elevated to the cabinet and, for her opposition to General Franco in Spain, be dubbed the "Red Duchess." The frolicsome side of English country life she left entirely to her aging husband who, Fanny soon discovered, could not be trusted at a distance of less than two feet under the table.

Quite a different type was Violet, duchess of Rutland. She was up to her delicate ears in court gossip: a lady-in-waiting to the queen, an accomplished palace painter with three works hanging in the Louvre, an inveterate romantic constantly engaged in promoting Fanny's love life. Politically, she was part of the ultraconservative Cliveden set; more uninformed than malevolent, Violet was capable in the middle 1930's of inviting her little Jewish protégée and Hitler's ambassador to England, Ribbentrop, to the same intimate tea party.

The Rutlands' main country seat was Belvoir Castle, a fairy-tale concoction of turrets, terraces and crenellated battlements perched on a hilltop in Lincolnshire. Its earliest masonry, matched by the Norman windows in the round towers, dated back to the eleventh century. Inside, beyond the vast entrance hall and Grand Staircase, the castle was a succession of superb rooms: Grand Ballroom, red-and-gold Elizabeth Saloon, lofty Picture Gallery and tapestry-hung 130-foot Regent's Gallery. Dotting the grounds were statues, stables and kennels. Human living accommodations seemed almost an afterthought.

A week-end in this splendid setting was Fanny's introduction to high living. It had its moments of low comedy.

First, there were the discreet inquiries from the house staff as to her preferences in room location. Fanny had no idea what they were talking about, even when hints were dropped that such-and-such a young lord "usually stayed" in the east wing: "I didn't realize that informal twosomes were the order of the day. An English country home is chilly — no central heating — so the natives defend themselves as best they can. Warm flesh is comforting — and gives everybody a topic for conversation the next morning."

Her next surprise was the washing facilities. A single tub served the entire rambling castle; it was accessible only by prior arrangement with the butler. In Brooklyn there were no butlers but three bathtubs. "You don't know how lucky you are," Fanny wrote home to her family, "not to have to live in a castle. I saw a place yesterday where Queen Elizabeth slept in the sixteenth century. She didn't know any better."

Invited on further jaunts, Fanny tried to check in advance on the primitiveness of the accommodations; but whatever her grumblings, she usually accepted. For the fact was that this was the England of her childhood imaginings, the land she had been reading about in Walter Scott novels at the back of the room while her classmates were reciting the capitals of the Dakotas.

She confessed her feelings toward the end of her second visit, in an article written at the request of the London *Daily Telegraph* and spread over a column and a half of its editorial page. A publisher's preface introduced her as "a New York lady of great distinction in the legal world," who "though young in years has risen to a very high place at the American Bar." Despite "the invitations showered upon her amongst the old nobility" and "close professional acquaintance made with many judges and leading lawyers" Fanny had found time to study English mores: "Her story is permeated with evidence of a profound regard for the old country and its people."

What followed from Fanny's pen was an adroit dissection of the stereotypes — blustering Yank, stuffy Briton — hampering relations on both sides of the Atlantic, and a balanced appreciation of the two national cultures.

Anglo-American understanding, she wrote, had been advanced markedly by the warm reception accorded to the visitors from the American Bar Association. "The road you have traveled is our history and our lesson. We look with a thrill in our hearts on all your venerable institutions, the foundations of our own civil liberty and self-government. It is the young country speaking to the old, whose heritages it carries on so successfully."

Very few Americans, in or out of office, were allotted two thousand words in the stately columns of the *Telegraph*. When the New York *Times* correspondent in London filed a story *about* Fanny's story, Jack cabled his congratulations.

Still, Fanny was not sure of her family's wholehearted approbation. On her return home a week later she brought a trunkful of sweaters, gloves and silks: partly out of affection, partly from inability to pass up a bargain — but perhaps fundamentally as a peace offering.

Whatever the response of her family, the British triumph had an enlivening effect on her office routine. The theatrical atmosphere remained. And Fanny continued to manage matters from behind her massive carved desk, one foot tucked under her in the Spanish-grandee armchair as she chatted away on the telephones that had become a physical extension of her personality.

But now a new, made-in-Britain note was added. It had become *de rigueur* for Englishmen arriving in America to stop in at the Bar Building. "Did you see Fanny in New York?" was a routine but eager question on their return; a "yes" answer established one as part of a special inner clique.

There were theater people like young Noel Coward, a fervent patriot who was quite overwhelmed by Fanny's status among the nobility. Noel's brittle wit, until she knew him better, made Fanny uncomfortable; he seemed ready to cut up anyone for a successful joke. Less breezy gentlemen telephoned before coming by, mumbling high-sounding titles in strangled voices (an uninstructed office boy hung up in disbelief on the duke of Rutland).

At news of a major transatlantic docking, the office adopted an extravagantly British manner, in effect donning a collective bowler-and-Burberry. New York accents were softened, questionable hairdos modified, ceremonial bows exchanged. Everybody fell into the game with great good humor except the blunt Joe Hochman, whose noisy nose-blowing and cackling laughter were calculated to jar British sensibilities.

"When we went into our Mayfair number," recalled a secretary of the period, "we had to keep Hockie out of sight on some errand."

Fanny, buoyed by a quick instinct for falling into the ways of anyone she was dealing with, had unconsciously picked up a variety of telephone accents. She could swap tough Broadwayese with the Shubert crowd, solemnly quote Latin to a law professor, and lapse into a homey, Yiddish-spiced vernacular with movie producers, many of whom had immigrant backgrounds. With Park Avenue matrons, nervous about impending divorce actions, she communicated soothingly in their own casual Bryn Mawr drawl.

Now, after exposure to the inflections of Belgravia, she glided into the speech of a cultivated Englishwoman. "One must always be careful," she reminded her staff with a straight face, "to keep one's vowels open." Ten minutes later, when some footloose baronet arrived, secretaries and clerks would be convulsed to hear her shift from earthy informality to the lofty diction of Buckingham Palace.

Whatever the reactions of her staff, Fanny was, in Broadway terms, boffo with the British. The visitors who came to tea always spoke with nostalgia of Fanny's previous trip and wanted to know when they could have the pleasure of rolling out the red carpet for her again.

These flatteries, combined with the accumulation of business matters and her restlessness at home, had the desired effect. Within fifteen months she was on her way back to London, in what would soon settle into a pattern of virtual commuting.

Between her second and third crossings, Fanny had slipped in a trip to California, where she made it a point to send her British friends cards postmarked from Hollywood: "They'd all had mail from America before, but never from Hollywood." She was now London society's acknowledged authority on the movie capital. Among the journalists of Fleet Street, she was something more: a good camera subject, an attractive dinner companion, and a source of lively quotations.

As the decade wore on, and Fanny shuttled frequently between the West Coast, New York and England, her interviewers broadened their praises and her reputed areas of expertise. The *Sunday Graphic*, under a striking photograph ("She is young, fascinating, beautifully gowned and thoroughly feminine"), complained that Fanny would not say a word about famous new clients like John Gilbert and Ina Claire, then went on solemnly to record her observations on prohibition ("the greatest thing ever invented for attorneys, but it ought to go") and American manners: "When English people visit America they may be shocked by the free-and-easy speech of New York taxi drivers. But they must not confuse it with bad manners. It is simply the result of living in a democratic country, where the words 'sir' and 'madame' are unknown."

A *Daily Express* interviewer too gave evidence of a personal susceptibility to his subject. He noted that despite her well-established refusal to share Hollywood secrets, she looked "much too pretty to be discreet." Her eyes were "enormously large, velvety brown, surrounded by a field of white"; they resembled those of Joan Crawford, and "like Miss Crawford's, they have much the same hypnotic effect."

Since these news stories reached into every corner of Britain, they had interesting repercussions. A stiff little man in spectacles and high collar turned up one day at the Savoy Hotel, where Fanny was staying, and introduced himself as Rudyard Kipling. Was it true that she had direct access to Irving Thalberg, chief of production at MGM?

Fanny laughed. "I don't know what you mean by 'direct access,' but I used to see a good deal of him and Norma Shearer socially."

"Would you — could you — do something for me?" Kipling was terribly upset. He explained that he had sold the film rights to his classic *Kim* to MGM, but had been totally frustrated in his attempts to convey certain ideas about its treatment to Thalberg: "My letters never got past the palace guard."

Fanny promised personal delivery of his comments —"on anything up to ten thousand words." And she meant it: "Movie stars I could take or leave — but how many ex-bookworms from Brownsville get a chance to do a favor for Rudyard Kipling?"

He wasn't her only literary giant. John Galsworthy broke up a whist game to seek out Fanny in a Belgravia drawing room. The conversation went erratically — he was intent on exploring legal complexities, she on discussing his play *Justice*, in which John Barrymore had appeared on Broadway — until he raised a specific copyright problem, and Fanny made an incisive recommendation. The next morning he sent flowers to her hotel.

There were always business reasons to justify a trip to England — tax and immigration cases, a new Cochran production opening in the West

End — but mostly Fanny went to relax and be fussed over. By the late 1920's she had become quite attuned to England's stately mansions — but not without occasional tremors, dilemmas and mishaps.

British society floated on a pool of high-proof brandy, and Fanny's tastes ran to nothing stronger than malted milk. The only alcohol she ever drank was the sweet wine prescribed for Passover services, and even that left her a trifle dizzy. Besides, she had a terror of developing a liking for liquor; knowing the intensity of her own nature, she had visions of winding up as a hopeless alcoholic.

But she didn't want to be marked as a blue-nose spoilsport, so she hit on what struck her as an ingenious solution: She would mournfully announce herself as a member of Alcoholics Anonymous, a past tippler so fiercely dedicated to the bottle that she had been obliged under medical orders to forswear it. The ruse worked. Her hosts, thrilled by the hint of bygone wickedness, never pressed the matter further.

Hunting was another feature of manor life for which Fanny had not been prepared. Once, on vacation in Scotland, she managed to avoid the grouse-shooting — but not the grouse. One of the birds, "still warm with life," was served for dinner. During the carving, the hunters related with gusto how they had spotted and brought down half the covey. Fanny blanched: "I felt like a cannibal." Pushing her plate away, she explained with a feeble smile that she was a devoted vegetarian.

"But Fanny — we had steak together a month or two ago —"

"It's a recent decision. Forgive me."

Inevitably, as part of a set that spent a lot of time riding to hounds, Fanny got caught up in a foxhunt. She had been able to dodge several such excursions until the morning when she was staying at a fourteenth-century showplace near Melton Mowbray, 105 miles north of London, and visitors from all around the countryside came clattering up for a hunt. Unable to make arrangements to return to the capital —"as for communications, you might as well have been in a Peruvian mountain village"— she decided to go along.

Fanny had progressed somewhat as a horsewoman since the Tex Austin days, mainly through lessons in the San Fernando Valley; she liked the rocking-chair comfort of the curved, roomy Western saddle.

Suiting up in a borrowed ensemble, she felt a mild exhilaration. She would be riding off to hounds with duchesses and earls, historic personages whose names read like the characters in a Shakespearean tragedy. True, the long-faced, bony women mounted in the courtyard below looked alarmingly like the horses they were riding, but the men had the proper dash and color. As for posting in the flat, bare English saddle, she was willing to take her chances. Presumably the fields of Leicestershire were included in surveillance by the angel patrols of heaven.

The only available equipment, alas, turned out to be a *side*saddle. Brawny hands swung her aboard before she could protest. This was a totally new, totally disconcerting experience. Precariously balanced, maintaining her seat more by determination than by technique, Fanny felt that each jolting step might be her last.

After a mile along a wooded trail, glad cries from up front assured the stragglers that there were "splendid jumps" ahead. Fanny decided not to count too heavily on the angels. She developed a convenient "chill" and retired as a huntswoman undefeated.

As a rule, the weekend guest lists were predictable, but there were exceptions. At a tea party in central England, a slender man idling at the piano was pointed out to her as T. E. Lawrence, "the chap who united the Arabs." Hovering nearby was a larger man with a sweeping moustache who suddenly detached himself from Lawrence and approached Fanny. He said something in a language that sounded foreign but dimly familiar.

As Fanny hesitated, groping for a reply, her hostess interceded: "My dear, this is Ronnie Storrs, governor of Jerusalem." At once Fanny recognized the not-so-alien tongue as Hebrew. Her own Hebrew vocabulary was meager, but her capacity for aplomb was not.

"*Shalom*," she responded to General Storrs, falling back on the catch-all term that served for hello and goodbye as well as for peace, its original meaning.

To her relief, Storrs fell into chatty conversation in English. When Fanny mentioned that she was the daughter of a pioneer Zionist, Storrs invited her to be his guest in Jerusalem. As matters turned out, it was Storrs who later came to visit the Holtzmanns in New York.

The familial note was struck again at a party given by the duke of Kent. Fanny was introduced to a very old, courtly Austrian nobleman who was busily telling fortunes — whether as a professional entertainer or a fellow guest she could not be sure. His name, a Teutonic clutter of *von*'s and *zu*'s, rang a distant bell. Comparing notes, she discovered that the count's estates included Zaida's hometown of Rohatyn; Zaida's mentor, the fabled Uncle Itzik, had been steward to the count's father. The old man bent low over Fanny's hand: "My dear, we are practically related!"

Fanny felt "like the Countess of Mittel Europa." She hoped Zaida was looking down from his heavenly perch.

All these diversions were momentarily ego-building but fundamentally unsatisfying. Fanny could not, as her sister Clara put it, "really share in the extravagances" of the ultrarich. As the financial depression reached England, Fanny would look out from her second-floor suite in the Savoy at the homeless men and women sleeping along the Thames: "Only the lucky ones had benches. And I had just come back from country places completely screened off from this world of poverty. Something was terribly wrong."

Brooklyn offered at least the comfort of shared values. At St. Mark's Place, where Fanny had installed her parents in a sprawling penthouse, she could argue politics with the elevator man, cut her own hair, and raid the refrigerator for the ethnic foods she prized. Being home, however, also meant submerging herself in the lives and interests of her large family — and sliding back to her own insignificant status there. The lovely gowns she had acquired at Chanel in Paris were, like her opinions, disregarded; most of them wound up in Clara's closet. And each return to New York underlined an increasingly disquieting reality: with Rita and now Stella married, only Clara and she answered to "Miss Holtzmann."

Fanny was haunted by the blunt advice of the elderly shipbuilder Sir Alfred Yarrow, who amid the general adulation in England had urged her to "get married and have a normal life." Yet she had discouraged intimacies with the young men about town who squired her to the London theater and had formed no serious attachments there. She knew that courtship at the Savoy Grill was game-playing, that these gallants were not of her real world.

Was she held back also by lingering feelings, however muted, for Eddie Goulding? Her friend the duchess of Rutland thought so, and in short penciled letters protested: "It's purely a mother's love to improve and help the old friend. He will ever grieve you — unless you can always be at his elbow — or you can 'care' elsewhere."

Through the 1920's, she did not really care elsewhere. Propelled by an inner restlessness never completely assuaged by her British triumphs, she became increasingly involved with Hollywood.

Chapter 5

*F*ANNY FIRST DESCENDED on Hollywood on a bright January morning in 1926 amid the fragrant orange groves of San Bernardino, at that time the train terminal for important movie-colony arrivals. Although the dawn was barely breaking, she was greeted with everything but a twenty-one-gun salute. Boutonniered MGM executives clambered down from their chauffeured limousines; giggling secretaries rushed forward with flowers. The formal welcome on behalf of the studio was extended by Harry Rapf, the vaudeville agent-turned-producer who had snared Goulding for MGM via transatlantic telephone negotiations with Fanny in London. Rapf presented "creative chief" Irving Thalberg, who apologized for the unavoidable absence of Louis B. Mayer himself.

Eddie Goulding, tanned and vigorous, swept Fanny off in his white Packard convertible and brought her to the Ambassador Hotel. In her suite more bouquets were waiting: from John Gilbert, Norma Talmadge, Joan Crawford — virtually every star on the MGM roster.

Behind this effusive welcome was the spectacular success of Goulding's first picture, *Sally, Irene and Mary*. Working on a low budget and in the comparative anonymity of the Harry Rapf production unit, Goulding had taken over the director's megaphone for the first time and from his own screenplay had fashioned an unmistakable hit.

Even more important from the studio's perspective, he had shown an instinct for star-building, for drawing performances out of women, that would become legendary. When he began rolling his cameras, it was on three unknown players: Joan Crawford, Constance Bennett of the New York stage, and Sally O'Neil. Eight reels later, the studio had a trio of new stars who could be marketed around the world.

Thalberg, ever alert to a fresh touch on the set, started wooing Goulding for his own select stable. Mayer was equally impressed. He saw in the English newcomer a source of pictures that would combine the Mayer banners of box office and moral rectitude.

Everybody at MGM knew of Goulding's dependence on Fanny. Far from being secretive about their daily exchanges of telephone calls, letters and telegrams, Eddie had continued as in New York to broadcast the wisdom of his young attorney. Clearly the path to his allegiance lay through Fanny.

But the studio brass, like Goulding himself, were immersed in dawn-to-midnight story conferences and casting sessions; they could hardly give the visitor from the East the proper attention. A companion-guide-liaison operative was desirable for another reason: with geographical separation, Fanny and Goulding had reached a plateau of relative detachment.

By collective inspiration, it was agreed that Fanny should be placed in the hands of Ruth Harriet Louise, the head of still photography at MGM. Although not yet out of her twenties, Ruth was a key figure in the Culver City operation; still photographs were the indispensable link between the studio and star-hungry exhibitors, as well as a lure to audiences. By the deft shift of a spotlight, Ruth could erase a neck wrinkle or give sculptured perfection to a bulbous nose. Her skills were real; but they were abetted professionally, Fanny soon learned, by membership in the intricate network of personal ties peculiar to MGM.

Ruth's maternal uncle, Rabbi Israel Myers, was the leading religious figure in the southern California Jewish community and founder of the Reform synagogue in Beverly Hills where Louis B. Mayer and his wealthy friends attended services. The rabbi's English-born, highly cultivated wife, Anna, had for several years provided guidance on entertaining to Mayer's wife Margaret, a small-town girl previously little instructed in the social amenities.

Through her aunt and uncle, Ruth Harriet Louise therefore enjoyed status at court. As she whisked Fanny along the palm-fringed boulevards — to studio lunches, picnics at the beach, Mexican curio shops, grandiose dinner parties at mountaintop hideaways — the convoluted structure of the burgeoning Mayer empire gradually unfolded itself. The first figure to emerge clearly for Fanny was the monarch himself, Louis Mayer.

On her initial visit to the studio, as Mayer's luncheon guest, Fanny was struck by the silence that fell over the vast dining hall the moment he crossed the threshold. Screen idols sat self-consciously with their forks in midpassage; comedians broke off their anecdotes until the great man had passed.

Mayer stalked to his table-throne in the executive section, head thrust forward in weighty concentration, hands clasped behind his back. His short, chunky body suggested reserves of crude strength; above his sharp nose, equally sharp brown eyes glinted behind steel spectacles.

He seemed indeed the personification of the MGM lion: a lordly, benevolent (if he wasn't crossed) autocrat battling the New York money-men for bigger budgets and better pictures on behalf of his protégé

Thalberg. Fierce, pompous, shamelessly histrionic, he roared in mock rage and wept saurian tears; once he punched Erich von Stroheim in the nose when the director asserted that all women were whores.

More commonly, he kept an appropriate distance between himself and his hirelings. He never, of course, read a script or a story treatment. Prospective stories had to be told to him, with suitable élan. Frequently his reactions seemed as capricious as those of a child.

Actually, L.B. knew exactly what he wanted. All the stories of his choice pursued three paths that were in effect road maps to his character: "decency," by which he meant an Old Testament–Puritan approach to sex; "Americanism," which he defined mainly in terms of the three men whose warmly inscribed photographs graced his desk — President Herbert Hoover, General Douglas MacArthur and Francis Cardinal Spellman; and "family," a concept that was as broad for Mayer as his patriotism was narrow. He doted on tales of self-sacrifice and rewarded loyalty. His own fervent paternalism embraced blood relatives, cousins by marriage, genial bootleggers and the entire personnel of the huge MGM lot.

To Fanny, Mayer was no enigma. His stern moral attitudes had a visible religious basis. Mayer's father was a pious Talmudist, his father-in-law a kosher-slaughterer. On High Holy Days, whenever Fanny was in California, the studio boss plied her with tickets to the elegant Reform temple he belonged to on Wilshire Boulevard. He himself, he confided, would be praying farther downtown at the orthodox Temple Israel favored by his father: "There, I put on a *tallis* [prayer shawl]. I stand with other Jews as my people have done for thousands of years — and I feel closer to God."

There were those who felt that in his fanatic stand on purity in films he saw himself as God's deputy. He was fond of quoting his mother on the obligation of men to "behave with respect toward women." He told Fanny: "I don't care what De Mille does, with his naked slave girls. No Mayer picture will have bedroom scenes, even where couples are married."

He showed typical elasticity, however, on the subject of Eddie Goulding's escapades among the extras and bit players. "No matter what Eddie does offscreen," he intoned to Fanny, "his *pictures* are models of decency."

Mayer had another reason for looking upon Goulding indulgently: he and the Englishman saw eye to eye on the social and political impact of films. Long before his colleagues in "the industry," Mayer was highly conscious of the movies' power to influence people and to sway entire populations. He knew and approved of Goulding's intense involvement, during World War I, in promoting Anglo-American understanding through the screen.

Of Mayer's third fetish, the family, he talked to Fanny freely and without apology. In the twenties, at least, he was a model son, husband, father and brother. He encouraged the marriages of his two daughters,

Irene and Edith, and was no less energetic in setting up jobs for relatives, both close and distant. When a local wag said MGM meant
"Mayer's ganze mishpocheh" ("Mayer's whole family"), he cited the
bon mot with pride. "Sure," he told Fanny, "my nieces and nephews work
here, and all my wife's relatives, too. Why shouldn't those with *mazel*
[luck] in a family help out the others? It's not as if I tried to pad the
payroll with *nudniks* [pests]. They have to make good, or out they go."

In his fervent campaigning for the MGM family, Mayer tried even to
bring Fanny within the fold.

His crown prince at MGM — "the son I never had" — was Irving
Thalberg. Mayer thought the boy wonder from Long Island and the
girl lawyer from Brooklyn would make a splendid match. So did Thalberg's adored mother, Henrietta, who was eyeing uneasily her son's
interest in Norma Shearer.

But the principals felt otherwise. Fanny liked the frail, soft-spoken
Thalberg who — an anomaly among Hollywood producers — actually
read books, and who opened his mouth only when he had something to
say. She appreciated his sensitive handling of Goulding, and felt at home
with his parents and his sister Sylvia. But that was it. Thalberg in turn
was clearly in love with Norma Shearer, in Fanny's eyes "a sweet, unpretentious girl who worried about his health and shared his interests."

So, far from trying to break up the Thalberg-Shearer romance, Fanny
lent a conspiratorial hand in it. She came to the Thalberg home as
Irving's dinner guest, thereby lulling his mother's apprehensions about
the actress; she did not resist Henrietta's lavish attentions.

Thalberg took quick advantage of the situation. Slipping away from
the studio for a few hours with Norma, he would intimate to his family
that he had been out with Fanny.

Once the ploy nearly backfired, when Henrietta pressed Fanny for a
full report on a concert she had ostensibly attended with Irving. Fanny
asked her "suitor" to brief her more carefully in the future.

She was back in New York in 1927 when Norma became Mrs. Thalberg.
Mayer, like Henrietta, reconciled himself to a good plan gone awry.
Naturally, in the nominal role of best man, the head of the MGM
family dominated the wedding proceedings.

Apart from an occasional brush with the front office in New York,
Mayer ran a tightly personal ship where mutiny was scarcely contemplated, let alone brooked. Every MGM regular was expected to stay
strictly within the family circle, socially as well as professionally. Fraterni-
zation with the personnel of other studios was frowned upon; the morning
after Fanny dined with several Paramount executives, she was peremp-
torily challenged in the MGM corridors: "What were you doing in Jesse
Lasky's house?"

The anticontamination policy grew even more pronounced when
MGM moguls ventured forth from their lair. Mayer and his entourage

whisked from California to New York to London and the Riviera talking only to each other, locked in an endless card game. Fanny ran into one group of producers and directors in Vienna, and ten months later saw the same half-dozen men gathered around a card table overlooking the Thames. They traveled like maharajahs, entertained in every capital by the resident MGM representative who, thanks to his control of preview tickets and autographed photos, was always an influential figure in the community.

Periodically, Mayer and other studio heads crossed party lines to badger each other at poker games or on the Hillcrest Country Club links. At these summit sessions, talent loans were negotiated, business intelligence exchanged, and the careers of "difficult" hirelings casually demolished. But mainly life at MGM was self-contained. The triumphs of each week were celebrated every Sunday during an all-day brunch at Mayer's waterfront home in Santa Monica.

Fanny found the weekly ritual a fearful strain. The women played gin rummy, retailed the latest gossip in the movie columns, and could be roused from their languor only by such items of hot controversy as the appropriate length for toenails. The men drank and played pinochle, drank and shuffled poker decks, or just drank. Fanny felt out of her milieu.

Amid the backslapping throng, she noticed two other guests who seemed equally bored. One, massive and smiling, she recognized as her amiable adversary of early Broadway days, William Randolph Hearst; the other, shrunken and dour under a black *yarmulkah* (skullcap), was Mayer's elderly father, Jacob.

The three misfits instinctively gravitated together, chatting through the long afternoons about politics, religion and philosophy.

Hearst, like Fanny, was there to advance a career for which he had long since assumed responsibility. His Marion Davies films had originally been released through the Goldwyn organization. When this was absorbed into MGM, Hearst had at first held back. Then Mayer came up with a new proposal: he would put up production financing, Miss Davies' salary and a percentage of the profits for her sponsor, in return for special treatment of MGM stars and pictures in the nationally powerful Hearst press. The arrangement was not exactly a founding-fathers approach to objective journalism, but it suited the two tycoons. It also gave unique authority to Hearst's movie columnist, Louella Parsons.

Fanny, while no admirer of Hearst sensationalism, was taken with the gentle, ruminative manner of the sixty-seven-year-old publisher. She found him positively touching in his devotion to the young mistress with whom he lived in the beach house next door. "I never saw two people more completely different. He was polished, well-read, self-assured; he made a persuasive argument for Christian Science and asked penetrating questions about my impressions of the British nobility. And he wouldn't touch liquor.

"Marion contrasted with him on all counts. She was the original dumb blonde, and a nonstop drinker. She couldn't play canasta any better than I could, so she would just sit there with a glass in her hand, constantly refilled by Louella or some other satellite. She didn't speak much, and when she did it was with a terrible stutter. I found Marion pretty unnerving, but Hearst was very patient with her. It was clear that he adored her."

At the other extreme from the gin-toting ex-Follies girl was old Jacob Mayer. Solemn, bookish, L.B.'s father seemed lost in the slick glamour mill of Hollywood. But he was always there, always treated by his son with a respect that to Fanny was genuinely impressive. "No matter who came to dinner — and over the years that included prime ministers, generals, scientific geniuses, because Hollywood, not New York or Washington, was the mecca for foreign celebrities — the old man alone presided at the head of the table, *yarmulkah* on his head. 'I don't give a damn who is being honored,' Louis used to say. 'If he doesn't like it, he can leave!' "

Behind this stubborn affection was a story that the old man recounted with pride. Fanny was aware that Mayer, since 1924 head of the Hollywood colossus created when Marcus Loew's Metro studio acquired the lavish Goldwyn physical plant in Culver City, had started in pictures as a nickelodeon exhibitor. Now she heard the intimate details of his rise from the man who knew them best. Louis was reared in New Brunswick, Canada, where his father, an immigrant from Russia, had built up a successful business as a junk dealer and enjoyed a solid reputation in the community. "My Louis was always my best son. The oldest boy, Rudy, was smarter, but he gave me trouble; from Louis I had only *naches* [dividends of pride]. He worked hard, he was reliable."

Traveling down to Boston on business for his father in 1904, the eighteen-year-old Mayer decided to stay. He got married, met a nickelodeon owner, and in 1907 saw a chance to acquire his own theater — a former burlesque house — in Haverhill, Massachusetts. By scraping together a fifty-dollar deposit, he acquired a three-day option against a total price of $600. He appealed to his father: "It's a business with a future, Pa."

"*Sindele* [Sonny], if you say so — all right."

A decade later, with two theaters and many distribution contacts, Louis was ready for the big leap into production. He put in a telephone call to Canada: "Papa, come down. I want to show you the picture I'm running: And the crowds it's pulling in."

Jacob came to the Colonial Theater in Haverhill, where his son was showing a film starring Anita Stewart. Lush and bosomy, with chestnut hair, Anita had been a Vitagraph attraction for several years. A line of waiting customers stretched to the corner.

"Did you like the picture, Pa?"

"Never mind the picture. For stories, I have my Talmud. I liked how many customers."

"Listen, Pa — this girl will soon be free from her contract. If you give me the money, we can sign her up."

"How much money?"

"A lot, Pa. But with her, I can start my own movie company."

The old man, as he put it to Fanny, "didn't know nothing about movies." But he knew his boy. "My son Rudy, of course, was against it. But I remembered how Louis would be out all day scavenging metals along the seashore, while Rudy talked about real estate deals. So I borrowed and mortgaged and that's how Louis got to Hollywood."

Jacob Mayer was no Zaida; he substituted bookishness for wit. Yet there was enough nostalgia for Fanny in his Talmudic erudition to endear him to her. And that in turn was enough to endear Fanny to Jacob Mayer's son. With or without a Thalberg romance, he treated her almost like a daughter, often inviting her to dinner on the servants' night off, when he and Fanny could enjoy Margaret's pot roast together in the kitchen.

Fanny did not share the prevailing harsh opinion of Mayer. His foresight and courage were undeniable; his less attractive qualities she could understand. L.B. had come to the New World as a young boy and had suffered through the self-conscious adolescence of an outsider. Mayer's furious impatience to shed the the past, his ghetto-based hunger for power, were familiar to her.

So she knew without deliberate reflection how to deal with him. If she tried to upstage Mayer, to play the intellectual lady lawyer, he would regard her as an enemy and unleash his trunkful of histrionics tricks. But by simply being herself, matching Mayer in bluntness and gusto, lapsing into Yiddish as he did to make a pungent point, she would serve her client best.

They talked about Goulding one Sunday over a gourmet brunch in Margaret's kitchen. "Did Eddie do a good job for you on the picture, Louis?"

"Yeah, that sonofabitch."

"He doesn't *shikker* [drink], give you any problems?"

"Not while he's working. As long as he brings in a picture on schedule, who cares if he goes on a bender later?"

"You're paying him a thousand a week, Louis. I think he's worth fifteen hundred."

Mayer nodded vigorously. "So do I, Fanny. But those *momzers* [bastards] in New York — I can't do it. Not yet."

"He needs twenty-five thousand to bring over his mother from England."

"I can't just hand out a bonus, Fanny. We have stockholders."

Long pause, as the two munched reflectively. Then, from Fanny: "Try this poppy-seed bagel, Louis. It's good."

"Mm . . . you're right."

"Listen, Louis . . . Eddie has this terrific new story. About a young couple who are crazy for each other, but they have five children. And when — get him to tell it to you, Louis. *Shadow Lane.*"

The next day, Mayer called Goulding into his office and listened, spellbound, as the Englishman ad-libbed his way through the four-handkerchief miseries of *Shadow Lane.* By nightfall, Mayer and Fanny had agreed on a purchase price of $25,000. The picture never got beyond the outline stage, but the deal brought Eddie's mother and sister over from London to Beverly Hills, where he set them up in proper movie-colony fashion.

It was not long before Goulding had his salary hike, too. Greta Garbo, after two tepid early entries, burst upon the public's consciousness in *Flesh and the Devil,* aided by well-circulated reports of a steamy off-stage romance with her leading man, John Gilbert. As the suddenly-brightest star in the MGM firmament, she could call the tune on her next picture. She demanded $5,000 a week, a classic story, and the best director on the lot.

Thalberg chose Eddie Goulding. With a prescient eye, he urged Eddie to leave the screen adaptation in other hands and concentrate his energies on atmosphere, pacing, camera movement and the myriad other nuances of direction, not least of them the handling of the star. The studio had a Derby winner and wanted to be sure of its jockey.

It was a brilliant decision by Thalberg and a liberating step for Goulding. Directing was the perfect milieu for his quicksilver talents, fecund but not always orderly. As an author, he sometimes went astray in his plotting, carried off course by the sheer multiplicity of his fancies. But with a story line crafted by such masters as Tolstoy, Somerset Maugham (*The Razor's Edge*), James Hilton (*We Are Not Alone*) and even lesser lights like Vicki Baum (*Grand Hotel*), Goulding could give free rein to his inventive resources. Solidly moored to theme and character, he was able to focus on the small decorative touches, poignant or amusing, that became his trademark.

Anna Karenina, released under the title of *Love,* was everything Thalberg had hoped for. It established Goulding indisputably as a major director, with the result that his world shifted from the drafting pad and the story conference to that of the movie set and the star dressing rooms.

Fanny did not entirely welcome the change. It meant that on every visit to Hollywood she would be obliged to maroon herself for hours on a hot, crowded movie stage while property men, electricians, make-up people and sundry assistants milled around between "setups." In her first brush with film-making, during her course in production at Columbia, she had as the only girl in the class been chosen for the lead in their Saturday-afternoon experimental film: "I told them I hated acting, but they went ahead anyway. The whole scene had to be thrown away."

She found Hollywood sets no more stimulating. The actual shooting was brief and repetitive, even with a sure-handed director like Goulding, who knew exactly how he wanted his footage edited. Tourists might gawk, but for Fanny the mechanics of movie-making were stupefying. Her retainers with actors always stipulated that she was not obliged to be on hand during filming.

Because she rarely tolerated boredom, and never hesitated to approach strangers, Fanny became chummy with the "real" people on the set: the lowly "juicers" who ran the lights, the camera crew. From them she picked up unvarnished comments on their alleged betters. She was proud, but not surprised, to learn that Eddie Goulding was the most popular director on the lot: thoughtful of his crew, open with his checkbook to anyone in need, never known to exercise arrogantly the make-or-break authority of his position.

Later she would hear much the same from the stars he directed. Although they were dreary company, these dwellers in the American pantheon could not be entirely avoided. The dullest evening of her entire life, Fanny claimed, was spent some years later on a Hollywood triple date with Gertrude Lawrence and Betsy Drake. Their escorts were Cary Grant, Errol Flynn and Sir Cedric Hardwicke. During dinner, Fanny could hardly keep her eyes open; only Hardwicke's wry asides kept her from falling asleep.

Sir Cedric delivered her to her hotel. "Well," he said, "you've had your glittering evening with the stars."

There were one or two exceptions. During a formal dinner party at the home of a woman writer, Fanny fell into conversation with a "lovely, well-bred Englishman" sitting on her left. In the usual fashion of introductions among the famous, she had merely nodded vaguely when her hostess said, "Of course you know — ?"

Over coffee, the interesting Englishman asked where Fanny was staying; perhaps they could have lunch?

"Forgive me — but I didn't really get your name."

"Ronald Colman."

Fanny gulped. "I'm so sorry." She had never, she explained, been much of a movie fan; the only pictures she saw were the prints run by producers in their homes. "And I haven't been in touch lately with my friends at Paramount."

Colman was properly gallant. "In that case, Miss Holtzmann, I am doubly flattered. You were listening to me for myself."

Then there was Garbo: not Garbo the glamour queen, whom Fanny regarded as the synthetic product of the MGM publicity machine, but Garbo the private person. "She was very non-Hollywood; direct and natural, loyal to Mauritz Stiller, the Swedish director who had brought her over. She couldn't stand crowds, noisy parties, the usual superficial chatter; she was always saying, 'I vant to go home.' "

What Garbo did like was art, including, many years later, a painting by Fanny on display at Clifton Webb's home in Beverly Hills. She told Fanny gravely, "This is good work. You must never give it up."

Fanny's regard for her was heightened by an evening with the Webbs at a plush restaurant on the Sunset Strip. Originally, Clifton had planned to dine there alone with Garbo, but his ever-jealous mother Mabelle had put up such a protest that he agreed to take her along if Fanny would join the party and make a foursome.

Garbo was, "for once, dressed to the teeth," in a stunning black chiffon gown that Fanny suspected had been designed at the studio. She looked ravishing. Mabelle, unequal to this kind of competition, sat in sullen silence, pouring down double martinis. Suddenly she let out a wail of distress; the martinis had been too much for her bladder.

Her son tried to console her: "It's just an accident, Mabelle." To Fanny he added defensively, "After all, she isn't doing anything Louella doesn't do."

It was Garbo who took charge of the situation, busying herself with a napkin and helping Mabelle to her feet. Gently as a daughter, totally disregarding the stares and whispers rippling through the restaurant, she guided the older woman to and from the ladies' room. It was a demonstration of dignity and compassion that Fanny never forgot.

By the late twenties, Fanny was a veteran of the Hollywood scene, entraining across country as frequently as she sailed to England. Her contracts with the home offices in New York, where the money decisions were made, gave her a special prestige. She knew the movie capital from the inside, its people and its foibles. It was a community built on sand, of rich, frightened transients who might be swept away by the next shift in the tide of public approval. The drive for cash and recognition while the sun shone was obsessive; the denizens of Hollywood were, in Fanny's words, "trapped at the bottom of a gold mine; the more they dug out, the more hopelessly deep they sank down."

In a less benign mood, she likened them to "animals in a circus, who need a lion tamer to keep them in line." Such expert services were hard to come by. West Coast lawyers were few in the twenties, and imbued with the mores of the movie colony. Once, occupied in England, Fanny passed on to a California attorney the tribulations of a much-married blond star. Months later, inquiring about her referral fee, she was told, "I should send *you* a bill. I wound up keeping that dame. It cost me a fortune in diamonds."

It was in these dubious conditions that the first crop of Hollywood agents emerged. Most had built-in ties to the reigning studio chiefs, either as relatives or former providers of personal services: bootleggers, barbers, masseurs. They were presumed to make up in loyalty what they lacked in business experience. Unhappily for their clients, the loyalty was frequently directed to the studios that set them up in business.

Under these circumstances, Fanny's reputation could only grow. The guidance she gave her clients was unique. Studio heads sometimes turned to her for an informed opinion uncolored by local rivalries.

*Fanny-in-Hollywood, as captured by the MGM studio photographer
Ruth Harriet Louise*

Closest among them remained Mayer. In one of their kitchen conferences he mentioned the difficulty of finding reliable escorts for his women stars. Fanny told him to create a pool among the titled Europeans in Hollywood: "Treat it as a casting situation; it won't add that much to your budget." Another time he asked Fanny how she would handle the "problem people" who plagued every studio: big stars given to drinking, ostentatious womanizing or questionable associations. It was the custom to surround such employees with spies and bodyguards, and hope for the best. Fanny proposed that instead the studio should write into their contracts a "morality clause," violation of which would be grounds for automatic dismissal. She was as pleased at Mayer's gratitude as he was by her suggestions.

Others high on Fanny's list were David O. Selznick, who in 1930 became Mayer's son-in-law; B. P. Schulberg, the former newspaperman who ran Paramount; and the suave, Dartmouth-educated Walter Wanger. She was also on cordial terms with the Warners, and somewhat less so with the Cohn regime at Columbia.

Harry Warner collected race horses; by Fanny's diagnosis, he "had illusions of being Harry Payne Whitney." His brother Jack, while more earthy, fancied himself as a performer; Fanny sat through a long lunch at which he competed for punch lines with Al Jolson.

Her prejudice against Columbia dated back to the early days in the Astor Building, when Jack Cohn was among her booking-agent neighbors. Jack dropped in often to report the rise of his brother Harry in Hollywood — and his own aversion to getting involved in the Columbia operation. Later, when Harry Cohn made a bid for Goulding's services, Fanny told Eddie: "Nothing doing. He treats his brother Jack shabbily. Anyone who can't maintain a good relationship with his own brother isn't likely to be trustworthy with you."

On minor issues related to her movie practice, Fanny was adaptable. She detested the bon voyage bouquets ("What is this, a funeral?") that attended her every departure from New York, but dutifully accepted them at Grand Central and then stepped down to unload them into her sister Bertha's arms at the 125th Street station. Because a good deal of business was transacted around swimming pools in southern California, she put childhood fears aside and learned to do the Australian crawl. And she was unfailingly mindful of her movie-struck nieces and nephews, especially the then-adolescent author of this book. From every visit she brought back precious autographed photos of such unapproachable goddesses as Clara Bow and Billie Dove.

The coming of sound hit Hollywood like a baleful tornado, leaving patches of glamorous wreckage in its wake. The storm had been in the air for some time, but nobody wanted to notice it. In 1925, Edward Marshall had sent to Fanny's office the electronics inventor Lee De Forest,

94

who claimed AT & T was infringing upon his basic patent for a talking-picture machine. A visit to his midtown laboratory convinced Fanny that the thin, harried De Forest had a workable device.

On her first trip to Hollywood, she approached Louis Mayer about it. Mayer snorted his disbelief: "I'm surprised at you, Fanny! Every day some crackpot comes to my office with a story like that. Even if it worked, who would be interested in hearing somebody speak off the screen?"

Ben Schulberg, usually imaginative, shook his head; Paramount wasn't going to rock the boat. And Richard Rowland of First National explained: "People go to the movies to dream quietly among the shadows on the screen. If the shadows speak, the illusion is broken. Besides, it's the bankers who make this kind of decision."

So Fanny went to her old friend A. H. "Doc" Giannini, a source of fatherly guidance ever since her early days in the Astor Building. As chairman of the board of the Bank of America, "Doc" was heavily involved in movie financing. He smiled at her naiveté: "It would mean a revolution, Fanny — new theaters, new training and equipment all around the globe — and instant obsolescence for the silent machinery. The audience for the silent screen is universal. Once you introduce language, you have to use many languages. Hollywood would lose its monopoly. What's the rush?"

Nonetheless, the new technology gradually crept in. At the end of 1926 the Warner Brothers introduced sound effects and a synchronized score in *Don Juan*, which starred John Barrymore. A year later they brought out *The Jazz Singer*, in which musical sequences were supplemented with live dialogue, and followed it with *The Lights of New York*, billed as the first "all-talking feature."

MGM buckled; the long lines pulled in by Jolson in *The Jazz Singer* were too much for either Mayer or the front-office boss, Nicholas Schenck, to resist. They hired fifteen sound engineers to midwife *Broadway Melody*. Early in 1930 the Roxy Theater opened in New York with the Fox feature *Happy Days* blaring songs and dialogue from a screen forty-two feet wide, and the new era was entrenched.

Its impact on Hollywood was shattering. The death of silent films altered not only the status of directors like Eddie Goulding, but the character of the town itself. Describing the transition more than forty years later, Joan Crawford said: "In 1929 everybody panicked at Metro, but I mean everybody — stars, producers, directors — everybody but starlets. Starlets didn't know enough to be scared." Producers reached out frantically to New York and London for theater performers familiar with handling dialogue. Along Broadway, Hollywood was no longer viewed as a distant barnyard where theater people went to pick up quick money before returning to the boards; it was a place where serious talent came to stay.

Most desperately affected by the change, of course, were the big stars of the silent medium. The majority had coasted to glory on the strength of their devastating close-ups, leaving the business of storytelling to the title writers.

The new rules demanded a sense of characterization and the vocal equipment to project it. Most of the stars found the switchover beyond their powers. Some found it impossible to combine memorizing lines with displays of emotion. In other cases, the timbre of the spoken voice was fatal, and despite the furious ministrations of coaches, unchangeable.

One such victim was John Gilbert. Caught up in Gilbert's downfall was a client of Fanny's whom he had lately married, the Broadway star Ina Claire.

Gilbert was the prototype of the American romantic hero, circa 1920. Tall and slim, he had dark ringlets and Pepsodent teeth. To Fanny, he looked like the perfect floorwalker at Macy's: "The only thing missing was the white boutonniere in his lapel." His conversation was bounded by Louella Parsons, *Hollywood Variety*, and his irritation at Irving Thalberg for letting Ramon Novarro use his make-up man. Nor did Fanny admire his idiosyncrasies: in his cups, he was wont to make maudlin capital of his "great love affair" with Garbo (the lady's explanation to Fanny of her surrender was simple: "I spoke no English — and I was lonely").

But that was a minority view of Jack Gilbert. To the silent-picture majority he was the Great Lover incarnate, an intoxicating blend of dashing ardor and roguish charm, most irresistible in his pairing with Garbo in *Flesh and the Devil*, repeated in *Love* and *Woman of Affairs*. Clearly the inheritor of Rudolph Valentino's mantle, Gilbert flashed his smile, strutted about in magnificent uniforms, and enraptured millions. By 1920 he stood at the peak of his career, rivaled as a box-office attraction only by Garbo herself, Clara Bow and Emil Jannings.

That was the year when the screen started talking, and Hollywood began looking to Broadway for help. Among the legitimate theater stars lured westward was Ina Claire: sleek, blond, elegant, a former *Follies* beauty who had developed into an outstanding performer of high comedy.

Ina Claire was the personification of Broadway, Jack Gilbert the king of Hollywood. They met soon after she reported for work in *The Awful Truth*, and in May of 1929 they flew together to Las Vegas to formalize what the press acclaimed as a "union of perfect lovers." It was his third marriage, her second.

For several months euphoria reigned at their Tower Road mansion. Gilbert was proud to have acquired a brainy beauty who traded quips with the most brilliant playwrights of New York and London; Miss Claire, weary of critics who hailed her intellect, reveled in the attentions of the nation's leading male sex symbol.

In the late fall, a certain edginess crept into Gilbert's behavior. He became moody and began to wonder aloud if he and his bride were temperamentally suited to each other. Finally he told her that she got on his nerves, and asked her to leave the house.

What had happened in between was MGM's conversion, over the summer, to full-scale sound production.

Cockily, as befitted the Gable of his day, Gilbert had entered the lists with the romantic comedy *His Glorious Night*. It wasn't. The picture opened at the Capitol Theater in New York on October 4, to a chorus of catcalls from the audience. Critics described the voice of the Great Lover as "squeaky" and "freakish." Suddenly MGM, bound to Gilbert by a long-term contract, had a multimillion-dollar liability on its hands; and Gilbert had the shell of a career.

His wife tried loyally to help. There were techniques for voice production, she pointed out, and effective ways of reading lines that could be mastered. She understood the difficulties he faced; her own arsenal of craftsmanship was at his disposal.

The more she talked, the more irritated Gilbert became. He already had the studio on his neck. Now this arty theater woman was lecturing him.

Hence the demand that she take up residence elsewhere — rescinded, then intermittently repeated, over most of the following year. In August of 1930 Ina Claire went to New York to fulfill a movie commitment there, and turned in despair to Fanny. Her husband was vain, truculent, unpredictable; they were never together for more than a few days at a time; and yet —"And yet I love him, Fanny!"

Fanny was deeply sympathetic. She knew very well the emptiness of Ina Claire's life in the pre-Gilbert period: "Here was a woman at the top of her profession, sought after by society to be worn like a Legion ribbon at parties and receptions, and yet she had no life. A bitter quarrel had split her off from the two people closest to her, her mother and her brother. She spent the summer weekends entirely alone."

Out of that vulnerability, Ina had invested everything in her second marriage. Because her suffering was painful to behold, and because Fanny regarded divorce as a last resort, Fanny tried to salvage the relationship. That involved swallowing her distaste for Gilbert: "I could understand a woman preening; but for a six-foot male to be preoccupied with his masseurs and his profile . . ." She helped Ina draft conciliatory telegrams, and herself phoned Gilbert at Malibu Beach.

From his answers it was clear that Gilbert considered the matter closed, a temporary aberration by "two nice people," and further, that he entertained hopes, once free of Ina, that he could resume his *grand amour* with Garbo.

Reluctantly, Fanny told Ina she had better put Gilbert out of her mind and her life. "You can't hold a man by chasing him. And you have too much to offer, more than he can appreciate. Retain your dignity, Ina. Go back to the stage."

Ina nodded. She would do as Fanny said. But she didn't want any money — she had married for love — or any fuss, either: "I couldn't stand people being sorry for me."

"I understand, Ina. We'll move quietly."

Fanny had expected to operate with her customary discretion, proceeding from a separation to a tidying-up of financial accounts and then to the necessary court action. She even persuaded the presiding judge at Los Angeles Superior Court to have the case heard, if not in chambers, at least with the courtroom cleared of spectators.

But she had reckoned without the MGM publicity department. Fanny's filing of divorce papers, on grounds of mental cruelty, was trumpeted by banner headlines two inches high in an extra edition of Hearst's *Evening Herald*. When Ina Claire took the stand a few weeks later, an army of press people, their seats carefully allocated by Howard Strickland of MGM, were on hand to record her anguish. Between sobs, she quoted a letter from Gilbert: "I am not for company, nor do I want anyone about me." The decree was granted.

That same evening, Fanny held a big party at the Beverly-Wilshire Hotel for Clifton Webb, who was in town and wanted to meet the stars. Prominent among them was the newly divorced Ina Claire. Her escort? John Gilbert. Apparently the date was an inspiration of Howard Strickland's, its rationale only too evident to Fanny: "Mayer hated the idea of scandal tainting his stars. This was to prove that Jack Gilbert was a decent fellow, civilized. Changing one's partner was no more terrible than changing one's shoes."

Mayer had more serious worries about Gilbert — and vice versa. Several days later, when preparing to depart for New York, Fanny had a call from the actor. Could she come to lunch? No, not at the studio; this was confidential. He would send his car to bring her out to his beach house. Gilbert indicated he wanted her advice about something.

It was not the first time a former adversary in court had sought her services. Fanny postponed her train reservation and went out to Malibu. She found Gilbert flushed and unshaven; evidently he had been drinking. "Fanny, my life is a hell. I'm earning more than half a million dollars a year — ten thousand a week, every week — and I can't even enjoy a good meal. This stuff"— he indicated a bottle outside on the patio — "is all I can put away."

The studio, he explained, while ostensibly looking for new properties for him, was actually trying to force him into a settlement. "They're not even going through the motions of offering me junk any more. They figure the silent treatment will wear me down."

He went to the window and stared out at the billowing Pacific. "I can't trust agents, they're all in Mayer's pocket." Suddenly he turned. "How about you, Fanny? Would you take on a fight against L. B. Mayer? Or are you committed to the studio's side, too?"

"I'm not committed to anybody except my clients, Jack. But I don't think a fight is the answer. There's more to be gained by quiet discussion. MGM would prefer not to wash their linen in court."

Gilbert's eagerness was almost pathetic. "Then you'll give it a whirl?"

"On one condition. That you don't cut the ground from under me by drinking yourself silly or stumbling into some morals scandal."

Gilbert nodded. "I'll be careful, Fanny. You be smart."

In view of the sums at stake, talks with anyone but Mayer were pointless. The studio boss would only do business while eating. So Fanny sipped coffee at Dave Chasen's one afternoon while Mayer wolfed down crêpes suzettes.

Admittedly, she agreed, Jack Gilbert's voice sounded like pebbles rattling on a tin roof. But why advertise that fact to the world by firing him? "It doesn't make sense, Louis. You don't spit in the soup you have to eat. You still own thousands of feet of Gilbert footage usable in many parts of the world. You can keep sending out stills, preserve the illusion in those places. Why throw away the assets in your vaults?

"Then there's the public relations aspect. How do you think movie fans would feel about Louis Mayer throwing out the former idol who did so much for him?"

"Ha!" snorted Mayer. "He did so much for me, that *shikker*, if I have an ulcer he should get the pill!"

"So leave him alone, and maybe he'll drink himself to death. Or let him take a swing at somebody in public, and you'll have legal cause. But don't try to break the contract unilaterally. It'll cost you a lot more than just to keep paying him. Let him go away and be forgotten."

Mayer frowned. 'Some of the boys feel we could dub in another voice on that flop of his."

"That," Fanny said gently, "I would not recommend doing without Gilbert's consent. You'd be wide open for damages. But I *would* suggest that in all future contracts with performers your legal department reserve that right to the studio."

Mayer shook his head admiringly. "Like I always said, a female Solomon!" He thrust his plate back. "All right, Fanny, we won't push Gilbert out. The sonofabitch ought to give you a nice fee for this."

Gilbert took a different view. He was immensely relieved, but expressed surprise at the notion that any compensation was due Fanny. "I thought you'd be happy to do it for the publicity," he told her on the telephone. "After all, I'm a big star. And you were really doing a favor for your old buddies, the management at MGM."

"It's *you*, Jack, not Louis Mayer, who are going to be collecting half a million dollars a year as a result of my efforts."

"Well — that's true. Okay, send me a bill."

It was her office policy, Fanny explained, never to fix an arbitrary fee but to discuss the matter with the client, who was free to pay what he felt the services were worth. For example —

"I understand," Gilbert cut in haughtily. "I don't need lessons from Louis Mayer in how to do the right thing."

Fanny returned to New York. She heard nothing more from Gilbert, nor did any check arrive. Making inquiry through the actor's divorce lawyer, Judge Peyton H. Moore, she was told that Gilbert disclaimed any knowledge of a debt, moral or otherwise.

At long last, she received a token of his esteem: an eight by ten glossy photograph bearing the stamp of the John Gilbert Fan Club, and inscribed: "For Fanny, with my very best wishes."

For Eddie Goulding, with his theater background, his composing talents, and his crisp singer's diction, the new era was on the face of it a bonanza. No other director on the lot could boast his combination of resources. When the studio decided to leap aboard the talkie bandwagon with *Broadway Melody*, it was to Goulding that its crucial sound tests were entrusted.

However, he was less happily affected by the improvement in Irving Thalberg's position. With the shift from gaudy epics and melodramas to more complex musicals and realistic "women's stories," Thalberg acquired heightened stature vis-à-vis Mayer. No longer content with the role of favored "son," he began challenging his erstwhile protector for authority. Tensions rent the studio, abetted by the doubling of movie income to $110,000,000 in 1929, and the swarm of agents now hovering on the fringe of production.

Goulding, caught in the middle of the Mayer-Thalberg struggle, became nervous. For four years he had been an obedient hireling, garnering laurels for his superiors. Now he wanted to make a picture of his own, free from the "creative" intervention of Thalberg.

To Fanny's annoyance, he launched upon endless lunches with palpably self-serving agents. He never quite committed himself; but he kept looking for the contact that would enable him to make a picture off the lot.

And then he found it, in the person of Joe Kennedy. Joseph P. Kennedy, Sr., was an intriguing figure — in both the good and bad senses of the word. Harvard-educated, tall and athletic, he had the fresh good looks and bonhomie that would endear his son John to millions. Joe Kennedy had been at twenty-five the youngest bank president in the country. After a successful foray as an insider on Wall Street, he entered film distribution, acquiring a chain of thirty-one movie houses; soon he was a financial adviser at Pathé, and in 1929 chairman of the board. All this was accomplished through a bewildering series of stock purchases, syndicate deals, over-the-counter transactions and under-the-table arrangements carried out with the aplomb of a Boston-born Houdini.

Fanny had some knowledge of Kennedy through a woman stockbroker who was a mutual friend. She regarded Kennedy as a personable promoter, glib and dangerous, the last man to be recommended as an associate for the easygoing Eddie Goulding.

But she was in London. And to Goulding, always in flight from his unpretentious origins, Joe Kennedy was the incarnation of wealth and social position. Furthermore, Kennedy had an interesting scheme. He was itching for recognition as a maker of movies, not merely as a manipulator of capital. If Goulding could get him together with Gloria Swanson, who as a senior founder (along with Charles Chaplin and Douglas Fairbanks) of United Artists could provide distribution without studio overhead costs, perhaps a three-way merger could be worked out.

Goulding was off and running. He had a story idea that he was sure would appeal to Miss Swanson; he suspected that his urbane friend would appeal to the lady, too. Both surmises proved well founded. Miss Swanson, thoroughly disillusioned with the chaotic dispersal of authority on her recent *Queen Kelly*, was looking for a cool head to take over production responsibilities. The fact that in Kennedy's case the head came equipped with affable blue eyes did nothing to diminish her enthusiasm. Goulding assured her she could henceforth forget about business matters; she was joining forces with "the richest man in America." Kennedy in turn assured Goulding that there was no need to obtain Fanny's blessing for their new setup: "What do you need her for?" The three-way partnership was sealed.

There was, of course, the little matter of the story to be squared away. So far, *The Trespasser* existed only in Goulding's imagination — and the shrewd Miss Swanson knew what an unreliable storehouse that could be: "I'd heard Eddie rattle off a story at dinner, usually with a few cocktails under his belt, after which some producer would come up to him with a check, saying 'Give me a synopsis tomorrow.' At that point, he would have quite forgotten what he said, and have to invent something else.

"Eddie was in the same category as Charlie Chaplin: like a radio that could be turned on to any subject just by pressing a switch. Put him among a group of engineers, and in two minutes he would be getting off brilliant observations about construction, surprising himself by the things he was saying. But he was *too* prolific; he needed somebody to regulate the flow of his ideas."

What Fanny had done for the drafting of *Fury*, Miss Swanson resolved to do now for her picture. The writing of *The Trespasser* was a typical keep-Goulding-on-the-beam operation that resulted in a solid screenplay. For a transitional sequence, Goulding composed, to lyrics by Elsie Janis, the later-famous "Love, Thy Magic Spell Is Everywhere." His music was as evanescent as his dialogue. He did not know how to commit it to paper, so it had to be set down by a copyist from his whistled rendition before it got away.

Although Kennedy would be billed as formally "presenting" the film, it was agreed that the actual production would be left entirely in Goulding's hands. No contracts were signed; who would question the integrity of "the richest man in America"? Goulding had delivered the star, the story and the music. He was providing a first-class crew on a depression budget, and his own directorial skills; he assumed that he and Kennedy would be splitting profits, apart from Miss Swanson's share, on a fifty-fifty basis.

According to Goulding's account to Fanny, just before the commencement of shooting he wondered aloud to Kennedy whether some memo of business agreement shouldn't be drawn up. The banker shook his head. "Let's not bother with details. That can all be taken care of when your lawyer gets back from Europe."

"But I need something to live on, Joe. I have expenses."

"Oh, sure. Let's say, a thousand a week."

For ten days, Goulding rehearsed his players intensively on a bare sound stage, until he felt they were ready. Then, lining up a dozen cameras, he guided them through long, smoothly integrated sequences. Gloria Swanson, a no-nonsense professional who had worked with the best, was permanently awed by one scene that ran uninterrupted for nine minutes. The entire production was completed in a record twenty-one days.

Goulding telephoned Fanny in London: when would she be back in New York? He and Kennedy were ready to go there from California to screen *The Trespasser* for her.

"It's the *contract* I want to see, Eddie — not the picture!"

"Don't worry about that, Fanny. Joe's going to work it out with you."

But Joe Kennedy, arriving in New York after Fanny was back, showed no hurry to sit down with her. After several postponements, he finally took her to lunch at the Iroquois —"as if he couldn't afford the Algonquin"— where he conveyed the astonishing information that he had no further debt to Goulding. "I paid him a thousand a week while he was working; I can show you the vouchers."

"But that was just expense money, Joe! Something to tide him over. After all, Eddie provided you with a great story. And he put the whole project together. Why, he gets more money than that for —"

"Listen, I did the bum a favor. He was on the skids in Hollywood, for running out on MGM. No other studio would touch him. I gave him a chance to get back on the screen."

"I can't believe my ears, Joe. Eddie had a deal with you, a clear verbal contract. You were partners."

"What contract?"

The "merger" was dissolving rapidly. Kennedy had also parted company with Gloria Swanson, amid bitter claims from her side of unfair treatment, financial and otherwise.

Ironically, at this point *The Trespasser* opened in New York. The *Times*, noting that the picture had been "wildly acclaimed" by London critics, found it "gifted with originality from beginning to end." The encomiums for Goulding did not stir Kennedy in the slightest. Goulding, desperate, told the banker he would be obliged to take his grievance to court. Kennedy fixed him with a chilling eye: "You have that Jew-girl go after me, and I guarantee you'll never be on a screen again. I'll tell a federal jury about some of those wild Goulding weekends, and you'll be deported for moral turpitude!"

The "Jew-girl" slur would take on more significance ten years later; it was ominous enough now. Nonetheless, Fanny pressed for some further compensation to Goulding. In a reluctant burst of magnanimity, the successful producer permitted his author-director-composer to retain the music royalties from "Love, Thy Magic Spell Is Everywhere."

Fanny and Goulding were at a second personal crossroads. Having failed at the critical moment to move together, they were inevitably drifting apart. Goulding, harassed by the demands of his mother and sister, longing for an "independence" he was unable to sustain, sought refuge increasingly in bacchanalian extravagances and haphazard friendships.

And Fanny, ever in quest of her storybook knight, ran into her second major entanglement of the heart.

This time her suitor had curly brown hair, and a quiet rugged charm unmarred either by alcohol or a difference in religious faith. Stanley was first brought to Fanny's office by a fellow writer who explained his friend's predicament. Stanley had captured the affections of a lady considerably his senior. There had been some ardent embraces, and evidently some promises or expectations. In either event, the lady was demanding matrimony, on peril of a lawsuit. As the recital proceeded, and Fanny extracted some essential details, her would-be client fidgeted on the couch, full cheeks reddening.

Perhaps the circumstances of their meeting lent a provocative aura of intimacy. If so, this only added to an already-present constellation of favorable factors. Fanny was in her prime as a woman if not yet as an attorney. Stanley, about the same age, was strong-jawed and sturdily masculine, as attractive as Goulding but in a way that suggested pipe, slippers and a paneled study rather than the marquee glitter of the West End. He used words with beautiful precision. If his creative flair was not quite so volcanic as Goulding's, it was better controlled; his humor had bite and depth. He had had a play produced on Broadway — unsuccessfully — and was writing a novel while taking a graduate degree in literature. On family background, he could not be faulted. His father was a reputable Manhattan businessman and a member of an established uptown congregation.

From their first interview, it was evident that Stanley was captivated. His eyes met Fanny's, and thereafter, as she jotted down notes with simulated detachment, never left her face. When the meeting ended, he contrived to lunch with her the next day, ostensibly for strategy discussions.

For a few days Stanley kept his distance, leaving her to unravel his legal problem. With a tactful mixture of sympathy and firmness, Fanny worked out a financial settlement.

Stanley turned up late that afternoon at the Bar Building to insist that Fanny cancel whatever plans she might have for the evening, and join him in a celebratory dinner. Fanny, who had no plans, let herself be persuaded.

From then on, the courtship moved rapidly: telephone calls and flowers, evenings at the theater, Sunday walks in Prospect Park. Stanley brought around his manuscript to the Holtzmann penthouse, where he and Fanny sat up until two in the morning discussing it. She had some thoughts about a publisher.

Stanley invited her to his parents' home: a momentous step forward. The evening went smoothly; Fanny's shyness in intimate social situations was wearing off. She reported in a letter to her London confidante, the duchess of Rutland, a definite brightening of the romantic horizon.

Her closest friend at home, however, sounded a note of restraint. To Lucy Schneeberg, who had met Stanley twice, he seemed a little touchy about Fanny's prominence, a little insistent on his masculine right to dominate. "Artistic people," she pointed out, were apt to be proud, self-centered. Must it not be galling for Stanley, knowing that Fanny gamboled among the lions of the Algonquin set, to contemplate his own position at the bottom of the literary ladder? "He undoubtedly thinks he's as good or better." Also, Stanley was a conspicuously handsome man; Lucy suspected that on that account alone he might be correspondingly vain.

Fanny conceded that Stanley's ego was not exactly invisible, and that the issue was a delicate one. But they had tackled it forthrightly, she declared, and had reached a reasonable understanding.

In fact, the two had started from quite different premises. Fanny, very aware that for the moment at least she overshadowed Stanley in income and public recognition, had taken pains to give importance to his work. She apologized for any intrusion on his writing schedule, and treated his opinions with deference. Theirs would be, she indicated, an equal partnership.

Stanley lost no time in making clear that such an arrangement would not be enough. He did not want, even temporarily, to appear before the world as a successful lawyer's husband. If she took his name, she would have to take her chances on his ability to maintain a household.

Fanny protested. This was a rigid and highhanded approach to a career that had been her entire life, had brought her honors and satisfaction.

There were tears and flare-ups; and finally, because both were deeply in love, a compromise. Stanley would expect her not to abandon her law practice at once, but to soft-pedal it gradually until, as he was able to assume greater financial responsibility, the duties of wifehood and motherhood absorbed her completely.

Since this was projected not as an ultimatum for immediate action but as a blueprint for the indeterminate future, Fanny was happy enough to agree. With such an evident grasp of each other's viewpoints, it seemed inconceivable that her career could present a serious obstacle.

A week later, to the immense delight of the Holtzmann family, Fanny announced that she and Stanley were engaged. Henry in particular was pleased: his daughter would have the companionship she needed, the protection of a genteel, cultivated man for the rest of her days.

Fanny went out and splurged on a magnificent trousseau: gold slippers chosen by her friend and client Gertrude Lawrence; a negligee, nightgown, fine linens and all the trimmings. For once she did not stint herself. The wedding was to take place in a few weeks, followed by an extended fall honeymoon in Europe; then the couple would move into a house in Westchester.

Fanny was radiant. In ten short years she had accomplished her life's goals. She was going to have it all: recognition, career, and the happy home she secretly cherished most. She too would "bring forth children" — the first Talmudic injunction to women; her offspring would mingle with those of her sisters and brothers, and continue the family line. She breezed through her tasks at the office with a good humor that was impervious to crises. Stanley saw her every day.

One summer evening, with the nuptials practically in sight, Stanley was invited to Friday dinner at the Holtzmanns'. Fanny had gone to Philadelphia that morning for a court hearing — a client was suing the owner of the powerful Philadelphia *Inquirer* — but she expected to catch a midafternoon train back to New York.

Stanley arrived punctually at six, his arms full of flowers. He was disappointed not to find Fanny there.

It was a little after seven when the telephone rang. Fanny was calling from Philadelphia, breathless and excited. She had missed her train, she told Stanley, and wouldn't be home for another hour — but the good news was worth it! The court had handed down a $200,000 judgment in her favor, even though the *Inquirer* had thrown a battery of high-priced lawyers against her. And the judge had commented that —

Stanley cut in sharply: "I'm interested in *you*, Fanny — not your career." He slammed down the receiver.

He was still boiling over as he talked to Bertha's husband, Sam Berkman, while the dinner waited on Fanny's return. "I refuse to be 'Mr. Fanny Holtzmann,' " he declared vehemently.

Sam assured him he wouldn't be. "This is just a passing incident. Once you're married, things fall into perspective."

But Stanley refused to be placated. When Fanny arrived, he did not join in the general congratulations. And he had little to say during the meal.

Afterward, as the family melted discreetly into other rooms, Fanny and her fiancé went outside on the penthouse terrace. For the next three hours Theresa and Bertha heard their voices — Stanley's tense, bitter, staccato, Fanny's low and calm — mingled with the occasional creaking of the hammock.

Then Fanny came in alone. "It's all off," she told her mother. "There'll be no wedding." She went quickly to her room. Nobody ever asked her, nor did she volunteer to provide, the details of the conversation on the terrace.

Early the next morning, Theresa appeared at Fanny's bedside: "Go to Europe with Stanley anyway." Waving aside her daughter's protest, she went on: "All your life you've done for other people. It's time you had some pleasure for yourself. About Papa, don't worry; he knows. It's all right."

Fanny had met Judge Ben Lindsey in California, and had paid approving lip service to his book *The Companionate Marriage*, which advocated a trial union with full sexual experimentation before marriage. But acting on such a revolutionary credo would scarcely have been easier for her than for Queen Victoria; there was really not that much difference in upbringing between the two.

Had Stanley been less self-preoccupied and more understanding of Fanny's dilemma, had he been capable of assuaging the hurt to her pride by a generous declaration of love, their story might have had a different ending. But if she was untutored in these matters, he was unsure; his talent far surpassed his self-confidence.

Ironically, within a few years Stanley would soar to the top echelons of the movie world. He would no longer feel the need to fight, even against the woman he loved, for his identity. But all that came later, too late for Fanny.

From the duchess of Rutland the decline of the affair was recorded in a series of heartsick little notes. That summer: "I am disappointed with your letter, because there is no talk of the marriage that seemed so beautifully fair . . . and you talk of having wished often you had *my* sympathetic ear. It seems sad, if things stopped, and all that hope of perfect things should have faded. Poor little Fanny. . . . Oh, I'm sorry if you are sad."

A few weeks later: "I wonder how it is all going. I think him crazy to wish you to give up your career after these years of good and great work. *Don't* give in."

And finally: "I am sure you were right to hold to your good profession — and not to give way to someone who so little appreciated your cleverness and worth. He ought to have had huge ambition for you. I do hope you are not sad."

Fanny was more than sad. She had opened up emotionally, let herself be totally vulnerable — and had been trampled upon. She was deeply, grievously wounded; and because she would not let herself die, furious.

But she could not long be immobilized.

Chapter 6

*W*ITH COMMITMENTS THAT spanned the six thousand miles between Sunset Boulevard and Piccadilly, Fanny needed help. It turned up in the unlikely person of her younger brother.

David Marshall Holtzmann came to the Bar Building via a choppy route. Tall and slender, he had the blond good looks and insouciant manner of an Austrian guards lieutenant; he glided gracefully through a series of colleges and scrapes until suddenly, in his last year in law school, he was stricken with encephalitis. For three weeks he lay in a coma while a procession of specialists shook their heads. Finally the family was told: "Better pray for him to die; if he lives, it will be as a vegetable."

Theresa and Fanny prayed; but not according to the medical prescription. Instead, they took their entreaty to Zaida's grave. When they returned to David's bedside at the Neurological Hospital, his long lashes fluttered open and he whispered, "Get me out of here."

A month later he was on the way to California and a writing job at Paramount, through the courtesy of Fanny's friend B. P. Schulberg. Basking in the sun, far from the pressures of law clerkship, he recovered his strength.

In 1929 he returned east to take the bar examinations. Although he had been away from the law for a year, he breezed through on his first try, turning in his paper while most of the candidates were still gnawing on their pencils.

Fanny reached out eagerly for his services. She sensed in David a stability capable of keeping people like Eddie Goulding in line, as well as a powerful grasp of legal logic that would complement her own intuitive flair. Ultimately, she felt, David would provide a secure base for her global free-wheeling.

By now she had amassed a formidable array of weaponry for skewering her way through a man's world. She could play the stern mother with improvident show people, or the helpless floundering little girl with giants of commerce. To a retired judge she might epitomize Victorian reserve — and a moment later send a Hollywood agent cowering in flight from a verbal barrage.

She exploited these resources with the skill of a veteran field commander, ferreting out the Achilles heel of the opposition and then going for it. Her attack could be direct, head-on — as with Louis B. Mayer — or, at the other extreme, incredibly convoluted. No general ever gave more attention to the elements of maneuver: flanking movements, counterattack, surprise.

David, startled by these dizzying stratagems, at first retreated, then fell into step. But he never quite buried his reservations about Fanny's circuitous ways. When Anita Gordon, a newly arrived secretary, expressed amazement that he could follow the spirals of Fanny's reasoning, David replied with mingled vexation and admiration: "Miss Holtzmann's approach is always straight. Straight as a stock-market graph."

The fact was, Fanny knew just where she was going. She was girding herself almost consciously, like a female Charles de Gaulle, for the moment when history would again demand her special services.

When the crisis came, it was a big one. In the fall of 1931, two years after the stock-market crash in the United States, England went off the gold standard. The British pound had dropped to the basement; business came to a standstill; the future — if any — of the entire empire was a gloomy question mark. From Fanny's clients in London, especially those in the at-best-erratic entertainment world, rose unmistakable cries for help.

The first call, paradoxically, came from the least panic-prone of her charges, Jack Buchanan. Although an international musical comedy star — a heftier, more virile Mayfair version of Clifton Webb — Buchanan was immune to the romance of grease paint. In contrast to theater-creatures like Noel Coward and Gertrude Lawrence, who from Fanny's observation "didn't really come to life until they were backstage, like fish returning to water," Buchanan regarded performing as "just a job."

What did interest him was business; so in 1930 Fanny had set up an elaborate corporation through which he could engage in real estate as well as theatrical production. A year later he was heavily involved in building the Leicester Square Theatre in London when the financial crisis struck. His American backers withdrew; disaster loomed.

Fanny went to her friend at the Bank of America, Dr. A. H. Giannini. On her personal assurance of Buchanan's reliability, Giannini extended without collateral a loan of 100,000 precious American dollars. Buchanan could breathe again.

Fanny took the first available boat to England to follow through. Many of her fellow passengers were worried industrialists with major holdings in England: Mr. Waterman had fountain pens there; Mr. Hoover, vacuum cleaners. Fanny had people.

Chief among them, with Buchanan taken care of, was her prime English client and longtime sponsor, Charles B. Cochran. "Cockie's" angels had vanished and his creditors were descending. His sole remaining asset was *Cavalcade*, a new play by Noel Coward that was completing dress rehearsals in the West End.

Cavalcade was a gentle panorama spanning three decades in the life of an upper-class English family, beginning with New Year's Eve of 1899. It interwove the changing fortunes of empire with the enduring personal relationships, above and below stairs, peculiar to the British household. The play opened at the Drury Lane two days after Fanny arrived, in a setting of high emotionality. Britons were being urged to stand firm together against the monetary squeeze; "Buy British" signs flooded Trafalgar Square. Coward's nostalgic paean spoke directly to the popular mood.

Fanny, watching in rapt absorption from the fourth row, thought it did more than that. "It's touching, honest, beautifully written," she told Cochran. "This is a story for everybody."

The London theater critics agreed. The movie scouts at the opening, alas, did not. When Fanny called them the next morning to read aloud from the notices, they were unimpressed. "Strictly fish-and-chips stuff, Fanny," sniffed the man from Paramount. "Wouldn't bring in a nickel from American audiences." The others echoed this view. There were five Hollywood scouts in London; five negative reports had been filed. Most crushingly, for Fanny, the Warner Brothers representative pointed out that even John C. Wilson, Coward's most intimate friend, had dismissed *Cavalcade* as an "animated British newsreel."

Coward himself, convinced there would be no movie bids, had boarded a cattle boat for a long slow voyage to South America. He cabled Fanny that he had no objection to her plugging for a *Cavalcade* film sale, but no hope, either. He was quite as broke as Cochran — playwrights did not get rich in the low-cost British theater — but he did not have comparable overhead.

For Cockie, the situation was desperate. "Why couldn't Noel have written something that would bring in American dollars?" he complained to Fanny. "Even the Shuberts aren't interested, for Broadway."

"Hang on, Cockie. There's a thought percolating in my head."

Her hostess at lunch the next day was her politically minded friend, the duchess of Atholl. Among the guests invited to meet Fanny were a sprinkling of lawmakers and economists from the current Labour government of Ramsay MacDonald. Fanny sat politely through some opening talk of devaluation and economic theory — "things I couldn't follow."

At the first pause in the conversation, she spoke up: "It seems to me that if you need money, there's no richer source for dollars than the cinema box office. Now, I saw a play the other night which, if transposed to the screen, would bring a fortune into your treasury. It would also be the greatest imaginable piece of propaganda for England. Did anyone see the reviews of *Cavalcade*?"

Abashed silence. This was a company obviously not attuned to the theatrical pages. Nonetheless Fanny plunged on: 'You don't have to sell England to Englishmen. But if you put that story on celluloid, you could have audiences all over the world reacting as I did at the Drury Lane — tears streaming down their cheeks, good will flowing from their hearts to Britain. From there, it's just a small step to the acceptance of British products."

Fanny paused. "I'll even tell you how to make the picture — with the Union Jack waving through every reel. But it should be filmed in Hollywood, because they control world distribution. The trick is to combine their facilities with promotion by the British Empire Marketing Board."

This time there were several thoughtful nods, and a mumble or two of assent. Then somebody threw in a statistical observation, and in a moment figures filled the air. Fanny and her project were apparently forgotten.

Not quite, it turned out. After lunch, the duke of Atholl took her to see Major Walter Elliott of the Empire Marketing Board; and a few days later she had a letter from No. 10 Downing Street. Would she care to outline her proposal over lunch with the cabinet?

It was, as Fanny remembered it, "a typically dreary British lunch." Still, she preferred London lunches to dinner parties, where the women were herded together after dessert to prattle of cosmetics and divorces while the men disposed of more important matters.

At Downing Street, she was the only woman present. The leaders of the government listened as Fanny spun through her theme, this time adding the point that films were deserving of national subsidy: "You gentlemen are sitting on millions in untouched public relations assets, ranging from Shakespeare to Noel Coward."

Again the reception was excruciatingly polite. "But nobody said anything. Cabinet members never express opinions individually; they function as a group."

Fanny returned to the Savoy rather deflated. The *Europa* was leaving for America in thirty-six hours; her baggage had already been shipped to Southampton. Not too hopefully, she put in an overseas call to Louis Mayer in Culver City: "Look, Louis, *Cavalcade* has a built-in market. The colonies alone will give you back your negative cost. And you can get it cheap — I'll put it to Cockie and Coward as a matter of patriotism!"

"But we'd still be stuck with the picture."

In vain Fanny appealed to Mayer's public relations sense ("It would be a great investment in terms of goodwill"); to his vanity ("You'd be a cinch for a top decoration"); to his Empire sentiments as a man who came to the United States from Canada.

"You're wasting your time, Fanny."

Jack Warner merely laughed at the notion of buying *Cavalcade*, an expensive, six-thousand-mile laugh: "Come on, Fanny! You're not serious!" Ben Schulberg, who had a nose for properties, was no more encouraging: "I'll grant you it's probably a classic — but you want us to do an English propaganda play, in the middle of a depression?"

As Fanny was hanging up the telephone, a uniformed messenger arrived with a letter from Viscount Snowden, chancellor of the exchequer. The government had weighed Fanny's suggestion, was deeply grateful, wished her well in her efforts to obtain a Hollywood production for *Cavalcade* — but offered no concrete assurances of aid from the Empire Marketing Board.

Fanny Holtzmann had failed. The myth of the trouble-shooter who bridged the worlds of London, Broadway and Hollywood, never letting her clients down, had been pierced. Sighing, Fanny tucked the letter in her purse along with the original invitation from Downing Street. She would show them both to Papa and Mama.

She departed for Southampton with a heavy heart. Cochran's final words at the sailing did nothing to cheer her: "Not a crumb of interest from our own film people at Soho Square. I suppose I was a fool to hope for a film sale. But when one has nothing else . . ."

"I haven't given up yet, Cockie. I'll try again when I get home."

She was back in her office a few days later, poring over the *Cavalcade* review clippings, when a call came from Caruthers Ewing, the attorney who had been her adversary in the *Dancing Mothers* plagiarism suit. Ewing had been in touch with her about handling a matrimonial matter for a society woman named Marion Aubert. Mrs. Aubert was in town from the south of France; could Fanny possibly see her at lunch?

Fanny told him to send the lady along. Mrs. Aubert arrived, slim and elegant, shortly before noon. She was ushered into the big private office, where Fanny was firing away again over the telephone at selected targets in Hollywood. For ten minutes the visitor sat in silence while Fanny talked with Irving Thalberg.

Finally Mrs. Aubert piped up: "A friend of mine has just been made president of Fox Films. Ned Tinker. He used to be chairman of the executive committee of the Chase National Bank."

Fanny pushed aside her telephones and stared. Fox was the only non-operating movie company in America, on the edge of receivership after a program of reckless theater acquisitions. Chase National, with $120,000,-000 locked into the organization, was the caretaker.

"Ned is coming to my home for dinner tonight," Mrs. Aubert went on. "Perhaps you'd be interested in joining us."

That evening, Fanny whisked out of the closet a scarcely worn Chanel gown of rich and regal deep maroon, and set out for Park Avenue. Edward R. "Ned" Tinker, seated conveniently beside her by the obliging Mrs. Aubert, turned out to be a stocky gray-haired man in his early fifties. Fanny noticed that although he spoke deliberately and never raised his voice, he was alert to every cross-current of the table conversation. Tinker was a director, she had learned that afternoon, of no less than thirty-five major corporations.

Dipping into her madrilène, Fanny turned to him casually: "Pity about Noel Coward's *Cavalcade*, isn't it?"

"I beg your pardon?"

"I mean, that Hollywood has lost it."

" 'Lost' it? How? Has someone else bought it?"

"Well, naturally, they'll make it in England now. They're no fools."

Tinker reflected on that a moment. He could not, he admitted, see Fanny's point. What would be the advantage for Hollywood in making *Cavalcade*?

"Money," was the terse reply. "The British Empire sales alone would pay for the cost of making the picture, and the rest of the world would be velvet."

Tinker put his spoon down; he was listening.

"Why do you think your company has been operating in the red? Because movie people see their whole audience as living between Jersey City and Pasadena!" She shook her head. "Provincial, Mr. Tinker. You and I know better. Americans at this point have barely enough money to buy apples from their former stockbrokers.

"The real market is overseas, especially Britain and its colonies. They have an Empire Marketing Board that pulls the whole system together — you should see the signs in Trafalgar Square! When they put all that muscle behind a nationalistic story like *Cavalcade* — well, they'll have to build new theaters to accommodate the crowds."

"But you think the picture should be made in Hollywood?"

"That's where the technical know-how is, and the distribution. But — as I explained to the people in Downing Street — the production itself has to have an authentic British stamp, like the guarantee label on British woolens. That means using the original cast from the Drury Lane, and sticking close to the Noel Coward script."

Tinker looked down at his plate for several seconds; Fanny reached for a stalk of celery. Then the banker raised his eyes: "Miss Holtzmann, I think there may be some merit in your idea. I'd like to talk to my staff about it."

Fanny's large brown eyes grew larger. "Oh, I'm afraid it's a bit late for that. My clients — Mr. Coward has no taste for shilly-shallying. I'm to give the British government a go-ahead for a London production by early next week, unless . . ."

"This is Friday . . . I have a film man who, so to speak, runs the show for me. His name is Richard Rowland."

"I know Dick Rowland."

"I'll get hold of him tonight and tell him to be at the office tomorrow. Can you meet us at noon?"

"I can meet you at dawn," was on the tip of Fanny's tongue. But she merely nodded and said, "I'll bring the English notices."

She had a clear recollection of Rowland: hard-bitten, laconic, a white-haired veteran of the nickelodeon era. As head of First National Pictures, he had employed Goulding and another of her writer clients, Ernest Pascal. He had gone on to the presidency of Metro Pictures, where Louis Mayer was his restless subordinate; now he was bucking for the top operational post at Fox. His appointment, Fanny learned in hasty overnight research, had not yet been officially confirmed.

Rowland's expertise was in distribution; for script judgments he relied on his story editor, Florence Strauss. Fanny was pleased, on arrival at the Fox midtown office, to see Florence there with the two men. Slender and reserved, Florence spoke her mind — and it was a good one — fearlessly.

Florence came straight to the point: she had read the newspaper and trade journal reports on *Cavalcade*, heard about Tinker's discussion with Fanny, and was in one hundred percent agreement. Fox should do the picture.

Ned Tinker turned on his heel. "I leave you and Mr. Rowland," he told Fanny, "to discuss the price." He led Florence Strauss from the room.

Rowland drummed on his desk. "Well, kid — I'll give you five thou for your fancy piece of crap."

Fanny eyed him levelly. "Dick, I'm not here to shadowbox with you. I've got to deliver on this deal — and Noel Coward won't take a penny under two hundred thousand."

"*What*? Why, for two hundred grand I could buy the whole movie industry!"

"This property has built-in box office, all around the world. At two hundred you'd still be getting a steal."

Rowland shook his head. "Well — I'll have to talk to the bank."

"What bank? Tinker *is* the bank, and he wants to do it. He's scared to death an English producer will beat him to it. Why stick your neck out by going against him?"

Rowland, an old hand in the movie jungle, saw the Hollywood logic of that — as Fanny knew he would. "Still," he mumbled, "all that money for a lousy animated newsreel!" (Catchy phrases traveled fast and far.)

"To sweeten the deal, I'll throw in a couple of other Coward properties."

Rowland clamped his jaw. "All right, Fanny — you're holding the aces. But we'll have to dress up the deal for Tinker and his board. Now, here's what we'll do: you hold out for your top figure, and I'll knock you down to something we can both live with."

When Tinker returned with Florence Strauss, he found Fanny and

Rowland at apparent loggerheads. "I've cut my price to two hundred thousand," Fanny told him, "but Mr. Rowland doesn't know the difference between a piece of junk and a box-office bonanza."

Tinker turned to his negotiator. "Mr. Rowland, I think this property would be a very intelligent purchase for the new management."

"It has heart," agreed Florence Strauss. "And beauty. The world could stand some clean entertainment."

"But the price!" protested Rowland. "Nobody pays that kind of money for a story. Especially not in the middle of a depression."

"Show me another property that's presold," countered Fanny, "with the British government doing your publicity!"

"Well . . . I'll go to ten thousand."

"Not a chance. I could never face Noel."

Tinker motioned Florence to come with him from the room.

Alone again with Fanny, Rowland leaned back in his chair. "All right now, Fanny — how much will you take?"

"A hundred and fifty thousand."

"That will include a couple of other properties?"

"Definitely. You can have *I'll Leave It to You,* and I'll find something else."

"I need something to show these moneymen."

"I understand."

"What about that musical of Coward's that was on Broadway?" Rowland pretended to be fumbling for the title: "*Sweet* something?"

"*Bitter Sweet*? Oh, no. That's a hot property in its own right."

"Ah, who goes to movie musicals?"

"The same people who go to dances and concerts — everybody."

After some further fencing, Fanny agreed that as a "concession" growing out of the *Cavalcade* deal, Fox would have an option to purchase *Bitter Sweet* for an additional $50,000.

Cochran and Coward had been ready to part with the movie rights for $5,000.

Fanny typed out the agreement herself — there were no stenographers in the office — including the specification that the film of *Cavalcade* would be scrupulously faithful to the stage version. She had Tinker's signature on the letter-contract before going home at 2 P.M. She called Cochran.

"What?" he spluttered. "What's that you say? A hundred and fifty — am I dreaming?"

Fanny assured him he was not. Under producer-author arrangements in England, which provided a fifty-fifty split, he would soon have his hands on $75,000.

"In that case, my dear Fanny, would you please hold the phone a moment while I indulge in a mild heart attack?"

Fanny wanted a script of *Cavalcade* in a hurry, if only to convince Tinker and Rowland that they had acquired something tangible.

"We have no script, Fanny."

"What about your actors?"

"They only have their own sides [the lines for a particular part]."

"Get hold of Noel's secretary."

An hour later, Cochran called back. "Lorne Green says there was only one complete script, and the Master took it with him — presumably to 'make revisions.' So our precious property is somewhere between here and Valparaiso. I've sent Noel a cable."

Coward replied to Cochran with a long and merry cablegram, hailing Fanny as the wonderworker of the ages. His playscript would soon be in the mails from Chile; he didn't care in the least what happened to it en route to the screen; they could change it to *Bleak House* so long as they spelled his name right on the check.

To Fanny, Noel sent a wire that, even for the acknowledged master of understatement, set some sort of record for restraint. "I forgive you," he cabled grandly.

Industry wiseacres didn't. Trade-paper columnists, dubbing the purchase "Tinker's Toy," pounced on Fanny as the villainess of a project that would bury Fox Films forever.

Fanny was too busy to notice. *Cavalcade* still needed a capable executive producer: Winfield Sheehan, the best moviemaker on the Fox payroll, had fled from the company's financial troubles to London. Fanny took a liner there to lure him back.

Over lunch at Claridge's, Sheehan grinned at Fanny benignly. "I'll never touch *Cavalcade*," he told her. "Not with the crazy contract you cooked up. 'No deviation from the stage version': whoever heard of such a clause?"

"That was my promise to the British government."

"Come off it, Fanny. I know you from the Brooklyn days. You slipped one over on the studio."

Fanny shrugged. "So that was their blunder — not yours."

"Why should I pick up on somebody else's fumble?"

"Because there's an excellent chance you'll come out as a hero."

"What do you mean?"

"To begin with, you can bring in the production below budget. The Drury Lane cast will sign for practically nothing to get to Hollywood. And they'll work fast; they know their parts. You'll spend less for exploitation with this behind you." She produced a letter from Major Elliott of the Empire Marketing Board. "Now, let's say the worst happens, and you have a flop. Who's to blame? Not you. The bankers picked the story, didn't they?"

Sheehan nodded.

"But just suppose for a minute that I'm right — and I haven't always been wrong about picture properties, Winnie — suppose *Cavalcade* pulls them in at the box office. Who's the great producer, the man of the hour, the savior of Fox Films? Winfield Sheehan!"

Fanny could see that Sheehan was tempted; but he shook his head. "Nah . . . get yourself another sucker, Fanny."

Two days later he signed up.

Sheehan brought over a Fox camera crew from Hollywood to film the London production of the play. With that as a blueprint, and the able Frank Lloyd to direct, he launched into production in Hollywood.

As the weeks passed, the grumbling from the sidelines grew louder. The nearest thing to a "name" in Sheehan's cast was Clive Brook — not exactly a household word in Sheboygan, Michigan. Coward's theme seemed more and more remote from American interests. By the time Sheehan turned in his work print, all three of the front-office culprits in the presumed fiasco — Ned Tinker, Richard Rowland and Florence Strauss — had been fired.

Chase National, convinced it was hatching a turkey, invited no critics to the New York screening. Instead it filled the house with bank employees. Tellers, security guards and their wives shuffled in self-consciously, reconciled to a dreary evening. By the end of the opening scene the house was breathlessly silent. During the second reel there was audible sobbing. Later came bursts of applause, and at the close of the picture, prolonged cheering. Such a reaction was far beyond the call of duty. The moneymen were bewildered. Could their turkey possibly be a prize peacock?

This astonishing hypothesis was confirmed when *Cavalcade* opened in January of 1933. The New York *Times* pronounced it "most affecting and impressive"; the *Herald Tribune* hailed "a success that can only be described as magnificent." Fanny's "crazy" insistence on the original all-British cast had resulted in an authenticity totally new to movie audiences, not to be equaled until the postwar Italian directors began mixing untrained but vivid local types into their professional casts.

And the box-office chimes started ringing. Before they stopped, $4,000,000 was in the till. Sheehan had an Oscar and all the prestige Fanny had predicted.

More importantly, Chase National promptly poured another $15,000,-000 into the moribund film company. In a few years, Fox merged with Twentieth Century to become one of the giants of "the industry." If not for Fanny and *Cavalcade*, it might well have been swallowed up in the long list of bankruptcies.

The *Cavalcade* coup demonstrated Fanny's unique approach to the law. Like her most creative clients, she was interested in reshaping chaotic reality, bending facts into a new sculptural outline. Her methods often rested less on conventional logic than on flashes of intuitive perception; her mind, unfettered and freely associative as a child's, darted past obstacles to light on dimly sensed solutions.

Fanny's imaginative concentration on the grand design rather than the routine details of building a case allowed her to put an entire situation in a fresh perspective. So viewed, nothing appeared impossible. Instead of being restricted by precedent, she could create it.

New York now regarded Fanny with a new respect. In Hollywood the tributes were tinged with fear. And London was frankly adoring. Judge Cardozo, running into Fanny in the lobby just before assuming his seat on the Supreme Court, confessed: "You have fulfilled the ambition of my youth. I always dreamed of dashing around the world on mysterious missions for glamorous clients. You actually do it." Another testimonial came from Caruthers Ewing in a letter requesting her address in England: "I want it if anything should come up. I think you are one of the great lawyers of this country."

Equally gratifying, in its own way, was a plea from Sam Goldwyn over lunch: "Fanny, I believe in quality merchandise. The writer in pictures is everything: what you put into a *challa* [a sweet white bread] comes out. A person uses good raisins, he gets sweet *challa*. Now, you deal only in the best. Please, get me some of your fancy English clients."

In London there was a subtle change. Up to the fall of 1931 Fanny was still the subject of gushy newspaper interviews celebrating "the dark-eyed brunette to whom shattered stars take their most delicate problems, the lawyer-girl who guards the innermost secrets of Screenland." A year later she was being quoted at long and sober length in *Film Weekly* on the desirability of having a British "film ambassador" stationed in Hollywood to advise American producers about British audience reactions, and an opposite number from America posted in London. She was an Authority.

One letdown marred Fanny's near-perfect deal. The new management replacing Ned Tinker and Rowland at Fox had at first announced they were picking up the $50,000 option to buy *Bitter Sweet*; then, apparently nettled by the *Cavalcade* terms, had suddenly reversed themselves.

Down the drain went eight weeks of time and considerable trouble expended by Fanny in Central Europe, obtaining clearances from producers who had presented the musical there. It was a disappointment, but Fanny never let herself brood for long. Her brother Jack liked to compare her with his office elevator in the Woolworth Building, which would hurtle downward at a terrifying rate and then, just when disaster seemed imminent, suddenly bounce up again. This time her recovery of morale was aided by Fred Astaire, who came to her rescue by needing to be rescued.

In the early thirties, Astaire plunged from a professional crisis into an emotional impasse.

For fifteen years he had been half — the less assertive, less celebrated half — of a popular dance team. With his pert-faced, breezy sister Adele, he had starred in a series of Broadway and West End hits, including *Funny Face*, the *Ziegfeld Follies* and *The Band Wagon*. Although sister and brother were totally disparate personalities — she was zestful and free-wheeling, with a flavorsome vocabulary, and Fred was all gentle diffidence — they were a harmonious team who, in Fanny's presence at least, never exchanged a harsh word.

This Fanny attributed to their mother, a magisterial lady of instinctive breeding who "unlike most actual duchesses, really looked like a duchess." Under her aegis the humble Austerlitzes of Omaha, Nebraska, had swept up past the Algonquin crowd into the drawing rooms of Park Avenue and Mayfair. There "Dellie" encountered Lord Charles Cavendish, younger son of the duke of Devonshire, a slim dapper clubman who was by Fanny's description "a more brainy edition of the classic P. G. Wodehouse hero." Soon after, Adele departed the Broadway scene to become Lady Cavendish of Lismore Castle.

Suddenly Fred was unpartnered. His prospects as a soloist, even after a promising debut in *The Gay Divorce*, were dubious. London beckoned, but that might be a three-thousand-mile move in the wrong direction.

It was toward Hollywood that he cast a wistful eye. Hollywood squinted back, and was not too impressed by what it saw: lantern jaw, receding hairline, gawky manner. There was a certain resemblance to the recent MGM discovery, Clark Gable, but unfortunately it was confined to the outsize ears.

Fred brought his problem to Fanny, who a couple of years earlier had successfully extracted back salary from Florenz Ziegfeld for the Astaires after the stock market crash.

Fanny put in a call to the RKO studio, where Mark Sandrich, brother of the photographer Ruth Harriet Louise, had been taken on as a director of musicals. Fanny suggested that Fred be teamed up for pictures "with one of the girl hoofers on your lot, maybe Ginger Rogers."

Mark reported back that his boss, Ned Depinet, didn't think Astaire could carry a romantic lead.

But Fanny felt confident that her client, once exposed to movie audiences, would win them over with his shy charm. She put in a second call, to Louis Mayer's breakfast room in Santa Monica: "It's no gamble, Louis, because you're not investing anything. Give him a bit, a walk-on with dancing shoes. For that you spend nothing, and you get a name that means something in the big cities with the big movie houses. In England alone, the Astaires have always been a sellout wherever they play."

From that "what have you got to lose" challenge emerged Fred Astaire's first film appearance, a brief ballroom sequence in the Joan Crawford feature *Dancing Lady*. Word filtered back to New York that the MGM brass had seen the daily rushes and had been bowled over. Fanny promptly called Mark Sandrich: "Get a peek at that picture, Mark. Maybe you'd better try to sign the guy before MGM does."

Within the week Sandrich had made contact with Astaire and brought him to Ned Depinet. Agreement in principle and soon in fact was reached on a long-term association, to begin with *Flying Down to Rio*. Fanny, preparing to leave for London, forwarded the outlines of a contract to Astaire's agent in Hollywood, Leland Hayward; salary details were to be worked out between Hayward and Depinet.

After an uneasy year, the Astaire future seemed assured. Sandwiched between his first two pictures, in mutually beneficial reinforcement, would be a trip to London to repeat his success in *The Gay Divorce*.

Unexpectedly Fred Astaire, up to this point preoccupied with dance steps and polo ponies, found himself in love. The lady, Phyllis Livingston Potter, had youth, looks and fortune. She also had a four-year-old boy by a previous marriage who, under the terms of her divorce, could not be taken out of New York State without the express sanction of her first husband. The ex-husband, a broker named Eliphalet Nott "Bo" Potter, Jr., showed no disposition to grant such sanction. And Fred's work would require him to be in California, then London.

Fred's sister and mother had misgivings about the Babylonian luxury in which Phyllis had grown up, as sole ward of Henry Worthington Bull, a senior partner in the Wall Street firm of Harriman and Company. Fred's own feelings were harder to fathom. He sat across from Fanny's desk in a heavy brown leather chair, his long dancer's legs lightly crossed, a self-effacing grin playing across his face. "You see, Fanny, she's awfully nice . . . very good family . . . and she wants to marry me."

"What about you, Fred? Do you love her?"

"Well, uh . . . I think we could be happy. I mean, if it could be worked out about the child."

"You wouldn't mind raising the child?"

"Not at all. I mean, if a man cares about a woman . . ."

"Then you do care?"

"Of course. Didn't I say so?"

"All right, Fred." Fanny felt as if she had completed major surgery. "Now we know where we stand."

Her first move was to separate her client from what might be a sticky court battle. "Send me Mrs. Potter and Mr. Bull — with all the relevant documents. After that, you wait in the wings."

The divorce agreement, under which "Bo" Potter had full custody of the boy three months a year, had been ingeniously drawn by his counsel, the prominent firm of Davis, Polk, Wardwell, Gardiner and Reed. Fanny's only hope for revision was to establish that the child's welfare would be better served if other arrangements were made. For courtroom reinforcement, she brought along her redoubtable brother Jack.

The case reached the Brooklyn Supreme Court — and all the New York papers — in July of 1933. Under questioning by Jack, Mrs. Potter confirmed "published reports" that she had been asked for her hand in marriage by "a very prominent New York gentleman."

"He is in all respects acceptable to you?"

"Yes, in every respect."

"Have you given him an answer?"

"No."

"Why not?"

"I feared that if I remarried I might not be able to give my child all of my attention."

"Then you do not intend to remarry until that is finally determined to your satisfaction?"

"That is correct."

The boy received inadequate care during his visits to his father, Mrs. Potter insisted, with the result that he always returned home upset. By contrast, she herself stayed unfailingly at his side, and saw that he had the best of everything.

To the accompaniment of occasional incredulous gasps from the spectators, Jack led the witness through a meticulous catalogue of the facilities available to the children of the privileged. At the Bulls' town house on East Sixty-second Street, four-year-old E. N. Potter IV had an entire floor set aside for his use, specially designed to include bedroom and bath, nursery, a bedroom for his mother, and a sitting room for his governess (one of "about eight" servants at his disposal). Should these quarters prove insufficiently amusing, he had a large play yard in the garden.

Things got even better for little Eliphalet out of town, where the Bull mansions at Islip, Long Island (summers only), and Aiken, South Carolina (wintertime), were equipped with enormous gadget-strewn solarium playrooms.

A supplementary brief filed on behalf of the plaintiff pointed out that the child's relatively impoverished father could offer only the comforts of a $4,800-a-year East Side apartment, with "but one maid" and, shockingly, no private bath for E. N. Potter IV. This sort of thing made pretty ironic reading in the midst of a depression, but Fanny wasn't trying her case in the papers. She was aiming at Justice Selah B. Strong, and scoring points — especially when she reminded the court that "Bo" Potter had not even taken the trouble to attend the hearing (he had just remarried and was off on a honeymoon).

The upshot was that Justice Strong instructed the lawyers to draw a new arrangement under which the boy would remain essentially in his mother's hands, with a minimum of disruptive uprooting. Fanny wound up with a total victory: eleven months of custody for Phyllis and Fred, plus the all-important right to take the child not only out of New York State but out of the United States for a period of up to six months.

Only when the papers were signed did Fanny permit Fred to pop out of the wings. He hastened into the justice's chambers and to his beloved's side. "Is it all settled, darling? Can we get married now?"

Phyllis turned to Justice Strong, who said: "I see no bar to your marriage. I want to commend you on being such a devoted mother. I'm sure you'll be an equally devoted wife."

"And I want to assure you, sir," interjected Fred, "I'll be a good father to the boy. Just as if he were my own son."

Phyllis beamed at him. "I wish we could get married this very afternoon."

"You can," said the justice, "I'll perform the ceremony."

The groom skipped out the door and dashed to a novelty store on the corner, where he picked up a five-dollar ring for his heiress bride. Someone telephoned the Marriage Bureau and a messenger hurried over with a license.

The bride, in a filmy blue-and-white silk print, was given away by Mr. Bull. Witnesses were Justice Thomas Cuff of the New York Supreme Court and a trio of Holtzmann lawyers: Fanny, Jack and young David.

L'affaire Astaire still needed a couple of finishing touches, and Fanny was there to supply them. When Fred reported for work on *Flying Down to Rio*, he discovered that his agents had in following through on Fanny's arrangements committed him to a seven-year deal: not in itself ruinous, except that it fell in with the standard studio practice of minuscule annual increases. This meant that in event of a smash performance, it would be the studio, not the player, that reaped the rewards. Fanny was furious at what she considered a sellout of her client's interests.

However, she had a trump card, and lost no time in playing it. During the filming of *Rio*, she turned up in the office of Ned Depinet at RKO. Depinet greeted her heartily; Fanny had sent him Fred Astaire, and she currently held the strings on Francis Lederer, the much-coveted matinée idol of the international hit *Autumn Crocus*.

"*Mazel tov*, Ned," returned Fanny. "Do you know what that means?"

"Yes, I've heard it from my Jewish friends. At Bar Mitzvas and such."

"Well, I offer you one. I've just seen a rough cut on Fred's opening sequences."

Depinet smiled smugly. "Pretty fabulous, eh? The man's going to be a big star."

"That's right. And as soon as *Rio* is finished, you can say goodbye to him."

"What are you talking about, Fanny? We've got a seven-year contract."

"Including one small clause that I dictated before I left for London."

Depinet frowned. "What clause?"

"Fred's picture commitments can never take priority over his stage career. He's free to go back to Broadway any time. And he's just had a great offer."

"Any time?" repeated Depinet.

"Just check your contract. All he has to do is give notice. And I'm giving it."

Depinet went white. "Now, wait a minute, Fanny. Let's talk . . ."

The "seven-year swindle" — Fanny's term for the starlet type of boiler-plate contract — did not survive that conversation. When Astaire embarked on the first of his nine hits with Ginger Rogers, it was as a well-protected Holtzmann client.

With the contract disposed of, one delicate issue remained: the timing of the annual visit by Phyllis's son to "Bo" Potter. At the suggestion of Potter's lawyer, former Secretary of State Frank L. Polk, Fanny telephoned "Bo" on her return to New York and told him how well the boy, now called "Peter," was getting along in Hollywood.

"He readily agreed with me," she reported by letter to Astaire, "that it would be a pity to snatch Peter from school" before the end of the term. Speaking "not as a lawyer but as a woman," she went on: "I honestly believe you can get more from Bo by friendly discussion than by retaining the most high-powered legal minds." She herself would be a "volunteer liaison officer" between the two families.

This fairy-godmother role, gratefully accepted at both ends of the continent, for the moment dovetailed with Fanny's personal inclinations. Since the episode with Stanley, she had been taking temporary refuge from emotional entanglements in a setting where she could wander without a sense of pressure: the chic, brittle world of gifted homosexuals . . . Noel Coward, Ivor Novello, Clifton Webb, Somerset Maugham.

She was quite oblivious to the special bonds that existed between her friends and the so-called "secretaries" or "valets" who trailed them: "All I knew was that these people were wonderful companions: witty, attractive, aesthetically sensitive, with superb manners. They never failed to notice what I was wearing; that's flattering to a woman's self-assurance. And they were never vulgar or obnoxious; you could kiss them goodnight without worrying . . ."

With the handsome homosexuals, Fanny could relax. They were Prince Charmings who would never bring her joltingly down to earth.

Meanwhile, the celebrity clients kept coming. Anybody shuttling between Hollywood and points east sought Fanny out. A rising young singer was quoted as demanding wryly, "How famous do you have to be before you can get on Fanny Holtzmann's list?" And in the Bar Building, the office staffs along the ninth-floor corridor would intercept Anita Gordon every morning on her way to the ladies' room: "Who's coming in today?"

Sometimes even Anita didn't know. One afternoon it was a tall, pale Englishman in a rain-soaked trenchcoat. He stood in the doorway shaking the water from his hat and his lank blond hair.

"Your name, please?" she inquired.

The man glared. "Howard," he said huffily. "*Leslie* Howard." The star's angular features were all over the fan magazines. He had just scored a personal triumph in the film *Berkeley Square*, whose mystic overtones suited perfectly his wounded, wraithlike manner.

Two years earlier, Fanny had cut loose a snarl of red tape surrounding his tax and immigration status. Now Howard had a more complex problem. He was caught between a personal contract signed with Gilbert Miller, the theatrical producer, and a subsequent three-picture commitment to the RKO studio. The movie company was afraid that if he departed for England, Miller might tie him up on the West End indefinitely.

After some energetic calendar-juggling, and a heated cable or two, Fanny sprang him free to commence filming on Somerset Maugham's *Of Human Bondage*.

Another frequent visitor to the office was Francis Lederer. Curly-haired and pleasantly accented, the Czech star was displaying his knees and much manly charm in *Autumn Crocus*. He had been the sensation of the season in London, where friends had urged him to see Fanny in New York as a precaution against the pitfalls of Broadway.

Broadway was easy. What Fanny wanted for Lederer was Hollywood, where international prestige could be converted to gold. When she told Lederer how much she planned to ask for him, the Czech recoiled. It was exactly double what he had intended to propose.

"Come in Thursday at eleven," she told him. "Ned Depinet is sending over his Eastern talent man."

With Lederer hunched nervously in a corner, the negotiations began. Fanny named a figure, and the man from RKO told her she was crazy. She promptly asked him to leave.

From there, things got warmer, with shouts and gestures and promises of recrimination. Fanny, far from wilting, seemed to welcome the challenge.

After ten minutes or so, Anita Gordon noticed that Lederer was gone. An office boy was dispatched to the men's room: no luck. Nor was Lederer in the library. Finally Anita found him in the Alice Foote MacDougall restaurant downstairs, gulping large drafts of tea. Fearful of being hit by a stray bullet, he had fled the battlefield.

Anita brought him back. The stormy debate ended, of course, in handshakes all around. Lederer got his contract, but he never quite got over his shock.

Fanny's fierce partisanship for her clients was a source of awe to the show-business community. She was an all-out advocate, with no pretensions to dispensing even-handed justice. Noel Coward once remarked that he would "rather have Fanny as a friend than as an enemy"; and he expressed the sentiments of many who crossed her path. Those who

*The middle thirties: Fanny beneath the pundit section of her wall
gallery in the Bar Building. At upper right: Justice Benjamin Cardozo
of the U.S. Supreme Court*

Betty and Jimmy Walker

Louis Bromfield

Clifton Webb

PIRIE MACDONALD

Noel Coward

Fred Astaire

locked horns with her were apt to come away dazed and bruised, wondering what had hit them.

Sondra and Jay Gorney — he was the composer of "Brother, Can You Spare a Dime"— had vivid recollections of coming under Fanny's fire. They had rented their house in Beverly Hills to Eddie Goulding, a man never noted for his abstemious habits, and had incurred damages to floors and furniture that they estimated at $5,000.

Fanny, answering the alarm from her scapegrace first client, deluged the Gorneys with furious denials. Eddie could not possibly have held riotous parties, she insisted, or permitted Ben Hecht to hammer out sculpture in the garden music-studio; Eddie was an ethereal soul, a model of decorous respectability. But if Jay really felt put upon, Fanny would permit her brilliant client to write a hit song with him.

Gorney replied that he wasn't prepared to "settle for a song." He clung to his complaint, and got a fair settlement. But it didn't come easy. As Sondra Gorney sighed years later, "I kept wishing we had Fanny on *our* side."

Clients themselves could be intimidated by Fanny in her more fervent manifestations. One such was Alicia Markova, the exquisite ballerina. Timid, a semirecluse whose tax records were kept for her by a sister in a shoebox, the London-born dancer admired Fanny immensely but found her overwhelming. Markova was relieved to find shelter ultimately in David Holtzmann's hands.

The dancers had crept into Fanny's life one by one, then two by two; it was the middle thirties before she realized she was being inundated by them. This was high irony, if a triumph of sorts, because Fanny herself had always stumbled over her feet. Unlike Clara and Stella, who fell naturally into the dancing ways of their Vienna-educated mother, Fanny was as befuddled rhythmically as her father, who couldn't tell a waltz from a polka. Dancers and dancing made her uncomfortable.

It was Clifton Webb who made the first breach in these defenses — perhaps because he was also a polished singer and comedian. Then came Fred Astaire and Jack Buchanan, more unmistakably hoofers. They were followed by the English-Spanish ballroom duo, Marjorie Moss and George Fontana.

As Fanny's practice became increasingly international, so did her dancers. Anton Dolin leaped gracefully onto her doorstep, trailed by his partner, Markova.

Irish-born Anton "Pat" Dolin was a lifetime favorite of Fanny's. She first met him in London, where he was a main attraction at the Sunday soireés held in St. John's Wood by Edgar Cohen, an arts-loving merchant. Every society woman in London wanted to mother Pat, and Fanny could understand why: he was a "very beautiful young man," whose white-marble profile and supple movement were embellished by an impudent wit.

In 1930 Dolin came to America to appear with Gertrude Lawrence in the *International Revue*, presented by André Charlot, the Anglo-French manager associated with the early successes of Beatrice Lillie. By that time Fanny had attended a performance by Nijinsky in Paris —"it drove me out of my mind"— and was more open to serious dancing. But it wasn't until she saw Dolin on his home ground two years later, partnering Markova in *Giselle* at the Royal Ballet, that she became a balletomane.

Dolin was already a firm friend of Fanny's, thanks to a mutual affection for Gertrude Lawrence. He shifted to the client ranks, bringing along his partner, when the two required — and Fanny supplied — bailing-out from a one-sided contract with Billy Rose.

Dancers had chronic legal problems. Most of their bookings were made two years in advance: in the interim tastes might change, economies falter, theaters collapse. An impresario faced with the prospect of an empty house frequently tried to wriggle out of his commitment by charging artists with imaginary grievances.

It was in this slippery area that Fanny's younger brother came into his own. David had an ear for the language of contracts, and disarming warmth as a negotiator. He had gradually been assuming greater responsibility in the New York office, especially in playing financial watchdog to the erratic Gertrude Lawrence. He fell into an easy rapport with the brisk, good-humored Dolin, and could even handle Markova, who veered from shyness to sudden explosions.

When Dolin brought in other dancers, David inherited them. Fanny was happy to recede into the role of friendly guru, available for consultation on long-range career decisions. Nonetheless, even in fleeting appearances, she made a lasting impression. Pat Dolin was struck by her "incredible" tenacity: "Most people will latch onto something, stay with it a while, then forget it — especially if they encounter obstacles or disappointments. Not Fanny. Once she gets an idea in her head, she'll work that idea to its ultimate limit.

"And her talk! She wins half her cases simply by wearing her opponents down with a round-the-clock barrage. It's a clever, conscious technique — because when the occasion demands it, she can be quiet as a mouse, a very good listener . . ."

She could even disappear completely, as Sol Hurok discovered to his constant vexation. The Holtzmann office, guiding the fates of a half-dozen globe-trotting dancers, did a good deal of business with the ebullient Ukrainian-born impresario; but it was always David who sat down to iron out dates and terms with him on Saturday afternoons at the Russian Tea Room.

Hurok, the promoter of Pavlova, Chaliapin and Artur Rubinstein in the United States, had known some older members of the Holtzmann family before World War I. He was very curious about Fanny, particularly about her exploits among the czarist nobility of his Russian homeland.

This appetite was whetted when he began receiving enthusiastic messages from Fanny during his overseas journeys, congratulations telephoned from one European capital to him in another. For years she was a disembodied, mystery-laden voice, brushing aside his eager requests for a meeting.

And she took pains to keep it that way, explaining to David: "As a legend, I'm invaluable. Life holds few illusions for Hurok. He lunches with heads of state, gets no thrill out of meeting Stalin. But he still has a vision of Fanny Holtzmann, floating down a staircase in a royal robe and tiara. Let him cling to that illusion, nourish that unfulfilled desire."

Ballerinas and impresarios were all very well; movie stars had their place. But for Fanny, authors were the exciting part of her clientele, the people she felt had most claim on her skills and her contacts. In the twenties, she had lent a voluntary hand to P. G. "Plum" Wodehouse, who as an English writer living in Hollywood was beset with multiple-tax difficulties. Now she moved into furthering more directly the fortunes of two estimable literary figures: the Pulitzer Prize–winner Louis Bromfield and the Anglo-Irish historical novelist Francis Hackett.

It was at the Ritz Hotel in Paris — the Ritz Bar was practically American territory — that Fanny first crossed paths with Bromfield. She was alone in the dining room when a short, baldish man with a cavalry moustache strolled up to her table. "Miss Holtzmann? I'm George Hawkins, secretary to Louis Bromfield. And we've got a problem."

"Who hasn't?" murmured Fanny.

"The fact is, we've been sailing under false colors. Everybody in Paris assumes we know the great Fanny Holtzmann; indeed that we are all — excuse the expression — bosom buddies. But you know, and we know, that we are not on your list."

A tall rangy man, sandy hair falling in a cowlick over his right eye, materialized alongside Hawkins. He had a raw, likable quality. "What do we have to do," he drawled with a country twang, "to get you out to Senlis?"

Fanny laughed. "Try asking me, Mr. Bromfield. In New York I had to pay admission to hear you speak."

"Here it's we who will pay," said Hawkins. "And you don't have to say a thing. Just show up."

"You see," explained Bromfield, "I'm entertaining a society crowd from Newport this weekend, a whole collection of rich bitches. I've got to give them somebody new."

He was not, Fanny discovered, entirely kidding. Bromfield was an Ohio farm boy, elevated by a Back Bay marriage into an upper-crust social setting that he found both deplorable and irresistible. His rambling old manor house at Senlis outside Paris was the scene of weekly parties that brought together dowagers, chorus girls, gamblers, diplomats — a picturesque potpourri of celebrities and scalawags.

Secretly, Bromfield confided, he yearned to be what most people assummed he was: a New York Jew. He related with relish his signing of a writing contract with MGM shortly after winning the Pulitzer Prize in 1927 for his novel *Early Autumn*. J. Robert Rubin, counsel to the film company, warned him: "Of course, this short story of yours that we're buying will have to be entirely rewritten. We're only signing you for your name, Mr. Bromberg."

Bromfield was not at all discomfited. "Where I grew up," he told Fanny, "the Jews were the leading citizens in every community. They owned the big stores and were the main stockholders in the First National Bank. My mother was only a farmer's daughter.

"And when I came to New York, I found that the great writers, the wits of the Round Table, were all Jewish. FPA was really named Schlossman. Dorothy Parker was born a Rothschild. Edna Ferber taught me how to make chicken soup and *brusteckel* [pot roast]. Those writers who weren't Jewish, like Alec Woollcott, kept quiet about it."

Fanny went that weekend to Senlis. Sunday evening, after a superb dinner prepared by her host, the talk turned to Hollywood.

Bromfield grew suddenly morose. He was illustrious but broke, he told Fanny. There was no such thing as an "established writer." His epic and much-applauded novel of India, *The Rains Came*, had left the movie-makers cold. A series of agents had been rebuffed with the comment that the story would have no appeal in America: "Who wants a picture about a lot of foreigners?"

Upon her return to New York she made a date for lunch with Ned Depinet, the RKO studio chief with whom she had negotiated for Fred Astaire. "I know it's been hawked around without any takers, Ned — but that's only for lack of imagination on the part of story departments. You people like to make pictures with safe ingredients — cops and robbers, kiss and kill — well, here's a chance to wrap up the tried-and-true formula inside an exotic package. You give them maharajahs and elephants, gorgeous costumes, the clash of races — all done on a wide screen and in blazing color!"

"We won't live to see color movies, Fanny."

"That's exactly what everybody told my client Lee De Forest when he said he could make movies talk! The role of an executive is to look ahead, Ned — not to echo the babbling of the gossip columnists. Here's a property that has a glamorous background, a great love story and a visual climax that's unbeatable: the endless tropical downpour, washing away people, animals, the whole subcontinent."

She saw a flicker of interest in Depinet's eyes, and turned up the heat: "That is what movies are *for*, Ned. The story couldn't be told on such a scale in any other medium."

"Hm . . . What kind of money is he asking?"

"Plenty. But he's leaving that entirely to me. And I can ask him to make a special price for an old friend."

Depinet nodded. "Well — let Lily take a look."

Like Mayer, Depinet did not himself deign to read a book or a script. His story editor was Lily Messenger, formerly the RKO representative in London, where Fanny had dined with her often.

Lily agreed that *The Rains Came* would make an exciting film, especially after Fanny pointed out its affinities with Somerset Maugham's short story "Rain," which had been adapted into a highly profitable movie. Lily had an aide prepare a synopsis emphasizing these commercially attractive aspects.

Depinet thumbed through the synopsis and came up with an offer of $50,000. The sale financed Bromfield's return to America and his purchase of Malabar Farm in Ohio, converted by the author into a showcase for advanced agricultural techniques.

For the rest of the decade Fanny kept up a spirited correspondence with the Bromfield menage, sending them kosher delicacies along with reports on Bromfield's parents, who lived on the East Coast. George Hawkins, writing from the farm after a visit to Europe, reported: "The salami was still intact when we got here. Jewish food must be just like our Jewish friends — never goes bad or spoils." But Louis' reconstruction projects were soaking up thousands: "What are we going to do about getting the boss some dough — quick?"

Fanny tried hard to interest the studios in old Bromfield properties. "Frankly," she advised her friends in Ohio, "I've never known of a common-sense purchase of a story by a film company. They must always go around corners — so I'm trying to create corners for them. More discussions with Paramount; they'd like a Bromfield story but you know how they function now. The dictatorship policy of the old Thalberg-Schulberg-Zanuck days had its advantages; one could get an immediate 'Yes.' Now the Coast must pass on it, and then the New York office must okay it — and after all the efficiency theories are lived through, they cannot blame any individual for the flops they are having."

Finally Bromfield took an eight-week writing assignment in Hollywood, from which he sent Fanny rueful little notes: "Wish you were coming out here. It might liven up the life, which I find very monotonous."

Their friendship was genuine and close. It was to be strengthened even further during the war years.

Fanny was recommended to Francis Hackett by Justice Felix Frankfurter of the U.S. Supreme Court, who at the time knew her only by reputation. The author, plump-cheeked and scholarly, had a major claim against Alexander Korda and United Artists; according to Hackett, Korda's film *The Private Life of Henry VIII*, starring Charles Laughton, was plagiarized from Hackett's earlier book, *Henry the Eighth*. There were unmistakable parallels in incident and characterization; even some historical flaws in the biography were carried over intact into the movie. And Hackett professed certainty that his book had been read twice by

Laughton, as well as by the actor's secretary, and by the screenwriter Edward Knoblock.

Korda countered that the material was all in the public domain, a matter of historical record for four hundred years. He refused to consider a settlement or even to see the author. Fanny, warming to the battle, set about preparing a brief. Copyright had been her special domain since law-school days. Korda filed a reply through his attorneys, meanwhile dropping hints to Hackett that if he separated himself from Fanny Holtzmann some adjustment might be worked out. Hackett held firm.

At this point Fanny discovered that the author was developing a new work, a fictional treatment of Henry VIII's second wife, Anne Boleyn. She reasoned that if interest in *Queen Anne Boleyn* could be stimulated in Hollywood, Korda might be stirred to competitive bidding, perhaps leading to an overall settlement embracing both Tudor properties. It was a farsighted notion; and, Hackett thought, far-fetched.

By contrast, he was enthusiastic about the "amazing results" of Fanny's spadework in Hollywood, where Mervyn LeRoy was panting to see a synopsis of *Queen Anne*. But no sale materialized on the Coast.

Meanwhile Fanny had met several times with Korda's lawyers, and built a working relationship. "Look," she told them, "this is a very controversial issue. A court could rule either way — and one of us get badly hurt. On the other hand, my client has a property that's a natural for a follow-up to your *Henry the Eighth*. Why don't we put together a settlement that will give my man some cash and your man the most valuable gift in the world — peace of mind?"

London Films was amenable. For a minimum guarantee of $25,000 in cash against 5 percent of the producer's gross, screen rights to the still-unwritten *Queen Anne* would go to Korda; in return, Hackett would drop his claim regarding *Henry VIII*. Hackett, who stood to make up to $75,000 if the film rights were sold to a third party, cabled his delight with this "wise amicable solution."

Hackett ultimately collected only in part because Korda went bankrupt. Years later his widow, with the easy wisdom of hindsight, questioned whether Fanny was right in encouraging him toward a stage version of *Queen Anne*. But the author himself had already gone on record feelingly with his appreciation of Fanny's six months of labor, and of the earnest dedication behind them. Fanny too, Hackett noted in a letter to her, had been in a position to gain if the $75,000 ever came through, but he realized well that it was not "the twenty-five percent which motivates you, any more than the seventy-five percent motivates me.

"Your power, and your power alone, converted my defeat by Korda into a victory. . . . You could not have given me this chance if you had not spent your fierce energy and perception on it. You tried one solution after another, and you finally hit on the solution that had the maximum of possibility in it. With your amazing insight you changed defeat into opportunity.

"I am at heart no more reconciled to the orthodox now than I was twenty years ago, but to do a good job I needed material help, and now I can be just as original, just as independent, just as free, as lies in me. It is my belief that you, in your innermost self, value these things in my work, and it is this respect for my integrity as a writer that warms me when I think of what you are and what you have done."

The Hackett settlement had an amusing aftermath. Some months later, an English producer had a falling-out over a coproduction deal with Korda, who departed the next day for New York. His aggrieved associate took the next plane out and caught up with Korda at the Plaza Hotel. There the Hungarian, still several years away from his knighthood but imperious as an archduke, dismissed him contemptuously for his pains.

Much vexed, the Englishman called his solicitor in London for advice. He was told to "get hold of Fanny Holtzmann."

He telephoned her in the late afternoon, eager to rush right over. But Fanny had just left her swimming club; her hair was damp, and she didn't want to look less than her best when receiving a new client. So she made an appointment for two the next afternoon, which would allow her time to see the hairdresser at Stern's department store across the street in the morning.

When she came in from Stern's a little before noon, there was a brief message waiting from the client: "Plans changed, can't make it, will phone again."

At three o'clock a splendid bouquet arrived from the Plaza, with the English producer's card. A few minutes later the telephone rang; it was the producer, with the cheerful report that he was en route to the airport to fly home. Clearly he was in fine spirits.

What, Fanny inquired, had happened to his dispute with Korda?

"Oh, that . . ."

Well, it seemed that after breakfast that morning he had stepped into the elevator and found Korda already there. The lanky Hungarian shook his mop of gray hair impatiently: "Must you stay at the same hotel, to haunt me? Move somewhere else!"

"Don't worry," he had replied, "I shall. I'm turning the whole matter over to Fanny Holtzmann."

Korda stared hard. The *Henry VIII* episode was undoubtedly still fresh in his mind; perhaps he had visions of his own head being lopped off, like the heads of the monarch's unfortunate wives. The elevator soared upward with the two men.

Finally Korda spoke. "My dear fellow, that is silly. It's not necessary to go to Fanny. Besides, she and I are old friends."

The elevator stopped, and the door slid open. The operator turned to Korda. "Twelfth floor, sir."

Korda beckoned his erstwhile associate. "Come in and talk. We can settle this ourselves."

And they had, on terms more than satisfactory to the Englishman. Two words had done the trick: "Fanny Holtzmann."

Mention of Fanny's name was enough to inspire *premières danseuses* and chill movie moguls; yet to the public she was by choice unknown. She still made her home with her parents, since 1931 in various apartments in Manhattan. And she lived as inconspicuously as any of the millions with whom she disappeared into the subway every day. The occasional trip to the hairdresser at Stern's was one of her few indulgences. Usually she cut her own hair before a mirror and washed it under the shower ("part of the good sensation is not paying"). She wore no jewelry, scrubbed her own nails, picked up her everyday wardrobe in the girls' departments of the big stores, and seldom paid more than six dollars for a hat. When not lunching with a client at the Ritz or the Algonquin, she patronized the short-order counter at Stern's.

Fanny was celebrated only in the private haunts of celebrities. She might long have remained that way, if not for a lurid figure who had dominated the imperial court of the last Russian czar and who a generation later returned ghostlike on the screen to spark a new and bitter controversy: Rasputin.

Chapter 7

*T*HE RASPUTIN AFFAIR began at a Mayfair party attended by Fanny in the summer of 1933. A fellow guest, blond and tipsy, announced that she was an illegitimate daughter of King Edward VII, and intended to entrust her life story to that most expert of professional ghosts, Frank Scully.

Fanny turned her head. "The man from *Variety*? He's my favorite columnist."

"My dear, he's everybody's favorite everything. His place on the Riviera is headquarters for all of your American compatriots, from Ernest Hemingway down."

That, Fanny mused aloud, was interesting; she would be in Nice herself on business the following week.

"In that case, you must look Frank up at Menton."

"But I don't know him."

"You will, I assure you — in a matter of minutes." Scully, the lady explained, was the friendliest of creatures — a man with enough ailments to sink a half-dozen ordinary mortals, who transmuted his endless hospital adventures into humor books and his ardent Catholicism into political reform. In bouts with polio, other microbes and various surgeons the New York–born columnist had lost one leg, one lung and part of his hearing — but never his passion for life.

The next morning, Fanny sent Scully a fan letter. By return post she had a warm invitation to stay with Frank, his wife Alice and their infant son Skippy.

Fanny was met at the railroad station in Nice by Alice Scully: brisk, comely, very Norwegian and very pregnant. Alice spoke a thickly accented English spiced with *Variety* slang. She had first seen Frank in the hospital at Nice, had studied English and nursing to be at his side, and now ran his car, his correspondence and his household.

Alice drove eastward some ten miles along the picturesque Corniche road; the Scully villa at Menton was close to the Italian border. Walking up the path, Fanny saw suitcases and packing boxes scattered around the veranda. From behind a typewriter, a silver-haired man with strong Spencer Tracy features slipped a crutch under his arm and hauled up his broad frame. "Welcome, Fanny," he said in a sweet clear tenor. "We're off to the States in a couple of days. The house is all yours."

"Complete with no water," added Alice. "Our plumber laid an egg."

Fanny, accustomed to the splendors of her Savoy suite, suggested she might better accomplish her business at the Grand Hotel in Nice. She stayed for a few hours, helping the beleaguered Alice to deal with a procession of visitors, collaborators and doctors.

She returned the next morning when she had disposed of her legal duties. Over breakfast Scully recalled that he had an urgent message for Fanny. He had just completed a memoir for Olga Tchirikova, a czarist aristocrat living in nearby Roquebrune. Olga's closest friend, the Princess Irina Youssoupoff, had some sort of libel grievance against MGM; the princess was expected on a visit momentarily.

Scully had mentioned that Fanny too would soon be in the area, and Madame Tchirikova had seized on the news with great excitement. Frank must promise to let them know as soon as Fanny was free.

"All right, I'm free. Give them a call."

"Nix," said Alice. "Olga doesn't horse around with telephones."

One sent a note, it was explained. Frank hobbled over to his typewriter.

After several confused exchanges, Fanny established contact with Olga and her royal guest. Princess Irina was a slim handsome woman in her late thirties. The niece of Czar Nicholas II, she had been known before the first World War as "the most eligible girl in the Empire"; at her wedding to Prince Felix Youssoupoff she was given away by the czar, who added to his blessings a bag of twenty-nine large diamonds.

The princess told Fanny that a movie had reportedly been made by MGM in which a character recognizable as herself was portrayed as the mistress and sponsor of the notorious Rasputin, the crafty Siberian peasant who wormed his way into the czar's household. She had not seen the film, but understood from Russian émigrés in America that it had been widely shown there. Since she had never even met Rasputin, she was outraged at the association; but she was leaving all details of redress to her husband, Prince Felix — himself deeply involved in the historical record as the acknowledged killer of Rasputin. Prince Felix, she said, was anxious to discuss the matter with Fanny.

"I'll be at the Ritz in Paris," Fanny told her.

The day after Fanny arrived in the French capital, Prince Felix Youssoupoff came calling. He was slender, jaunty, elegant, with the cockiness that might be expected from a man brought up to regard the czar as a poor relation. In 1916, the prince had become heir to seven palaces and an oil-based fortune in south-central Russia valued at $500,000,000. His father, on a whim, once gave his mother the highest mountain in the Crimea as a birthday present.

Nearly all of Prince Felix's riches, of course, were wiped out by the Russian Revolution; he escaped to Europe in 1918 with a mere million in jewels and a couple of Rembrandts. He claimed he turned up his nose at a German offer to install him as czar if he would sign the Treaty of Brest-Litovsk, and took his wife to settle in Paris. There, with his orchidaceous lifestyle and his noblesse-oblige generosity to other refugees, he was quickly reduced to the genteel poverty that was the common lot of Russians in exile. But his manner was not in the least affected. Ornaments dangled from his wrists and fingers; behind his cool gray eyes, screened by long lashes, lurked the mocking humor that had led him once to unloose a crateful of small farm animals in the austere lobby of the Carlton Hotel in London.

Despite prewar "studies" at Oxford, where he cut down his entourage to a spartan five servants, Felix had a less-than-Oxonian command of English. Fanny's Russian was nil, her French choppy. At the end of their first meeting — the dinner check at the Ritz was signed by Fanny — she knew only that there had been some exploration of starting legal action in New York, and that Felix "ate like a prince." Still mysteries to her were the exact nature of Princess Irina's complaint, the historical background on which the MGM film was based, even the title of the picture.

These bothersome details, the prince managed to convey, would be imparted by his wife's mother, the Grand Duchess Xenia, who was the czar's favorite sister. The Romanoffs, he explained, thanks to their Danish mother and their cousinly connection with the British throne, spoke excellent English. Prince Felix indicated that a few visits to his mother-in-law would be more useful to Fanny than a doctorate in Russian studies.

Thus began Fanny's trips to Frogmore House, and her successful passage under the scrutiny of King George.

The grand duchess was, as Felix had assured her, a splendid source: an intimate witness to the disintegration of the czarist regime. Fanny quickly perceived the clue to melting Xenia's royal reserve. Members of ruling households, shut off from outside contact, were less interested in affairs of state than in each other. In the gilded ghetto of Petrograd, an eight-year-old grandchild was more important than the new French ambassador; the mood of a beloved big brother far outweighed the ceremonial launching of a battleship.

And when it was a question of the brother, Xenia's adored "Nicky," falling into the clutches of a dim-witted German princess, Fanny could see at once where Xenia's sympathies — and antipathies — lay.

"That woman," Xenia said bluntly of her sister-in-law, the empress, "made a rag out of Nicky. She was never really one of us. She wouldn't speak a word of Russian unless she absolutely had to."

It all sounded terribly familiar, a rerun of the family feuds in Louis B. Mayer's Hollywood or among the Holtzmanns of Eastern Parkway. As Fanny reported it later, "I simply equated her family with ours." She told the grand duchess at their second meeting that the pot roast and kasha served at Frogmore were the *pièces de résistance* of her own parents' table. Xenia was much gratified.

But before matters got quite so cozy, there was something Fanny had to get out of her craw: the anti-Semitic Russian pogroms which, even if officially discouraged by Nicholas II, were deeply rooted in late czarist history.

That, said Xenia, was something she simply didn't know about. Rampaging Cossacks were not part of her world. As for Jews, "All I know is they're very intelligent. In St. Petersburg, if someone was sick, you sent for a Jewish doctor. Every duke had a Jew to run his business affairs. The really talented people — concert violinists, chess masters — always turned out to be Jewish. That's why, when we heard you were Jewish, we wanted to consult you."

Xenia fixed her earnest brown eyes on the young American lawyer, and Fanny saw no reason to doubt her.

In pursuit of an inside slant on Russian history — the official accounts, after all, were available in any library — Fanny asked Xenia how she and her family had escaped the fate of the czar, slain on the eastern slope of the Urals with all his immediate household by a Bolshevik execution squad in the summer of 1918. Xenia answered in personal and graphic terms.

She and her mother, with other members of their family, had taken refuge in a castle on the Black Sea when word arrived of the royal slaughter. Red Army troops were closing in on the Crimea. Xenia's mother, the Danish-born Dowager Empress Marie, flashed a message across Europe to her sister Alexandra in Buckingham Palace, the mother of King George: "Send a ship!"

According to the family account, the king ordered HMS *Marlborough* rigged up for the rescue trip — and ran into an angry protest from Lloyd George, first of the Labour Party prime ministers: "You'll have us at war with the Bolsheviks, Your Majesty! There will be a storm of anti-monarchist reaction here. Are you trying to topple the throne, and bring down your cousin's fate on yourself?"

The king was in turn confronted by his tall and imperious mother, the widow of Edward VII and the daughter-in-law of Queen Victoria: "Do I understand that you are placing the wishes of that Welsh miner above your concern for your family? Just what do the letters 'H.M.S.' on a warship mean? Who is the ruler of England — King George or Lloyd George? Your cousin Nicky, at least, went down fighting. He was not content to be a puppet!"

The *Marlborough* was duly dispatched, and on its arrival was loaded up with refugees in a boarding that combined desperation with high comedy. As Xenia explained: "Naturally, there wasn't room for all the people who wanted to get away. The Russian custom in making long journeys is to take lots of good cooks along; in exile, especially, chefs took priority over chancellors. So suddenly everybody was claiming to be a great chef, an undiscovered genius in the kitchen. Quite a few generals and engineers got aboard that way."

For Fanny's purposes, this was all essentially prelude; she still had to be briefed by Xenia on Rasputin. That would entail more visits to Frogmore, and perhaps meetings with the grand duchess in town. Meanwhile, there would be a good deal of communication by telephone — and hotel operators had notoriously long ears. The grand duchess had heard Fanny Brice's radio portrayal of the willful Baby Snooks. With a flash of her grave humor, she suggested that her telephone name be "Mrs. Snooks." Fanny thought that was too much of a demotion. They settled for "Lady Snooks."

"Ah, that Rasputin!" Xenia shook her head. "We all warned Nicky, again and again."

Xenia's account, supplemented by those of her children and Prince Felix, filled out the legend of the peasant-adventurer but did not substantially alter it. Rasputin (literally, "The Dissolute One") wandered into the imperial court from Siberia soon after the turn of the century, when there was a great vogue for the occult among the sensation-seeking aristocracy. Smelly, unkempt, with coarse features and a squat tough body, he announced himself as a *starets*, an ascetic man of God with prophetic and healing powers; and indeed the effect of his fierce gaze, blazing out of blue eyes that "changed to steely gray," was hypnotic. Court ladies in particular, perhaps jaded with their perfumed consorts, were susceptible to his influence. Many a titled head was led to his pillow by the assurance that "for true redemption, one must first commit sin; I am not polluting you, I am purifying you."

Rasputin would have remained merely a foxy seducer, lost in the bypasses of history, if not for a tragic coincidence: Nicholas and Alexandra had a son named Alexei, then about six, who carried the not-uncommon royal inheritance of hemophilia. Doctors could do nothing for the ailing czarevich, but Rasputin was able with a few calm words at least to soothe the boy.

And so the empress, superstition-prone and desperate, came to see the "holy monk" as the savior of her child. He had the run of the court — wenching, drinking, dispensing "petitions," and even recommending ministers — especially after war broke out in 1914 and the czar went off to the front. Thereafter, "good" politicians, in Alexandra's mind, were those who got along with "our Friend."

The old aristocracy seethed: rumor said Rasputin was planning a sell-out to the Germans. Finally a "patriotic conspiracy" was formed to dispatch the intruder, and in December of 1916 Rasputin was drugged, shot and clubbed to death in the cellar of Prince Felix's Moika Palace.

Against this background, the distress of Princess Irina and her family was understandable. Rasputin was, if reports of the MGM movie were correct, portrayed as the court protégé and sexual master of the princess.

By now, Fanny and Xenia were on intimate terms. The grand duchess indicated that the remaining Romanoffs had other legal problems, including the whereabouts of enormous assets reportedly held overseas by the late czar.

Fanny was frankly intrigued. The Romanoffs were a romantic flash-back to an era the world would never see again. And as clients, they gave promise of staying power. Fanny had a hunch that "for once I'd met a family that had a lot of legal work and not a single relative to do it. In Brooklyn every family had an Uncle Sidney or Cousin Abe tucked away somewhere with an attorney-at-law shingle tacked on his door; in Buckingham Palace there were no lawyer cousins and none likely ever to be."

The grand duchess's hint of unfinished business was soon followed up by a call to Fanny, in some agitation, from "Lady Snooks." Could Miss Holtzmann please come to tea at Frogmore at once?

It seemed that Xenia's late husband, the Grand Duke Alexander, had sat to a sculptor named Yourievich, and later adopted a less formal posture with Yourievich's wife, Helene. The lady had amassed, and was apparently planning to publish, a collection of love letters, political articles, and family reminiscences written by the grand duke. Xenia was not optimistic about the impact of such an event upon her daughter Irina and her six sons. She had consulted her cousin "Geordie," and the king had told her: "Let us see what Miss Fanny recommends."

For Fanny, this was a relatively routine assignment: "I never had a big-name actor for a client who wasn't sooner or later faced with a similar situation in dealing with a former girl friend. I knew I could play it by ear."

She invited Mme. Yourievich, an opulent blond with a Wagnerian figure, to drop in on her at the Hotel Splendide in Piccadilly. The dialogue between the ladies was brief but pungent.

Fanny (innocently): Are you living in London, madame?

Mme. Y: Of course. Where else would I stay as a refugee?

Fanny: Do you like it here?

Mme. Y: Very much. I have many friends, people of my own background . . .

Fanny: I understand you also have some letters from an important personage.

Mme. Y: Ah yes, the Grand Duke Alexander! Sandro was an amazing man, the love of my life. He was a great bon vivant, you know — the czar's companion at those midnight suppers with ballerinas in their bachelor days. He hated being tied down to that dreadful Xenia —

Fanny: Who, if your letters ever appear in print, will emerge as the heroine of the story — the maltreated wife! (Her tone hardening.) But let me advise you of something far more serious: if you make *any attempt* to use the material in your possession, you will be ruled an undesirable alien practicing blackmail. You will not spend another day in this country.

That same evening, Mme. Yourievich signed papers abandoning all rights to the grand duke's writings and correspondence, including his appraisals of the two strong-minded Danish sisters, Alexandra and Marie, who became respectively queen of England and empress of Russia.

Advised of the news, Xenia sighed her relief. "Fanny, you really are incredible! No — don't send anything by messenger. I'll pick up the papers myself. And I'll tell Geordie."

After reflecting on the *Rasputin* movie claim, Fanny decided it might be a sticky case to prove. Besides, on principle she preferred settlements to court battles. She put in a call to J. Robert Rubin, the MGM vice-president and general counsel in New York, and told him of her conversations at Frogmore: "The princess and her family are very upset, Bob. They're determined to press for damages."

Rubin laughed.

"You don't understand, Bob. Royalty looks at these things differently. If I don't take the case, they'll get someone else."

"It wouldn't make any difference if they got God Almighty. There *is* no case, Fanny. The movie is fiction, and we're protected by clearances. Anyway, the damn thing stinks. Audiences won't go near it."

"Could I see it?"

"Why not? Call Sam Eckman [the MGM manager in London] and tell him to cable me for a print. He'll arrange a screening."

"I'll need a shooting script, too, to prepare my case."

"You'll need a miracle to build this into a case. But I'll talk to the story department."

The private screening of *Rasputin, the Mad Monk* (in America it had been released as *Rasputin and the Empress*) raised more questions for Fanny than it resolved. She saw the picture with Prince Felix at the MGM executive theater in Upper St. Martin's Lane. The scenario unfolded a tale of suspicion, seduction and revenge, revolving around a gallant nobleman who mistrusted the peasant-healer from the outset; the prince's innocent sweetheart, reduced by the lecherous Rasputin to a fallen woman; and the conspiracy, evidently born of personal as well as patriotic motives, that after many failures finally resulted in Rasputin's death.

The cast offered a parade of Barrymores: Lionel in the title role, sister Ethel as the hapless czarina, and John of the noble profile as one "Prince Chegodieff" — an invented name — seen as the dispenser of summary justice to Rasputin. The prince's fiancée, played by Diana Wynyard of *Cavalcade* fame, was dubbed "Princess Natasha." This was the character held by Russian émigrés in New York to be unmistakably recognizable as Princess Irina.

When the lights went up, Prince Felix turned to Fanny: "*Voilà!* Eet ees clear. *Le prince, c'est moi* — '*Natasha,' c'est Irène!*"

Fanny wasn't so sure. The names had been changed; probably the details of Rasputin's death and his amorous intrigues had been deliberately muddied. Nothing less than an exhaustive comparison between historical facts and fictional treatment could establish points of identity. And according to Sam Eckman, the studio had a deskful of clearances from former court figures of the period, obtained by payments of sums ranging from one hundred to five hundred dollars.

On the other hand, she saw a hook for possible action in the silent title flashed on the screen at the beginning of the film: "This concerns the destruction of an empire brought about by the mad ambition of one man. A few of the principal characters are still alive — the rest met death by violence." This seemed a flat negation of any claim to fiction. And with Rasputin slain as well as the czar, the czarina and the czarevich, which of the principal actors in the drama could be "still alive" except Felix and Irina? Furthermore, the sexual episodes in the picture were hardly ambiguous; if "Natasha" was indeed a thinly disguised Irina, then Irina had grounds for libel.

Meanwhile, there was a tactical question to pursue. Papers had already been filed against MGM in the New York Supreme Court, but the picture was scheduled for imminent general release in England. Some two thousand theaters in King George's own backyard would be displaying an overheated narrative objectionable to the royal cousins. Should deletions be requested or an injunction be sought?

Xenia talked it over with "Geordie." The king, somewhat dubious about linking the crown to the *enfant terrible* reputation of Prince Felix, decided he wanted the advice of his lord chamberlain, the earl of Cromer.

Cromer, slight but regal-looking, had exercised a quasi-paternal interest in Fanny since her first trip to England. As official censor of all productions on the West End, he was involved from time to time with some of her clients.

Cromer invited Fanny around to St. James's Palace to hear her analysis of the case. She told him that Prince Felix would make a responsible and impressive witness, capable despite his limited English vocabulary of describing graphically his murder of Rasputin. But if the palace wished to go ahead with court action in England, she as an American could not handle it; and she did not want the responsibility of selecting British counsel.

Cromer pondered overnight, then sent her to see Sir Reginald Poole, a member of the firm of Lewis and Lewis, His Majesty's personal solicitors.

Sir Reginald took unkindly to the project from the first. Short and pompous, he scowled at Fanny from behind heavy black-rimmed glasses. It was obvious that he disapproved of taking up such matters with an outsider from America, who was a woman to boot. He declined even to discuss the case until he had seen the film.

When he emerged from the screening room, his head was waggling negatively. "Not a chance," he reported at a later conference with Cromer and Fanny.

"A woman's chastity —" Fanny began.

"We'd be laughed out of court. The princess has been married for more than twenty years. It's an awkward business — but they've covered their tracks. No specific identity — just a photograph with a fictional name attached. Rasputin had dozens of women. It could have been anybody."

"I still think it's worth bringing suit, if only to force a disclaimer about any living person being intended."

"In America, perhaps," said Sir Reginald cuttingly. "In this country, the prospects wouldn't justify the risk of public scandal."

Fanny looked appealingly toward Cromer, but the lord chamberlain was nodding in gloomy agreement.

Fanny was caught in the middle. She had invested time, money and reputation in the Youssoupoffs, against a contingency fee on actions instituted outside of England. At this point all she wanted was a graceful way out. She made a second transatlantic try with Bob Rubin: "Look, Bob, there *is* a case here, but the protocol complications just aren't worth the trouble. I can't afford to spend the next month lunching with the lord chamberlain. So here's a simple solution for both of us: Pay the princess some minimal settlement — say, five thousand dollars — and put in a notice with the credit titles on *Rasputin* that the picture doesn't refer to any living person."

"Five thousand dollars? You must be out of your mind!"

"It's peanuts to MGM, Bob. But it will cool off the royal hotheads here — and spare both of us a royal headache."

"I can't do it, Fanny. I have to think of our stockholders."

"Which includes protecting them against possible disasters. Look — I don't care how much you pay. Make it a thousand; five hundred, even. Just so we can both get off the hook, and I don't have to go back to my clients empty-handed."

"I am ashamed," intoned the MGM counsel — how like her brother

Jack he was! — "that an American lawyer should be so concerned with gaining the goodwill of the decadent Russian aristocracy. This is what comes of your running around castles all over Europe and hanging out with those titled loafers." There was more in the same sorrowful vein, about Fanny turning her back on the native land which had been so good to her.

"At these prices," Fanny interrupted, "I don't need a lecture, Bob."

She hung up and told the operator to get her Louis B. Mayer at the studio in Culver City. Mayer listened briefly, then said: "Come home, Fanny. We'll talk about it."

Ten days, eight hundred dollars and six thousand miles later, she sat in Mayer's beach house at Santa Monica. The studio chief had been tied up in conferences all day, so they were taking potluck dinner together in his kitchen. Mayer tore into a bagel: "What kind of *tsouris* [trouble] are you bringing me, Fanny? Haven't I got enough to do here without fighting New York? Besides, what the hell do you want to get mixed up with those lousy Romanoffs for?"

"They're not such bad people, Louis. Believe me, this bunch didn't run any pogroms on your people and mine. That was the previous Romanoff — Alexander III. This crowd all had Jewish stewards and advisers. Do you think our people are so much better off now under the Bolsheviks?"

"Anyway, the legal department tells me your clients are never men-tioned in the picture, and we have clearances from everybody else. So there's no case."

"I wouldn't count on that, Louis. Libel can be a tricky business. This is one of those situations where anything can happen. Just look at the elements: beautiful princess thrown into exile by the Revolution and now held up to the world in your picture as the worthless plaything of a wicked seducer. Robbed first of her fortune, then of her good name."

"We don't even mention her name!"

"You don't have to — if a jury concludes she's the one you mean. And naturally, I'd have to do my best to persuade them. The grand duchess and the princess are counting on me."

Mayer frowned.

"Why take a chance, Louis, when you may be able to head it off by paying a few thousand dollars?"

Mayer swallowed a chunk of brisket and put down his fork. "You're a good lawyer, Fanny — which is the main reason I'll go along with you. I'll call Bob Rubin over the weekend, and tell him to work out the details with you in New York." He pushed back his chair.

In the plush MGM offices overlooking Broadway at Forty-fourth Street, Bob Rubin was waiting. Before Fanny could speak, Rubin held up his hand: "It's no use, we're not going to settle."

"But L.B. said he would explain to you —"

"Nick Schenck [head of MGM in New York] is taking charge of this one, personally. And he absolutely refuses to pay a penny. In fact, he gave me this message for you." Rubin glanced down at a paper on his desk. " 'Those sonofabitch czarists can't get their hands on us over here, especially not with a fake trumped-up case!' " Rubin stood up. "And you know something, Fanny? As MGM general counsel — the lawyer on the premises — I agree with him, one hundred percent!"

Spinning through Fanny's mind was a case she had recently stumbled on while in the office of Charles L. Wagner, the concert manager. Fanny had been there to discuss a schedule change for a client when Wagner's attorney-accountant, Meyer Kurz, emerged much shaken from an inner office.

Kurz told Fanny he had just been assailed as a "Jew bastard" by Simon F. Peavey, Jr., the attorney for a disgruntled pianist.

At this time Hitler was gaining ground in Germany, and Jews all over the world were very sensitive to racial slurs. Fanny jumped to her feet: "You should sue Peavey. It's too bad your mother isn't alive — you could both sue."

"But she is!"

"In that case — why not teach him a lesson?"

Fanny, fascinated since law school by the nuances of libel law and the rarely invoked Civil Practices Act, swiftly outlined her reasoning. By calling Kurz a "Jew bastard," Peavey had challenged Meyer's legitimacy and thereby impugned the chastity of his mother. A brief should be drawn up, stating and documenting meticulously the circumstances of his mother's marriage and his birth. Every available record, such as rabbinical and birth certificates, should be included. With the matter of legitimacy thus established, damages should be claimed on behalf of both Meyer and his mother.

Young Kurz followed her advice. One of his older brothers brought suit for him in the New York Supreme Court, affirming that Meyer was "one of nine children born in lawful wedlock, issue of the marriage between Abraham and Esther Kurz." Esther was "at all times prior and subsequent to said marriage a chaste woman and has never given birth to any children out of wedlock nor cohabited with anyone other than said husband." Five thousand dollars in damages were asked for Meyer on the grounds that he had lost a retainer with Charles L. Wagner — and one hundred thousand dollars for Mrs. Kurz on grounds of "slander per se."

Peavey responded with a motion to dismiss, ridiculing the claim. Everybody knew, he declared, that the term "bastard" was merely a "common epithet," without literal meaning, especially when hurled in the course of an angry discussion.

Justice William Harlan Black, in a sharply worded opinion quoted in the *Law Journal* of New York, rejected these arguments as "sham, frivolous and irrelevant." The imputation of unchastity, Judge Black ruled, was indeed "slanderous per se," since it "deliberately attacks the honor of a person whose good name is dearer than any other possession."

Peavey was nailed to the wall; but the Kurzes weren't interested in drawing blood. They agreed generously to drop the case in exchange for costs and an elaborate written apology. What mattered to Meyer and his family was that their point had been upheld in court. And that likewise was what mattered to Fanny, weighing her next move on behalf of the Youssoupoffs.

If a humble immigrant housewife was worthy of the law's protection, should it not be extended also to a czarist princess? Should Irina be open to besmirching merely because her family had fallen from grace?

Surely the question would be answered most sympathetically in Great Britain, where royalty still had status as well as sentimental backing, and where the princess's cousinly connections would count. Furthermore, the British sense of privacy — and hence of infringements upon it — was far more developed than its counterpart in the United States. Libel laws were taken seriously, and rigidly enforced.

Fanny could not conduct the case in England but she could orchestrate it. The barrister appearing in court on behalf of her royal clients would have to be distinguished both in appearance and reputation. A sense of drama was indispensable, and also a rich voice capable of wringing the last ounce of pathos or indignation out of a situation.

Fanny's casting requirements were rigorous. Only one man in England could meet them, but luckily that man was within reach, a longtime member of the Cochran circle.

Sir Patrick Hastings, ten years before, had been the leading disciple of Sir Edward Marshall Hall. Wiry and articulate, with careless Irish good looks, he had once entertained dreams of writing and performing for the stage. Instead he had risen rapidly at the bar, to the eminence of king's counsel, a coveted honorary title conferred on outstanding barristers. Sir Patrick had charm, nerve and imagination; to execute Fanny's plans, he would need all of them.

She arranged for a quiet after-dinner talk at Cochran's house. "Pat, this trial can be the greatest show in history — and for once, not produced by Cockie. It's the drama of an innocent young girl, the greatniece of a queen of England, disgraced before the world as the cast-off mistress of an unscrupulous scoundrel, a man she never even laid eyes on. All for the commercial aggrandizement of a movie company."

"A heartless, Hollywood movie company," amended Hastings dryly.

"You get the picture — in every sense. We'll have titles and tiaras dripping from the witness stand: ladies-in-waiting fished out of their mothballs at Hampton Court, ambassadors from imperial Petrograd. The princess herself will testify to her purity.

"And at stage center, the eloquent Sir Patrick Hastings: sketching in the background, drawing out the witnesses, plucking at the heartstrings of the jury . . ."

Sir Patrick nodded. "There's a play-within-a-play here," he pointed out. "The old Rasputin melodrama refurbished for modern audiences."

"Exactly. And we can dredge up all the authentic details: the gullible czarina, the furious aristocrats, leading up to a murder scene more paralyzing than anything conceived in fiction. Imagine this grubby peasant who held the empire in his hand, being poisoned — shot — clubbed — and still refusing to die. We'll call the prince to the stand, the only man alive who can tell the story — and in the first person!"

Hastings leaned forward. "Fanny, I can't wait to appear in your production. But first, could I see the MGM version?"

Sir Patrick's reaction to the film was unequivocal: "This is a solid case of libel. And we can make it stick."

To round out her team, Fanny needed a firm of solicitors, the attorneys entrusted under British law with handling briefs and other pretrial procedures. She went to Harold Brooks of Langton and Passmore, who had been her associate in the Tex Austin case.

Brooks was not enthusiastic. The case seemed to him flimsy. And the Youssoupoffs were penniless foreigners, vulnerable to the demands for posting security and other delaying tactics that would undoubtedly be employed by MGM counsel.

The princess had solvent relatives, Fanny pointed out. And Sir Patrick Hastings was committed to presenting the case in court.

"The best of barristers is limited by the strength of his arguments. There's nothing in the books to go by, no precedent."

"I don't follow precedent," retorted Fanny. "I establish it."

Reluctantly, Brooks agreed to sign on. Fanny felt that his uneasiness might be traceable to an air of disapproval seeping down from the offices of Sir Reginald Poole. Even her friend Lord Cromer seemed skeptical about her plan.

She went ahead anyway, in long quiet meetings with Hastings at the Goulding town house in Kinnerton Studios. Sir Patrick slipped in at odd hours from neighboring Knightsbridge, avoiding teatime to minimize the possibility of running into inquisitive newsmen; Fanny stayed out of sight completely.

But behind the shades in the ancient drawing room she and her ally drew up plans. He would be charged with projecting the grand design of their case: blameless noblewoman linked with satanic adventurer just to fabricate a "good story"; precious privacy sacrificed to box-office sensationalism.

For the details of his legal argument — the identification of the fictional "Princess Natasha" with the live Princess Irina, and the specifics of the cinematic seduction — the barrister would rely on the staff of solicitors at Langton and Passmore. Fanny herself undertook to supply further background material on the actual history of the period. During the weeks ahead, when her British colleagues would be occupied with the usual preliminary jousting of briefs and motions, she would be involved with research in Paris and elsewhere on behalf of the Grand Duchess Xenia.

In 1918 Xenia had been named administratrix for the estate of her brother, the czar. For fifteen years a treasure hunt had been in progress all over the world, with lawyers and investigators in every country angling for a percentage of assets variously described as gold bullion, real estate and stocks. Now Her Imperial Highness placed the whole affair in Fanny's hands, except for litigation already in progress in Germany and Finland.

Fanny leaped to the task with enthusiasm, seeing an opportunity simultaneously to pursue inquiries about the czar's estate and to gain more information about Rasputin. She dispatched a dozen confidential letters to highly placed friends in government, and herself set out for Paris, the main gathering-place of Russian émigrés.

Most tantalizing of the rumors surrounding the alleged czarist fortune was the story that Nicholas, at the urgent request of his embattled cousin King George, had put $50,000,000 in gold bullion aboard a British warship. The money had never been delivered or otherwise accounted for. Questioning the royal survivors and their retinue, Fanny ran into a maze of conjecture and contradiction.

Heavy investments in the United States were also attributed to the czar, mainly in railroads, steamship companies and timber; the New York *Sun* estimated the aggregate at $120,000,000. But as Fanny methodically checked out each lead, it slipped away into insubstantiality.

Gradually a different picture emerged, of a czar and czarina whose resources in Russia were confiscated or sold after the Revolution and whose overseas assets were quickly swallowed up: by the collapse of the mark in Germany, and in England for the purchase of trains and medical supplies. A private letter to Fanny from a War Office official in close touch with the Bank of England provided a gallant footnote to history: "From a person well placed to know, I gather that *the very* high personage you mentioned, far from depositing funds abroad in 1914, actually sold and repatriated all their foreign deposits, investments, etc., as an act of patriotism. This I have confirmed elsewhere."

Although the treasure hunt yielded no treasure in bullion, it did, as Fanny had hoped, fill out her picture of life in the imperial court. Making the rounds of the émigrés in Paris with Princess Irina and two of Xenia's sons, Princes Dimitri and Fyodor, Fanny was led to a modest building on the rue de Pompei. "Four flights up" — Dimitri pointed — "lives one of the best-informed men of Old Russia. Arkady Roumanoff. He was counselor and aide to my father — and a friend of Rasputin." Fanny followed the prince up the stairs. She found herself in a small apartment crowded with children and flea-market furniture. Everybody was congregated, Russian-style, in the dining room. Dimitri presented Fanny, then went back with his sister and brother to wait in the corner café where they had all dined earlier.

Arkady Roumanoff greeted Fanny with a ceremonious bow. He had a fine beard, a cultivated voice, splendid manners: the very prototype, she thought, of the White Russian in exile. He was little instructed in English. After Fanny disposed of her few phrases in Russian, the conversation was limping along in French when a boy of six or seven straggled in and tugged at the functionary's elbow: "*Tati . . .*"

" *Le zein sha!*" ("Shut up!") , bawled Roumanoff vigorously. He glared at the boy, who slunk away.

Fanny waited a moment, then asked quietly: "Parlez-vous Yiddish?"

After that, the conversation gathered speed and animation. Fanny had arrived at nine in the evening; an hour later she was still upstairs. The corner café locked its doors, discharging the royal exiles into the cold December night. At eleven Prince Dimitri began to get nervous. Had his mother's American lawyer run afoul of some terrible plot? Did they dare to notify the gendarme strolling across the street?

Finally they did. The policeman found Arkady and Fanny sipping tea-with-lemon in the kitchen, exchanging tales in Yiddish of two households, the Roumanoffs (Petrograd) and the Holtzmanns (Brooklyn).

The czar and his family, according to Arkady, lived an insular existence. They knew nothing of the intrigues and corruption at court, and less about the lives of their Jewish subjects. Rasputin, on the other hand — and here was a startling turn — was actually a benefactor of the Jewish community: not out of compassion or principle, Arkady explained, but because he leaned heavily on Jewish advisers and was content to give them a free hand. "All Rasputin wanted was to go his own way, without anybody interfering with his drinking and wenching. So he left the petitions and the politicking to people like his secretary, Aaron Simonovich. Yes, Aaron is very much alive, I'll see that you meet him."

The man who had dispensed Rasputin's favors was slight, clean-shaven, quick of eye and speech. He spoke an earthier Yiddish than Arkady Roumanoff, but what he had to say of his former boss was much the same: "Rasputin was a threat to a lot of people at court: the insiders, the established grafters and racketeers. He broke up the entrenched pattern of corruption. For instance, before he came the Jews were fair game for murder, stealing, extortion — they had to pay a fortune for exit permits. Rasputin opened things up; he would make deals with *anybody.*"

This indirect, offhand liberalization was actually a factor in Rasputin's murder, according to Simonovich: "I don't say he was killed only on account of that; he made many enemies, for many reasons. But certainly it was one of the things that made the old court crowd anxious to get him out of the way."

Simonovich did not include Prince Felix Youssoupoff in this "old court crowd"; the prince, he agreed, undoubtedly had patriotic motives. And Rasputin, he hinted, possibly had a lecherous eye on Felix, known in his youth as "the most beautiful boy in Europe."

From other refugees, Fanny was absorbing additional intriguing tidbits about the protean Felix. His mother had desperately wanted a girl child; like Clifton Webb, he had been dressed in dainty frocks for several years. Not surprisingly, in his teens he was parading through the streets of Petrograd in his mother's finery, drawing — and accepting — dinner invitations from bemused officers of the guards.

In his twenties he had dabbled in opium, erotic literature and the gypsy guitar, a bored dilettante who could have anything he wanted merely by clapping his hands. It was bewildering, now, to hear his careless, "Ah, Fanny, do you have a few pennies for the Green Line bus?"

The pretrial skirmishes in London were growing faster and hotter. As anticipated by Harold Brooks, MGM demanded the posting of $5,000 as security against costs by the princess; and, as predicted by Fanny, the bond money along with initial fees for British counsel materialized quietly from the direction of Buckingham Palace. For her own compensation, Fanny was gambling on follow-up judgments against the movie company in other parts of the world, where she had sole representation of the Youssoupoffs.

A preliminary affidavit from Princess Irina declared that far from introducing Rasputin to the royal family, "with all the consequences historically held to have resulted," she had never even met the debauched "holy man"; to portray her as Rasputin's sexual pawn was "not merely grossly untrue but grossly defamatory." MGM countered that *their* princess could not possibly be Irina because "Natasha" was only a lady-in-waiting at court. To cancel current bookings at two thousand English theaters would cost them $200,000.

As defense counsel, MGM had hired the only barrister whose reputation rivaled that of Sir Patrick Hastings: Sir William Jowitt, a future lord chancellor. The two had appeared as opposing counsel in many major cases; the hiring of either was the signal for an adversary to engage the other.

With a sharp legal wrangle over the "particulars" to be spelled out by the plaintiff before trial, the case broke in the British press late in 1933. ·

Sir Patrick began his complaint by citing the clear admission at the start of the film that "a few" of its principals were still alive. Hastings then reeled off his grounds for identifying "Princess Natasha" with Princess Irina. The princess in *Rasputin* was referred to as "Her Highness," a niece of the czar in constant attendance at court; Nicholas had no such niece other than Irina. The two were of the same approximate age and both were betrothed at the three-hundredth anniversary celebration of the Romanoff dynasty. The nurse's garb worn in 1916 by "Natasha" was very like the wartime costume of Irina. Rasputin was killed cinematically by "Natasha's" fiancé, "Prince Chegodieff," and historically by Irina's husband, Prince Youssoupoff — in both cases in the cellar of a palace on the Moika River. The plaintiff's brief argued that the film virtually revolved about the relationship between Rasputin and "Natasha."

The battle lines were drawn; there was nothing more Fanny could contribute. Her continued presence might becloud the coronets-and-ermines atmosphere being cultivated by Sir Patrick. She slipped quietly aboard a liner bound for New York.

The trial opened on Tuesday, February 27, 1934, before a special jury and an equally special judge, the stern, widely respected Sir Horace Avory. It instantly wiped all competition from the front pages of British newspapers. Typical was the streamer carried by the *Evening News*: "Princess Sues a Film Company: Ex-Kaiser and Rasputin as Co-Plotters."

Sir Patrick, opening for the plaintiff, concentrated his early fire on establishing the lofty rank of his clients, the unutterable wickedness of Rasputin, and what he suggested was the scarcely less reprehensible callousness of the defendants. He introduced Princess Irina as "one of the few surviving members of the royal family," a favorite of the czar, surrounded since childhood by grand dukes, now "living on memories." From the witness stand, Irina affirmed that she was presently staying with her mother at Windsor Castle, and had been entertained frequently by members of the British royal family.

Irina's husband was described by Hastings as a descendant of the "reigning monarch of Tartary," who killed Rasputin "as a public duty" upon learning that the Siberian was in league with the German Kaiser to seize control of Russia.

"People who make love stories out of history," Sir Patrick said, "always take a liberty." To make John Barrymore as Prince Paul Chegodieff more attractive to audiences, the barrister proposed, the prince's marriage to Natasha was deferred in the script until "after the audience left the theater"; and he was given an additional, romantic motive for killing Rasputin: vengeance for the rape of Natasha. "The defendants may have thought that from English audiences a man who killed another, even out of a sense of deep and almost religious duty, would not get the sympathy that John Barrymore would desire."

As a consequence of this and other distortions of history, "whenever it was not sufficiently dramatic," concluded Hastings, "this film shows Princess Youssoupoff, if it is her, as a woman who has been sleeping with a man so utterly degraded as Rasputin; and then in the end her husband, as he is, and lover as he was in the film, begs her to marry him.

"She turns round and says, 'I thought this man was a man from God, and I now know he was only a man, and I am not fit to be your wife.'

"What does that mean? If ours is the true view of this film, what can you think of it? Why have such a story? Who gains by it? Why take the unhappy lives of these people and make them into a film?"

The next thirty-six hours belonged to Prince Youssoupoff. Coolly, the noble assassin mounted the stand to describe his bizarre adventure with Rasputin. The faultless tailoring of his English morning clothes gave added height to his slim figure; his low musical voice and detached manner increased the dramatic impact. Even the veteran correspondent of the New York *Times*, which ran the story on page one under a two-column headline, was chilled. The prince's calm recital, he reported, "spread a thrill of horror" through the courtroom.

In halting English, Felix told how, in order to gain Rasputin's confidence, he permitted himself to be mesmerized. He learned, he testified, that Rasputin's curative powers over the ailing czarevich derived from Tibetan herbs unknown in Europe and that the mystic intended to force the abdication of Nicholas so that he himself could rule in the name of the czarina.

After gathering together a few trusted friends, including Vladimir Purishkevich, a leader of the Duma (the Russian parliament), Felix invited Rasputin to the Youssoupoff palace on the Moika River. There he fed Rasputin cakes and wine heavily sprinkled with potassium cyanide, and when these failed to take effect, shot him through the heart. Purishkevich added four more shots.

"Was he dead then?" demanded Sir Patrick.

"Not yet."

"In the end, did you do anything to kill him?"

"Yes."

After Rasputin had been felled in the snow outside the palace, Felix testified, servants dragged the still-writhing body back to the cellar, where he himself battered out the last vestige of life with a loaded stick.

It was a climax hard to surpass. In the editorial words of the New York *Times*, "To have the Rasputin story repeated by one of the players in the matter-of-fact question-and-answer of the witness stand carries an effect that no Hollywood scenario can quite produce."

Yet the most awesome moments of the prince's macabre tale did not come until the next day, under cross-examination by Jowitt. Seeking to undermine the witness's credibility, and also to show that the actual killing was not, as distinct from the MGM version, a solo act, defense counsel led the prince through passage after passage of Felix's book *Rasputin*, published in 1927.

The prince confirmed that on the fatal night — December 16, 1916 — he arranged to have Rasputin secretly driven to the wine cellar of the Moika Palace. The mystic, attired with unusual care in a white silk blouse, black-velvet trousers and new long boots, his straggly hair slicked back and his body "smelling strongly of cheap soap," was hopeful of meeting Princess Irina.

Three slabs of poisoned chocolate cake — enough to kill as many ordinary men — were consumed by the thick-set peasant with great relish; three glasses of lethally dosed Madeira brought only a complaint of slight throat irritation.

The prince felt the small gray eyes of his guest boring into him: first with defiance, then with "fiendish hatred"; Rasputin had boasted frequently of being indestructible. "A mute and deadly conflict seemed to be taking place between us. Another moment, confronted by those satanic eyes, and I should have gone under."

Actually, Jowitt suggested, Felix's account was open to serious question. Wasn't the prince under such nervous strain that "you hardly knew what you did?"

"This is quite natural," came the cool rejoinder. "I am not, how you say, professional murderer."

Nonetheless, at Rasputin's insistence, he got out his guitar and sang gypsy songs for half an hour. Then he briefly joined his colleagues upstairs, taking a revolver from the Grand Duke Dimitri Pavlovich. Facing Rasputin before a crystal crucifix, he fired point-blank at the heart: "There was a roar as from a wild beast, and Rasputin fell heavily backwards on the bearskin rug." A red splotch appeared on the white silk blouse. The seamy features twitched a moment, then fell still. "There could be no doubt about it; he was dead."

Ten minutes later, upstairs with Purishkevich while the other conspirators were disposing of Rasputin's clothing, the prince felt an inexplicable compulsion to check on the body. He went back to the cellar. Rasputin lay motionless but still warm.

In terse monosyllables the prince and his questioner spelled out a fearful moment in history.

"You felt his pulse?", inquired Jowitt.

"Yes."

"There was no beating?"

"No."

"You believed him dead?"

"Yes."

"In your book, you add this: 'I cannot explain why, but I suddenly seized him by both arms and violently shook him.' "

"Yes."

"As you did that, his eyes trembled and lifted?"

"Yes."

Sir William read aloud from Felix's text: "Then the incredible happened. With a violent movement, Rasputin jumped to his feet. His fingers, convulsively knotted, flashed through the air; like red-hot irons they grasped my shoulder and tried to grip me by the throat. His eyes were crossed; he was foaming at the mouth. In a hoarse whisper he constantly repeated my name. It seemed that the devil himself was holding me."

Felix tore himself loose, leaving his left epaulet in Rasputin's hand, and staggered upstairs to Purishkevich: "Quick, quick, the revolver! He is alive!"

Behind him, Felix heard furious sounds: "Rasputin, on all fours, was rapidly making his way up the staircase, bellowing and snorting like a wounded animal."

Felix rushed into his study and picked up a loaded stick from the writing table. He turned to see Rasputin charging out into the courtyard, with Purishkevich in pursuit. Two revolver shots rang out, then two more; Rasputin pitched forward into a snowdrift.

This time he seemed definitely dead; yet, returning to the scene a few minutes later, Felix found the monk crumpled in a different position. Afterward, as the body lay in the cellar, the prince rushed at it once again.

Sir William professed to be shocked. "You mean you had some sort of paroxysm and so far forgot yourself that you battered this dead man?"

"Not dead, no. At this moment"— the prince made a small gesture with his hand —"moving. I saw he was moving."

Precisely when the coup de grace was administered, Felix insisted, and by whom, was not important: "Public opinion is that Youssoupoff killed Rasputin."

Jowitt did wring a few concessions out of the prince during his long, relentless questioning: four men, not one, had been involved in the murder; the "Prince Chegodieff" of the movie was in several respects more like the Grand Duke Dimitri, another of the conspirators, than like Felix; the fictional "Natasha" had qualities found in court ladies other than Irina.

Against that, Sir William had to weigh the emotional effects on the jury of having taken Felix once again through his harrowing first-person account. Suddenly, on the verge of dismissing the witness, the celebrated barrister changed tack. "I suggest," he exclaimed, "that an American lawyer, Fanny Holtzmann, has been exploiting your wife!"

The prince registered puzzlement.

Was it not true, Sir William persisted, that Miss Holtzmann had been "trying to take advantage of the situation" to persuade Princess Irina to bring proceedings?

The prince said no, and Sir Patrick protested, so Jowitt dropped the subject.

However, in opening the case for the defense an hour later, he raised it again, and more resoundingly: "It is not in the least easy," Sir William told the jury, "for two foreigners, however high-born, to form an opinion as to whether or not they should commence litigation. Do you think the possible view of this case is that it was Miss Fanny Holtzmann who thought to herself: 'I will persuade these people to bring an action. It may add to my reputation?'

"The result was that there has been litigation all over the world. I do not say a word against the princess, but what I say is against the woman who, we assert, persuaded her to bring this action, which the princess would have been better advised not to bring."

It was, in the words of the Paris *Herald Tribune*, a "characteristic" and shrewdly calculated stroke by "one of England's leading lawyers," delivered "with eloquent and suave persuasiveness." Sir William followed it up with an extemporaneous attack on Fanny during recess, telling newsmen the trial was a travesty of British justice; it was really a dispute between a pair of outsiders — a Hollywood film company and an ambitious lawyer. He would give anything for a chance to rip apart the American interloper on the stand.

Within minutes, Fanny had changed status from a discreet backstage adviser whispering cues over the transatlantic telephone, to a legal luminary in the international spotlight. Her picture flashed across front pages from New York to Singapore ("Object of a long-distance legal rebuke was attractive Fanny Holtzmann," began the photo caption circulated by the NEA syndicate), and stayed there as Jowitt's fulminations continued.

Fanny's family was appalled. This was the kind of notoriety against which Jack had always warned. Did she have to drag the Holtzmann name into such an unsavory debate? Papa Henry declared he was "ashamed to show his face" at Borough Hall in Brooklyn.

Chagrined, Fanny nonetheless issued a spirited reply: "I am sorry to note that Sir William Jowitt, despite his eminence as a barrister, is not above resorting to the shopworn trick of abusing an adversary when finding himself with a weak case on his hands, even though that person is not present to defend herself. It may seem safer to attack one who is thousands of miles away than to meet the issue involved directly."

Both sides closed with secondary witnesses who testified that "Natasha" unmistakably was — or was not — recognizable as Irina.

In final arguments, Sir William insisted that nobody could confuse the regal Princess Irina with timid, naive Natasha; Sir Patrick averred that his client — a married woman with a daughter — had been depicted to the public "as a woman who has been defiled by a blackguard." His voice rose in indignation: "I wonder who is going to ask an English jury to say that is not defamatory?"

Then the presiding justice, Sir Horace Avory, delivered his summation to the jury. Small, desiccated, precise, Avory was celebrated as a master of forensic reasoning; his decisions were studied in law schools all over the world.

The action portrayed in the film, Sir Horace instructed the jury — "a virtuous woman locked in a 'Chamber of Horrors' in St. Petersburg with a brutal libertine"— was indisputably libelous. The only question for them to decide was whether, no matter what the producers of the film intended, a substantial number of reasonable persons would conclude that "Natasha" represented the plaintiff.

The judge reviewed the case made by the plaintiff, noting the film's opening announcement of historical verity, and laying stress on the many parallels of age and circumstances between "Natasha" and Irina. No one denied, he pointed out, that the chief figure in the death of Rasputin was Irina's husband or that the murder setting in the MGM film was modeled on a room in the Moika Palace.

The jury had to weigh the confirming testimony of "sensible, responsible persons" like Sir Aubrey Smith, of whom Sir Horace commented: "You know a man does not become an Admiral in the King's Navy without he is a person of level head and sound judgment." By contrast, Avory cited the hesitant, varied opinions of the defense witnesses, two of whom had conceded on cross-examination that in the death scene they had assumed that "Chegodieff" was Prince Youssoupoff.

Perhaps the least expected, and thereby most devastating, position taken by Justice Avory came in connection with the scene of Natasha's subjection to Rasputin. Sir William Jowitt had argued that the ravishment depicted could not come under the Slander of Women Act since that statute was confined to imputations of "unchastity or adultery" on the part of a woman; in support, he had cited Shakespeare's classic *The Rape of Lucrece.*

That, observed the justice, was an "unfortunate reference," because it prompted him to reread the poem and find in it "a verse which is direct authority for saying that a woman who has been ravished has been deprived of her chastity."

" 'Pure chastity is rifled of her store,' " reiterated Sir Horace. "That is the description Shakespeare gives."

Before departing the subject, Avory remarked on one other line found in the poem: "All orators are dumb when beauty pleadeth."

"Not so Sir William Jowitt," he observed dryly.

As to the question of damages: if this was a libel, declared Sir Horace, it was a "gross, insulting and injurious one"; it would be "difficult to imagine any worse." A film, even more than a newspaper story, could "circulate calumny through every region of the globe"; retractions rarely caught up with the original negative impression.

The jury, after an hour of deliberation, returned with a judgment for the plaintiff of £25,000 (about $125,000). Justice Avory ordered that an initial £5,000 be paid to the princess at once, and also granted an injunction against any further showing of the film "in the manner complained of in this action."

The defense girded itself for an appeal, but the *Morning Post* lost no time in recording a satisfaction probably shared by the general public. The paper's leading editorial of March 6, 1934, looking back with a delicious shiver on "such a tale of desperate murder as had never yet been heard in an English court," hailed the successful intervention of British justice on behalf of "truth and decency."

For Fanny, the verdict was both professional triumph and personal vindication; but she was still smarting over Jowitt's assault on her integrity. She blamed Bob Rubin, the MGM general counsel. Rubin knew better than anyone of her repeated efforts to effect a modest settlement, and as an experienced American lawyer, he also knew very well that contingency-fee arrangements such as she had made with the Youssoupoffs were an approved democratic device for enabling a poor man to bring an action.

MGM now faced the prospect of multiple judgments being levied against them around the world. Fanny put in a call to Rubin: "Bob? Are you holding any MGM stock? Better sell it short!"

"We're not finished yet — we're appealing. We'll beat you in the House of Lords."

Fanny told him not to bet his retirement money on it.

She returned to England to supervise the appeal preparations and plan her next move, taking along her brother Jack. The technicalities of computing costs and working out payments to her English colleagues promised to be complicated, and Jack was an old hand at the conference table.

While Jack was closeted with Langton and Passmore, Fanny submitted to a low-key press conference at the Savoy. Asked to confirm the report that she was the wealthiest of all women lawyers, she made what the *Daily Sketch* called a "characteristically adroit" reply: "I am not interested in the earnings of my colleagues at the Bar. Success at the Bar is not judged by the yardstick of money, but by a barrister's ability."

Whatever the criterion, Fanny's status was smashingly upheld when the Court of Appeal handed down a decision on July 17.

They found unanimously against the appellants. In his written opinion, Lord Justice Scrutton observed with some heat that the claim "solemnly put forward" by the defense to the effect that rape by a blackguard was not defamatory "took courage" to argue: "I only wish the jury could have expressed what they thought of it." He himself had "no language" sufficient to the occasion.

As to damages, the assembled justices nodded sympathetically while Sir Patrick Hastings recited historical precedents. He had searched the records to see "if any member of *our* royal family" ever took similar court action, and discovered that in 1684 James, duke of York, brought suit against Titus Oates, winning judgments of £100,000 from each of two defendants; the third, Sir Francis Drake, fled abroad.

The justices agreed that royalty — even fallen royalty — was entitled to heavy damages. They ordered MGM to pay over an additional £5,000 installment of the original £25,000 verdict ("You have had a second try and been beaten — is that clear?") — and gave them three months to enter an appeal with the House of Lords.

The Court of Appeal ruling became a landmark case on defamation, working its way into law-school textbooks everywhere. As the *Law Journal* put it, never before had a libel victory been attained through a deliberate confession of murder.

There were profound repercussions in America, where the giant communications media, suddenly alert to their vulnerability, pushed through new modifying legislation at the state level. Fanny had made good on her assertion to Harold Brooks: she did not follow legal precedent, she created it.

The immediate effect was to put MGM in terrible jeopardy. *Rasputin, the Mad Monk* had been shown in half the countries of the world. Since the libel was now a res adjudicata — a judged issue — before the most prestigious bar in Europe, the movie company and its exhibitors were wide open for further damages. In every theater that showed the film, if the projectionist had run it four times a day that meant four separate libels, each bearing an established price tag of $125,000. Should Fanny choose to sue everywhere, the cost to MGM would be astronomical; overseas showings in the British Empire alone would be enough to put the parent company, Loew's, Inc., out of business. All this was apart from the pending action for $2,000,000 in the United States.

MGM executives took a quick look and shuddered. Their vaunted appeal to the House of Lords gave every prospect of being an empty and expensive gesture. Bob Rubin sent Fanny a cable suggesting that they talk things over.

Slightly dizzied by the large numbers whirling around her head, Fanny asked Jack to take up initial negotiations in America with Rubin, Mayer and Nick Schenck. Jack reported back that he had a settlement for well over a million in prospect, but that Mayer's cries of anguish were gnawing at his conscience. The next morning Mayer called Fanny in London:

"Fanny, Fanny — my dear young friend!" The sobs rose and fell eerily over the erratic amplification system of the radio-telephone. "What did I ever do to you, Fanny, that you should cast me aside like an old *shmatte* [rag]? Is it right that the family of the Russian czar should get rich at the expense of good Jews? That a fine company" — more audible sniffing — "a company that has given America clean entertainment, millions in taxes, should be crushed against the wall?"

"I tried to get you out of this long ago, Louis —"

"So Bob Rubin is a *shlemiel* [poor fool]! Already he's paying for it. He had a bad heart attack."

Fanny winced. "I'm sorry to hear that, Louis."

"I believe you. I know you like a daughter, Fanny. That's why I'm begging you: don't squeeze us. You know what the Bible says about squeezing someone. In case you forgot, ask your father . . ."

A royal victory: Fanny faces the press with her clients, Princess Irina and Prince Felix Youssoupoff, after winning the biggest libel judgment England had known since 1684

It was one of Mayer's best, and perhaps most genuinely felt, performances. But Fanny had a client to represent. She cabled Jack: whatever settlement he made, she would accept.

On August 10 it was announced simultaneously in New York and London that the litigation had been ended. MGM would not go forward with its appeal to the House of Lords. And in return for payment of an undisclosed sum, all actions by the princess in the United States and elsewhere in the world would be dropped.

The settlement touched off a spontaneous "victory party" at Fanny's Kinnerton Studios apartment where, in the words of the Paris *Herald Tribune*, "more than one hundred members of the English aristocracy and the Hollywood screen world mingled." With the Youssoupoffs as guests of honor, Violet, duchess of Rutland, scrambled up from early slumbers to attend. Gertrude Lawrence was there, along with Rebecca West, Sophie Tucker, Douglas Fairbanks, Jr., Jimmy and Betty Walker, and the Count and Countess Kleinmichael. A complete list of the guests, the *Daily Sketch* reported, "would present a cross-section of London society: literary, artistic, theatrical, legal, medical and merely 'society.' It was remarkable evidence that London is not really empty when it is supposed to be; and also a striking testimony to a hostess from abroad who could call together such a varied assembly at short notice."

The next morning the journalistic guessing game began. How much had MGM paid to get out of its international jam? Three-quarters of a million dollars, flatly declared the New York *Times* — "believed to be the largest amount ever resulting from a libel action anywhere." Fanny, pressed for a statement, issued an "official figure" of $250,000 plus costs, but declined to spell out the costs. Told on her return to New York aboard the *Berengaria* that a Russian émigré had estimated the total at "about $900,000," she was quoted as replying wearily, "He seems to know what he is talking about."

The *United States Law Review* noted that no American libel award had ever dealt in such figures; "considerable credit" must go to the princess's counsel. Others agreed. Justice Avory had invited Fanny to a chat in chambers. One of the historic Inns of Court in London elected her to membership — an honor that she ultimately declined because it would have involved registering her name as "Frances." Another accolade that she rejected was a bid for her services by Queen Victoria Eugénie of Spain, wife of the deposed Alfonso III. The queen asked the duchess of Rutland to approach Fanny for her because the lawyers engaged by the queen in New York had, deplorably, "turned out to be Jewish." Fanny forwarded a brief reply: "I would not replace another lawyer. And — I am Jewish."

More pleasing was the discovery that something like a Fanny Holtzmann Fan Club was flourishing at Windsor Castle. Prince George, who would later become the duke of Kent was constantly badgering his Russian cousins for news of the American lawyer; and once as Fanny was signing the guest book at Frogmore, Prince Nikita brought out an autograph book and diffidently requested her signature on behalf of seven-year-old Elizabeth, daughter of the duke of York. Fanny graciously obliged the future queen.

More than ever, she was irresistible newspaper copy. Rhapsodic interviews appeared in *Paris-Midi* and the *Neues Journal* of Vienna. *Good Housekeeping* of London, in an editorial chiding Sir William Jowitt for "what sounded like a courtroom sneer at a woman lawyer," praised Fanny as "one of the most mentally alert lawyers alive," adding: "She is as modest and unassuming as she is charitable and clever, and all women who take pleasure in the achievements of other women should be very proud of her immense legal victory."

O. O. McIntyre led off an outpouring of syndicated encomiums in America. "A chit of a woman lawyer," the columnist wrote, "with flashing black eyes and a magnificent sense of humor, has become the toast of London's Mayfair. No outsider has so tilted the collective lorgnette since Michael Arlen peacocked his mignon way into celebrity. After her libel victory, crowds followed her along the streets in the manner of a prize fight champion. . . . A satisfactory exemplar of the new freedom of women."

A five-column, lavishly illustrated feature article by Irene Kuhn, hailing Fanny as "overnight London's most talked of hostess," was spread across the feature section of the New York *World-Telegram.* Fanny's mews apartment, Miss Kuhn reported, was headquarters for "every important theatrical and social name, resident or transient," in London. When she held open house, "rows of empty tables" showed at the Savoy and the Dorchester.

"Musicians try out their compositions on her grand piano; Viennese psychiatrists demonstrate thought transference. Fanny sits on the raised window seat under the huge studio window munching cookies, and looks on with the air of a pleased child at a surprise party."

Parties, Fanny was discovering, really *were* fun, perhaps because they had been so long denied her. Here was the personal acceptance she had always craved. If she couldn't get it from Jack or Clara, she would have to make do with dukes and Nobel Prize winners. Fanny had an instinctive knack for mixing people; she never compiled a guest list on the basis of repaying social obligations. Now her doorstep was swarming with the rarest assortment of friends and admirers imaginable.

The titled foreign colony, en masse, adopted her; they found her rambling apartment more homelike than their hotel bedrooms. So did the wandering royalty of Hollywood. Bored with card-shuffling studio chiefs and the weather, the George Burnses and Jack Bennys hustled over to Kinnerton Studios, where they could swap jokes with cabinet ministers, foreign correspondents and the duke of Atholl. The nabobs of Beverly Hills and Mayfair found each other mutually endearing. Often, in the small hours, people would curl up on sofas and window seats; Fanny might wake after a party to be greeted by half a dozen hungry celebrities clamoring for breakfast.

A staple of her entertainments was Felix Youssoupoff. With the strain of the lawsuit behind him, the prince emerged in his natural colors as a prankster and omnidirectional flirt. Felix could be irksome. He had no regard for possessions — other people's or his own: he had disbursed his fortune to his fellow refugees. But he was a great charmer and raconteur, especially in spinning tales of the Rembrandts he claimed to have cached behind castle walls all over Russia.

Felix was the top-ranking regular at Fanny's parties until the advent of George II, the exiled king of Greece. The Hellenic monarch was an inspiration of the duchess of Rutland, who never ceased to think of Fanny's romantic interests as her own special domain.

George was a presentable bachelor of forty-four. Although not wealthy compared with the royal houses of England, Italy, Belgium and Holland, he was not exactly poor, and some people thought he had prospects.

Others weren't so sure. The Greek crown was one of the most slippery

PLANET NEWS LTD.

David squires Fanny to a royal garden party at Buckingham Palace, 1935

in Europe. Since the establishment of the monarchy in 1830, the country had known a frenzied succession of coup d'etats, royal exiles, plebiscites and returns. George's grandfather, the Danish-born George I, had been assassinated in 1913; George himself had been deposed in favor of the Second Republic in 1924, after a single turbulent year on the throne.

The king's demeanor reflected this somber history. Neat, dark and unobtrusive, he was popularly known in Athens as the "no-smile man." Since infancy, he had been guarded constantly against possible assailants. With his thinning black hair and carefully waxed moustache, he looked respectable — and miserable.

Fanny and King George met over the duchess's tea table, where the king was attended by his suave Master of Ceremonies and aide-de-camp, Colonel Dimitri Levidis. Afterward, Violet phoned to report that His Majesty had been favorably impressed; he would like to take Miss Holtzmann to dinner.

"Tell him he's welcome to come around to Kinnerton Studios."

The next morning the phone rang. The king wondered if he might drop by that evening.

"With or without the colonel?"

"Alone."

The royal visitor arrived around nine. There was some initial awkwardness; his palace-bred formality did not blend with the casual air of Kinnerton Studios. "Your Majesty," his hostess cut in, "please call me Fanny."

"In that case"— a moment's hesitation —"you might as well call me George."

"Why not? It's a familiar name at Buckingham Palace."

"The king and I are related." George explained that his Danish grandfather had been the brother-in-law of King Edward VII of England, as well as the uncle of Czar Nicholas II.

The talk turned to Greece. George was restless and depressed. For a decade his country had been the scene of bitter Republican-monarchist struggles, while he languished abroad, royally unemployed. He was staying at Brown's Hotel on Dover Street, studying intelligence reports, speculating whether he would be taken back. He wasn't sure he wanted to be. "My advisers," he told Fanny, "say I should return to Athens now."

"What, and be a sitting duck for some hothead with a gun? From what I read in the papers, Athens today is like Chicago in the middle of a gang war!"

"But what else am I trained for?", George protested.

"Okay — you're a king, so be a king! But you don't have to put your head in a shooting gallery." After all, Fanny argued, he wasn't the only one out of a job. "There's a depression on! Look at the ex-millionaires selling apples on Wall Street. Or Whitney, who headed the Stock

Exchange and wound up in prison. You're lucky — at least you don't have the police after you."

Things could change overnight; nobody knew what opportunities tomorrow might bring. Fanny's counsel was in effect to keep the royal chin up and the royal eyes open.

The friendly scolding seemed to be just what the downcast monarch needed. Departing, he asked Fanny if he might see her again.

"I go to the theater a good deal. Perhaps we can catch a play together."

Through Charles Cochran, Fanny had house seats everywhere in the West End, usually, by her own choice, for Tuesday second-nights rather than the ceremonial openings. She began inviting King George to be her escort. He always sent a thank-you note the next day, along with an elaborate bouquet that wound up in the quarters of Mittie Hawkett, Fanny's chirpy little housekeeper. Fanny regarded flowers as funereal.

Once, Fanny was invited to the theater by a visiting couple from Boston, and asked George to be her companion. In the limousine that picked them up at Kinnerton Studios, George sat up front with the chauffeur.

Her hostess, sitting in back with Fanny, indicated the small quiet figure. "What does your friend do?" she whispered.

"He's out of a job right now."

"Poor fellow. I suppose he had to rent the dinner jacket and tie."

"Not exactly . . ."

"What sort of work is he in?"

"He used to be king of Greece."

Whenever the reports from the Greek capital were discouraging, the king took to seeking refuge at Fanny's. Lonely, he would pick up the telephone: "What are you doing, Fanny?"

"I'm about to make myself a chop."

"Have you got another?"

"Sure, just take the number 9 bus."

"No, I'll be right over by taxi."

A London newspaper, getting wind of these visits, reported that Fanny often broiled chops for her royal friend. Years later, in New York, Fanny's indignant denial was quoted in *Time* magazine: "I don't go to London to broil chops for anybody. The king of Greece knew where the saucepans were; when he came to see me, he broiled his own chops."

One noonday when the larder was low George telephoned to say he was coming. Eddie Goulding's niece Lydia, visiting from India, hastened out to Harrod's and picked up three small boxes of raspberries at the equivalent of a dollar each. Chided for her extravagance, Lydia retorted: "He *is* a king, you know."

Fanny treated her royal guest to a non-British lunch: lamb stew à la

Zaida, and crisp potato *latkes* (pancakes). The potatoes were rubbed down personally by His Majesty, a towel tucked in at his waist.

As he rose from the table, George remarked: "They tell me Fanny is a great lawyer; I don't know. But about her cooking, I can testify."

Mostly, King George seemed dazzled by the ambience of glamour and unexpectedness surrounding Fanny. He sat in awe at the Savoy as the reigning figures of the West End stopped by at her table, and was positively overjoyed one evening to find George Burns and Gracie Allen puttering around the Kinnerton Studios kitchen.

In rare moments, he gave evidence of more personal feelings. Calling for Fanny one evening, he found her in a breathtaking evening gown from Loehmann's, one of those fabulous discount-models that she and Gertrude Lawrence were always looking for. The king stared, blinking his small black eyes: "You look like . . . like the most beautiful of queens that a man could imagine."

"Hold on, George. Remember, you haven't even got a job!"

She teased away his few such approaches. He was a nice chap, Fanny told His Majesty, but he was in the wrong business. The king profession did not appear to have a rosy future. There was the mortality risk, for one thing. Perhaps he ought to consider getting into some other line of work. What would he like to do if he didn't go back to Athens?

"Be a builder of some kind," George told her earnestly. "Maybe a carpenter or wood-worker. I enjoy working with my hands."

"How about making popcorn? I could probably get you a job with the Skouras theater chain!"

While in London, King George had royal competition in his modest attentions to Fanny. Prince Frederick of Prussia (known as Fritz), the grandson of Kaiser Wilhelm, was tall, fair and blue-eyed . . . anybody's version of a young storybook prince.

There were murky indications that a pro-Hohenzollern group in the United States was trying to whip up a match between Prince Frederick and Fanny. Apart from her personal attractions, Fanny's contacts within the British ruling circle were better than those of any conventional princess; and she was reputed to be worth millions.

The prince conveyed his gallantries in a mangled English that was about as close to pure Oxonian as Fanny's answering Yiddish was to high German. He hovered about Kinnerton Studios a good deal.

Fanny regarded the handsome if unexciting prince as a kind of household pet. At a party given for her by the Youssoupoffs, she presented Fritz to Princess Irina; it was, according to the United Press, the first meeting between a Romanoff and a Hohenzollern since World War I.

She also superintended a breezy introduction of Prince Frederick to King George. "All I know about European history," she told the pair, "is in the glossary on my desk. But the duchess [of Rutland] tells me you two are related. Say hello, cousins!"

A sometime partner of the royal duo at the Holtzmann dinner table was an even more celebrated expatriate in London: the former mayor of New York, James J. Walker.

Fanny had first met Walker during her hectic visit with Frank Scully in the summer of 1933. The former mayor, after resigning from office in the fall of 1932 at the height of the anti-Tammany Seabury investigation, had gone directly to the Riviera with his longtime inamorata, Betty Compton. The two had been married there a few months later. Fanny liked them: slim, insouciant Jimmy looked like an ageless musical-comedy juvenile; Betty — dimpled, black-haired, lissome — seemed in perfect harmony with her husband, twenty-three years her senior. When Jimmy said they would be coming to London, although hoping to stay out of the newspapers there, Fanny gave him her telephone number.

Walker called after the Youssoupoff trial. He and Betty were in Dorking, Surrey, about an hour's ride from London, where they were renovating a small cottage. Urged by Fanny to jump into a taxi and come for dinner, Walker chuckled and said: "Dinner's fine, if we can make it Thursday. That's our day in town. But taxis are out. We're on a budget, Fanny. I used to laugh at the commuters who ran for the five-fifteen; now I'm running, too, and pinching shillings harder than pennies."

The cottage, it developed, was being financed by a loan from Betty's English-born mother. Obviously the rumored fortune in graft carried off by Walker was nonexistent. Nobody who rode buses as regularly as Jimmy Walker, Fanny was quick to conclude, could have a hoard of tin boxes stashed away. If there was one thing about the Walkers as evident as their devotion to each other, it was their poverty.

What happened next is recorded by Gene Fowler in his biography of Walker, *Beau James*. Fanny, says Fowler, showed "an immense zest for people having a rocky time of it"; she promptly invited the couple to stay at Kinnerton Studios. Fanny's own explanation was characteristic: "Jimmy and Betty thought royalty were the very last word. I had two royal guests; I wasn't going to waste that on *myself*."

The spare room adjoining the kitchen upstairs was small but available: Mittie Hawkett slept out. The Walkers moved in. As far as Fanny was concerned, the gesture was hardly a hardship: "Jimmy's being bounced out of office was a windfall for me; I've never known a wittier man — or a more honorable one."

By Gene Fowler's account, her hospitality transformed the status of the Walkers overnight. They had been living under a cloud, as not particularly welcome refugees from a political milieu regarded in England with suspicion. Suddenly, via Fanny's affectionate sponsorship, they were installed at the pinnacle of the British social structure. As Fowler pointed out, it was a long jump from City Hall and Tin Pan Alley (Jimmy was the lyricist of "Will You Love Me in December?") to the manicured gardens of Belgravia.

The former mayor, once noted for his ten-dollar perfumes and three-changes-a-day wardrobe, was delighted with his simple new quarters. There was running water in the room, a loo outside in the foyer, and just down the hall that most English of luxuries, a huge bath. "Where else could we get that?" Jimmy crowed.

Sharing the bath — the only one in the apartment — was worked out in elaborate "political deals," although arrangements went awry one weekend when Prince Felix slept overnight on the window seat. The prince took possession of the bathroom at 8 A.M. An hour later the impatient Walker, peering through the half-open door, was aghast to discover the heir to Tartary preening before the mirror, applying makeup to his long eyelashes.

Walker's one point of touchiness, although he joked about it, was his financial condition; he shrank from any intimation of sponging on Fanny. Out of respect for his feelings, Fanny contrived to find amusements that would cost nobody anything: the stalls at Covent Garden, a stroll through Petticoat Lane. Discovering that the Walkers were on a cautious hunt for antique furniture, Fanny introduced them to Sir Louis Sterling, a peppery little former Grand Street Boy who had made a fortune in British gramophones. Sir Louis was glad to place a Rolls-Royce at the disposal of his fellow New Yorkers.

On one chauffeured expedition along Portobello Road, Fanny and her guests stumbled upon an antique shop. It was run by a picturesque crone who, swathed in a billowing low-cut gown, insisted she was a reincarnation of Nell Gwyn. Jimmy bent low, kissed her withered hand, and paid two pounds for an allegedly "certified" Holbein.

When the Yiddish Theater brought *Yoshe Kalb* to London, Walker looked wistful; he was dying for a whiff of Old New York. But he didn't want Annie Oakleys for the play: "I can pay my own way. We just won't sit up front."

A discreet note from Fanny to the play's producer brought a written invitation, a pair of tickets, and a follow-up telephone query: "Shall we send a car for Mr. Walker?"

Fanny decided that Jimmy and King George ought to be brought together, if only to commiserate over their respective exiles. She arranged a dinner party for eight at home, warning the king to leave his monocle behind: "I don't want Jimmy and Betty to be intimidated." Also invited were Prince Frederick, the duchess of Rutland, and a titled elderly couple from Wales.

As the guests assembled over cocktails, Fanny made the introductions, giving Walker full billing as the retired "First Magistrate of the greatest city in the Western Hemisphere."

Jimmy raised his glass. "Everybody," he announced, "has a title here. So I am about to confer one." His gaze traveled around the room: "Your Majesty . . . Your Highness, Prince Frederick . . . Your Grace . . . Your

Lordship and Ladyship . . . may I present the one and only, the non-pareil and incomparable . . . *Princess Fanny from Brooklyn!*"

The prince roared his appreciation. He made a remark in German to which Fanny responded, shrugging, *"Wer weisz?"* ("Who knows?"). Jimmy professed to be admiring of her erudition: "You're a great scholar, Fanny. Even I understood your German."

"You should," Fanny shot back. "It's Yiddish."

Betty Compton, across from Jimmy, was trying to get him to unravel the family ties between King George and Prince Fritz.

"Darling," Jimmy pleaded, *"don't hok me a tchynik."*

The duchess looked up, eager to expand her store of "Americanisms." "What does that mean?"

"'Chop me not a teacup,'" Fanny translated daintily. "In other words — although I don't pretend to understand why —'don't bother me with nonsense.'"

Jimmy and King George kept exchanging reflective glances. Finally, as Fanny had anticipated, they fell into conversation about the "ingrati-tude" suffered by public figures. It was a relief, Fanny later wrote her brother David, "to see the king *krechtz* [complain] on somebody else's shoulder."

At the end of the evening, Jimmy addressed the fallen monarch with mock gravity: "Sir, you and I made one terrible mistake."

"What was that?"

"We both forgot to take out unemployment insurance."

The more Fanny saw of Walker, the more convinced she became that he was the victim of trusted associates who abused his good nature: "Care-less he may have been, in handing out city contracts. But not a dollar ever touched him personally. The worst you can say about him is what the British say about their King Charles II: he was too busy with his love life to keep an eye on the rascals in his administration."

It was typical of Fanny's erratic political leanings that despite her family-rooted Republicanism she chose to befriend a hard-pressed Tam-many Democrat. Except on truly central issues, her loyalties were to individuals, not to parties or theories. And almost always they were with the underdog.

Jimmy Walker, cleared of charges, made a hero's return to New York in 1935 (just before his fellow exile King George was reinstalled in Greece). But a few years later Walker's marriage inexplicably broke up. He went back to the Catholic Church and lived ascetically until his death at sixty-five in 1947.

The titled Russians refused to go away, literally and metaphorically. Felix was always around in London, and the Grand Duchess Xenia, as a frequent guest at Buckingham Palace, had issued a standing invitation to Fanny to drop by when she was in the neighborhood (Fanny's

American friends never quite got used to the spectacle of liveried foot-men bowing before Fanny as they swung the palace gates open, and announcing her name with the hauteur of centuries).

In New York, a delegation of footloose Romanoffs was apt to be on hand in the Bar Building, smoking and reminiscing about bygone days at the dacha.

It was inevitable, therefore, that when an alleged "Princess Anastasia" made one of her periodic appearances, claiming to be the youngest daughter of Czar Nicholas and a miraculous survivor of the slaughter at Ekaterinburg, Fanny was called in. A New York lawyer asked her, as official counsel for the czar's estate, to join forces with him in pressing "Anastasia's" claim to unspecified millions. The lady's story had apparently impressed several members of the Russian colony in America.

Fanny checked it out with her own sources. A former aide to the czarina, reached in Paris, declared that the would-be princess was no princess at all. Aaron Simonovich, who had been Rasputin's secretary, reported that "Anastasia" was an East European adventuress fronting for a syndicate of down-at-heel princelings.

Fanny declined to get involved. Six months later "Anastasia" was branded a pretender in New York Surrogate Court, where her petition was dismissed.

At one point, Fanny tried to see what Russians were like on their home grounds. In the winter of 1935, she applied for a visa at the Intourist office in Paris, where she was told to head eastward; an official decision would be issued later. Vaguely in her mind was a claim on behalf of the Grand Duchess Xenia, as the widow of Grand Duke Alexander, to a vast stretch of woodland between Minsk and Pinsk. She outlined the possibil-ities in a breezy letter to her parents: Her brother-in-law, Dr. Sam Berkman, was "the only real *Litvak* [Slavic Jew]" in the family. "Let's make him the duke of Minsk, and Bertha can be the duchess. Can't you see them strutting down Eastern Parkway, with Bertha wagging her tail?"

Fanny took a train to Vienna, and then shifted to a less commodious rail line for the trip through Slavic Europe. Czech trains had only a handful of private compartments. She took the available second-class facilities, expecting to share her compartment with another woman.

In the dead of night, gazing out over the lantern-lighted snow-covered landscape, she was joined by a gigantic bearded Russian who silently began shedding layers of fur. As the intimations of underwear appeared, she fled into the corridor, bawling for help.

Strangers materialized, jabbering excitedly at her in Czech, Russian, German — and then, blessedly, there was a voice in English. It belonged to a strapping man with a leathery cowpuncher face who identified him-self as Chuck Johnson, a fellow Yank.

Fanny fell into his arms. "Where are you from, Chuck?"

"Aw, a place you never heard of. A little town in a state nobody ever goes to."

"Try me."

"Pocatello, Idaho."

"Pocatello? Of course! I stayed at the Grand Hotel there in 1928, when our car broke down on a trip to Yellowstone Park. Greatest food in the West."

Chuck got her a private compartment.

The next morning Fanny arrived at the Russian border — and a flat turndown. She could not, the Soviets had finally decided, enter their workers' paradise; she was too closely associated with the decadent czarist aristocracy.

Commented Fanny, in recounting the incident to her mother: "Zaida, with his long *payess* [ear curls] and his memories of Russian pogroms, must be turning over in his grave!"

Meanwhile, publishers were trying to zero in on Fanny's story. The first bidder was Max Schuster, a Columbia classmate and ardent follower of Frank Scully. Schuster came to London in the summer of 1934, bearing a letter from Scully, who was staying at the Holtzmann home in New York, and some personal belongings for Fanny. She included him in her parties, where he was captivated in turn by Jimmy Walker and young Prince George of England. She set up a meeting at her home with P. G. Wodehouse, who thereby became a prize acquisition of Simon and Schuster; but she shook her head at the thought of an autobiography: "My eyes are on the future, not the past."

Her reticence had a practical aspect: as the mysterious "Garbo of the Bar," a keeper of momentous secrets who moved in unfathomable ways, she enjoyed an above-the-crowd exclusiveness.

On her return to New York, she was invited to lunch by Blanche Knopf, who brought along Katharine Cornell and Clifton Webb for support. Once again a book was proposed; once again Fanny said no.

With so much curiosity prevalent in publishing circles, something had to find its way into print. *The New Yorker,* whose lively profiles of the period were chronicling such personalities as Henry Luce, James B. Conant, Benny Goodman and J. Edgar Hoover, assigned Margaret Case Harriman to tell its readers about Fanny. As the daughter of Frank Case, manager of the Algonquin, Margaret had a fast inside track.

Her chatty account, complete with an artist's sketch, appeared in two lengthy installments. Fanny had mixed feelings about it. Such attention in so distinguished a forum was very flattering; but there were inaccuracies that could have been avoided, and a certain feline flavor colored the author's wit. Besides, as the cloak-and-dagger boys would say, it "broke her cover." Instead of being privately revered, with the rolling of *The New Yorker* presses she became publicly famous.

Famous, and yet . . . The peaks of Olympus were lonely. Although she could guide the fortunes of Russian princesses and English playwrights, she could never really share their lives. And at home, all her sisters except Clara were married and bringing up families of their own. One night Rita, the youngest of the Holtzmann girls, now a schoolteacher living in Flatbush with her lawyer husband and two children, stayed overnight in Manhattan, sharing Fanny's twin-bedded room. In the darkness she whispered, "How does it feel to reach the top, Fanny — really to be a success?"

Rita was startled by the soft, bitter reply: "You ought to know. You're more of a success than I am."

Emotionally, Fanny was at an impasse. Stanley was a still-poignant memory, too painful to contemplate. Eddie Goulding was a chimera, impossible either to escape or to pin down. He was constantly getting into scrapes, pleading for advice — then disregarding it. Eager to "run with the big boys," he embroiled himself with a succession of agents and even, to Fanny's disgust, made peace with Joe Kennedy.

In 1931, under punishment of silence from Fanny, and sleepless with the tensions of preparing to direct Garbo, Crawford and John Barrymore in *Grand Hotel*, Goulding was introduced by Ivor Novello to the dancer Marjorie Moss. Marjorie, in failing health, had just parted company with her partner, George Fontana. Two weeks later Goulding made Marjorie his bride.

They had little time together; Marjorie was an early victim of cancer. Goulding bought an estate for her in Palm Springs, where he cared for her gently until her death in 1935.

Soon afterward Irving Thalberg died, and Louis Mayer took his revenge on the "Thalberg men" at MGM. Despite Goulding's brilliant record, which included *Love, Devil's Holiday* and *Riptide* as well as *Grand Hotel*, he was abruptly replaced as director of *Maytime*.

Of course, at three-thirty one morning he called Fanny and wept his apologies: he had never been in love with Marjorie; he had stumbled into matrimony in an alcoholic stupor. Moved in spite of herself, Fanny restored their old unspoken contract: "Yes, you can call me again, Eddie . . . any time." So it was to remain with them over the years: a closeness that could not be expunged, a distance that could not be breached.

Restless, craving reassurance of her femininity, Fanny was primed for a romantic adventure. Brian D. met her full catalogue of requirements.

Brian floated between England and the United States on a silver-lined cloud of glamour. A big man, fleshily handsome, he had amassed a fortune from the sales of medicines developed in his chemical laboratory. He had also acquired three wives, two children, and many rounds of notices in the international society columns.

Fanny met him through Angela R., the sister of a Hollywood friend. Angela was interested in becoming Brian's fourth wife; she wanted

Fanny's assistance in helping Brian shed the third, a likewise much-married Park Avenue beauty.

Brian and Fanny were mutually attracted on sight. But Fanny discouraged his hints of interest; Angela had priority here, and besides the man was Gentile. Fanny left for Paris on business.

Brian followed. The messages that he left at her hotel were oblique but unmistakable. Finally, consenting to see him for dinner, Fanny admitted that she too was ensnared.

They went back together to London and a three-way confrontation with Angela, who promptly staged a "suicide attempt." Fanny offered to withdraw but Brian wouldn't hear of it. It was agreed that she would sail home as scheduled on the *Berengaria,* and return to England to marry him as soon as he was free.

For a few months there was high excitement. Fanny confided her plans to only a handful of people, among them the duchess of Rutland and, oddly, her usually critical big brother Jack.

The duchess was predictably enthralled. "Poor thing," she wrote, "your new romance, I hope it knocks out all the others. Your mother mustn't mind a *short* history instead of a long one — new blood is good sometimes — with more energy and push!" The duchess invited Brian to tea: "How nice he is. I was not alone so could not say, 'Did you "fall" for her'?"

But it was Jack's backing — he cast a beaming eye on Brian's social and scientific position — that finally emboldened Fanny to approach her parents.

Henry and Theresa did not pretend to be overjoyed; nonetheless they made it clear they would not stand in her way. "If it will make you happy, daughter," said Henry, "then it is what we want."

Fanny was left with no hurdles to surmount but herself. That, however, hardly meant the matter was ended. With time and distance, two considerations were taking new shape in her mind: Brian's matrimonial record, and her own Jewishness. A man who at forty-two had been married three times, and who even at the moment of meeting and courting her had been engaged to someone else — such a man might be a dubious prospect for a long-term relationship. If she were going to commit herself, she did not want to end up as another divorce statistic.

And — Hitler's bully boys were on the march. In all conscience — and Fanny had a lot of conscience — could she simultaneously be concerned about the future of her European coreligionists and be deserting their common faith? Was this the time to deplete the ranks of Judaism?

Brian's divorce process in England dragged on, and the thrill of Fanny's conquest seeped away. In a few months she was writing the duchess of Rutland: "The 'Heart' interests are disappointing. The object of last summer's romance is in New York . . . I believe Paris was a more romantic background.

"As for the others — they are still about, but a bit monotonous, I fear."

Foremost among the "others" was Max Schuster. Stocky, earnest, aggressive, Max was much taken with Fanny. He listened as she described how the Tauchnitz Edition paperbacks were spreading through Europe, where hard-cover books were beyond the economic reach of the masses. Why not, she mused, introduce the same concept in the United States, starting with classics in the public domain where the publisher would not even have to pay a copyright fee?

Max Schuster snapped up the idea. He also gave every indication of wanting to snap up Fanny.

Fanny's reaction was curious. Schuster's reputation as the pedantic *wunderkind* of his Columbia class did not exactly inflame her. The son of poor immigrants who ran a candy store, Max had devoured the literary magazines on the racks and had been admitted to college in knee-pants at sixteen. He was constantly being teased for his unworldliness by such ribald companions as Morrie Ryskind, the librettist for *Of Thee I Sing*.

On the other hand, his publishing venture with Dick Simon, another Morningside Heights alumnus, had achieved instant success. He was a power in the publishing world, widely respected as a businessman and an innovator. Nobody questioned his character; even the ribbing by his classmates was affectionate.

What tipped the scales against him was the reaction of Fanny's family. In her childhood, anything had been considered good enough for Fanny; now, ironically, nothing was. Theresa sniffed; what was so special about this Max Schuster? "For such a fellow you have to be Fanny Holtzmann?" Clara, who never missed a chance to pass a judgment, thought Max was "not polished enough, unsophisticated." Henry simply shrugged without enthusiasm.

"What do you people want?" Fanny protested. "He's a nice man — decent — established."

"Yes," came the unanswerable argument. "But how does *he* come to *you?*"

Clearly they, even more than Fanny, were scanning the horizon for a knight on a white horse. And just as clearly, the present suitor did not qualify. Chunky, nearsighted Max on a white horse? He'd be sure to fall off.

Ambivalent about the familiar, unsure of her own judgment, Fanny accepted theirs. With halfhearted bravado she sent Max on his way, "just another general in the horn-rimmed brigade."

Fanny's final emotional flurry of the 1930's grew out of a visit to Francis Hackett. At the author's home near Dublin, she met the great Irish-Jewish physician Bethel Solomons, whose family in the British Isles dated back to the return of the Jews under Oliver Cromwell. Dr. Solomons was the subject of a superb bust by Jacob Epstein in the

Dublin Museum, and in person was no less striking; his massive, craggy features radiated intelligence and authority.

The doctor was master of the Rotunda, the world's first maternity hospital, and president of the International Obstetrical Association, but his interests far transcended his profession. As a founder of the Abbey Theatre he was an intimate of O'Casey, Yeats and George William Russell ("A.E."). He kept a fine stable in the country and rode to hounds.

Dr. Solomons came to Hackett's for a sober discussion of the Nazi menace with the celebrated lady lawyer from America. He stayed until 2 A.M., plying Fanny with questions far more personal, and on his next visits to London came several times to her flat for tea.

But the white-maned and magnificent Solomons had a wife of many years' standing. After Fanny returned to America, a few letters were exchanged and then the physician faded from Fanny's life.

He was briefly replaced by a gangling "Right-ho!" Englishman, Sir Anthony Lindsey-Hogg, of whom Fanny wrote to Louis Bromfield: "He is one of those Mayfair fellows who is no doubt all right, but not in my life or yours."

At this somewhat sensitive juncture in her emotional history, Fanny had an uncomfortable encounter with the world-famous Swiss psychiatrist Carl Gustav Jung. The occasion was a dinner-lecture by Jung at the Hotel Plaza, under the auspices of the Analytical Psychology Club of New York. Fanny as a luminary of the bar was seated on the dais, by chance or design beside the guest of honor.

Jung had been briefed on her accomplishments. A bulky, stern-looking individual with what Fanny considered a "rather accusing manner," he went about methodically trying to determine the nature of her sex life. His questions were brief and blunt: what, with whom, how often?

Fanny managed a few evasive replies, then excused herself, saying her father was unwell at home. She hurried to a telephone booth and put in an SOS for the family chauffeur.

Back in her own kitchen, she told her mother a "dirty old man" had been asking her a lot of prying questions. Jung was over sixty at the time, Fanny in her mid-thirties.

Out of touch with her own kind, out of place in her acquired world, Fanny was beginning to fend off sexual approaches and turn with a kind of relief to family and friends.

The Scullys had become important to her. Watching Frank hobble along to some left-of-center political rally, a beret perched jauntily on his head and a wisecrack on his lips, it was impossible for anyone to indulge in self-pity. On their arrival in New York in 1933, Fanny had arranged for them to be put up in her home with every facility from baby bottles to a uniformed chauffeur. "Her hospitality," Alice Scully summed up later, "was absolute." Fanny's mother, learning that Frank had once been a fellow patient of her own departed Eddie, treated him with tender affection; the Scullys responded by putting up Jewish *mezuzahs* beside the crucifixes in their bedroom.

When winter came and Frank's crippled body yearned for the Riviera sunshine, Fanny bearded Winfield Sheehan in Hollywood: "Why don't you do yourself a favor, and hire a really sharp, objective film man to punch holes in your scripts *before* you blow half a million dollars on a scene you don't need? I'm talking about your Irish compatriot, Frank Scully."

"The columnist? Do you think we could get him?"

"I think it could be arranged."

A month later, after a leisurely boat trip through the Panama Canal, Frank was installed at Bedside Manor in the Hollywood Hills. The Scully home quickly became headquarters for visiting eastern literati and the local intellectual set. Whenever Fanny came to town, it was her first port of call. She was welcomed with a huge tureen of bouillabaisse and an instant rundown on the Hollywood scene.

If time permitted, the reception was more elaborate. In 1936 the guests honoring her included the master director John Ford, Groucho Marx, Judge Ben Lindsey of *Companionate Marriage* fame, Mrs. D. H. Lawrence, actors Harry Carey and Carl Brisson and scenarist Dudley Nichols, along with columnists Sheilah Graham, Sid Skolsky and Louis Sobol.

Frank was a beacon of integrity in the moral murk of the movie colony. He preferred sportswriters to pundits, he declared, because "you can't juggle a basketball score." When he delivered a favorable judgment at a preview and an eager studio flack asked, "Is that your honest opinion, Mr. Scully?" he hauled himself up on his crutches and demolished the man in five words: "What other kind is there?"

In terms of career advancement at Fox, Scully's honesty was his undoing. His critiques were cherished until it became evident that they would spare no one. By that time, happily, Scully was well launched in the California sun. He ran for mayor of Hollywood in 1934 during Upton Sinclair's EPIC campaign, picketed the Hollywood *Citizen-News* on his crutches a few years later, and acknowledged one enemy in the world: Congressman Martin Dies of the House Un-American Activities Committee. Encountering Scully in an elevator during committee hearings, Dies cowered in a corner. "Relax," Scully told him. "I wouldn't contaminate my crutch on you."

Through it all, Fanny remained his sponsor, sometime financier, and friend. The Scully children, multiplying rapidly, paid a simple tribute to the generous lawyer-lady from New York. They called her Aunt Fanny Claus.

It was through the Scully set that Fanny had her single adventure as a landowner. During a Christmas party at Bedside Manor, a writer named Nat Ferber was moaning about a priceless paradise he had discovered in

Southbury, Connecticut, that would be foreclosed in two days unless he deposited thirty-five hundred dollars.

On impulse, Fanny said, "I'll buy it."

Ferber's Eden proved to be as advertised: dogwoods, maples, a burbling stream — except that there was no road and no access to the water.

Fanny went ahead anyway, laying out an English-style stone house with a high pitched ceiling and an upstairs balcony giving onto several bedrooms. From a New Haven wrecker operating on the Yale campus she obtained masses of ancient vines — and "the worst case of poison ivy in New England history."

On a July weekend in 1938, Fanny held a mammoth housewarming. The day was hot, there was a heavy call for iced drinks and showers — and by midafternoon Fanny's hideaway had run totally dry. That night, Theresa missed her hot water bottle; Clara was "kept awake" by the chirp of crickets.

A month later Fanny turned over the estate to a group of young Jews preparing for the pioneer life in Palestine. Ultimately she sold the place at a fraction of her investment and gave the proceeds to the pioneers. She "never knowingly" entered Connecticut again.

As close to Fanny as the Scullys, but in a very different way, was the dowager duchess of Rutland. For the fiftieth wedding anniversary of Fanny's parents in 1935, the doting duchess did a charming, dreamy pencil portrait of her little American friend. After her death in December 1937, Fanny penned an emotional note to the duchess's daughter, Lady Diana Cooper:

"She was the truest of friends. I shall never forget her kindness, sympathy and loyalty. For over thirteen years she wrote me regularly, on all topics, and never once did she reproach me for failing to reply. She was such a sweet, understanding soul — never demanding, always ready to give. When she would ask me to dine, she'd invariably emphasize that I was not to hesitate to accept 'a more amusing companion,' as she would put it, at the last moment.

"With her passing, I don't look forward to a visit to England. To me, London will seem empty."

Ultimately, things came back to the family. Fanny's most consistent joys came from bounty shared with the widening circle of her relatives. Despite urgings to get her own apartment, she preferred to live with those closest to her. If familiarity had its strains, there were also compensations.

Clara had developed into a capable household manager as well as an indispensable counselor to Fanny on clothes, domestic help and other everyday practicalities. She pushed Fanny, always hesitant about spending anything on herself, into acquiring a wardrobe consonant with her professional status. Clara's scolding, big-sister manner, Fanny knew, was

The Holtzmann clan in the Brooklyn penthouse, 1931. Theresa and Henry are seated, flanked by Jack (left) and David. In the middle row, left to right, are Fanny's sister-in-law Lilian (Jack's wife), Selema, Clara, Bertha, Stella, Fanny, Helen Berkman (a niece), and Rita. The author is in the top row, second from left; next to him, at right, is his father, Samuel Berkman

a reflection of genuine concern; and it was more than balanced by her shrewd judgment.

Papa Henry was unfailingly docile and appreciative. "When the sun shines," Fanny once explained, "Papa thinks it's a special gift from God to him." A lifetime dandy, Henry reveled in the Sulka ties and silk shirts Fanny brought home from Bond Street; his particular treasure was a blue velvet smoking jacket. She also brought home gourmet tidbits for his intellectual dining table: Sir Ronald Storrs, Dorothy Thompson, the duchess of Atholl.

Papa found the former governor of Jerusalem a passable Hebrew scholar, but lacking in broad culture: "a typically rigid military mind, no imagination." He was much more taken with Miss Thompson, then a militantly anti-Nazi columnist for the New York *Tribune*; it was a big moment for him when, shortly after Fanny moved her menage to Park Avenue in 1937, Miss Thompson came up from the Algonquin to pay her respects.

Papa likewise admired the duchess, who had been equally outspoken against Hitler; but their meeting had to overcome a slight contretemps. The "Red Duchess" was staying across town as the house guest of the ultraconservative president of Columbia University, Dr. Nicholas Murray Butler, an arrangement that was embarrassing to all concerned. She did not arrive on the East Side until after 10 P.M., so Fanny led her into the huge kitchen for a casual cup of tea.

Papa, sauntering by in his bathrobe for a snack, saw Fanny at the table with a lanky grayish lady, very plainly dressed, a grassy deposit on her upper lip. "So," he said, "your duchess never got here, after all."

"Papa, this is Her Grace . . . whose speeches you've been collecting."

"Don't play games with me, daughter." He turned to Fanny's unprepossessing guest: "What is your name, my dear?"

"Katharine."

"Katharine *Atholl*," underlined Fanny.

Papa blinked, adjusted his robe, and rose to the conversational occasion. Theresa, curious at his long absence, came from the bedroom to investigate ("Fortunately," Fanny recalled, "both of them had their teeth in"). Theresa took command as hostess, and Fanny was all but forgotten.

It wasn't the first time. A year before, she had arranged a splendid formal dinner for the Francis Hacketts, with Harold Ross and Jane Grant of *The New Yorker* among the guests. James, the chauffeur, had exchanged his black jacket for the starched white of a butler's uniform; pine logs crackled cosily in the fireplace; roses danced in the candlelight reflected along a gleaming mahogany table.

Suddenly Theresa rebelled. "Why do we have to dine in darkness?" she demanded. "We were the first family in Brooklyn to have electric light. We always paid our bills."

"And that hot fire," echoed Henry. "Who needs it, when we have good steam heat? Put it out, James."

For once Theresa nodded in harmony with her husband. "What's more," she told Hackett, "in *my* home we don't usually eat from a bare table. Even in the worst times, I managed to have fresh linens. Maybe your Henry the Eighth didn't have such advantages, but *here* we're accustomed to tablecloths!"

More tractable were Fanny's nieces and nephews. Increasingly they became the focus of her shopping forays and her impulsive enthusiasms. The author of this narrative, as eldest nephew, scholarship winner, and incipient author-composer, was a natural target of her attentions.

My dormitory walls at Cornell showed off autographed photos of

Fanny's Hollywood friends. At the graduation ceremonies in 1933 I presented her proudly to the chairman of the Drama Department as the attorney for Noel Coward.

Several years later, when I was on the West Coast to report Mary Astor's diaried indiscretions for the New York *Daily Mirror*, Fanny introduced me to Walter Wanger. A story conference with the gifted director Fritz Lang led to a job offer at Wanger's studio, where I became the protégé of director William K. Howard. Howard, on returning to England where he had just introduced Vivien Leigh in *Fire Over England*, conspired with Fanny there to set up a contract for me with Alexander Korda. I wrote two screenplays at London Films, then was wafted back to Hollywood by Fanny for a Shirley Temple epic at Twentieth Century–Fox.

Although these interventions were clearly genuine attempts to promote my career, they reflected also Fanny's hunger for the loving recognition that within her immediate family steadfastly eluded her. In these outpourings of giving, she was able to ward off other feelings too troublesome to face. However, being not only generous but human, she could not invariably preserve a sharp distinction between altruistic motive and personal need, between what would advance a younger person's growth and what would gratify her own internal imperatives.

Here, as elsewhere, what brought things back into focus for Fanny and those around her was her unfailing sense of humor. Asked why she did not, like her sister Clara, take first-class train accommodations to visit their parents in Florida, she replied straight-faced, "Because I don't have a rich sister." Consulted by her brother Jack on the wisdom of traveling to the baths at Vichy, she suggested that instead he "drink four quarts of water from the faucet, take a stiff shower at Brighton Beach in Brooklyn — and give yourself a five-dollar tip!"

Generally, through the *Rasputin* decade of great external successes, Fanny covered her personal discontents with similar Zaida-flavored ironies. Only occasionally did a wistful note creep into her conversation or correspondence to signalize the emotional chinks beneath.

Writing to Louis Bromfield in the late 1930's, she expressed curiosity about Ina Claire's forthcoming new marriage: "Who is he? I thought she had told me about every romantic interest. I hope she's going to get some real happiness out of this one. A swell girl, Ina. She's entitled to a break."

Ina — or Fanny?

Book Two

Chapter 8

*G*ERMAN JACKBOOTS were on the march in Europe, ringing across a continent.

For Fanny, Nazism was no ideological abstraction. The Holtzmanns had relatives in Eastern Europe, a pungent crew with uncanny resemblances to their American cousins. Twice Fanny had journeyed into Galicia to explore the family roots.

Her first visit was in 1932, when she was accompanied on her usual European junket by her married sister Stella. As the pair were about to return home, Stella paused in her packing: "What about that village of Zaida's you keep harping on, Fanny? Do you actually know anybody there?"

The town of Rohatyn, population a few thousand, was not listed in any tourist excursions. The Cook's office in London finally found it tucked away in a far corner of "Austrian Poland," some thirty-five miles southwest of Lemberg (Lvov). Fanny, attuned to the glories of the Savoy, the Ritz and the Adlon, sent off a wire to Zaida's nephew Yoshe Kleinwaks requesting him to book a suite in the best local hotel, "preferably two separate bedrooms and bath." How should she know Rohatyn was innocent of running water? With their Mark Cross luggage, new movie camera and Harrod labels, the two American women started the long ride eastward by boat train.

At Lemberg they changed to an ancient local, wheezing into the station at Rohatyn in bright sunlight at six in the evening. The town looked like a Western movie set on the back lot at MGM: dusty, unpaved, ramshackle.

On the platform, packed together into a solid black mass, was virtually the entire population. Their faces had an eerie sameness: the consequence, Fanny later realized, of intermarriage over many generations.

A figure in the front row caught her eye: long white beard, blue eyes, patriarchal bearing. Stella was pointing toward the same man. "Zaida!" she whispered.

Fanny nodded. "Down to the last detail." The top fly buttons of the villager's trousers were not quite fastened.

The oldster introduced himself as Zaida's nephew Yoshe. Playing to the gallery of onlookers with Zaida-like élan, he noted that the American visitors were arriving with felicitous timing on September 1, the forty-seventh anniversary of Henry and Theresa's wedding.

A thin little man in a skull cap promptly detached himself from the crowd and shuffled toward Fanny, hand outstretched. He was a *klezmer* (musician), he announced in Yiddish, and he had been cheated of his rightful fee in 1885 when Theresa's wedding was canceled because she had run off with her fiancé's best friend.

Fanny was too stunned by this ingenious invention to resist it. She handed over twenty-five zlotys — and was instantly surrounded by a score of eager "musicians," all claiming to have been similarly deprived.

"The Rohatyn band," murmured Stella, "must have been bigger than the Philharmonic."

Fanny kept passing out zlotys until she found herself confronting a husky blond native who obviously had never seen forty. "You couldn't have been there," she protested. "You weren't even born in 1885!"

"True," came the bland reply. "The *gnädige Fräulein* is very clever. But my father, you see, was our town's leading fiddler. Would you let his untimely death — may he rest in peace — deprive an innocent family of their rights?"

Fanny reached into her purse again, shaking her head in professional admiration.

After several hours with Yoshe's family, Fanny and Stella hired Rohatyn's only car for a bumpy ride to Koslow a few miles away. According to report, a surviving sister of Papa Henry lived there.

Koslow "made Rohatyn look like a metropolis." It had a church, a synagogue, a general store and a combination post office and tobacco shop. This last was supposed to be the domain of their putative Aunt Frimme, who as the wife of a Chasidic Holy Man naturally relieved her husband of all concern with worldly matters.

Entering the little shop, Fanny stared at the buxom, sweet-faced woman behind the counter. It was hardly necessary to confirm that this was Frau Goldfeld: Tante Frimme was a virtual replica of Bertha Holtzmann Berkman, down to the brisk bossy wiggle of her bottom when she walked.

Tante Frimme, whose seven children included two eligible daughters, presented several of her brood.

One didn't wait on formalities. "Handsome Moshe," the twenty-two-year-old jewel of the family, leaped onto the running board of the visitors' car and offered his hand to Fanny in marriage. A black-haired youth with full, strong features, he was finishing a degree in accountancy at Lemberg. He would be a fine prize, he suggested, for cousin Fanny to bring back to America or, if she preferred, to Palestine. Anywhere but this backward rural ghetto of Galicia, where a Jew was doomed to poverty or worse.

Fanny was amused but also disquieted by the "proposal"; behind it she sensed a terrible desperation. Stella was annoyed: Galicia had too many favor-seekers and no bathrooms. She couldn't wait to shake its copious dust from her feet.

Within twenty-four hours they were back in Vienna, where Fanny called Papa Henry to report a gift more precious than any Sulka haberdashery: the sister he had not seen in nearly fifty years was alive in Europe!

The glimpse into the family past left a deep impression on Fanny. For a few hours she had actually entered the Chasidic world sketched so lovingly for her during her childhood; although her grandfather's "noble mansion" had turned out to be a decrepit farmhouse, other details rang true.

She felt closely drawn to these people whose faces held such familiar echoes; they might be planets apart from the New York Holtzmanns in life values and life prospects, but they were in fact just a generation away. She could so easily have been one of them.

Two summers later, Fanny was in Europe waiting out the appeal on the Youssoupoff case, and decided again to visit the Galician cousins. This time she reserved comfortable accommodations at the George Hotel in Lemberg, a landmark of Old World opulence.

From Vienna she wired Tante Frimme's daughter Ella Raizman, who lived in Lemberg with her husband Isaac and three little girls. Would it be all right if Fanny continued eastward the next day, Saturday, breaking the orthodox Sabbath?

Ella relayed the reply: "Travel on Yom Kippur if necessary — but come. Quickly."

In Lemberg, many lips poured forth the family crisis. "Handsome Moshe," in whose education the Goldfelds had invested their meager savings so that he might command an enormous dowry in the arranged-marriage market, had committed a scandalous, not to say unpardonable, sin. Moshe had had the temerity to fall in love with a poor girl.

Moshe's father, Rabbi Mikhail Goldfeld, was aghast at this betrayal of Chasidic tradition, in which such matters were the province of elders. His mother was worried about its practical consequences for her two unmarried daughters, Estelle and Angela. They were spirited, well-formed girls; but without a dowry, attractive appearance meant nothing. Moshe had been the repository of the family hopes. His dark good looks, buttressed by a university degree, would surely make him a catch a banker's daughter might covet. The resultant fine dowry, once in the family coffers, could be dangled as bait before prospective suitors of Estelle and Angela.

It was an excellent, logical plan, that took everything into account except Moshe's feelings. He had his heart set on twenty-one-year-old Regina, and his eyes fixed on Palestine. For a year he had been training intensively as a *chalutz* (pioneer), and had just received his certificate of immigration to the Holy Land. His group was to leave in less than two weeks.

But how could he go without Regina? And how could he marry Regina without destroying his sisters' lives?

It was a situation made to order for Fanny. At her invitation, Moshe and Regina came to the hotel for dinner. She saw a clear-eyed dedicated man and a healthy intelligent girl, two young people obviously in love.

The next day Fanny spoke with Tante Frimme: "Have you anything against Regina personally?"

"No, but — "

"How much would it cost to stake all three girls?"

"You mean, dowries for Estelle and Angela — and also for Moshe's Regina?"

"Yes. Plus two boat tickets to Palestine."

"*Gott in Himmel!*" Tante Frimme clutched at Fanny, tears welling in her eyes. Then she made some rapid calculations. Translated into United States currency, the total came to about twenty-five hundred dollars.

Although Fanny was supporting her parents and Clara, and intermittently the less prosperous members of her large family, she did not hesitate.

"Okay," she said. "You've got it. Just see that Moshe and Regina have a proper wedding."

Fanny gave Tante Frimme's unmarried daughters something much more valuable than dowries: a few days with her at Jerencia, a local summer resort that was the Galician equivalent of Grossinger's. Every matchmaker in the area canvassed the place regularly. Here the two sisters could make the most of Fanny's awesome prestige as their "millionaire American cousin," the only offspring of a native emigrant who had returned in the full flush of success. Riding in a carriage with Fanny and carelessly displaying German-language newspaper clippings about her, the girls were transformed into instant heiresses.

Fanny wrote home that she might personally negotiate a match for Estelle. "Don't laugh — that is how it is done here. It was shocking to me at first, but everything is in the point of view. They take it in the same manner as my royal friends who have their marriages arranged.

Lemberg, 1934: Fanny with her young cousin Angela Goldfeld, whom she later tried in vain to save from the Nazis

Works out better in the long run because the economic factor is weighed, and love follows. Look at Papa and Mama — theirs was a love match, so what?"

Moshe's wedding was still a week off, so Fanny returned to the George Hotel, holding court beside a constantly replenished buffet. Another nephew of Zaida's, the learned Moshe Zuckerkandel, turned up to gossip, nibble fruit, and marvel at her bathroom fixtures. "The first thing he does after greeting me," Fanny wrote, "is to poke his head into the bathroom. I told him it would be no desecration if he went in and tried it for himself!"

Then the children of the savant came, and that was not so amusing: "Mom, I could not restrain my tears — I'm crying now as I am typing this, merely thinking of them. THEY ARE THE SADDEST SIGHT I HAVE EVER SEEN. There is a boy of almost 16 — the most beautiful face — his stature is that of a child of eight or ten. And 14-year-old Basia, very very thin and tiny, but SO bright." The children were motherless; Basia and a younger girl had been at a sanitarium in the country until recently, when money ran out.

Fanny arranged for them to be sent back there immediately after Moshe Goldfeld's wedding: "I don't know how," she wrote, "but I simply MUST send them money for food hereafter. I don't mind making sacrifices if it means giving two kids a chance to live — as it is, they are condemned forever."

Meanwhile, she included the two little girls in a shopping spree for wedding outfits: "Believe me, it is a *mitzva*. And I am not defending my extravagance to ANYBODY [followed by a string of eleven exclamation points]. If you don't like it, any of you, that is just too bad. I am not depriving you of anything so don't worry. I should get dresses at Chanel's and have to apologize because I am clothing a few poor, helpless orphans!"

From her base in Lemberg, Fanny made forays into the countryside, checking ancestral gravestones and current larders. As word of her largesse spread, "relatives" popped up everywhere ("I am named Itzik, after your grandfather's famous uncle — so all right, maybe it's only my middle name . . .").

The acute need was for dowries. With the depression in America depleting aid from emigrants there, many girls faced the prospect of wearing old-maid braids for a lifetime. Impulsively Fanny decreed that for this one year, as in some Gaelic folktale, she would put up a small dowry for every orphan in the area.

The run on romance was — by Rohatyn standards — electrifying. Fanny herself reported back: "I have made two male conquests here — both marriageable men, both eligible prospects. One is the widower Zuckerkandel (he looks almost 70), and the other is Frimme's 20-year-old son who looks 15."

Impishly, she looked up Leopold Halperin, the man who made the mistake of showing Theresa's picture to his friend Henry Holtzmann half a century earlier (Theresa ran off with Henry, leaving Leopold at the altar). She informed the family that Leopold was now a successful lawyer, thrice-married, "young-looking," and still carrying a torch: "To hear that old boy still moon about Mom — well, it is safe with an ocean and a continent between them. But — don't be so independent, Pop!"

Back came a frantic cable from Jack: she'd better not revive that old triangle unless she wanted to give her father a heart attack.

The wedding was held at the home of Regina's boss, "the local Hattie Carnegie." It was preceded by Orthodox religious services that left Fanny fuming — when she was not being moved. The women were herded into a separate synagogue; they were banished also from the ceremonial Kiddush, where the men ate, drank and sang. "The Great One [Moshe's rabbinical father, Mikhail] does not shake hands with a female, nor walk with her, nor be alone in her presence — probably afraid I'll seduce him. A female here is lower than the worst dog."

This was one of Fanny's rare outbursts of feminist indignation. Typically, it came in a private letter to her parents. Strident public protest offended her. It was not by accident that Golda Meir, grandmother-diplomat, came to represent her ideal of personal fulfillment.

Even in Galicia, her resentment of male dominance was tempered by familial sentiment. When all the Goldfelds gathered for songs around the Sabbath table, in a setting that "Maurice Schwartz and his Yiddish Theater could not have improved upon," Fanny was strangely touched: "I looked at Frimme at one end of the table, her husband at the other. They have given their children a great heritage."

At the wedding, Fanny watched the men touch handkerchiefs in their Chasidic dance of celebration, and threw herself into a happy *hora* with the other outcasts of the Feminine Division. She shared knishes and exchanged blessings. It was "good to feel like a fairy godmother," and good to submerge her Westernized self in the tangy pleasures of Yiddish; she had spoken nothing else since leaving Vienna.

"My one worry now," she wrote, "is I must relearn English. Can you see me saying to the Duchess of Rutland that I have to run down to a *geveldel* [a small shop] to buy a frock?"

Two days later Moshe and his bride departed for the Holy Land via Trieste — Fanny's first, but far from her last, gift to the nascent Jewish state. The station was jammed with well-wishers. Moshe had only a farewell pittance in his pocket, but he couldn't have been more jubilant with a million. As Fanny explained to her parents: "For the Jews of Poland, in contrast to those of the United States and England, Palestine is not so much an ancient ideal as a practical chance to escape from a land without opportunity. The departing emigrants were like so many convicts set free from a life sentence."

Back in America, Fanny was approached by the *Jewish Daily Bulletin* for an interview on her *Rasputin* victory. Instead, she urged every reader to adopt a family in Galicia, where "beautiful girls age almost overnight," and even five dollars a month could fend off "starvation and disintegration."

For the next few years, Fanny kept the checks flowing: a few pounds from England, a regular monthly allowance from her office, extra gifts on holidays. In German and English her beneficence was acknowledged: "You are so prudent and kind-hearted like an angel."

In 1937 the tone of the letters from Rohatyn and Brzezany, her father's birthplace, changed: "Here is the time no good. In every way they try to ruin us, so they say here is worse than in Germany. I think you know everything from the papers."

And two years later, from Frimme's daughter Estelle, who had married a young Talmudic scholar: "Life here is insupportable. We Jews are exterminated in all ways. We live only with the hope of getting out."

Already Fanny had swung into action, spurred by a tip from friends in the British Foreign Office that concentration camps were being readied by the Nazis. American entry visas for East European Jews were limited by a strict quota system. In addition, applicants had to struggle through complex technicalities to prove the solvency of their sponsors. Understaffed American consulates in Europe could not cope with the mounting paper work, and the State Department visa desk under the ultraconservative assistant secretary Breckenridge Long did nothing to expedite matters.

Fanny threw her support to a Child Refugee Bill before Congress, under which the quotas would be relaxed to admit ten thousand children for each of two years, but despite the strong backing of Eleanor Roosevelt, the measure could not survive the opposition of the DAR and the American Legion.

On November 9, 1938, a German attaché in Paris was killed by a Polish Jew, and the reprisal terror of *Kristallnacht* (night of smashed glass) swept across Hitler's Germany. The next day Fanny went to Washington to confer with her friend Supreme Court Justice Felix Frankfurter.

Small, alert, with abrupt crackling movements that reflected the quickness of his mind, Frankfurter was in Fanny's phrase a "City College lawyer." He lacked the polish and gentleness of a Cardozo; his crisp Yiddish *"Nu?"* offended genteel Anglo-Saxons like Eleanor Roosevelt. But he was warm, open, approachable. To Fanny, Frankfurter was "my brother Jack with his hair down."

Fanny put her case bluntly: "You have great power among American Jews. Can't you get them to bring pressure on the president?"

Frankfurter became very bitter. "I have no power at all where it counts — with the smug, fancy Jews at the top of the economic pyramid — the ones who spend all their time trying to batter their way into non-Jewish clubs. They will sit in silence until their own skins are threatened. Nothing short of a personal *Kristallnacht* will wake them up."

If he was scornful of "Park Avenue Jews," Frankfurter loathed even more the "inside boys" of his own faith at the White House: "The Jews closest to Roosevelt, like Sam Rosenman and Dave Niles, are all thinking of their own careers; they're not rocking any boats. Don't blame the president; he thinks all Jews are like Dave Niles."

"Can't you talk to the President yourself?"

Frankfurter shook his head. "A justice is not free to engage in such discussions. You'd be surprised at the restrictions that accompany these chambers." Nor could he make a public statement challenging American policy: "It would only erect another wall between the president and myself. That would be counterproductive."

Still, he urged Fanny to pursue her contacts among interested Republicans, even such Roosevelt-dubbed "enemies of America" as Congressmen Bruce Barton and Hamilton Fish. "It takes courage to plug away, Fanny — but somebody's got to do it!"

Meanwhile, he would set up an appointment for her — not too optimistically — with Dave Niles.

Niles, born Neyhus forty-eight years earlier, was a man of medium height, medium looks, and medium intelligence, a tepid social-worker type who blended inconspicuously into the Washington bureaucratic background.

"You must understand," he told Fanny, "the administration can't just slice off a piece of America and hand it to the Jews. We're only a part of this nation — we don't own it. And when you talk of economic sanctions against Hitler —" He frowned. "That's a delicate business. After all, this is Washington, not Jerusalem. The way you people come to me and talk —"

"We're talking about saving human lives!"

"I know, I know." Niles threw in his favorite line: "Remember, I'm Jewish, too!"

"Hell," snapped Fanny, "you wouldn't *be* here if you weren't Jewish!" To her, as to Frankfurter, Niles was FDR's house-Jew, a professional religionist living off public funds. "I'm not asking you for Palestine," she went on, "just for some of those miles of arid desert I see out West every time I travel to Hollywood. The refugees will make it bloom, just as they did the Middle East."

"Congress won't hear of it. It's those anti-Semite Republicans . . ."

"Like Bruce Barton and Ham Fish? Don't give me that tired old story. Listen — I'd like to see the president."

"What? I mean, people can't just walk in . . ."

"Why not? Tell him I had an interesting private conversation with Ribbentrop at the duchess of Rutland's."

Fanny had reason to believe she was known to the President. A few months earlier she had been approached by his friend Morris L. Ernst to switch loyalties to the New Deal, but had declined out of distaste for FDR's immigration policy.

Reluctantly, Niles picked up a phone. A few minutes later he ushered Fanny into the president's office: "Miss Holtzmann thinks," he scoffed apologetically, "that because she had tea with Ribbentrop, she can solve the question of the Jewish refugees."

FDR smiled at Fanny. What could he do for her?

He could make a little room for the exiles in his big country, Fanny told him. A parcel of land in the dry, empty West. "Why do you permit Jews to go down in the sea, Mr. President? What crime have they committed, other than to be born Jewish?"

"My dear Miss Holtzmann, it is my Jewish advisers, not non-Jews, who are guiding me in these matters. I'm doing all I can."

The British, Fanny persisted, were exercising a quiet behind-the-scenes humanity toward the refugees. In the midst of the official boat blockade, they were making "discretionary" exceptions, admitting doctors and professors as ostensible "domestics."

FDR nodded. "Yes, very interesting, Miss Holtzmann. I'd like to hear more about it, but unfortunately —" He gestured toward the papers on his desk. "Why don't you talk to Dave Niles about it? Perhaps we'll have an opportunity to go into the matter again."

Niles, guiding her to the door, closed on his familiar note: "You know, Fanny, we can't halt the whole machinery of government just to look after the Jews . . ."

Fanny made a brief try with Bernard Baruch, who on one of her Atlantic crossings had displayed a grandfatherly pride in her achievements.

"It's not like the old days," Baruch told her, "when I could get Woodrow Wilson's ear. Roosevelt is immersed in a sea of frightened Jews. The man is wonderful, but he has to take the advice of his staff people."

That left Samuel Rosenman to tackle, the former Tammany politician who had become counsel to FDR during Roosevelt's service as governor of New York and was later made a judge on the New York Supreme Court. Rosenman, an adroit speech-writer, was closest of all to the president.

And farthest, Fanny discovered, from her reach. When she telephoned his office, she was told by Rosenman's secretary: "Oh, every Jew in the country calls him up. What organization do you represent?"

"None."

"Write him a letter."

Fanny reported the incident to Justice Frankfurter. He advised her not to waste any more time in that quarter: "The Jews around Roosevelt just don't want to get involved."

Many of Fanny's Gentile friends, ironically, did. Louis Bromfield and Francis Hackett expressed their outrage over Hitler in eloquent public statements; Louis would later become head of the Emergency Conference to Save the Jews of Europe. Marlene Dietrich declared that America should launch a strong economic boycott of the Nazis, starting with the withdrawal of all Hollywood movies. Leslie Howard, reportedly of Jewish background but officially an English WASP, denounced the Berlin regime and contributed heavily to refugee relief.

In Washington, Fanny had made no dent in the Democratic administration. So she went to the Opposition.

In the 1938 campaign, FDR had mocked the hard-core Republican isolationists with the derisive refrain "Martin, Barton and Fish." Now each of the trio, for whatever motives, responded sympathetically to Fanny.

Her first point of contact was Bruce Barton: congressman, churchman, former advertising executive and her neighbor in the so-called Silk Stocking District of Manhattan. Barton's son "Petey" (Bruce Jr.) and his daughter Betsy were frequent visitors to her home.

As she lunched with Barton in the House dining room, she mentioned the latest discouraging communiqué from Dave Niles: Jewish refugees should seek a haven in Africa; "they'll make fortunes there."

She herself was wondering about Lower California, the undersettled semitropical peninsula straggling southward across the American border from Tijuana. A part of Mexico, the territory held only 130,000 people in its 55,600 square miles.

"Excellent idea," said Barton. He agreed that it should be pursued privately — established organizations did not welcome unpaid crusaders

— and suggested engaging Linton Wells, a prominent Washington newspaperman who knew the area well.

Barton waved a greeting to a small, wiry man passing their table, and presented House leader Joe Martin. Told of Fanny's mission, Martin pulled up a chair: "I'm with you all the way — although personally I think it stinks that you have to look for land outside the United States when we have so much here."

However, he wasn't optimistic about administration backing: "They want to keep as far as possible from the Jews — they're surrounded by them. I suspect they'd resist Lower California for fear that, being so close to the border, Jews would slip in with the help of relatives and friends. They'd also drag in their red herring about Labor — the argument that illegal immigrants would depress the work market and stir up the unions."

The towering figure of Hamilton Fish appeared at the table. As an ardent America Firster, Fish was regarded suspiciously in the Jewish community. But Fanny knew him as a friendly congressman who since Bull Moose days had helped Zaida and later herself when problems came up with Jewish immigrants at Ellis Island; she was aware also that he was the sponsor in the House of the congressional resolution applauding the Balfour Declaration.

Fish offered his personal cooperation in anything Fanny proposed. He would be glad to sign a batch of visa affidavits for refugees and to round up more from such colleagues as Senator Robert A. Taft. But he, like Martin, thought a massive influx from Europe would be blocked by the administration.

Nonetheless, Fanny went ahead with her Lower California idea, gathering powerful sponsorship. She learned that Barton's friend Colonel Theodore Roosevelt was indignant over the refugee issue. She enlisted Roosevelt for her board, along with Bruce Barton, Louis Bromfield, Linton Wells, and Edward J. Nally, president emeritus of the Radio Corporation of America. The group was incorporated as "The Association for the Resettlement of Oppressed People," serving the dispossessed "irrespective of race, color, creed or political beliefs." It would seek the blessing first of the Pan-American Union and then of the Mexican government, on the grounds that Mexico would gain industrial resources, mineral rights, a protected coastline and global goodwill.

Linton Wells was an expert on Latin America who had also been involved two decades earlier in the Macedonian population exchanges affecting three-quarters of a million people. In January 1939, he was dispatched to Europe to confer with refugee-rescue organizations there. Fanny financed the trip herself, explaining in a letter to an Anglo-Jewish banker that the usual money sources would hold back until they were sure she wasn't chasing a rainbow: "Of course we are chasing a rainbow, a beautiful rainbow. But that is what all ideals are: rainbows." She did not want the Jews of Germany thrown upon the mercy of world charity: "We are not a pauper people. We are a proud, successful race who have been bled and robbed by gangsters, tyrants and thugs."

Wells came back with a token check for $30,000 from Amsterdam and pledges of aid from other capitals. He went on to Lower California, where a preliminary survey had reported that half a million immigrants could be sustained. After talking with engineers and ranchers there, Wells asserted that with proper dams and irrigation the area could support at least three times that number.

And then the project ran into ugly realities. Although Undersecretary of State Sumner Welles and J. Reuben Clark, a former ambassador to Mexico, were both personally enthusiastic, Welles intimated there might be difficulties with the White House. Clark warned that Mexico was extremely nationalistic, jealous of its sovereign rights; President Cárdenas would have to be approached cautiously, by Latins rather than *norteamericanos* — and not yet. At the Pan American Union, Linton Wells was told nothing could be decided before summer.

Events in Europe would not wait. A note from Linton Wells to Fanny sounded the epitaph of the association: "It is too bad there are not more great humanitarians in the world like your all-too-generous self."

Fanny had been careful to keep her bridges to England intact. Despite moments of furious indignation —"How brazenly," she wrote Louis Bromfield at the start of 1939, "they have tossed aside the Balfour Declaration when it suited their needs!"— she continued to feel that Britain and its allies were the front line against Hitler, without whom Western civilization and with it European Jewry would be swept away.

She had already been of service to the British government, although her first efforts at liaison fell on unreceptive ears. In 1933 the revue *As Thousands Cheer* opened on Broadway with a ribald sketch poking fun at the British royal family. Fanny, who was in London, heard that King George's sensibilities were much aroused, and also that the Foreign Office was going to lodge a formal protest in Washington.

She made a couple of telephone calls to New York, then got in touch with Whitehall through the duchess of Atholl: "May I strongly suggest you forget about a protest? My information is that the show is only fair. An official statement will simply give it tons of free publicity, without changing anything."

She was coolly thanked — and disregarded. The British were too outraged to concern themselves with consequences. They communicated their anger officially through the British ambassador in Washington. His protest was still being circulated around the country by the wire services when Sam Harris, the producer of the revue, issued a vigorous counterblast. The story reverberated for several days, exactly as Fanny had predicted, creating enough notoriety to generate a respectable Broadway run.

Two years later, with Fanny again in London, word reached her that Harris was rehearsing a new musical, *Jubilee*, in which Buckingham

Palace was caricatured even more broadly. This time, when she offered advice to her British friends, they listened. It was partly out of the recollection of their previous gaffe; but also because in the interim she had become the particular pet of the lord chamberlain, the earl of Cromer.

With Cromer's approval, she got busy on the overseas telephone. Her first call went to Harris. Fanny crisply ran through the consequences of "bucking the British government." He would imperil the position of Actors Equity on talent exchanges and invite a boycott of all Sam Harris productions in London. "And suppose you want to sell your lousy show to Hollywood, so what? So the British are laying for you, and they'll see that the picture is banned all over the British Empire!"

Then she called Cole Porter and Moss Hart, respectively responsible for the songs and script of *Jubilee*. "Your name is very big on this side, Cole — how many composers can point to 'Let's Do It' and 'Night and Day'? You run the risk of being blackballed wherever the Union Jack flies! That goes for you too, Moss."

Finally, she asked Dr. Giannini of the Bank of America and Eddie Goulding to make separate, discreet interventions.

Within a week she was able to advise Lord Cromer that the locale of the play had been changed from England to an innocuous "mythical kingdom," and the dialogue had been sharply trimmed to eliminate offensive matter.

When *Jubilee* opened in New York, the London *Daily Telegraph* noted with relief: "Fears that the play would attempt to caricature the British royal family were dissipated." Fanny's role in the revision was never revealed, although Walter Winchell, the gossip columnist, carried a typically garbled item attributing the cuts to a warning from unnamed "Washington officials."

The grateful Cromer told Fanny she had earned a substantial fee — she shook her head — or, if she preferred, a decoration.

"No," she told him. "That would put me in the position of being a defender of the British government. I'm more useful all around when I'm not labeled as anybody's agent."

In the four years since, Fanny had stayed in close touch with the Cromers, visiting them whenever in England and on her return home briefing the lord chamberlain regularly on the shifts in America opinion toward Britain.

Lord Cromer in turn confided the ruminations of His Majesty's government. In early spring of 1939, he wrote: "The tremendous strides in re-armament made both in France and this country since the September Crisis should convince Germany and Italy that, while a policy of appeasement and peace is the aim of the Democracies, there is a limit to what they will tolerate." And a little later: German expansion had "here in Europe been discounted beforehand as a foregone conclusion" of Hitler's policy. On April 28, Britain's rulers were still whistling in the gathering dark, comforted by the "moderation of tone" of Hitler's latest speech. Yet Cromer could not resist adding the disquieting postscript in longhand: "The real problem is whether he means what he says, and says what he means."

When a royal goodwill visit to the United States was projected, Fanny sent the lord chamberlain a series of letters analyzing and documenting isolationist sentiment, especially in the Midwest, and emphasizing the influence on American public opinion of syndicated columnists like Walter Winchell and Eleanor Roosevelt. Fanny enjoyed — or at least maintained — cordial relations with Winchell, who liked to be on a first-name basis with high-level insiders. She aroused the Hearst favorite, Westbrook Pegler, and even a columnist on the Anglophobe New York *Daily News*, to "missionary work" on behalf of the hands-across-the-sea cause.

Finally, with Gertrude Lawrence and the BBC correspondent in America, Felix Greene, she put together a hail-to-Their-Majesties radio program for June 9, featuring British theater personalities who were working in the United States. The program, retransmitted to England, proved to be the capstone of a successful visit.

A week later Fanny sailed for Europe, passing up a chance to head a federal investigation into monopolistic practices by Hollywood. War was too close, she told Thurman Arnold, the New Deal trustbuster at the Department of Justice, to permit any deviation from the task of rescuing refugees. She did not need Lord Cromer's admonition that "the next few months till, say, the end of September must be anxious ones for the world"; every news report and personal advice from the Continent pointed to a Nazi onslaught before autumn.

In London Fanny found trenches and bomb shelters under construction; the handsome old trees fronting Lord Cromer's home in Belgravia were being removed. Everywhere refugees were milling through the city. Their Mecca was the United States Embassy, where visas to safety were processed — if the obstacles of quota, sponsorship and other technicalities could be overcome. This was the task into which Fanny threw herself.

She faced a special handicap in the person of the American ambassador. Joe Kennedy, her old nemesis, had been in the post since December of 1937. His appointment had been received dubiously when first proposed to the Court of St. James's because the lord chamberlain was all too familiar, largely from Fanny's accounts, with his history: his shabby treatment of Gloria Swanson and Eddie Goulding, his stock deals, his friendship with the notorious demagogue Father Coughlin and his own open anti-Semitism (over a highball with Goulding, he had put it quite bluntly: "Sure, I've had Jews in my home — as tutors! How else could I get those dumb kids of mine to pass their exams? But I'll never let them *live* in Bronxville; Brownsville is where they belong!").

As Cromer explained the matter to Fanny, "We weren't too keen on accepting Kennedy, but your people pressured us, and we were in no position to argue." Behind the British capitulation, he intimated, was the realization that James Roosevelt, son of the American president, was slated to become a partner in Kennedy's enormously lucrative scotch whisky import business.

But the reason for the original British opposition remained a mystery to Kennedy until the royal garden party in July of 1938, when he encountered Fanny there. He knew she was not among the handful of Americans on his embassy guest list.

"How did *you* get here, Fanny?" Kennedy demanded.

"I know how *you* got here, Joe!"— a reference, not lost on the ambassador, to his heavy backing of the Roosevelt 1932 campaign and subsequent financial involvement with the president's son. "I came," Fanny added, "at the invitation of Their Majesties, extended through the lord chamberlain."

At the end of the afternoon, Kennedy asked if he could give Fanny a lift home.

"No, thank you. I'm going with Lord and Lady Cromer."

The astute Kennedy needed no further clues as to the source of the negative report on him. From that moment he let it be known that he wanted no favors extended to Fanny or her clients: "She may pull a lot of wires in London, but she's not running my embassy."

However, Fanny had good friends at the lower, working echelons of the American diplomatic staff — and that was where decisions about visas were made. John J. Coyle, the commercial attaché at the U.S. Consulate, was on close terms with the theater people whose interests spanned the Atlantic; he had been "Jack" to her since 1929. Quiet and knowledgeable, married to an English girl, Coyle had survived all personnel shuffles. He introduced Fanny to Consul Edward S. Maney, who ran the visa desk. Maney operated with more of an eye for people than for protocol.

Fanny also had aid from an unexpected quarter: the ambassador's first and second sons. Joseph P. Kennedy, Jr., and his brother Jack did not share their father's views on Hitler, refugees or Fanny. She met them in London through Bruce Barton's son Petey, who had been with them at Harvard; subsequent tragedy never dimmed her striking first impression: "I have seen good-looking men in my time — on Hollywood sets, in the theatre and elsewhere — but those brothers! Dressed alike in their straw boaters with the bright Harvard band — when they entered a room, it was like having the American flag walk in."

The dominant boy was unmistakably the elder: "It was always Joe and Jack, not the reverse."

Two days after meeting the pair, Fanny came across them in the visa section of the embassy, helping a crowd of bewildered East European refugees fill out applications. She could not suppress her surprise.

Jack shrugged and smiled. "What else can a fellow do, Miss Holtzmann?"

In August, Jack Coyle dropped by Kinnerton Studios with potentially disturbing news. A new consul general, John G. Erhardt, was being transferred to London from Hamburg, Germany: "He's a hell of a nice guy, you'll get along with him." Coyle wasn't so sure, however, about the new second secretary that Erhardt was bringing along, Alan Steyne: "Andover, Yale, a lot of money and I suspect big social ambitions."

This hunch was confirmed at Fanny's first meeting with Erhardt. "Young Steyne," he told her, "would really get a kick out of meeting some of your aristocratic friends. Like Lord Cromer."

She learned elsewhere that "young Steyne"— he looked far short of his forty years — now exercised active control of the visa desk; the amiable Ed Maney was no longer free to cut corners. Steyne apparently held his authority directly from the ambassador.

Fanny lost no time in bringing him to tea with the lord chamberlain.

The next morning, she went to see Steyne in his office. "Alan, we've got to get the Jews out of Europe." After all, in the last analysis the man was Jewish himself; surely he would help. "You carry a lot of weight here," she went on. "You're practically in charge of the embassy, and of every report that goes back."

Steyne, slim and self-assured, fixed her with a knowing look: "That's quite true, Fanny — but let's be realistic." He picked up a pouch of tobacco and very deliberately filled the bowl of his pipe. Again, the shrewd, calculating glance. "Of course we're aware of the Hitler program. But don't you see, that will only affect the East European Jews. After that, they won't touch anybody. For you and me, it will be clear sailing."

Fanny stared at Steyne, disbelieving. If she understood English — and she had no reason to doubt it — he was prepared to offer up the "kikes" of Europe as sacrificial lambs, for the greater security of gentlemen-Jews like himself.

She exploded, marched upstairs and became hysterical in John Erhardt's office. The consul general was sympathetic but not encouraging. "I'm afraid that's official policy. The only place to get anything done is at the White House."

Fanny couldn't quite accept that. There were other American embassies in Europe where both the need and the possibilities might be greater. She decided to make the rounds herself. To her delight, the two Kennedy boys and Petey Barton agreed to join forces with her in France.

For two days, her team haunted the embassy in Paris, gathering affidavits and expediting clearances. They had strong support from Robert D. Murphy, the nimble-witted embassy counselor. Elizabeth Arden, for whom David Holtzmann had handled some export contracts, telephoned Fanny at the Plaza Athenée: "If you have some refugees who want to stay in France, send them to me. I'll find work for them." Fanny knocked on many doors, and rang telephone bells from Neuilly to Los Angeles. In Washington, Dave Niles protested, "You're driving me nuts!"

"You, against thousands. What matters more?"

From Paris, the rescuers split up, with the Harvard contingent heading for Warsaw and Fanny going on alone to Berlin. She found an enormous queue lined up before the doors of a locked embassy. The American ambassador had been recalled, leaving matters in the hands of his chargé d'affaires, to whom Fanny had a letter from John Erhardt. Harassed and exhausted, the chargé had come to a dead end. He could not issue visas because sponsors in the United States had failed to enclose their income tax returns; mail service between Germany and America by boat was excruciatingly slow, compounding the bureaucratic lethargy at the State Department.

"These people are going to put me in the loony bin," the chargé complained to Fanny. "They never let up, day or night. Wherever I go, I'm hounded by Jews. They're irrational, hysterical."

"So would you be, or I, if we had Hitler breathing down our necks. Is it true that a declaration of war is expected soon?"

"A matter of weeks, maybe days." The time was mid-August. "That's why we have to be careful and not let any of these people out. We have enough complications on our hands already."

"You mean, you're deliberately slamming the embassy doors in their faces?"

"I have no choice."

"But what will happen to them?"

A brief shrug of the shoulders. "What do you expect me to do, Miss Holtzmann — worry about the Jews of the whole Continent? And it *will* be the Continent. Once Hitler gets going — well, it'll just be one of those things."

He is as dispassionate, Fanny thought to herself, as if he were talking about the extermination of a colony of cockroaches.

The next morning, picking up the Paris *Herald* in her hotel lobby, Fanny read that Congressman Hamilton Fish was in London en route to Oslo as chairman of the congressional committee to the Interparliamentary Union Conference, a last-ditch effort to preserve peace. She tracked him down by telephone at Brown's Hotel in Dover Street.

"Ham, you've got to come. Nobody here gives a damn about the refugees. They're being dismissed as 'hysterical Jews.' "

"What are they supposed to do," Fish roared into the telephone, "stand by calmly and wait for Hitler to kill them?" He had personal knowledge of the German plans, having conferred with Nazi officials in Berlin two days earlier: "Their 'solution,' Fanny, is concentration camps, where the entire Jewish population will be wiped out. If there's anything we can do together, I'm with you."

199

He canceled luncheon plans and took the next available plane back to Berlin. Fanny, meanwhile, drew up lists of names and prepared applications for Fish's signature. She also dropped word at the embassy that the powerful congressional leader was on his way. Doors, desks and typewriters flew open.

Fish came straight to Fanny's suite at the Adlon. They needed some technicality, he felt, to put a smooth veneer on his intervention, some rule-book quibble that would satisfy the foreign-service passion for "correct procedures."

A jest of young Jack Kennedy's flashed through Fanny's mind. "Why not," he had asked smilingly amid the throngs at the London embassy, "give them all temporary visas to attend the World's Fair in New York? It's running out of customers."

She repeated the quip to Fish.

"Perfect!" he cried. "We'll apply for three-month transit visas for as many people as can be processed. Curious visitors all, eager to enjoy the wonders of the World's Fair."

The two bustled down to the embassy, where Fish addressed the staff. He wanted a stack of three-month World's Fair tourist visas issued at once: no delays, no questions asked. Miss Holtzmann would provide names and papers; he personally would sponsor the first dozen. The congressman reached over and started signing blank application forms.

Only then did Fanny shift attention to the routine business of getting Jewish capital out of Germany. Several clients with heavy investments in Berlin had requested her help. The chargé directed her to "the most important lawyer around," Dr. Alois Westrick, who later turned out to have top connections at ITT and elsewhere in America. His contacts in Germany were no less imposing, and Fanny quickly found herself with released currency. She used her share of it to finance boat passage, clothing and other amenities for the homeless adrift in Berlin.

As August drew to a close, Fanny telephoned her brother Jack from London to discuss priorities for her next mission. She was deeply concerned about the European relatives, from whom nothing had been heard for months. Jack in turn was worried about Fanny herself. She had taken on a formidable enemy in Joe Kennedy; and a measure just passed in Washington specifically prohibited any "interference" by private persons with diplomatic procedures. War was believed imminent. He counseled caution.

Fanny's next move was not exactly cautious. Fighting was expected to break out momentarily, perhaps at the disputed seaport of Danzig on the northern tip of the Polish Corridor. In London, excursion parties were being formed; for blasé Britons of the sporting class, the event promised livelier excitement than Epsom Downs. Among those chartering yachts was an editor of the *Sunday Chronicle*. He invited Fanny along.

She promptly accepted. A British ship might be the perfect vehicle for whisking Polish cousins out from under the noses of the Nazis. She cabled Tante Frimme to book two first-class train passages and to come, with her unmarried daughter Angela, nearly five hundred miles northwest to Zoppot, a short distance up the Baltic coast from Danzig. Fanny would be arriving at the Casino Hotel there on August 28.

Fanny found Zoppot swarming with visitors: yachtsmen-sightseers from all over Europe and Nazi officers on grimmer business. The men in Fanny's party, including a Board of Trade executive and a naval lieutenant, were soon deep in conversation with uniformed Germans at the hotel bar. Fanny found their mutual bonhomie irritating, but decided it might be useful.

It was. The Germans, including an obviously high-ranking general named Forster, came aboard the yacht. They quickly perceived Fanny's VIP status among these influential Englishmen, and proceeded to treat her accordingly.

As the general bent low over Fanny's hand, she informed him that she was Jewish.

The general's gray eyes betrayed nothing. Reports on that subject, he replied, were greatly exaggerated. Could he be of any service to her here?

It developed that General Forster was a friend of Alois Westrick, the lawyer who had worked with her in Berlin, and was also a considerable movie buff; now he recognized Fanny's name from Hollywood stories in the German press.

As for exit permits for the relatives she was expecting, she must not give it a second thought. He wrote out a telephone number. "Tell my aide, Captain Werner. He will arrange everything."

Fanny was elated. An American visa would not be too difficult. Although there was no U.S. consul in Danzig or nearby Gdynia, the ambassador in Warsaw was her good friend A. J. Drexel Biddle. Tony Biddle, the theater-loving scion of a Philadelphia Main Line family, would do anything short of forging a passport for her.

Her one miscalculation was with the ladies themselves. They arrived on the evening of the twenty-ninth. Fanny took them shopping the next morning, and then to lunch aboard the yacht, where she outlined her plan. They would make the four-hour trip by car that afternoon to Warsaw, where Tony Biddle had been alerted to prepare the necessary documents, and they would return at once to Zoppot, embarking for England the next morning. Biddle, who spoke excellent German, was expecting war in "24 to 48 hours" (he was very close to the actual invasion date of September 1).

Tante Frimme shook her head. A very nice plan, and she appreciated the trouble Fanny had taken — but out of the question.

"You don't understand, Frimme! The Germans are coming. The German army!"

"I understand, I understand — better than you, maybe." She looked down at the deck a moment, then raised her eyes to Fanny. "But what is the *gedilla* [great joy] for me to escape without my husband, my children, my grandchildren? No, Fanny. It is not for us to interfere with the ways of God. What He wishes, He will accomplish. Whatever fate He has in store for the rest of the family, we will share. We could never be happy otherwise."

The young lieutenant, sitting quietly at the end of the table, suddenly joined the conversation. "But Angela is young and — and beautiful!"

The lieutenant begged everybody's pardon. It was really quite un-English, he admitted, but he could not stand by silently and see this lovely creature abandoned to Hitler. He himself would be happy to bring her into England as his wife: "I'll never touch you, mind you — but it's a way for you to be safe, to start your life over among friends . . ."

Angela trembled, the tears rising in her eyes. She had not followed every word, but she had understood enough. This stranger, this *goy* who had not known of her existence twenty-four hours before, was offering her his name. She was too moved to speak.

Finally the words tumbled forth, jagged fragments of thought. A daughter . . . by the side of her mother. A question of faith. The family was one; to break it for the purpose of escaping murder would in itself be a kind of murder.

Fanny emptied her purse and put them on a train to Lemberg: "Buy your way out. When I get back to London, I'll send more."

Fanny went on herself to Warsaw, where she found the by-now familiar mob surging around American diplomatic quarters. Tony Biddle, having been briefed by Ham Fish on the World's Fair visa formula, was following through energetically, and with the American consul general John Ker Davis, was doing a land-office business. Biddle's personal relief at finding a way around the income tax–affidavit requirements was evident: "Hitler is locking up Poland, Fanny. We've got to get them all out, every Jew that we possibly can."

The two Kennedy boys had been up all night assisting Davis; they were leaving as Fanny arrived.

By the time she caught up with them again in London, Poland was crumbling under the German-Russian squeeze. Air alerts were sounding in the British capital. Fanny moved from Kinnerton Studios to shelter-equipped Claridge's and Ambassador Kennedy found it prudent to spend less time at the embassy than in the safety of a country house in Epsom Downs.

Not so Joe Jr. and Jack. In early September they took over all-night duty on the busy visa desk, processing hundreds of applications before the morning office staff arrived. Over the next few days Fanny ran into them repeatedly at the embassy: cool, cheerful figures guiding a Hungarian exile through the mysteries of English, restoring a frightened child to its family.

Nearly twenty-five years later, when Jack Kennedy had reached the White House, Fanny was attending a dinner party in London. The subject came up of the American administration's opening its doors to Chinese refugees in Hong Kong.

Meyer Weisgal of the Weizmann Institute snorted his skepticism. "Where was the American president when millions of Jews needed a refuge from Hitler?" he demanded.

The slur annoyed Fanny — and triggered a memory. "You know all the answers!" she snapped at Weisgal. "What you don't know is that John F. Kennedy as a boy of twenty-two went into Poland on the eve of war to help penniless refugees get to safety! That he risked his life wandering around Europe putting his name on affidavits — and stayed up night after night as a volunteer issuing visas at our embassy here in London! There's nothing inconsistent about Jack Kennedy letting in exiles from Red China. He has *always* cared about *all* refugees!"

Weisgal, for once cowed, fell silent. Later, as Fanny was getting her wrap, an Englishman among the guests approached her. Was it really true what she had said about President Kennedy or had she been laying things on a bit thick?

"It was true, and more. I was there."

The next morning, a headline in the *Sunday Express* blared forth the story. Returning from lunch, Fanny was told there had been a call from the White House.

William Clark, chief of public relations at the embassy, had the explanation. He had been on the wire to Washington earlier in the day and had read the *Express* story to the president: "He was tickled pink, happy as a kid. I told him you were at the Savoy."

Fanny said it would be nice to have a more permanent record of the president's response. No, she didn't want to be photographed with him in Washington — she was a Republican — but a letter of reminiscence would be appreciated.

A few days later Clark called back. JFK was more than willing. She should telephone his office to get together on details next time she was in Washington.

Before Fanny got back to the capital, Jack Kennedy was dead.

The overrunning of Poland was followed by the ominous pause of the "Sitzkrieg" — a time of threat and buildup, but one of limited hostilities. For six weeks Fanny lingered in London, working on refugee missions and conferring with Lord Cromer and other British officials. In late September she crossed the storm-battered North Sea.

In neutral Holland she went to tea with Kaiser Wilhelm, grandfather of her prewar admirer, Prince Frederick. The Kaiser told her of his distress over the Nazi persecution of Jews.

From Holland, Fanny went to Berlin, trusting in her American passport and the protection of Alois Westrick. Chatting at random among visa applicants lined up at the U.S. Consulate, she ran across a slender man with thinning brown hair who identified himself as "Nachtigall," an artist-architect formerly associated with the Bauhaus. His daughters had gained entry into England — humiliatingly — as "domestics"; he could use no such pretext, and he lacked a legitimate sponsor.

Did he know Walter Gropius, founder of the Bauhaus School and now a professor at Harvard?

"But of course. He was my teacher."

Fanny went to the consulate's message center and got a call put through to Gropius in Boston, who agreed to underwrite Nachtigall.

The next morning the artist had disappeared, apparently picked up overnight by the Nazis. Either her telephone conversation had been tapped, or a German employee at the consulate had passed a tip to the Gestapo.

Fanny had other failures in her visa campaign, which at one point took her as far afield as Helsinki. But they were balanced by gratifying successes, among them the rescue of a Gentile school teacher who had befriended the Jewish children in his small German community. Altogether Fanny was involved, directly or indirectly, in the deliverance of hundreds from the Nazi cauldron.

On October 6 she wrote to Louis Bromfield from London: "You are quite right — I *have* been looping-the-loop all over the Continent. . . . Life is full, exciting, and really worthwhile, despite the pessimistic outlook." She was off to a meeting in Whitehall — "mustn't mention names" — but he would be pleased at the news "on how we are going to lick Germany. Because we are!"

Two weeks later, back in the States, Fanny's overriding worry was the European cousins. The Red Army had swept through their villages in early September; nothing had been heard from Tante Frimme or any of her brood since the meeting in Zoppot.

On October 25, Fanny launched a discreet letter into the void. "Are you all safe? We are happy that you are under the Russian government regime as everybody in America has great admiration for Russia." Five hundred dollars had been dispatched to a mutual relative in Moscow, to be converted into Russian currency and delivered to Frimme's husband, Rabbi Mikhail Goldfeld. Had they received it? A monthly check would be sent as soon as Frimme confirmed an address.

Silence, a silence that persisted for two years. In late 1941 a torn, grimy letter arrived at Fanny's office. Months in transit, written in a shaky Yiddish scrawl, it was from an eyewitness to the Goldfeld family's ending.

As the Red Army pulled back before the great German offensive in the summer of 1941, the towns of Galicia were left helpless in the path of the advancing Nazi troops. In Koslow, rampaging soldiers set out to destroy everything Jewish they could get their hands on. Rabbi Goldfeld, as the spiritual leader of his community, had been seized and, together with his family and his flock, thrown into his synagogue, which was then put to the torch. They died clinging together, with the classic *"Shema, Yisrael"* ("Hear, O Israel") on their lips.

Nothing ever hurt Fanny so deeply. As the rescue of many innocents was her greatest triumph, so the perishing of Tante Frimme's family was her greatest sorrow.

Chapter 9

*F*ANNY RETURNED TO AMERICA firmly persuaded of carrying a vital war-time mission. In late September she was lunching with the lord chamberlain, Cromer, and his wife at the International Sporting Club in Upper Grosvenor Street when Churchill shuffled over to their table. He had met Fanny several years before over tea at the House of Commons. "You should be at home," he told her, waving a fat cigar. "Home, helping to mobilize public opinion against Hitler!" Churchill's pro-Jewish sympathies were well known; his actress daughter Sarah was married to Vic Oliver, an Anglo-Jewish vaudeville star. "Here," he emphasized, "you're just another female for us to worry about!"

Cromer agreed. The war would last from five to seven years, he thought, exhausting every resource of the democracies. Fanny's contacts in government and the communications media at home would be invaluable.

The theme was reiterated to her by Prime Minister Neville Chamberlain when, a few days before sailing, she was invited to lunch with the cabinet at No. 10 Downing Street. She found the prime minister, in contrast to the ebullient Churchill, "a dried-up rod of an Englishman — all Empire, no compassion."

Upon her return to the States, Fanny was free to pursue her mission of building Anglo-American accord — largely because of the broader role assumed at the Bar Building office by her brother David. David ran day-to-day operations with a sure hand, while maintaining close relations with their key clients.

Being Holtzmanns, of course the two quarreled, mostly over Fanny's selectivity in clients and causes. David argued that by enlarging their office staff, they would no longer have to turn away lucrative cases. Fanny countered that, since every client was entitled to the services of Holtzmann and Holtzmann, and she spent so much time away from New York, too great a burden would fall on David. There were also other, less serious strains growing out of differences in temperament.

Fanny's mind was never idle, and her talk reflected its perpetual motion — sometimes with minimal regard for the impact on others: Lilian Birkan, a newly arrived secretary, was shocked to hear herself described in a loud whisper as "obviously a small-town mentality" who would "have to go" at once (she stayed for years, finally retiring to become a lifelong Holtzmann-worshipper).

Fanny's habit of chatting with total strangers kept David constantly unnerved, fearful that especially on a slow cross-country train ride she would sooner or later drop some casual bombshell. (He was later to hail air travel as "the greatest thing that ever happened to the office: how much ear-bending can Fanny do in a mere few hours?")

From Fanny's side, the main source of friction was something not directly related to work: David's reputation as the "soft touch" of the Bar Building. Fellow tenants in financial trouble, tipped off to David's penchant for inventing "emergency" assignments, would waylay him in the corridor outside Suite 914. Every time he asked one of the secretaries for a passkey to the men's room, Fanny would moan, "How much is this trip down the hall going to cost us?"

But David provided an indispensable complement to Fanny's effervescent style. He tempered her more fanciful flights and skillfully developed her improvisations.

Fanny's first liaison effort upon her return was on behalf of the newly arrived British ambassador, Lord Lothian. At the request of Cromer and the foreign secretary, Lord Halifax, Fanny undertook to brief Lothian on the American media and present him quietly to leading opinion-molders. She dispatched messages to a number of trusted friends in publishing, broadcasting and films, including Eddie Goulding, who had worked under Lothian in World War I.

As a result, the ambassador was invited for a weekend at the Sands Point estate of Herbert Bayard Swope, then executive editor of the New York *World-Telegram*, where he met Alexander Woollcott, Frank Scully and a score of other major columnists and communication executives.

Lothian's successor, Lord Halifax himself, was not so amenable to Yankee guidance. Although Fanny flooded him with suggestions for improving the British image in America, Halifax adamantly went his own way, gathering hostile press notices as a fox-hunting snob.

More responsive than Halifax was John Foster, first secretary at the British Embassy, a former lecturer in law at Oxford. Huge and convivial, with an attractive masculine awkwardness, Foster was by Fanny's description "the only British diplomat whose heterosexuality I never heard questioned."

When Fanny pointed out that war charity organizations were tumbling over each other competitively, Foster moved quickly to untangle the snarl. He tossed into her lap the question of extending to British forces the entertainment passes available to American servicemen: "I know you are very good at moving mountains, of red tape or otherwise." Fanny promptly had the necessary legislation introduced and pushed through the House by Ham Fish, who could not be accused of pro-British bias.

As Foster put it years afterward, Fanny was "unique, of an intellect much more general than that of a mere lawyer." The fact that she was a woman made no difference "except that she was tolerated to speak at greater length and without the introduction of any full stops or periods, for up to one hour without drawing breath (her own at least)."

Relatively easy for Fanny, but vital to her English friends, was the recruitment of Hollywood support. Traveling to the West Coast, she went first to Louis B. Mayer and asked him to act as bellwether in lining up the movie colony. Mayer had the biggest roster of British stars; and, sentiment aside, MGM had millions of pounds frozen in England. The studio responded by scheduling such Union Jack epics as *Mrs. Miniver,* and offering to help cast as well as distribute anti-Nazi documentaries.

With Mayer behind her, Fanny went to Jack Warner.

"When it comes to backing the democracies," intoned Warner, "I'll match Louis Mayer or anybody else." Fanny went back to New York with full pledges of assistance.

But these were pale victories. It was almost too simple to cajole producers, send Gertrude Lawrence whirling around the country in a storm of benefit rallies, find vacant storefronts for the British-American Ambulance Corps. Fanny yearned for a big challenge, something she could sink her teeth into.

In the summer of 1940 she got it.

Amid the oaks of suburban Chertsey, twenty miles south of London, stood the British Actors Orphanage, sheltering the homeless offspring of theatrical pairings, regular and otherwise. In the summer of 1940, with the Nazi blitz of the British capital reaching its crest, the orphanage lay directly athwart the path of Göring's bombers.

Cries arose in the West End for removal of the youngsters, aged five to seventeen, to sanctuary in America. Although the seas were infested with German submarines, at least a boat would present a moving target. English actors in Hollywood were asked to take responsibility for bringing the children across the Atlantic and looking after them till the end of the war.

The British movie colony, under fire in London newspapers as "deserters" (actually they had been instructed to stay put and promote goodwill), hastily agreed. Its leaders — Cary Grant, Sir Cedric Hardwicke, Basil Rathbone and Brian Aherne — organized a committee under Dame

May Whitty; every star would be asked to guarantee the support of at least one refugee child.

From London, the president of the Actors Orphanage was dispatched to expedite arrangements. By an ironic quirk of casting, the president was Noel Coward — who was childless, unmarried, and inclined to regard children as strange, vaguely terrifying animals.

Coward traveled to Washington, where the State Department brought him up short. As "institutional children," his wards were not eligible for individual entry permits; nor could they be quartered in private Hollywood homes.

The playwright-composer, so glib onstage or in the drawing room, was not equipped to cope with this wartime morass of overworked clerks and overlapping agencies. Near panic, he turned to Gertrude Lawrence, herself a vice-president and director of the orphanage.

Gertrude allowed herself briefly to enjoy Coward's discomfiture. "Sixty children?" she teased. "There aren't enough normal males in the West End to account for that number." Then she told Noel to put the whole thing in Fanny's hands.

He did — and things began to happen.

State Department officials agreed that the Republic would not be toppled by the use of simplified affidavit forms. The children could set out for a Canadian port as soon as space was available, and final details could be worked out with the U.S. consul general in Montreal, who would arrange their admission across the American border fifty miles to the south. Meanwhile, formalities would be channeled through the efficient United States Committee for the Care of European Children.

There was still an enormous job to do in rounding up affidavits and supporting documents, as well as operating funds. Many who were quick to sign pledges showed less alacrity in signing checks. Fanny rode herd on the Broadway crowd, while Dame May kept after the impulsive promisers in Hollywood. Correspondence flew back and forth: about "the Chaplin check" (for nearly $4,000), the new affidavit by Douglas Fairbanks, Jr., a copy of Edmund Gwenn's statement-of-earnings, an $800 check from Alan Mowbray collected in "the Gertrude Lawrence drive."

Dame May reported to Fanny on her adventures in trying to find a suitable place in Hollywood to house the children. She was being plagued by the "local ladies" of various welfare organizations, who insisted on setting up rigid living conditions for the newcomers: "Ye Gods, these welfare women!" But money was coming in and enthusiasm was picking up; she had raised $20,000 of the estimated $35,000 needed for the first year of operation, and had sent a check for $3,347 to the Committee for the Care of European Children, to pay the fees involved in bringing over fifty-four children. "I hope I have covered everything," she concluded. "The one thing I cannot cover adequately is our enormous sense of gratitude to you."

Fanny relayed the good word to John Foster, commenting: "What a lot of suppressed parental love exists in the film colony. There is a greater danger of the children being smothered by love than by bombs."

Early in September, a harrowing story broke in the New York *Times*. The waters around Britain had been alive with U-boats, which with deadly impartiality were sinking warships, tankers and merchant shipping. Now it was revealed that on August 30 the Canada-bound *Volendam* of the Holland-American Line, carrying three hundred child evacuees among its six hundred passengers, had been torpedoed off the English coast. By a miracle of advance planning and good luck, only one life, that of the purser, was lost. The children were plucked from open lifeboats in banana slings, or climbed up warship ladders. Yet, as the *Times* editorialized, "a sickening tragedy was barely averted."

Agitation swept Hollywood. Fanny's telephone rang incessantly: should the dangerous transfer be abandoned? On tour in the Middle West, Gertrude Lawrence soberly weighed the issues: "I personally am in full sympathy with both sides," she wrote Fanny. "It would be dreadful if we did persuade the children to sail and they were attacked or mined — their chances of escape from harm might be greater in England than at sea."

The New York *Times* pointed out conversely that in July alone, forty English children had been bombing victims; surely their chances were better in convoys, which had already brought more than twenty-six hundred across without loss.

The actors weren't so convinced. Nor was the British government. Four days later it was announced that the evacuation of children had been suspended indefinitely.

Fanny, buttressed by Noel Coward, went to the U.S. Committee for Refugee Children. The inmates of the orphanage, she argued, were a special case: parentless by circumstance, helpless by geography. Coward concentrated his vaunted charm and earnest concern on Elsa Castendyke, director of the committee. That evening Fanny wired him the results:

"Dear Noel: She came, she saw, you conquered. The very first thing the dear girl said was, 'How very understanding, how human he is.' So you win, pick up the marbles." Fanny cabled word of the arrangements to London, with the postscript, "Praying hard we are doing the right thing." The children must be guarded, she warned Noel, "against being publicized in any way in Hollywood. They could so easily be turned into copy, a process which has been known to ruin normal American kids."

On September 14, Fanny relayed word to Dame May that the "tour starts today." But nothing was to be said to anyone until the children were well on their way: "A leak may cause all kinds of trouble and postpone us again."

By this time an impressive roster of sponsors' affidavits had been assembled. Among the American signers, joining their friend Errol Flynn, were Fredric March and Robert Montgomery. Cary Grant undertook to support two youngsters, as did Alfred Hitchcock, Brian Aherne, Mary Pickford, her son Douglas Fairbanks, Jr., and Charles Chaplin. The heartiest backing came from Alexander Korda, who forwarded a triple affidavit along with a single pledge from his wife, Merle Oberon.

With twenty-seven affidavits in hand, all but eleven of the fifty-four incoming children were covered. Fanny advised Dame May: "To overcome the technical obstacles, I am furnishing my own affidavits for many of the children whose sponsors have failed to sign, and am getting Lynn [Fontanne] and Alfred Lunt for the others."

The orphans sailed on schedule from a northern port, but the cliff-hanger was far from over. Seventy-two hours after their departure, a German torpedo slammed into a passenger vessel during a violent storm six hundred miles off the British coast. Word trickled out that ninety children had been aboard, of whom all but a handful were lost.

It was six terrible days before the wrecked vessel was identified as the *City of Benares*, which had departed from the same port as the orphans, but a few hours earlier.

Meanwhile a new worry was developing in Hollywood. After an intensive survey of housing facilities, Dame May had settled on the Urban Military Academy. A bargain fee of $50 per month per child had been fixed; but this, Fanny and Elsa Castendyke noted from New York, did not include health care, clothing or books, which would swell the budget to nearly $50,000. And that kind of money simply was not coming in.

Equally disturbing to Fanny was the dubious outlook in Hollywood for the welfare of the children. Uprooted from a sleepy English suburb, they would suddenly be set down in a plush and artificial environment among well-meaning but not necessarily stable people notorious for living beyond their means. If the orphans became an economic burden, everybody would suffer. Accommodations in the East, on the other hand . . .

Fanny had learned to drive in California, if only in self-defense, and she kept a small car in the East in addition to the luxury model for her parents. She got behind the wheel and took off for the suburbs. She had looked at a waterfront mansion in Rye, the Harry Frank Guggenheim estate in Sands Point, and a girls' school farther out on Long Island, when one of Elsa Castendyke's assistants suggested the Gould Home for Children in the Bronx. Fanny searched out Pelham Parkway on a road map, and headed north again.

What she found was quite incredible: a children's paradise of intimate cottages, playgrounds and tennis courts, an admirable supervisory staff — and virtually no tenants! Spread over several secluded acres just north of the Bronx Zoo, the home had been created by the millionaire Edwin Gould as a memorial to a son who had died very young. It was dedicated to the support of children in distress throughout the world, and especially to the victims of social crises.

The home might have been designed for the refugees of the Actors Orphanage. It had a sparkling modern infirmary, a swimming pool, classrooms, even a separate cottage for toddlers, with mini-scaled tables and toilet seats. The cost for all this, including summer-camp vacations, was only eight dollars a week per child. At the moment, the home was being used as a transit facility for children from overseas, but its administration, the Gould Foundation, was quite willing to consider a long-term arrangement for the British Actors contingent.

The question was, would the actors go along? Fanny knew that for all of their hesitancies, the Hollywood crew with their flair for self-dramatization had begun to relish the role of child-saviors.

Noel Coward was the key. If she could win him over, the Charles Laughtons and Boris Karloffs would not resist.

Noel's first reaction was decidedly negative. He had been sent from England to assist his California colleagues, not to snatch responsibility from their hands. However, confronted with the economic facts, he agreed reluctantly to take a look at the Gould Home as a possible stop-gap enabling further exploration.

The auto trip up did nothing to improve his disposition. Chattering away about her plans, Fanny took the wrong turn on the Triboro Bridge, and landed in Queens. She wheeled merrily in and out of traffic, driving, as Noel later recounted it, "with only an *occasional* glance at the road. That trip to the Bronx was definitely the most dangerous leg of my overseas journey."

At Noel's insistence —"to preserve what was left of my nerves"— they stopped at a roadside hot-dog stand.

"Whaddaya want, bud?" demanded the counterman.

"Why, ah, we should like to have two frankfurters well done . . . with just a touch of mustard on the roll, please."

"*Two wit'*," bawled the man briskly to his cook.

What Noel found at the Gould Home, Fanny reported to Dame May Whitty, was something "so unexpected, so delightful, so ideal in every way that he immediately said, 'Perfect.' It was as though, after all our troubled days and nights, Aladdin's lamp had been rubbed and the problem solved."

Dame May took Fanny's eight-page letter to Laurence Olivier, who had voluntarily replaced the defecting secretary of the Hollywood committee. "Larry was immensely impressed and grateful"; he and Dame May, with the approval of their executive board, had dispatched to Fanny the $2,000 check necessary to nail down the agreement with the home.

As Brian Aherne recalled it in his memoirs, the link-up with the Gould

Foundation had magical overtones: "We never quite knew how this miracle came about, but we thanked God, Gould, Gertrude [Lawrence] and Fanny."

Soon after disposing of the British orphans, Fanny found herself running a virtual soup kitchen — Park Avenue style — for their elders. English visitors were streaming through New York; with Kinnerton Studios still a vivid memory, Fanny's home was a natural base. In New York, however, she had to circumvent parental feuding.

Henry and Theresa were nearing the end of the trail: Henry still gallant and unworldly, Theresa more than ever the prima donna. They wrangled over everything. Hospitalized in 1938 with a heart attack, Henry insisted on young, pretty nurses — and Theresa resented it.

"Why shouldn't I be free of Mama's tongue by this time?" Henry sighed. "After fifty years, even a slave is rewarded with liberty."

In the fall of 1940, when Fanny gave a party for Lady Grosvenor, an aunt of the queen, she consigned Henry and Theresa to her sister Stella's house for the evening. They came home early anyway ("Mama says she's dying," reported Stella, "and must have her bed"), and promptly took command. Theresa traded wisecracks with Dorothy Parker, while Henry regaled Alec Woollcott and the Fred Astaires with the wisdom of Spinoza. When he turned to Tallulah Bankhead, twirling his moustache engagingly, Theresa stalked off in a rage.

By the end of the year, she was a widow. The era of "Jenkie" began.

Mrs. Jenkins — nobody ever heard her first name — was slim and saucy, a white-haired woman of Dresden-doll elegance. She had a birdlike alertness and a great capacity for vicarious adventure; Fanny's household, with its changeable troupe of theater stars, famous authors and famished nobility, was her idea of heaven.

The wife of one of the elevator men in Fanny's apartment house, Jenkie had hired out for baby-sitting and other odd jobs since the Depression. She did a bit of cooking, hustled forgotten papers down to Fanny's office, would look after a stray grandchild. Far from regarding herself as a servant, Jenkie tended to boss Fanny around. Publicly, she was "Mrs. Henry Holtzmann's companion."

Jenkie had exacting standards, as Fanny and Adele Astaire were amused to discover. Adele, widowed in 1944 by the death of Lord Cavendish, remained mistress of his ancestral Lismore Castle — where, as it happened, Jenkie's mother had once supervised the linens.

When Adele came to dinner on Sixty-fourth Street directly from entertaining Allied troops in Europe, she was still imbued with the salty language of the barracks. As she recounted her adventures — uncensored — Jenkie served in frosty silence.

The atmosphere was tense until Fanny whispered a few words of explanation to her guest. With professional aplomb (and muffled laughter), Adele assumed at once the role and accents of a proper Lady Cavendish. Jenkie consented to be mollified.

Not, however, before she had indicated her displeasure at Adele's even momentary lapse from the demands of rank.

By contrast, another star had Jenkie's fanatic approval. From the moment Gertrude Lawrence appeared in the doorway — cool, mischievous, enchanting — Jenkie idolized her. The Lawrence gestures in *Susan and God* became part of Jenkie's repertoire. She wore Gertrude's cast-off gloves; and when Gertrude, who had remarried in the summer of 1940, battled with her husband over a new hat, Jenkie retrieved the discarded headpiece. One evening Gertrude came to dinner in a tailored black suit and white tie; Jenkie tracked down a similar outfit in a Third Avenue charity store and came in wearing it two days later.

Moved by such fidelity, Gertrude yearned to have Jenkie on her payroll. She tried it for a day and was cured. Jenkie's cavalier approach to housekeeping offended Gertrude's sense of meticulousness. But the actress regarded Jenkie as infallible "litmus paper" for trying out new theater material, thereby confirming Jenkie's own lofty view of her aesthetic judgment. (Years later, rebuked for retouching the figures in one of Fanny's paintings, she expostulated, "But I did you a favor, they looked wrong!").

Jenkie's true realm was the kitchen. Every afternoon at two she would check with Fanny by telephone, employing the theater jargon of her beloved G.L.: "What kind of house are we having tonight? Heavy bookings? A benefit crowd again?" The "benefit" referred to the many English visitors struggling to feed themselves in New York in the face of currency restrictions.

To appease ration-whetted appetites without going overboard on budget, Fanny and Jenkie concocted wartime specialties. Staples of their fare were canned soups, stuffed cabbage and similar delicatessen products from Jenkie's neighborhood on the West Side, adroitly doctored and blended. The star item was Rokeach's barley-and-mushroom soup, strained, slightly sweetened with cream, and garnished with a sprinkling of chives. Served by candlelight, with splendid silver and china, it pleased palates accustomed to the *haute cuisine* of the Riviera.

Syrie Maugham, former wife of the acerbic author, pronounced the dish "divine." Could Jenkie possibly be persuaded to part with the recipe?

"Never. Not for ten thousand dollars."

But, Jenkie relented, she would be glad to whip up a fresh batch tomorrow and send it to Syrie's pregnant daughter, Liza, at their Park Avenue hotel. To Fanny, Jenkie whispered, "I'll slaughter another can."

Syrie was Fanny's steadiest customer — and not only because she liked the menu at East Sixty-fourth Street. Syrie, herself an internationally known decorator, was in bad financial straits, growing out of a long and bitter matrimonial battle with her husband.

The trouble began more than a decade before, when she first brought suit against "Willie," and had the bad taste (in the eyes of their cosmopolitan set) to name his gentleman friend–secretary as corespondent. The author of "Rain," *Of Human Bondage, The Moon and Sixpence* and *The Razor's Edge* never forgave her.

Since the divorce their daughter Liza had been the focus of Syrie's happiness — and fears. A tall, blue-eyed blond beauty, in contrast to her physically unprepossessing parents, she had been given over to Syrie's custody under the terms of a settlement in the late 1920's. But plump, gentle Syrie lived in terror that her husband would reopen the custody issue. Well aware of Maugham's vindictive ways, Syrie was careful whom she saw and what she said: anything might be seized upon as an excuse for challenging her fitness as a mother.

Yet she never criticized Willie to Liza. As she explained to Fanny, "I wanted her to love and admire her father, to feel secure about him." During her trips to America, she always left Liza with Willie: "It wouldn't be right to deprive her of that contact."

In 1933, at eighteen, Liza met Vincent Rudolph Paravicini, the personable son of the Swiss Minister to the Court of St. James's. Their marriage three years later was the prime affair of the London season, and filled a whole issue of *The Tatler*.

Before the ceremony, Liza's parents engaged for once in a civil discussion. Willie had been paying Syrie £2,400 (about $12,000) annually. She agreed to a reduction of that figure to £2,000 in consideration of cash payments and an annuity from Willie to Liza.

Syrie went further. "I think we should march down the aisle together, Willie. For Liza's sake. She's entitled to that, even if it's just an act. And — I don't care how much you hate me — I want you to behave affectionately."

According to Syrie, Maugham performed like a trouper in one of his West End successes: "It was the first time since our courtship that I ever knew Willie to be so wonderfully thoughtful toward me. And the sweetness he displayed to our child! I found myself positively in danger of falling in love with him again!"

That danger was soon enough dissipated. Early in the war, after the fall of France, Maugham left the villa he had occupied for fourteen years at Cap-Ferrat. Returning to England, he informed Syrie that he intended to stay there for the duration. Since this meant suspension of his heavy overseas earnings, would she be a good sport and temporarily reduce her stipend to £1,500?

Soft-hearted Syrie, perhaps still bemused by the memory of Liza's wedding, agreed. A few months later Maugham was on a freighter bound for New York, where the Bank of England authorized him to collect $250 a week in publishing royalties from Doubleday. He took up comfortable residence at the old Ritz on Madison Avenue.

Syrie arrived in America as a refugee soon after, with her daughter and her grandson Nicholas — but no income. Liza's husband was at war; she was expecting a second child. The trio moved into a kitchen-less hotel room, while Syrie tried to pry loose some dollars from the British Exchange Control authorities. She was entitled to some $666 a month from Willie if they would let her substitute Doubleday royalties for frozen sterling.

But the British Treasury declined to involve itself in domestic squabbles, and Willie showed no inclination whatever to intervene: "Government regulations, my dear. What can one do?"

In despair, Syrie asked Fanny to bring court action. Months dragged by. Meanwhile Syrie and her brood survived through Fanny's soup kitchen, long weekends among friends at Tuxedo and Westbury, and the personal generosity of Nelson Doubleday, who extended repeated loans.

Finally, with the publisher's patience wearing thin and Maugham hiding implacably behind legalisms, Fanny decided to confront the monster herself. She had sipped tea with him a few times in the early thirties on the Riviera, and had disagreeable memories of the experience. Although part of the sprightly Noel Coward–Cecil Beaton clique, Maugham was not one of its personable charmers. "A cold, withdrawn man," she told her brother David, "absolutely without lift or sparkle. Brilliant on the written page, but deadly in company. You have to struggle to extract a word from him — and then it's usually malicious. He seems consumed with hatred."

Warily, she picked up the telephone. "Willie? It's Fanny Holtzmann. I —"

"You're talking to the wrong party, Fanny. My lawyer is Mr. Black."

"I'm quite aware of that, Willie. But it's you I want to see."

Icy silence. "What about?"

"It concerns personal matters."

"I have nothing to say about Syrie."

"I'm not speaking as Syrie's lawyer — but as Liza's friend."

"Well . . . come have a cup of tea tomorrow."

She found Maugham playing solitaire at a table, his features craggy and impenetrable. More than ever, with the wrinkles creeping up his neck, he resembled an ancient turtle. He looked up sourly, a venomous glint in his eye. "*La belle dame* of the courtrooms. Did you b-b-bring your Blackstone?"

Fanny ignored the jibe. She knew that Maugham was ill at ease with people — the stutter was a giveaway of the torment beneath his calm. She knew also that Liza was important to him, "a boutonniere in his lapel," one of his few sources of pride. There was no point in bandying sarcasms.

"I'm here because I care about your daughter, Willie — and I have reason to believe you do, too. This isn't just a case at law for me. It concerns the happiness of a young girl who is my friend. Whatever you and Syrie have between you is not my business; you've settled it, in your own way. But the two of you are partners, and will always be partners, in the matter of the child you both love."

Quickly, Fanny sketched Liza's situation: physically frail, thousands of miles from her adored husband, with one infant clamoring for attention and another on the way. "During the week, *my cook* is the only one who stands between Liza and outright hunger. We keep a special section in our pantry, with strained foods, marked 'Liza's shelf.' Jenkie prepares dishes and takes them over herself to make sure they don't spoil. Do you think that's right, Willie? Is that the way you want things for your daughter?"

Maugham's lips clamped into a thin red line. He seemed in pain, but unable to speak.

"I don't want to go into details with you, Willie. Mr. Black and I can work those things out. All I want is your understanding."

Maugham's nostrils quivered. At long last he managed a nod: "Very well. You s-s-s-see Black."

A few days later, when arrangements had been completed for relieving the situation of Maugham's womenfolk, Fanny received an autographed book from the famous author. It was apparently as close as he could come to an expression of gratitude.

Although Fanny played no role in the later adventures of the Maughams — Liza's divorce and remarriage, Willie's wild attempt to challenge his daughter's paternity — she had succeeded in extracting a human gesture from one of the unhappiest, most encapsulated of men.

Other sons and daughters of the British Empire unloaded their problems at the Bar Building. John Foster faced an unusual embarrassment in the person of one Prince Bishnu, a British protégé whose family ruled over a strategically important Himalayan sovereignty. Bishnu was careening around the New York entertainment district with an entourage of expensive blondes, at a time when Americans were being urged to empty their pockets for British war relief.

The prince arrived at Fanny's office trailed by four long-limbed goddesses. On the pretext of shielding his amours from "jealous" journalists, Fanny persuaded the royal rake to retire with his playmates to a secluded estate at Oyster Bay, Long Island.

But Fanny's star client — in every sense — was Gertrude Lawrence. Lawyer and client were an extraordinary pair, linked by vitality, humor and a kind of mutual envy. To Fanny, as to half the males of the English-speaking world, Gertrude Lawrence was the epitome of alluring sophistication. As Fanny's new secretary, Lilian Birkan, observed, "Gertrude was the Fanny that Fanny herself never felt she could be; not only gathering the gallants of several continents at her feet — Fanny had managed that herself, in a modest way — but poised, self-assured, *knowing exactly what to do with them*."

Gertrude, in turn, was awed by Fanny's law degree, her negotiating finesse, her prestige in London's most august circles. Who but Fanny could chat on equal terms with Supreme Court justices, Hollywood pashas and diademed royalty? Who but Fanny could elicit paeans of thanksgiving from the acid-tongued Noel Coward?

It was Noel who had first brought the ladies together, so that Fanny might rescue his comrade of dancing-school days from bankruptcy or worse. A woman of staggering charm, talent and compassion, Gertrude had one failing that threatened to override them all: she spent money like a fleet of drunken sailors. Usually it was money she didn't have, tossed recklessly after clothes and jewels that she quickly discarded.

By 1929, although a leading star of English musical comedy, Gertrude faced enormous unpaid taxes both at home and in the United States. Behind that was a harrowing record of buying sprees, bill collectors and frantic auction sales, climaxed recently by eviction from her apartment in the West End of London. Her fans had wanted to stage a benefit for her, but Noel felt that something less humiliating and more enduring was in order.

To Fanny, it was obvious that Gertrude needed total control, à la early Goulding; she could not be permitted small purchases any more than an alcoholic could be permitted a small drink. However, first she had to be kept out of jail.

The tax men were agreeable, once Fanny outlined a plan for deferred payments. Hattie Carnegie, to whom Gertrude owed $100,000, took more persuading. But one by one, from Beverly Drive to the rue de Rivoli, creditors were staved off, and in the early thirties Gertrude sailed blithely into *Private Lives* with dear Noel.

All was well, till the play ended its international run in New York. Now Gertrude had time on her hands and Cartier pounding on her door.

The dean of Fanny's British clients, Charles Cochran, was likewise "at liberty" and chafing for action. Fanny learned that Cochran was sitting on a script called *Nymph Errant*, adapted by Romney Brent from the novel by James Laver. The chronicle of an English girl's wide-eyed wanderings through the seduction parlors of more exotic lands, it was, Fanny thought, a perfect showcase for Gertrude's varied talents.

Fanny took a ship to England. Would Noel kindly cook up a score for *Nymph Errant*, to round out the production?

No, he would not. He had something in mind for himself and Gertrude (it emerged ultimately as *Tonight at 8:30*), but plays could not be created at the push of a button, and he saw no point in writing music for someone else's libretto.

Thumbing through the Paris *Herald*, Fanny noticed that Cole Porter was in the French capital. She knew Porter socially through Clifton Webb and as a composer who had strengthened the career of another client, Fred Astaire, with his songs for *The Gay Divorce*.

She went to Paris and put it to him directly: "I don't like lawyers or bankers to pass judgment on creative matters. But in this instance I have to speak up for my client. Great talents like Gertrude's deserve the very best — and to me that means Cole Porter."

Porter read the libretto overnight and was at work the next morning. For several months Cockie relayed his bulletins to Fanny. He was having the time of his life with this score, and had never written better.

At Manchester, the tryout audience heartily agreed. Haunting Porter ballads like "It's Bad for Me" were balanced by the racy, nimble wit of "The Physician." A West End smash was assured. Fanny spun breathlessly from London to Hollywood, urging a combined film-theater package on *Nymph Errant* with the Broadway production financed by a major studio; the film, she pointed out, could be shot on location in various countries by using frozen funds.

But the film project collapsed when Cole Porter joined Fanny in insisting that Gertrude be retained as the star. As a result, Porter's magnificent score never crossed the Atlantic. But Fanny had the satisfaction of knowing she had helped bring it into being — and in the process, kept the enchanting G.L. in funds as well as out of mischief.

Fortunately, Noel was now ready with *Tonight at 8:30*. Afterward, Fanny shepherded Gertrude through the contractual intricacies of *Susan and God* and *Skylark*.

Over the course of the decade, Fanny became increasingly involved with the star's roller-coaster emotionality. Gertrude and her eighteen-year-old daughter, Pamela Gordon-Howley, had all the problems predictable between a hard-working divorced actress and a child reared in the best Swiss boarding schools. When Pam suddenly announced her engagement to an India-based officer, Fanny wrote to her client, who was vacationing in Bermuda: "It seems to me life turned a bit of a trick on you. Heretofore so much of your life outside your work must have revolved around your child, planning your holidays together months in advance . . . and now just when you two could share so much together, Fate steps in and she is headed for another road.

"Oh dear, I do wish the right man would turn up and fill your own life. You have reached the top rung of the ladder professionally — now give the private life of Gertrude Lawrence a chance. Your life has been no bed of roses, and while you are still young and beautiful and the most envied woman in the world, I hope the new season holds more than professional glory for you."

In the late 1920's, at her father's urging, Fanny had been helpful in getting a Broadway hearing for a play written by the young drama coach at the Brooklyn Jewish Center. The play turned out to be *Once in a Lifetime*; the drama coach, Moss Hart. Now, after a decade of spectacular collaboration with George S. Kaufmann (*You Can't Take It*

with You, The Man Who Came to Dinner), Hart had written an unconventional musical of psychoanalysis, *Lady in the Dark*. Only Gertrude,
he declared, could capture its wide-ranging fantasies.

Hart came to Fanny's apartment on East Sixty-fourth Street with
his composer, the diminutive German refugee Kurt Weill. Fanny hated
auditions —"I'm usually bored to death"— but she liked Weill's gentle,
modest air and his respectful references to her refugee work in Berlin.
The shy, bald little man sat down at the piano and ran through the songs
—"like most composers, he had no voice"— while Hart acted out the
plot: "brilliantly, especially as the leading lady, Liza."

For once, Fanny was impressed: not with the show as a Pulitzer
Prize contender — a matter of minor interest to her — but as a vehicle
for Gertrude. "That's what a star is always looking for. And this story
gave her a chance to do everything, from broad comedy to throbbing
drama." Fanny read the script in bed that night and phoned Gertrude in
the morning: "This one is for you, Gee."

There was, however, an obstacle, in fact, six feet four inches of obstacle. Richard Aldrich, the blue-blooded theatrical producer, was in
gentlemanly pursuit of Gertrude, who could hardly wait for him to
catch up; and Richard didn't think much of Moss Hart's project.

"Broadway gimmickry," he insisted. "Gertrude shouldn't be wasting
her time on such stuff. She has developed far beyond the music hall, into
a fine dramatic actress capable of playing Shaw or the classics." Besides, Aldrich warned, Gertrude's voice was the least of her theatrical
assets, and the Weill score had some tricky pyrotechnics. If it was a
question of playing a spirited lady, he intimated, Lady Macbeth would
be more suitable.

Richard's opinion was not to be swept aside lightly. The lanky New
Englander was enormously eligible, and, as Theresa observed, it was
"no disgrace to be related to the Chase National Bank."

Fanny struggled to reconcile conflicting goals: "I wanted nothing
more than to see Gertrude settled in a loving marriage; yet, this show
would be good for her." So she repeatedly postponed giving Moss Hart a
definite answer, hoping meanwhile to soften Richard's opposition.

Every time Hart thought his commitment from Gertrude was firmly
set, Fanny popped up from the woodwork with another excuse. "I had
to preserve that part for Gertrude, and vice versa — but I was having
a hard time getting her to override Richard's judgment."

From Hart's viewpoint, Fanny's delaying tactics of course appeared
very different, not to say maddening. A year later, just before *Lady in
the Dark*'s rhapsodic reception at the Music Box, the playwright unburdened himself in the Sunday drama section of the New York *Times*.

His article, filling the center of the front page, recounted at length
how Gertrude, after swooning over his opening scenes, had invoked first
the counsel of her astrologer, and then the approval of Noel Coward, to
whom Hart had been obliged to read his entire script.

Would Gertrude now kindly sign? But of course not! She never made a move without her lawyer.

"The next day," Hart reported, "Fanny Holtzmann came into my life. In the following weeks and months all of the life I had lived before, I could only dimly recall. I could only remember that at four o'clock I must see Fanny Holtzmann and be sure to have enough sleeping pills by my bedside that night.

"It is a sore temptation to set down here a life-size portrait of Fanny Holtzmann, but for one thing Fanny is a little larger than life, and for that reason quite unbelievable, and for another, I shall probably do a play about Fanny some day and I do not like to waste ammunition. Suffice it to say that Fanny is a small, delicate, mouselike creature given to wearing floppy hats in the Spring and creating a first impression of wistful helplessness. Helpless, indeed! Fanny is about as helpless as the Bethelem Steel Company and as delicate as 'Jack the Ripper.' "

According to Hart, Fanny listened to his show and liked it. At a meeting with Hart, Kurt Weill and the lyricist Ira Gershwin, she declared that terms would be worked out by the weekend. Then she began negotiations. " 'Carried on' is what they were, amid Fanny's various other activities — such as bringing over boatloads of child refugees, running the war for England and constant calls to the British Embassy. I would leave after a two-hour session, limp and bedraggled, only to be called to the telephone fifteen minutes later, no matter where I was, for at least a forty-five-minute conversation. Fanny is a telephone girl and how the British Embassy ever stood up under it I still have no idea."

After a few days, Fanny's demands were satisfied: her client was to receive "The Music Box Theatre, Sam Harris's house in Palm Beach, my farm, half of Metro-Goldwyn-Mayer, a couple of racehorses and five thousand dollars a week." The contract was drawn up.

The next morning, Fanny telephoned to report a slight delay: Gertrude had gone off to Cape Cod for a week of summer stock.

Hart tried to strangle the telephone receiver. Fanny had better go up to Massachusetts over the weekend, he screamed, and come back with a signed contract by Monday, or the whole deal was off. Meanwhile he told his agent to look for a replacement in Hollywood.

On Monday there was a bulletin, but not the one he was looking for. Gertrude had been married the night before to Richard Aldrich. "I suppose," Hart noted sourly, "it was utterly beyond her to sign two contracts at once."

The next two days were a blur of luncheon meetings, forgotten initialings, overlooked clauses and mad scrambles to Gertrude's dressing room where she was preparing to go on tour in *Skylark*. As Hart was collapsing in a sodden heap, the contract arrived from Fanny, "beautifully signed . . . just as she had always told me it would be if only I had a little patience."

Fanny shed no tears for the playwright. By delivering the star he needed, she had ensured Hart's triumph. More importantly, her tightrope act had snared a wedding ring for Gertrude (in a typical bravura climax, Fanny had persuaded the Commonwealth of Massachusetts to waive documentary formalities on the grounds that Richard and Gertrude had a "constitutional right to the pursuit of happiness").

Gertrude's play ran for two years; her marriage, movingly recounted in Richard Aldrich's *Gertrude Lawrence as Mrs. A,* lasted till the end of her life.

Not, it must be added, without an assist or two from Fanny. As the blitz on England grew more severe, Gertrude chafed increasingly at being on the safe side of the Atlantic. A near-orphan, she looked upon George V as her father: "I must go home, Fanny. They need me."

Gertrude and Richard were just beginning to get used to each other. If she raced off to one end of the world while the U.S. Navy was shipping him off to another, their untested marital ties would never stand the strain. As Fanny saw it, "Dick would lose a wife, Gertrude an indispensable husband, and Holtzmann and Holtzmann, incidentally, a valued client."

There was plenty to do on behalf of the British cause in America, and Fanny made sure Gertrude did it. Between performances, Gertrude was literally all over the map, doing benefits for the Red Cross and the Stage Door Canteen, selling emblems for British War Relief, serving as hostess at blood-bank rallies and bond drives. In Washington, she dissolved Ham Fish's suspicions about the arming of merchant ships; in Minnesota, she handed out plant production awards.

After Pearl Harbor, she and Fanny established an American branch of ENSA (Entertainments National Service Association), the British equivalent of the USO, with Gertrude as president and Fanny as counsel. To conserve Gertrude's energies, Fanny devised tie-ins with major women's stores for the display of Gertrude Lawrence Fashions, all royalties from which would be channeled to British War Relief. A similar arrangement with Columbia Gramophone enabled Gertrude, in exchange for an advertising photo, to provide army camps with thousands of disks and record players.

Fanny and Gertrude worked closely together, reviewing each day's schedule in long morning telephone calls, sharing the dreary waits at airports. Once, en route south, they saw Ernest Hemingway being interviewed in the lounge. Gertrude, never averse to meeting an interesting male, asked David Holtzmann to round up some Hemingway titles from the airport bookstalls.

David hurried back with three books, but Gertrude waved him away. She had already been chatting with "Mr. Virility," and found him exceedingly dull: "As far as I'm concerned, he saves it all for the inkwell."

At the end of 1941, Fanny was in Los Angeles on war business. *Lady in the Dark,* an indisputable smash, had been sold to Paramount for filming, but not yet cast. Although Gertrude was the obvious choice, Hollywood was wary of her unorthodox profile and un-American accent. There were some cautious offers to the British star relayed through agents — if Gertrude would submit to the usual screen tests.

From Arrowhead Springs, Fanny set down her reaction in no uncertain terms: "I plead, pray, beg, urge, implore you NEVER to submit to a test here or anywhere. Tests are what the word connotes — for others; you are YOU — GERTRUDE LAWRENCE, first lady of the Drama — a Goddess! To submit to a test means that you go into competition in a Hollywood projection room, or the drawing-room of any fat-bellied producer after he has been well fed at dinner.

"These uninformed producers compare you with some Mary Glutz who has no acting ability but whose sweater appeal stands out because she is seventeen years of age . . ."

Fanny cited a test unreeled for after-dinner amusement at a producer's home, where she watched Gertrude and Noel Coward do a scene from *Private Lives* "without benefit of proper lighting" or other accommodations to film.

"And what did the ignoramuses say? 'Oh, how different they look on the screen!' Not a word about the great performances." Fanny was determined not to compromise her star's status for mere money; her patience was rewarded years later in Gertrude's stunning film performance as the mother in Tennessee Williams' *The Glass Menagerie*.

Meanwhile, Fanny's impatience with the Hollywood value-structure was running over: "It is now New Year's Eve. How they can drink and make merrie downstairs when most of the world is soaked in bloodshed, you and I do not know. Hollywood people are strange. The news broadcasts, when I put them on, seem to annoy them."

Gertrude not only listened to the news; she made it. In the spring of 1944, with Richard on war duty in England, she flew across to embark on a bug-ridden, sleepless tour of RAF bases and fleet units there, then went into Normandy on an LST behind the infantry. She continued on under shellfire to Brussels and Antwerp until sent back in October with dysentery. Six months later she was off to camps and hospitals in the Pacific.

In between these military hops, Gertrude tried out a new play and started on her autobiography, *A Star Danced*. She also spent money; so much of it that in May of 1945 Fanny was constrained to write her a twenty-five page letter dwelling on her past extravagance and future prospects.

Gertrude, with her penchant for incorporating into her personality fragments of every part she played, was once described by Fanny as "a woman who wears six hats." Fanny, in her roles of counselor, companion, inspiration and sometime reproving mother to her less disciplined clients, wore one or two hats herself.

A prime concern of Fanny's British friends at the outbreak of war had been the support of America's labor unions, vital to the production of armaments. In 1939, Fanny didn't know any labor leaders. By 1942 she was on a first-name basis with Philip Murray of the CIO, had won important concessions from William Green of the AFL, and was engaged in heated argument with John L. Lewis, head of the United Mine Workers.

The breakthrough into labor came via a chain of contacts starting with Frank Scully. One of Frank's admirers was the reformist priest Father Flanagan, founder of Boys Town in Omaha. When the son of a prominent Nebraskan ran into serious disciplinary trouble in the army, Flanagan appealed to Frank for help; the health of the boy's mother's was being imperiled. Frank referred the matter to Fanny, who on her own recognizance obtained a parole for the boy.

Father Flanagan was deeply grateful. Was there anything he could do for Fanny, perhaps in Washington where his friends included J. Edgar Hoover and Philip Murray?

Fanny told him to stop right there. She'd like a private chat with the CIO president. A few days later she was in Murray's office near the Mayflower Hotel.

Murray was rugged and direct, a devout Catholic; he got along at once with Fanny. He had worked for her friend Sir Alfred Yarrow in the shipyards of his native Scotland and had succeeded to the presidency of the CIO in 1940, when John L. Lewis fell under Nazi influence.

The two key issues worrying the British were strikes and the resistance to overtime, which was rooted in AFL-CIO jurisdictional disputes. Both Murray and James B. Carey, the slender, youthful secretary of the CIO, were against work stoppages and other muscle-flexing by unions: "We should be sharing like all other civilians the sacrifices of the men at the front," Carey declared.

The most effective way of spreading the word to stay on the job, Murray suggested, would be through Father Flanagan and his network of contacts in the Catholic Church. Pulpits should be informally advised to remind workingmen that a Fascist victory would destroy labor along with God and Church.

Jurisdictional quarrels posed a thornier problem. As long as the two big labor bodies bickered over rights of representation in overlapping areas, it would be impossible to institute any comprehensive program for extra shifts and accelerated production. Murray was gloomy about getting cooperation out of "that crazy Baptist" Bill Green: "He's limited, narrow-minded; he sees only local interests." Jim Carey thought that instead of approaching Green through Father Flanagan, a "Protestant detour" might create a more favorable climate. Fanny enlisted Louis B. Nichols, a ranking official of the FBI, as her intermediary.

Green came to lunch suspicious, defensive. He was not isolationist or anti-British, he insisted; his only concern was the welfare of the United States.

"Fine," Fanny nodded. "But what if England falls? What's to stop the Fascists from hooking up with the Communists and overrunning us here? You and Phil Murray had better stop your squabbling, or Hitler won't leave you anything to squabble about!"

Green wouldn't commit himself right away; but he did accept an invitation to a British Embassy reception, where he was treated with ceremonial respect. Soon after, the AFL leader agreed to bury the hatchet.

The capitulation by Green, Fanny discovered, carried no weight with John L. Lewis. "He's a megalomaniac," Phil Murray had told her. After visiting Lewis in the UMW office, where he delivered a nonstop tirade against the British, Fanny saw no reason to dispute the judgment. She left after a few minutes: "Discussion is a waste of time when you're up against a dictator mentality."

As proof of his open-mindedness and sense of fair play, Lewis later circulated a story on Capitol Hill to the effect that Fanny, "the CIO's lawyer," was a member of the Communist Party. Confronted by Fanny on the canard, Lewis waved his "evidence"— a newspaper clipping. It turned out to be about a quite different person of faintly similar name.

Word of the smear by Lewis had come from a Holtzmann admirer on the other side of the economic fence: the 1940 Republican presidential candidate, Wendell Willkie. From big labor, Fanny had turned her attention to big capital, many of whose leaders she felt were holding out for exorbitant wartime profits. Willkie had been brought to her home for drinks by Bruce Barton. Husky, tousle-haired, mildly flirtatious until Fanny signaled that he was on the wrong track, he lingered to become a receptive conduit for her ideas.

Over a year of "Dear Wendell"–"Dear Fanny" exchanges, she urged Willkie to crack down publicly on "industrial saboteurs" who "stage their own sitdown strike by simply not accepting the government's terms on war orders." Such profiteering was unconscionable: "We are asking millions of young men to give up their lives for $21 a month. Is it too much to ask everyone in the United States to live on a limit of $25,000 a year while our boys are prepared to die for $252 a year?"

Fanny's Union Square rhetoric was perfectly compatible with her family's Theodore Roosevelt Republicanism. Besides, party labels counted for less with her than personal values. In fact, her politics were so much of the heart that in the fevered climate of wartime she was able, under special circumstances, both to win freedom for an alleged German spy and to rejoice at the death of a fellow-Jew.

Alan Steyne, the Joe Kennedy disciple in London who regarded Polish Jews as expendable, had, so far as Fanny knew, been swallowed up in the elephantine machinery of the State Department. Shortly after the collapse of Japan, she was in Washington on business. The fighting had ended, but the tribulations of its survivors had not. Europe was bulging with refugees, most of them Jewish, bottled up in dismal camps. Fanny was bending every effort to spring them loose toward Palestine or the United States.

On her perennial hunt for visas, she was in the basement of the State Department building when she noticed Steyne's name on a door. From his title — Special Assistant to the Director, Office of the Foreign Service — he was in a position to be helpful. On impulse, she knocked and went in.

Steyne was at his desk, sucking at an empty pipe. He greeted Fanny cordially; he had always been impressed by her contacts in Downing Street.

Fanny came straight to the point. Wasn't there something they could do together to ease the refugee situation: cut through the red tape, speed up the cumbersome processes of bureaucracy?

Steyne smiled tolerantly. "Sometimes bureaucracy serves its purpose, Fanny. The hasty action isn't necessarily the best."

"What do you mean?"

He took a leather pouch from his jacket and slowly tamped some tobacco — Fanny remembered the gesture from London — into the bowl of his pipe. "The Jews have been an abscess on the body politic for centuries. Giving them a homeland won't solve anything. And we certainly don't need more of them in America. Perhaps, you know, Hitler in his way has done us a favor. Why interfere with history? Let nature take its course."

A band of crimson flashed before Fanny's eyes, and with it an inspiration. "I'll let nature take its course, all right," she screamed. "Through Walter Winchell! I'm going to feed him the truth about your un-American, inhuman behavior: how you turned your back on the helpless refugees in London, how you couldn't wait for Hitler to get rid of those terrible 'undesirables,' the Jews of Eastern Europe! Tune in this weekend, Alan, and you'll hear the whole disgusting story!"

She imitated Winchell's shrill staccato: " 'Good evening, Mr. and Mrs. America and all the ships at sea . . . we have at a key desk in the US State Department the biggest rat this side of Berlin . . .' He'll spread your record around the world. You'll be despised, hounded." Hysterical, Fanny slammed the door shut behind her.

Of course, she did not intend to go to Winchell. That, as it turned out, didn't matter.

In Steyne's mind, the vivid broadcast was apparently as real as if the gingery columnist had spewed it out to the universe at his famous 227 words a minute. The next morning Fanny picked up her *Herald Tribune* to read that Alan Nathaniel Steyne had shot himself fatally in the basement of the Metropolitan Club, where he lived.

At the other end of the emotional scale from Steyne was Karl Voll-moeller: feeble, aging and a citizen of Hitler's Reich. World-renowned twenty years earlier as the author of the gigantic pantomime *The Mira-cle*, Vollmoeller had been arrested in California in 1942 as an enemy alien and was languishing in an Oklahoma internment camp. His ac-cusers claimed he was a dangerous spy who had worked for German Intelligence in World War I. His defenders — and they included Max Reinhardt, Father Flanagan, Eddie Goulding and the German stage beauty Eleonora Mendelssohn — insisted he was an apolitical poet who had befriended countless Jewish victims of the Nazis, and who faced certain death unless released for proper medical attention.

Reinhardt, the Austrian-born master of theater spectacle, brought the case to Fanny. He told her that Vollmoeller had the warm backing of Secretary of War Henry Stimson and Stimson's law partner, Bronson Winthrop; both had been classmates of the German author at Heidelberg.

"Then why come to me — knowing how I feel about the Nazis?"

"Because Stimson's hands are tied by virtue of his position. Two appli-cations for parole have already been turned down. Everybody feels you're the only one who can get a reversal."

Fanny paused. She knew from Alois Westrick, the Berlin attorney, that Stimson's connections in prewar Germany had been extensive. "All right," she told Reinhardt. "I'm a lawyer. If Winthrop and Stimson are really behind this man, let them come to me."

The following week, Bronson Winthrop walked into her office. Tall and straight, with a thick crown of white hair, he looked far younger than his seventy-odd years. Winthrop painted an ingratiating picture of old college acquaintance ripening into lifelong friendships. Vollmoeller, he declared, was the mildest and most sensitive of men; Secretary Stimson had been deeply distressed when duty obliged him to sign the papers of incarceration.

"Could I talk with the Secretary myself?"

Winthrop put in a call to Washington. Everything he had said was confirmed by Stimson, who added that Vollmoeller was in "really desper-ate shape" physically: bad lungs, weak heart, failing kidneys. "If you can help, Miss Holtzmann, the Lord will bless you."

Fanny put down the phone, one thought gnawing at her mind. From his friends' descriptions, Karl Vollmoeller might have been her own father: sweet, unworldly, a frail elderly poet (Henry, too, wrote verses in German) adrift in an uncaring world. If Henry Holtzmann had been an American writer traveling in Germany at the outbreak of war, would not he too have been interned?

"I'll see what I can do," she told Winthrop. She set one condition: she would not be acting on her own. "This has to be a retainer from your law firm."

"Of course. We can't appear as attorneys of record. But retaining you is what I came up here for."

Fanny had to move fast: according to Stimson, oxygen tents were keeping Vollmoeller alive. First, his claims to artistic status had to be substantiated. She found that *The Miracle*, his 700-actor pantomime depicting the wondrous salvation of an errant medieval nun, had received eighteen separate stagings in Europe, the first by Max Reinhardt in Vienna in 1911. A dozen years later, Morris Gest had transformed the Century on Broadway into a vast Gothic cathedral for what the critic George Jean Nathan pronounced "the biggest and most beautiful thing the walls of an American theater ever housed."

Afterward, Vollmoeller was credited with the screenplays of *The Blue Angel*, which started the Marlene Dietrich vogue in the United States, and *The Shanghai Gesture*. Clearly, the German was an established professional.

No less legitimate, according to his supporters in America, were his credentials as a humanitarian. Testimonials were submitted to Fanny from California, Oregon, New York and Washington, D.C. They detailed a consistent record of philanthropism, friendliness toward England and America, and opposition to Hitler; one gave an eyewitness account of how Vollmoeller had, on the point of death in the internment camp at Stringtown, Oklahoma, rebuffed a Nazi delegation offering repatriation.

A statement from Vollmoeller himself stressed that as a man of independent means, with homes in Austria, Switzerland and Italy, he had sheltered artists of every nationality. Over the years his guests had included Charlie Chaplin, Marie Dressler, Thornton Wilder, Sinclair Lewis and Mary Pickford. He sat out World War I in Switzerland rather than "fight against people who had been kind to me."

In the Nazi era, his affidavit affirmed, his homes became "havens for artists and intellectuals fleeing the blight of Hitler. . . . I hated every Nazi for the misery inflicted on my friends, and for plunging the land of my birth into such disgrace." After helping others obtain visas for freedom, Vollmoeller made his own departure to the United States and applied for citizenship papers in California in 1938.

His sudden arrest, he suspected, was based on his frequent visits to the German consul in Los Angeles — all made, he insisted, on behalf of Jewish friends with relatives stranded in Europe.

Since then he had been suffering in heatless barracks and makeshift tents. Repeatedly warned that he had only a day or two to live, he clung to one "burning" ambition: "not to die under a cloud in an internment camp and be martyrized by the Nazis whom I so despise."

Fanny wove the material on her desk into a powerful forty-page petition. The petition led to a rehearing; the rehearing, to a reversal of the two previous negative rulings. Karl Vollmoeller was free.

The day he was due to arrive in New York, Bronson Winthrop came to Fanny's office. He took out his checkbook. "Henry said to fill this out for any amount you ask. We appreciate what you've done — and that nobody else could have done it."

Fanny toyed with the silver inkwell on her desk. "Under the rules of the Bar Association, I am to give you a referral fee of one-third."

"Oh, we waive that."

"I will take," Fanny insisted, "two-thirds of what you're going to get."

"But we aren't being paid, Miss Holtzmann!"

"I know that. You got into this case to do a good deed — what we call a *mitzva*. I want two-thirds of the good deed you've done."

Winthrop stared a moment, and bowed his head. "It's been a great honor," he said, "to meet a great lady."

That Christmas, Vollmoeller brought to East Sixty-fourth Street a copy of his famous pageant, inscribed "in sincere admiration" to Fanny Holtzmann — "who sometimes makes miracles."

But the story was not over. Vollmoeller was sitting in Fanny's living room a few weeks afterward when Syrie Maugham dropped by. The Englishwoman turned abruptly and without a word departed.

Fanny followed her into the hall.

"*That man is a spy*," Syrie whispered. "I can't go into details." She would say nothing more.

Two years later, after the war ended, Fanny was at Claridge's in London for preparatory sessions of the United Nations. With England still suffering severe consumer shortages, her well-stocked diplomatic suite was a magnet for ration-weary Londoners. Among her visitors on a cold rainy Sunday was Charles Cochran, the impresario. Lolling back before a roaring fire, a good roast beef dinner in his belly and a glass of brandy in his hand, Cochran reflected on the late hostilities.

"You Americans did a superb job — except in one area. Your intelligence services. Really quite stupid."

"Why do you say that?"

"Well, one case in particular comes to mind. It upset us very much over here, but we had to sit tight; apparently some powerful people were involved. Chap named Karl Vollmoeller, a writer. He had excellent connections in theater and business circles, and was using well-meaning friends like Max Reinhardt for a cover."

"A cover for what?"

"Well, my dear, Vollmoeller was notorious as a German spy in World War I. We had a dossier on him. Naturally, we tipped off the Americans in the late thirties. And don't you think the idiots let him in?"

Fanny felt a chill that had nothing to do with the clammy breeze outside. "How do you know so much about it, Cockie?"

Cochran sipped at his brandy. "I'll tell you exactly how. In 1920 I went to Austria to see Vollmoeller's pantomime, *The Miracle*. I brought it back to Hammersmith, where we played to thirty thousand people a day. Vollmoeller came to England, and I gave him a big reception. All my authors were there, including Willie Maugham.

"Well, Willie and Karl fell on each other like long-lost brothers. It seems they had been in Switzerland together during the First World War at a tuberculosis sanitarium in Davos, near Zurich. Both were ostensibly writing plays, having been rejected for bad lungs by their respective armies.

"Later, Willie told us what was really going on. Vollmoeller had been filing secret intelligence reports in code. Willie was assigned by the War Office, on the pretext of suffering his old chest trouble, to stay in Davos and keep an eye on him."

It was almost too plausible: Willie Maugham and Karl Vollmoeller, each slight, shy, the antithesis of the swashbuckling cloak-and-dagger hero, and hence the ideal undercover agent.

On the other hand, might not the two playwrights have been whipping up a colorful scenario to enliven a formal evening?

Who was right about Vollmoeller: Cockie or Max Reinhardt? Intermittently over the next twenty years, until one by one the principals in the case died off, Fanny pursued the question with friends in the State Department and the British War Office. Always the trail ended in mystery.

If Vollmoeller had indeed profited from the fallibility of a Holtzmann hunch, he would not be the last to do so. Adrian R. was a geologist and hydrologist, married to one of the most prominent young society women in New York. Fanny met the couple at the home of a wealthy publisher and was charmed.

A blond Adonis with beautiful children, a doctorate from Witwatersrand University in South Africa, and a fine family background — his mother was dean of a college in California — Adrian had everything, except ready capital. However, that seemed a passing detail. He had roved the globe as a consulting engineer, and was aglow with intriguing projects: new crops for Africa, irrigation schemes for the Middle East, a chemical invention that would revolutionize the packaging of scientific instruments. He even had inside connections with that classic of lures — a gold mine — in Ecuador.

Fanny, caught up in his enthusiasm, placed her wide-ranging contacts at his disposal. Before long she was dipping into her pocketbook: Adrian had "forgotten his cash," or "left a taxi-man waiting"; one day he was "momentarily strapped" for the rent on his large East Side apartment. Ignoring David's scowls, Fanny wrote out a check to stave off eviction.

As proof of good faith, Adrian turned over to Fanny his packaging patent. Soon he was borrowing also from Clara, signing over to her 17,000 shares of a Philippine marble-cutting company as security.

Several years later, when his patent had proved worthless and numerous loans remained unpaid, the Holtzmanns made claim to the stock. They discovered that Adrian had reported his 17,000-share certificate as "lost" and been issued a new one; their claim could not be honored.

Fanny conceded she had been taken, but insisted on looking at the bright side: "I really learned a lot about agriculture and water problems from Adrian." The tutoring cost her about $10,000 in cash.

Halfway through World War II, King George of Greece turned up again on Fanny's doorstep. With his country under Nazi occupation, he had been brought to America for public-relations purposes by his British protectors. Shuttling from fund-raising luncheons to political rallies, he was more than ever hemmed in by security guards, advisers and the entanglements of protocol.

Through his aide Colonel Levidis, now elevated to grand marshal of the court, George telephoned Fanny at home (Theresa, informed that "the king" wished to speak with her daughter, inquired loftily, "*Which* king?" before she would put Fanny on the line).

George told Fanny he was well but drowning in mushroom soup and oratory. He sighed feelingly for the good old Kinnerton Studios days in London. If only he could unwind for an evening again at one of her casual supper parties. But of course she could hardly be expected, in the middle of a war —

"Why not? There are plenty of people around. Even a king is entitled to some fun."

"Out of the question," interposed Colonel Levidis on the extension phone. His Majesty could not be exposed to a roomful of strangers, where a single shot from a hidden pistol could change the course of European history.

"We'll clear the guest list with the Secret Service in Washington," countered Fanny. "And post guards at every door."

What began as a whimsical impulse developed into a major outing for the king and a full-scale security project for his sponsors.

George, eager to display his democratic approachability, went to De Pinna with Mrs. Douglas Fairbanks, Jr., and for the first time in his life bought a suit "off the peg." The sleeves dangled to his knuckles, but he was much too pleased to notice.

Meanwhile squadrons of beefy young men descended on Fanny's apartment, scrutinizing doors, windows and the pedigrees of the domestic staff. Carefully they diagrammed potential lines-of-fire from neighboring rooftops. A few hours before the party, demolition experts combed through every closet. One let out a bark of triumph: his "bomb" discovery proved to be Zaida's leather phylacteries.

The guest list, naturally, was subject to equally cautious review; Henry Charles Spruks, chief protocol officer at the State Department, did everything but X-ray it.

This complicated an already touchy situation. Everybody wanted to meet the king. Even leftist authors and isolationist politicians were willing temporarily to put principle aside, just this once.

Fanny submitted her names alphabetically, leading off with Lieutenant Richard S. Aldrich (Gertrude was out of town) and the novelist Michael Arlen, who had wheedled his invitation through Eddie Goulding. Others from the entertainment world included Constance Moore, then the reigning beauty of Broadway, Clifton Webb, Moss Hart, the Ray Bolgers and the youthful Danny Kayes. Syrie Maugham survived the final cut, as did Wendell Willkie and the William Rhinelander Stewarts.

In deference to His Majesty's yearning for a relaxed evening, all of Fanny's guests were requested to dress informally. Nobody, of course, complied. Invitations to tête-à-tête with royalty were not commonplace in New York. Dinner jackets mingled with dress uniforms everywhere, and society figures like Mrs. Stewart came in glittering like chandeliers.

The result was that King George in his De Pinna lounge suit wandered through the elegant throng aimlessly, a worried-looking medium-sized man with thinning black hair, looking like someone who had strayed off the elevator on the wrong floor. People stared past him or elbowed him aside, whispering, "Which one is the king?"

Louis Bromfield and Eddie Goulding, who had brought the king uptown from his hotel, were not much help. Both had fortified themselves heavily with bourbon before taking on the royal assignment.

When Fanny came to the rescue of her guest of honor, there was a flurry of excitement. Several of the ladies lined up for formal presentation to His Majesty. Much to George's discomfiture, they insisted on delivering well-rehearsed curtsies.

Fanny's mother was not part of the admiring line. Eyeing George from the doorway, she commented with her usual acrid directness: "Where does he come to Fanny? A small man with a little moustache, losing his hair . . . If he wasn't a king, he would be maybe a headwaiter in a Brooklyn restaurant."

Things took a still less promising turn with the arrival of Spyros Skouras. King George had not been enthusiastic about having Skouras at the party, but he recognized that Fanny could hardly pass over a man who was simultaneously the overlord of Twentieth Century–Fox and head of Greek War Relief in the United States.

As Skouras came through the door, bulky and bald, the king nudged Fanny's elbow: "Look at that boor — a white tie, no less!"

"Shh! You may want a job from him soon."

"I never know what he's talking about. He speaks to me partly in English and partly in Greek — and I can't understand him in either."

As if on cue, Skouras approached, voicing a hearty greeting in what Fanny assumed to be Greek. The king frowned, screwing up his eyes in puzzlement.

From the punchbowl nearby, a tall blond young man spoke up with a modified version of Skouras's phrase.

King George brightened. "Ah yes," he nodded. "That is the correct expression."

Skouras wheeled on the man at the punchbowl. "*I* was born in Greece, Danny. Where did you learn that?"

"I suppose," offered the king, "Mr. Kaye came to modern Greek via classical studies at the university."

"Not quite, Your Majesty," the comedian said with a grin. "I learned my Greek from a soda jerker in the Brownsville candy store where I used to hang out as a kid."

That broke the ice. Five minutes later Danny's pert and gifted wife, composer-lyricist Sylvia Fine, was at the piano and he was racing through her specialty song "Tschaikowsky," a tongue-twisting breathtaking potpourri using the name of every Russian composer who ever put an eighth note to paper. As a nightly feature of *Lady in the Dark*, the song was second in audience appeal only to Gertrude Lawrence's "Jenny."

Danny had been known to gallop through "Tschaikowsky" onstage in forty seconds. Now, pausing to repeat the chorus, he handed a stopwatch to the king: "Time it."

According to Leonard Lyons, who led off his New York *Post* column the next day with a long account of the party, Kaye was inspired — possibly by the royal collaboration — to a new record of thirty-six seconds.

Later Johnny Green, of "Body and Soul" renown, took over the keyboard, and Peggy Wood sang a *Bitter Sweet* medley starting with "I'll See You Again." King George, sitting beside Constance Moore, was in raptures; this was a far cry from the solemnities of his official role.

A final flutter of uneasiness came at midnight, once again precipitated by Skouras. The film magnate, accustomed to early-morning conferences, started for the door without waiting for the king's departure; by European standards, this was a gross offense to His Majesty. Fanny suggested that to save face all around, King George take Mary Lee Fairbanks home — and then come back to the intimacy of a smaller group.

He did, and the late-stayers cavorted with mounting hilarity until six in the morning, by which time, as Fanny reported in a letter to Frank Scully, various impromptu exchanges had "thawed out whatever was left of dignity."

King George was sufficiently revived by his evening off to endure several more months of speech-making; and sufficiently grateful to stay in touch with Fanny regularly until his death in 1947.

The little king was succeeded on Fanny's wartime horizon by the Little Flower. Fiorello La Guardia, as lively a tenant in his own way as Jimmy Walker, had been in occupancy at City Hall since 1934. Early in the war Fanny had needed his cooperation on a school project for British War Relief. She had had no trouble obtaining it.

Half-Jewish and totally earthy, La Guardia delighted in displaying his command of Yiddish. "It's a *fargehneegen* [pleasure] to chat with you," he told Fanny. "You know, I had an Italian father and a Yiddishe mama. My parents made only one mistake. To produce the perfect mayor of New York, they should also have stopped off in Ireland so I could be born there."

One night in 1943, the mayor dropped in at Fanny's home with Newbold Morris, the president of the City Council. La Guardia, squat and rumpled, found amusement in lobbing Yiddish colloquialisms over the austere dome of Morris, who fancied himself a connoisseur of New York argots.

The mayor leaned toward Fanny: "Our *shlemiel* here"— he indicated Morris —"wants to have a city theater, Fanny."

Fanny looked at the council president, who was beaming: "You know what a *shlemiel* is, Newbold?"

"Oh yes. It means a bright fellow."

"*Very* bright," amended Fanny. "Really exceptional."

La Guardia burst out laughing. One of his favorite themes was the difference between a *shlemiel* and a *shlimazl*: "A *shlemiel* spills hot soup on the boss's best customer; a *shlimazl* manages also to burn himself." He wagged his heavy head at Fanny: "You're really a *momzer* [bastard]."

"That," Fanny informed Morris, "is a special term of flattery."

At City Hall on business at the end of the year, Fanny ran into the mayor in the corridor. "My *shlimazl* is stagestruck worse than ever," La Guardia told her. "*Weisz nicht sein kopf von sein tochus* [doesn't know his head from his behind]. Maybe you can get him a job as an usher? He has a new project: the city is stuck with a foreclosed piece of property on Fifty-fifth Street. Go to lunch with him, he eats at the best places; let him bore you with the story."

Over madrilène and shad roe, Morris explained that the ornate Mecca Temple auditorium, a huge house with an ample stage, had fallen into the city's hands by tax default. His plan was to present top-quality plays and musicals, under municipal auspices, at popular prices. So far, unhappily, the town's moneymen had scoffed at the notion as a kind of "postcollegiate amateur night." Wouldn't it be nice, he suggested, if Gertrude Lawrence could open his New York City Center for Music and Drama?

It might be not only nice but practical, Fanny responded — if he would assign all receipts to British War Relief. With Morris's eager agreement, Fanny obtained permission from Rachel Crothers for a special two-week showing of her *Susan and God*. Gertrude, awaiting transfer overseas by ENSA, was happy to oblige in the starring role.

Since the Mecca Temple needed repairs, rehearsals were begun in a hotel ballroom. The night before opening, a run-through on stage was ordered — and it became evident why the auditorium had been abandoned by its owners. Acoustics were so poor that dialogue was inaudible beyond the first three rows; onstage, echoes bounced so hard that the actors could not hear each other.

Fanny remembered an AT & T sound engineer, a Mr. Wolfe, she had met on a boat crossing to France. With Gertrude at her side, she telephoned Wolfe's office the next morning. He was out of town, but ten minutes later a call came back from Dr. Oliver Buckley, president of Bell Laboratories. Playing a hunch, Fanny put Gertrude on the line.

The cool, enchanting Lawrence contralto worked its magic; Fanny could almost see Buckley wilting at his desk. Although Bell Telephone was forbidden by the War Production Board to sell electronic equipment, he agreed that there was nothing in the regulations to stop him from *lending* materials to Miss Lawrence. She could in turn lend them to the city . . .

By lunchtime, the first survey team was at Mecca Temple. They were followed by a stream of cable-layers and microphone specialists bringing the latest equipment. In twenty-four hours, they advised Fanny, well in time for the next day's matinée, everything would be installed and ready.

But the opening, widely advertised and heavily subscribed, was for that night!

The engineers shook their heads. Unless — unless those stony echoing walls could somehow be padded over. With quilts, blankets?

"We'll borrow them," said Gertrude firmly. "The show must go on."

Fanny agreed: "The very idea of a dark house makes me furious!"

From Gertrude's maid, Fanny's friends, the mayor's guest room, bedding of every description was assembled. The padding was covered over with dark draperies provided by John Golden and Lee Shubert.

As the curtain went up that night on an opening performance that might or might not be intelligible, La Guardia, sitting next to Fanny, grumbled of Morris and his crew: "*A shlock zoll zay treffen* [a blow should strike them]."

His fears proved groundless. The production went like a dream, foreshadowing the creation two decades later of the magnificent Lincoln Center theater complex. The mayor was hailed as a pioneer of civic culture.

The next morning, identical bouquets from City Hall arrived at Gertrude's and Fanny's homes. Gertrude's flowers were addressed "To my Commissioner of Sound"; Fanny's, "To my Commissioner of Fury."

When La Guardia, ailing, stepped down in 1945, an ex-policeman named William O'Dwyer decided to make a second try for the mayor's job. O'Dwyer was a political natural: bluff, square-jawed, self-made, with a strong prewar record as district attorney of Brooklyn and important army service capped by a brigadier general's star. But as the Democratic nominee he wasn't so sure of his edge over his Republican-Liberal-Fusion rival, Judge Jonah Goldstein, and La Guardia's *shlimazl,* the maverick Newbold Morris.

A couple of weeks before the election, with the newspapers predicting an O'Dwyer landslide, Fanny was sitting at a booth in the "21" restaurant with Eddie Goulding when a heavy-set gray-haired man slid in beside her. He introduced himself as Eddie Rosen, a friend of the Holtzmanns from Brooklyn days, and insisted that good citizenship as well as self-interest obliged her to join the O'Dwyer camp. She was noncommittal.

Some days later, with Goulding back in Hollywood, Fanny's telephone rang. It was Rosen, reporting that Bill O'Dwyer wanted to have a private word with her. Would lunch at "21" be convenient?

"No — but if he'd like to come around to my house for a drink, I'll be home on Sunday."

"Okay. Bill is anxious to meet some of your friends. He's convinced you could bring in heads of government if you wanted to."

But prime ministers were not what O'Dwyer had in mind. He called himself a day later, to say he understood Fanny's delicate position vis-à-vis her Republican contacts, but did she know any of the top people in the mass media?

"A few. Bill Paley, Dave Sarnoff. . . ."

"Oh God! The two major networks! If I could meet Sarnoff . . ."

Fanny called the NBC chief, explaining that she was getting a small group together to meet the man who would probably be the next mayor of New York. Sarnoff said his wife Lisette was away, but he would come with his press aide, Roy Norr.

The candidate arrived early, stood around chatting with the media men for an hour, then disappeared into the kitchen to share a cold-meat dinner with Fanny and Gertrude Lawrence before going on to a speaking date.

Afterward, Fanny talked to O'Dwyer by telephone several times, but she did not see him again until the day of his victory, when with Adele Astaire and Gertrude she drove down to City Hall for a champagne celebration and much picture-taking. Her few exchanges with him, however, established a rapport that would profoundly affect the headquarters location of the future United Nations.

One side of Fanny's life remained untouched. Marriage had come to many in her circle, including her star client and her eldest niece, but Fanny, increasingly shy of entanglements, was taking refuge behind a façade of indifference. The occasional bold spirit who persisted was told she was "too busy running the war."

And yet the hunger remained. Hearing from friends in Hollywood that Louis Bromfield had promoted the romance between Lauren Bacall and Humphrey Bogart, who were married at Louis' Malabar Farm, she wired the novelist in May of 1945: "Dear Cupid Bromfield: When will you do the same thing for Fanny Holtzmann?"

Chapter 10

S o far, fanny's exploits had been limited — she had no reputation east of Suez. But in the spring of 1945 the oldest and most populous country on earth became a client of 914 Bar Building. The Chinese delegation to the founding sessions of the United Nations, held in San Francisco, included Fanny Holtzmann as special counsel.

Fanny's appointment grew out of the finesse with which she had handled a delicate contretemps several years earlier. Oei Hui-lan, the attractive wife of V. K. Wellington Koo, the Chinese ambassador to the Court of St. James's, had written a racy, intimate account of life in the loftiest circles of the Kuomintang (Nationalist Party), of which Chiang Kai-shek was the head. She depicted with nostalgic affection the extravagant ways of a "let-'em-eat-rice-cakes" hierarchy.

In the eyes of Allied diplomats, the issue was not the validity of Mrs. Koo's description but its timing. Americans were being asked to make sacrifices for China War Relief, to give their all for "our gallant allies in Asia," and the book's negative propaganda effect could be devastating: it would be welcome ammunition for isolationists and other critics of Roosevelt's policy, and might seriously hamper the Allied effort. A major American publisher was preparing the book's publication, newspaper serialization was scheduled, but promotion had not yet been launched.

Ambassador Koo, constantly moving between Allied capitals, had scarcely been aware of his wife's excursion into literature; now he was in Washington and in low spirits. A distinguished jurist, he knew that technically he had no legal recourse; the publisher had fulfilled a contract and was free to publish.

Dr. Koo turned to his lifelong friend Harry Hussey, the Canadian-born architect who built the Rockefeller Medical Foundation in Peking.

Hussey relayed the SOS to the British Embassy, where he was advised to consult their American troubleshooter-at-large, Fanny Holtzmann.

The Canadian came to the Bar Building, a trim blue-eyed septuagenarian whose white hair was complemented by a sharp Van Dyke (the Chinese transliterated his name into Hu Shih, the "bearded one" or "old wise one"). Hussey had an intriguing history. Sent to China by John D. Rockefeller I soon after Sun Yat-sen reopened the doors of the country to the West in 1911, he had become the confidant of all political factions, the detached outsider whom everybody could trust. His home was a neutral meeting ground; his young boy had grown up both with the sons of the great banking families and with the future leaders of Red China.

Hussey told Fanny he had come to her because he had reason to believe that as an American patriot she would extend herself for the Allied cause; and no country had a greater claim to her sympathy than China, which had been fighting longer than any other nation against tyranny. He then outlined the book and its explosive potential.

Fanny asked him to bring in Mrs. Koo and her contract.

Afterward, she went directly to the head of the publishing house. "I'm not telling you how to run your business," she said. "Nor am I trying to bring unfair pressure. But I think that you, as a conscientious American, are entitled to know what is at stake here . . ."

When she finished, the publisher waved aside her offer of a cash payment. "There will be no settlement," he said. "There will also be no book. You can inform Ambassador Koo, and he can inform the secretary of state, that every copy now on the shelves will be pulled back and destroyed."

"What about the newspaper syndicate?"

"My dear Miss Holtzmann, if you are even half as persuasive with them — no, wait. You've done your share. I'll handle them."

Fanny, like the publisher, declined any compensation. Dr. Koo invited her to dinner at his Park Avenue home. He seated her at his right hand and placed a chicken foot, complete with claws, on her plate: "This is what we give our special guests. It brings good luck."

Koo, the dean of Far Eastern diplomats, had held virtually every position of consequence in his country's government, from acting premier down. His talk with Fanny ranged over Chinese customs, the British legal system and Washington politics, lasting well into the night. A few days later, Hussey brought the draft of a speech by Koo to Fanny's office for her perusal. Thereafter she was gradually absorbed into the Chinese inner councils, attending one or two meetings a month in New York or Washington. Most of the discussions concerned Chinese relations with the West, but there was some heated debate on internal matters. Hussey, arguing for "peace with the Communists now, or you'll be kicked off the mainland," was secretly accused by ardent Kuomintang people of being a double agent.

Theresa Holtzmann was an amused observer of her daughter's new interests. Walking with Fanny to Bloomingdale's department store one afternoon, she saw a Chinese man approaching with a couple of laundry bags slung over his shoulder. She nudged Fanny: "Straighten up. Here comes one of your fancy new clients."

Theresa changed her tone when she read in the Hebrew-language weekly *Hadoar* that Wellington Koo, as chairman of the trusteeship section of the League of Nations, had been charged among other things with overseeing the creation of a Jewish national home in Palestine. Since her husband's death, she had taken over Henry's passion for Zionism. "Concentrate on this man Koo," she told Fanny. "As his lawyer, you may be in a position to do something about a Jewish homeland."

Toward the end of the war, Koo asked her to his office in Washington. As a key figure in the defunct League of Nations, he had been approached to take a leading role in forming the new world body, the United Nations. Charter meetings would soon begin in San Francisco. Would Fanny like to formalize her connection with his country and accompany the Chinese delegation to California? And if so, in what capacity?

"Well, Dr. Koo, I'm a lawyer . . . perhaps 'legal adviser' to your delegation?"

Koo smiled and read from a note on his desk: "How would you like 'special counsel to the Republic of China'?"

The core of Fanny's education, as she liked to point out, came from the direct questioning of her clients. In the case of the Chinese, "I started from a total vacuum."

Fortunately there was no shortage of sources. The Chinese were sending to San Francisco a bipartisan delegation drawn from both Nationalists and the Communists, who were challenging Chiang Kai-shek's regime. Traveling from New York with Koo and Foreign Minister T. V. Soong would be the country's intellectual leadership, including judges, economists, and academicians like Y. C. Yang, president of Soochow University. Fanny would be locked up with them in a private railroad car; she intended to make those four days the educational equivalent of four years.

Most Americans, she felt, were like herself vaguely aware of their country's role in defending militarily helpless China against the encroachments of the colonial powers; a few knew that American democracy had inspired Sun Yat-sen's overthrow of the Manchus. But beyond that they were uninformed. Fanny hoped to put together a capsulized story of Washington's Eastern ally.

From Harry Hussey, widely traveled and copiously read, she obtained a broad overview of Chinese history. Then, notebook in hand and secretary Carol Tunberg at her side, she went through the railroad car quizzing delegates on particular eras and issues. Unburdened by preconceptions or political dogma —"my inadequate schooling was my salvation"— she soaked up sagas of ferocious warlords, lovelorn princes, culture-laden imperial courts; of countless invaders whose civilizations were swallowed up in the unfathomable depths of China.

One morning she was dictating "And then China decided," when Y. C. Yang stuck his head in the door. "My dear Miss Holtzmann," the elderly scholar protested, "it wasn't that simple, a clear decision for the whole country —"

"I have to make it simple," Fanny replied, "or the people I'm preparing this for — congressmen, journalists — will get totally lost. I must cut through to the heart of what happened."

"*Hen hau* [very good]," nodded Yang.

"*Shieh shieh ni* [thank you]."

Her report on China, stubbornly pursued, flowered into eight compact pages that later served her well in briefing fellow Westerners.

The Chinese were carrying a sackful of worries to San Francisco. They no longer could count on an absolute ally in the West. Britain, under the strong influence of Clement Attlee, was making overtures to the Soviet Union. The United States had permitted arms shipments to Japan, China's archenemy, in the 1930's. Later, Roosevelt emissaries had, while fuming at Chiang Kai-shek as "an old son-of-a-bitch," flirted with the Chinese Communists. ("A terrible mistake," Wellington Koo told Fanny. "Mao and his people have abandoned the principles of Sun Yat-sen for tyranny. When we are wearied from fighting the Japanese, they will inherit our Chinese earth — to the world's regret.") Worst of all, in Oriental eyes, they had been rudely ignored when the decisions were being made at Casablanca, Teheran and Yalta. Roosevelt, in his eagerness for harmony with Russia, seemed ready to forget them.

The Chinese felt isolated, helpless in the path of an increasingly ascendant Soviet Union and a reconstituted militaristic Japan.

In this mood, the Chinese delegation at San Francisco pinned their hopes, first, on a strong charter, which no nation could prudently defy ("Noble idealism is not enough," Koo told Fanny; "that is the costly lesson of the League"); and second, on permanent veto-wielding representation for their republic on the Security Council.

As the nations of the world gathered at San Francisco, similar considerations preoccupied all the big powers and many of the forty-odd smaller ones. The consequence was that although the delegations were confronted by such urgent issues as the allocation of authority under the charter and the use of force, they put off until their fall meetings in London the actual business of hammering out a tangible approach to the world body. For the moment, they engaged mainly in political infighting, which eventually crystallized into a serious clash over the veto.

Soon after the conference began, Fanny wrote to Gertrude Lawrence, who was on tour in the Pacific: "The whole world seems to have descended on this Conference; they must have expected a six-ring circus. Most of the curiosity crowd and pressure-groupers have now left, which enables us to carry on quietly and more intensively. It is a good thing that no particular personality dominates the Conference; it enables the merits of a Plan, rather than the persuasive ability of a personality, to be considered."

The role of the Communists in Koo's delegation fascinated and puzzled Fanny. Ideological differences put no visible damper on their social relationships. Wou-Saofong, a mordantly witty radical lawyer, roomed and often dined with Yang, who was a Methodist minister. To her further bewilderment, Wou and his confrères were openly contemptuous of the Soviet Union. Obviously there were cultural and historical forces at work here that she didn't know about.

She went to Harry Hussey for elucidation, and found herself led into a morass. The Communists were patriotic theoreticians (Hussey's Monday version) but were also unscrupulous masters of *Realpolitik* (his emphasis on Tuesday). The Kuomintang was the legitimate inheritor of Sun Yat-sen's democratic doctrines, yet it had lost touch with the people and let itself be identified with unpopular Western missionaries.

Hussey's mixed sympathies, she discovered, left both factions uneasy and mistrustful. He was kept on out of gratitude for past services (years before, he had helped smuggle Koo out of hostile territory in women's clothes) and because, as the ambassador explained, "We had to have somebody as a bridge to the West."

Now they had Fanny — and suddenly circumstances combined to send her spiraling dizzily up the diplomatic ladder.

To begin with, she had the official sponsorship of the Chinese. She also had close ties to London, having been registered as a British agent during the war; and as a native American she had good connections in Washington. That gave her a pivotal position among three of the five great powers. To this was added an unexpected bonus early in the conference: the cautious regard of a fourth.

Fanny's first contact with the Russians came at one of their caviar-and-sturgeon soirées soon after her arrival. As she entered the room she was conscious of stares and whispers. What was this all about? "Then it dawned on me. The Youssoupoff case had made a big splash in the Russian papers. Nobody worships royalty like a Communist; they've never laid eyes on a grand duchess. Here they were rubbing elbows with an intimate of Prince Felix and Xenia, and the private attorney for the estate of Czar Nicholas. To them I was practically a Romanoff!"

Wellington Koo presented her to Foreign Minister Molotov — he reminded Fanny of the socialist theoreticians at Reiser's Restaurant in Brownsville — and Molotov's Jewish wife. Mrs. Molotov and Fanny fell into animated conversation in a blend of Yiddish, Hebrew and Russian. When Fanny apologized for her *gehackte* (chopped-up) Russian, left over from a wartime crash-study course, Mrs. Molotov countered that it was no worse than her own "Red Yiddish." Lesser Soviet officials circled around the pair at a deferential distance. Celebrity status among the readers of *Pravda* was something Fanny hadn't counted on, but was glad to have.

Piled onto these international credentials was Fanny's special position in the city of San Francisco. She was an established personality in California, a movie-world luminary well known to the state bar and the San Francisco Press Club. Although the Clift Hotel, where most of the Chinese staff were staying, had more than adequate accommodations, Fanny Holtzmann was offered nothing less than an enormous suite in the Mark Hopkins.

Just down the hall was the British delegation, headed by Foreign Minister Anthony Eden. To Fanny, Eden was little more than an accent and a profile: "The only thing in his favor was his consistent opposition to Hitler." More important were the Labour people from the coalition government: Clement Attlee and his brilliant deputy, Francis Williams. According to embassy insiders, it was Williams, once a prominent journalist in Fleet Street, who actually shaped policy. Fanny had always found him an attentive listener.

Across the street at the Fairmount were the Americans, top-heavy with State Department conservatives. Their mien pleased her Chinese clients, still wincing from the blunt remarks of "Vinegar Joe" Stilwell. To Fanny, Secretary of State Edward Stettinius was a "dull Rotarian," unable to weld the individual talents of his delegation into an effective unit. She considered the United States team inadequate to its task.

The one American in San Francisco who knew his business, by her standards, was the secretary general of the conference: a rock of stability in a sandstorm, patient, courteous, on duty day and night. His name was Alger Hiss. Subsequent events never changed Fanny's opinion of him as "an honest and honorable American."

On a lower floor at the Mark Hopkins was the star to which her wagon was attached, Wellington Koo. It was to him that seekers of wisdom and benefaction gravitated, and he would see no one of consequence without Fanny at his side. She would place her contacts and her inventiveness at his disposal.

Toward the end of the first week, Koo was approached by an informal Anglo-American group for urgent consultations. He suggested that in the interests of privacy the meeting be held in Fanny's suite — and was pleasantly astonished when Francis Williams loped across the living room to throw his arms around the "Chinese lawyer." The Americans present were also obviously on familiar terms with Fanny, creating a salon ambience conducive to relaxed conversation. Word quickly got around that for an off-the-record exchange of views in congenial surroundings, there was no place like Fanny Holtzmann's suite at the Mark Hopkins.

One could count on meeting men of influence there — key members of the leading delegations. One could also count on the curtain of confidentiality essential to frank negotiation. No leaks emanated from the Holtzmann suite because the press corps, for all of their long-standing interest in Fanny, were at first unaware of its existence. Fanny maintained the lowest of profiles, staying generally clear of the cocktail parties and rarely appearing even in the hotel dining room.

So modestly did she melt into the background of her clients that a workman, summoned to the suite of the "Chinese lady lawyer" to repair a typewriter desk, marveled aloud: "You sure could have fooled me. I'd take her for an American any time." When newspaper friends finally descended on her from the Palace Hotel, she asked them to find copy elsewhere, and except for the San Francisco *Chronicle*, they did; no extensive account broke into print until late in the session, when Elsa Maxwell devoted a column to Fanny in the New York *Post*.

Fanny herself, the self-styled "catalyst," took an increasingly active role: devising compromises, breaking deadlocks. As her secretary, Carol Tunberg, remembered it: "She had a fantastic way of slicing through red tape. She refused to be deterred by what she called the 'garbage' of protocol, the endless burrowing through layers of subordinates; she went straight to the top. Her directness shocked a lot of people, especially the State Department types; but our Chinese clients didn't mind a bit. They had a way of assimilating whatever came up."

Two weeks after her arrival in late April, Fanny was spinning along in high gear. Her Chinese clients, she wrote to Gertrude Lawrence, had "generously acclaimed" her results. Still, she realized "only too well that the pinnacle of success has a slippery floor, and that one false word, or move, might topple me off the dizzy heights on which I now find myself."

Instead she was toppled, albeit briefly, by bad news from home. Her mother, though ailing, had wanted to go along to California. Challenged by Fanny —"What will I do if you die on me?"— Theresa had retorted, "Don't worry, there are undertakers everywhere!"

Now word came by telegram of her passing, followed two hours later in the morning mail by her last letter: "When you receive this, I don't want you to mourn me. I am not dead, but going to my reunion with Papa Darling. When a fruit is ripe, it should fall to the ground. If it sticks to the branch, it rots the tree . . ."

Fanny had an appointment that weekend at San Simeon: Hearst wanted to salute the Nationalist Chinese for their long opposition both to Japan and to Asian Communism. She canceled her plans and retired to her bedroom, where she telephoned to Lucy Schneeberg in New York to pour out her sorrow.

But she would not be persuaded to return for the funeral. She wanted to remember her mother alive.

For some time Fanny had been hearing reports of a mysterious "Jewish general" high in the councils of the Kuomintang. One morning she had a call from the slight, dignified foreign minister, T. V. Soong. "That general I've told you about," Soong said in his impeccable Harvard accent. "He's just got in from China. We're giving him a party this evening." Soong assured Fanny she would like the new arrival: "He's one of our last living links with Sun Yat-sen, the George Washington of China, and a great favorite of my sister, Madame Sun."

On arriving at Wellington Koo's suite, Fanny found a sprinkling of Western dignitaries, including Senator Jacob Javits of New York in his colonel's uniform, milling around with a score of Chinese.

Her eye was caught by an unfamiliar figure talking with Harry Hussey. Tall and powerfully built, with a thick chest and battered features, the man might have emerged from the old Madison Square Garden world of Damon Runyon. Edging closer, she heard him speak a few words in a sharp cockney accent. Proper casting for this fellow, she decided, would be as bouncer in a tough Soho bar.

At that point T. V. Soong caught her by the arm. He introduced Hussey's companion as General somebody — a Chinese name that apparently ended in "Mo."

The big man thrust out a brawny paw. "To you," he said exuberantly, "I am Moshe Cohen. *Shalom alekhem* [peace be with you]!"

"*Alekhem shalom* [to you, peace]," responded Fanny.

"*Kol Israel chaverim* [all Jews are brothers]!"

Heads turned. The lively exchange in Hebrew, although limited (both had probably exhausted their vocabularies) startled the crowd. Moshe Cohen looked down at Fanny approvingly. "So you are the Fanny 'Oltzmann," he said in his clipped, choppy singsong, "that ev-ry-bo-dy is talking about! The generalissimo said some ve-ry nice things about you. I am really proud of you, for what you have done for my country."

"Your country? What country is that?"

"Why, China, of course. The most wonderful people in the world. I love them — and so will you."

"I've found them very gracious up to now. And appreciative."

"My dear girl, they're just like our own Jews: kicked around all through history, used by others and abused. When can we 'ave a chat?"

Fanny invited him to dine the next evening at her Mark Hopkins suite, where the aging but still-hardy general unfolded his story. He had been born in London, among the fish markets and crowded alleys of the East End. Very religious, very poor, he had in his youth fought as a professional boxer. Shortly after the turn of the century, in search of more agreeable employment, he had emigrated to Canada — where fate threw him across the path of Sun Yat-sen.

The Chinese revolutionary leader, perennially hounded by Manchu authorities, kept traveling around the globe in search of political and financial support. He had many admirers in Canada, some of whom were concerned for his safety. In 1911 they hired Moshe Cohen as his bodyguard.

Sun's lofty vision for China stirred Moshe's Talmud-nurtured idealism;

the former boxer's simple devotion endeared him to Sun. London slum-survivor and Asian intellectual became fast friends. When it came time for the leader to make his bid for power at home, Moshe went back with him.

After Sun's victory, Moshe shadowed him everywhere, acquiring "good everyday Chinese with a Yiddish-cockney accent." When Japan invaded in the thirties, Cohen had been commissioned into the Chinese army, rising rapidly to important field commands. As the one unpurchasable man among a horde of greedy generals, he developed a reputation of total incorruptibility.

His political standing, if equally exalted, was more complicated. Over the years Moshe had remained extremely close to the leftward-leaning Mme. Sun Yat-sen. This put him somewhat at odds with the other half of the once-legendary Soong sisters, the glittering Mme. Chiang Kai-shek, who did not share her sister's high regard for the Communists. However, Chiang himself enjoyed and trusted the jovial general, giving Cohen the extraordinary status of being acceptable to both contending factions in China, and hence an irreplaceable go-between in sensitive negotiations.

After his evening of reminiscence with Fanny, General Cohen popped around to the Mark Hopkins suite often. If she wasn't in, he left a calling card bent at the upper left edge to indicate, in accordance with the most formal protocol, that he had been there "in person" ("the first 'high diplomat' I've ever seen," Fanny commented to Carol, "who could pass for a Sunday fish peddler in Petticoat Lane"). If the two ladies were at home, he took them out to dinner, alternating impartially between White's Jewish Restaurant and some place of his fancy in Chinatown. Cohen had access to the innermost recesses of Chinese politics; but whether from guile or — as Fanny considered more likely — a certain cheery incoherence, he conveyed no useful insights. He had been originally chosen, after all, less for intellect than for muscles and integrity.

Carol Tunberg was getting restless. Homesick, exhausted by the whirl of round-the-clock secret meetings, she talked of returning to New York. Fanny could not afford such a defection. Signs were shaping up of an East-West impasse over the veto, and Wellington Koo would be the likely mediator. Alarmed, Fanny put in a call to her friend the secretary general. Alger Hiss counted on her, with her strategic position at Koo's elbow, for many small favors; in turn he was quick to supply anything from a trade encyclopedia to an out-of-stock typewriter ribbon.

Fanny explained that she needed someone to distract Carol from thoughts of home: "I don't want her straying off the reservation."

Hiss pondered a moment. "Well, there's Archie MacLeish. He's got some time on his hands . . ."

"A poet I don't need — especially a poet who's assistant secretary of state! It should be somebody who won't attract attention; quiet — and safe. I promised her parents I'd look after her."

"I don't know, Fanny. I've had some strange requests in this job, but really —"

"Look, Alger, why don't you do what the boys in the movie studios do when one of their stars gets restless? They just dip into the public relations pool — pick out somebody who's not too vivid a personality, but competent and soothing. In Carol's case, he should be well educated; she's very intelligent. Does that ring any bells?"

There was a pause, a chuckle, then a new lilt in Hiss's voice: "I think, Fanny, I may have just the man for you."

The caller at the other end of the phone sounded calm and cultivated. "My name is Stevenson," he told Fanny. "Alger Hiss asked me to stop in and see you."

"You're not a poet, are you?"

"No, I'm a lawyer."

"Are you free for a drink at six?"

"I can be."

Promptly at six he was at the door: a medium-sized man in baggy Brooks Brothers clothes, with a retreating hairline and a tentative manner. He settled into a chair, accepted a scotch, and began talking about Archie MacLeish.

"Never mind him," Fanny interrupted. "Tell me about yourself. What's your first name?"

"Adlai."

"Adelaide? But that's a girl's name!"

"A-d-l-a-i," Stevenson spelled patiently. "I'm named for my grandfather, who was vice-president under Grover Cleveland. The original was an Old Testament character, a shepherd of King David."

Fanny was not terribly interested in Bible lessons or Democratic vice-presidents of another era. "Are you married, Mr. Stevenson?"

"Yes. I have three boys."

"Good!"

A faint, engaging smile: "I'm rather pleased myself."

"What sort of law do you practice?"

"Whatever comes my way. Mostly corporate. I'm a junior partner with William Sidley's law firm in Chicago." For the moment, Stevenson explained, he was on leave to Secretary Stettinius at the State Department, handling daily briefings to the American news media. He did not add that he had been drafted to organize an elaborate "leak" operation after Stettinius despaired of promoting policy agreement among the wrangling prima donnas of the United States delegation. Nor did he mention that he had been president of the Chicago Council on Foreign Relations, the key wartime assistant to Secretary of the Navy Frank Knox, and author of a widely praised analysis in 1944 of the Italian politico-economic scene.

Stevenson didn't volunteer any of this, and Fanny didn't ask. To her he was a struggling not-so-young lawyer from the vast and colorless Middle West, a terrain not nearly so familiar as London, New York or Los Angeles. Up to her ears in smiling Chinese with unpronounceable names, she was not about to explore the biography of a part-time PR man. She went directly to the point that mattered: How did he feel about Jewish cooking?

"Why, quite affirmatively. We have kosher restaurants in Chicago, you know."

"Fine. The first thing I'd like you to do is take my secretary to White's for dinner tonight. And be sure to give me a petty cash voucher for the bill." How should she know that Stevenson had been brought up in the luxury of European travel, Choate and Princeton, before marrying a multimillionaire heiress?

The circumstances attending that first meeting set the tone for the future relationship between Stevenson and Fanny. At San Francisco, she outranked the future presidential candidate by light-years; a delegation press spokesman was scarcely within hailing distance of the special counsel to Wellington Koo. In earning power, the gap between them was even wider. Stevenson was a temporary civil servant in something under the $10,000-a-year class.

Even the timing of the moment conspired to Fanny's advantage. She was in her most buoyant phase, the world on her doorstep; Stevenson, harassed by the impossible task of letting out exactly the right amount and quality of information among seventy-five competing newsmen every day, was weary and subdued.

Against this background, Fanny's suite was for Stevenson a haven of relaxation and amusement, and Fanny herself a pixy-ish sorceress. With a stroke of the finger she summoned movie chiefs out of conference, badgered book publishers into gigantic advances, settled divorce cases by telephone — while keeping a brace of foreign ministers entertained in the living room. The traffic flowing through her apartment was exhilarating: Gertrude Lawrence on her way back from touring the Pacific in *Blithe Spirit*; Baltimore newspaper nabob Paul C. Patterson traveling in the opposite direction; Frank Scully up from Hollywood. The jangling telephone might be Orson Welles in the lobby, seeking help with a room, or the duchess of Atholl from London, worrying about the veto.

It was a far cry from the tedious routine of the Washington bureaucracy; much closer, actually, to the dreams of Adlai Stevenson's youth. A lifelong romantic, he had after Princeton been deflected from a ranching career to the law only by heavy paternal pressure.

Now he seized eagerly on the chance to get in on the fun. When Fanny suggested that Gertrude might appreciate being met at the dock, he fairly flew through the door. He carried out the assignment with a thoroughness, courtesy and tact that made Fanny take another look at him.

Would he be interested in taking on occasional liaison chores for her at the conference and following through on the informal approaches launched in her suite?

He most certainly would, Stevenson responded. He believed firmly in what she was doing and liked the way she was doing it.

Because he seemed to have an affinity for the English, dating back to adolescent travels, Stevenson became her expediter of contacts with the British delegation. Fanny found him deft, resourceful, reliable. By temperament and training he was a superb associate, more comfortable behind the scenes than in the glare of the spotlight.

He was, however, a skilled negotiator. When the showdown with the Russians over the veto came early in June, "Adlai was invaluable. He understood their stubbornness, their dependence on Moscow for instructions, their traditional mistrust of the West. Koo consulted him often."

Stevenson became a fixture around the Mark Hopkins suite. In a letter of the period, he referred to himself as "not a statesman but a mechanic" helping to build the United Nations. No task was too challenging and no chore on behalf of a fellow toiler too menial. One afternoon, when Fanny was laying out her clothes for a Chinese formal luncheon the next day, she noticed with dismay that the heels of her dress shoes were worn down.

Stevenson cheerfully tucked the shoes under his arm: "I'll drop them off at Angelo's. Carol can pick them up in the morning." To Fanny the gesture was a measure not of his servility but of his strength: "The greatest people I've ever known — Cardozo, Felix Frankfurter, Frank Scully, and later Eleanor Roosevelt — were the humblest."

By early summer, the San Francisco charter sessions were over. The following fall, Fanny and Stevenson were separately urged to proceed to London for the meetings of the UN Preparatory Commission, which would flesh out the actual structure of the world organization and also choose its permanent site. The request to Fanny came in a cable from Wellington Koo; Stevenson was named by the State Department as deputy to former Secretary Stettinius, head of the American delegation. In a note advising "dear Fannie" that he had once more "succumbed to the blandishments" of Washington, Stevenson did not mention his elevation to the rank of minister.

In the interim before Fanny's arrival in November, Stevenson had replaced the ailing Stettinius and put in distinguished service as chairman of the commission's executive committee, jousting successfully with Andrei Gromyko of the Soviet Union. Nonetheless, he was waiting in person on the dock at Southampton on the rainy Sunday night when she debarked from the *Queen Mary*.

"Good news, Fanny. The hotels are stuffed, but we managed to get you a room at the Dorchester."

"What, where the American tourists go? My wire said Claridge's. Can't you read?"

"You don't understand — people are putting up tents. *Nobody* gets into Claridge's."

All the way to London, Fanny sulked in the recesses of the State Department limousine. "No," she told the chauffeur. "No Dorchester."

At 1:30 A.M. she was delivered to Claridge's, where the head porter stumbled to his feet in sleepy recognition. True, he confirmed, the prewar manager of the hotel, an Italian, had been drowned while under internment; but his replacement also dated back to the old days . . .

Fanny telephoned the manager: "I'm at the desk, and they're turning me away."

Back came the reply: "I'll give you my own bed — and I won't be in it!"

The manager invited her and Stevenson up for a drink, then scurried around and found an emergency room. "The next morning," as Fanny remembered it, "he booted out an ex-king, Yugoslavia I think it was, and gave me one of the royal suites. My old chum George of Greece was just across the corridor."

Fanny's hotel bills were of course covered by her Chinese hosts. Otherwise they could have been classified as an allowable tax deduction, thanks to a sucessful encounter with the Internal Revenue Service in the thirties. The agents had challenged her write-off of an expensive suite at the Savoy as a business expense, asserting that only a bedroom was essential.

Fanny indignantly took issue. Demanding a full formal hearing, she pointed out with a straight face that the services she purveyed were not the sort rendered in a bedroom; in fact, to suggest otherwise via a tax ruling would carry overtones inimical to her purpose: "I am a counselor-at-law, gentlemen, not at love. I require a parlor for the dignified conduct of my profession."

The Revenue men wavered; ocean-hopping lady lawyers were not a daily experience. There was no precedent —

"Then let us set one."

They did — Fanny's way.

So she could settle into her royal rooms at Claridge's with the knowl-edge that her bank account would not be imperiled, and Adlai Steven-son would ease her social obligations. Each afternoon, as darkness fell, Stevenson hurried from his duties as ranking American delegate to Fanny's suite for drinks and conversation. He had lots of company. London was welcoming Fanny back like a long-lost daughter; she was the pet of *Rasputin* days, newly beribboned with the loyal services of wartime and the laurels of San Francisco. "My place looks like a Mafia boss's funeral — drenched with flowers," she wrote to her brother David. "Anybody who can get his hands on a piece of chocolate sends it to me. Love is pouring in."

And the scotch was pouring out. Although no Englishman could buy a bottle, Fanny was plentifully supplied by the Chinese Embassy. The Chinese also stocked her larder, as did Ben Goetz of MGM, and Gertrude Lawrence with steaks flown from New York. When to all this were added the blessings of two sumptuous baths, and toaster-smooth heat flowing from the walls, it was no wonder, as Fanny observed, that she was the most popular hostess in Mayfair.

Stevenson circulated beamingly among the guests, answering the door, making introductions, mixing drinks — and drinking in the atmosphere. He enjoyed the admirals and publishers, the academics down from Oxford — and most of all, the theatrical flavoring. After a day of hammering out the details of trusteeship, it was a relief to sit around a fire with Noel Coward, Laurence Olivier and Vivien Leigh. Although politely attentive to Lord Cromer, he obviously relished more the close-up view of Jack Buchanan and Charles B. Cochran.

In London, the UN conferees moved forward from political skirmishing to businesslike debate; Stevenson and Fanny were usually pursuing separate subissues. However, he kept her informed of general developments at the American Embassy, as did Alger Hiss, who was gaining further stature in Fanny's eyes by his "sensitive treatment of black leaders from the 'new' countries."

Less cooperative was the American delegate John Foster Dulles, Eisenhowever's future secretary of state. Fanny found him a stony-faced ideologue, pompous and forbidding.

One morning Stevenson telephoned to say his wife was in London. Could Fanny join them for lunch at Prunier's?

"Oh, Adlai, that's so expensive! You don't have to —"

"It's all right. You're the one person here she wants to meet."

Fanny liked Ellen Stevenson at once. Tall and handsome, Adlai's wife dressed offhandedly in old oxfords and well-worn tweeds; her brown hair was tucked in absently behind pink patrician ears. She had the air of a careless duchess, except that, Fanny reminded herself, Adlai had spoken of a home in the Chicago suburbs. Ellen's clothes, then, must be a mark of bookishness and frugality. More than ever, Fanny's impression of Stevenson as a man just a notch above genteel poverty was confirmed.

Other impressions, too, gained strength during their London association: "Adlai was unswervingly honest, deeply idealistic. It was impossible not to regard him with affection."

How Stevenson felt about it was conveyed a few months later in a note scribbled aboard the Twentieth Century Limited as he returned home from an intensive series of UN meetings in New York. He lamented his failure to see Fanny during the "nightmare" week of labors: "I count you as one of the most refreshing features of these international conferences — and to miss a glimpse of you was just *another* thing that was wrong with this one!" He concluded with the assurance that they would meet again. He was quite right.

A few steps down the hall from Fanny's corner suite at Claridge's were the quarters of the most illustrious American delegate to the Preparatory Commission, Eleanor Roosevelt. Fanny had met the president's widow more than twenty years earlier at the home of Elisabeth Marbury, a pioneering female in Democratic national politics.

When Mrs. Roosevelt began her travels and her "My Day" column from the White House, Fanny was among the many who cast a questioning eye. As she wrote to Lord Cromer in the late thirties, "At first we all thought it was infra dig, the mixture of little sermons about flowers with deadly serious political comment. Gradually we came to appreciate the potency of her writing. Mrs. Roosevelt is a good influence, and more popular right now than FDR himself."

In London, Mrs. Roosevelt filed her copy through Tosti Russell, a veteran Scripps-Howard correspondent. Russell, a slender, animated Anglo-Italian, had covered the Youssoupoff case and frequently hunted out background color at Fanny's flat in the Kinnerton Studios. He was happy to bring the two distinguished ladies together.

Fanny went to tea in Mrs. Roosevelt's suite. Surrounded by photos of the late president, the two talked for more than an hour. Later in the week the former first lady returned the visit.

By January, a more or less regular end-of-day ritual had evolved. After Mrs. Roosevelt turned in her column —"she was very conscientious about deadlines, and not only wrote but typed every word herself"— the two American women would slip into their lounging robes and relax over a cup of something warm. Usually it was Mrs. Roosevelt who padded down the hall to Fanny's "because neither of us drank, and I had a bigger stock of cocoa and malted, along with *nosherei* for nibbling."

Mrs. Roosevelt brought back to Fanny's mind that other earnest lady-in-politics, the duchess of Atholl: "Like the duchess, she was essentially humanitarian in her outlook, no more politically oriented than myself. Her militancy was on issues like child labor and the fate of the democratic Spanish Republic; she was very conscious of her public image, and it distressed her to be in the White House at the time of Franco's victory."

Fanny listened, introduced Mrs. Roosevelt to the Cromers, and passed along small thoughtfulnesses: some American hairnets, the services of her cleaning woman, a column-worthy newspaper clipping about the hardships endured by London housewives. When Mrs. Roosevelt fretted about getting a birthday gift home to one of her grandsons, Fanny dug up an accommodating traveler.

Ultimately their talk became more personal. Mrs. Roosevelt referred resentfully to Basil "Doc" O'Connor, the late president's former law partner, who had told FDR to "get the pants off Eleanor." And Fanny mentioned her frustrating interview at the White House over the clampdown on Jewish immigration.

Mrs. Roosevelt sprang vigorously to her husband's defense: "You must understand, Franklin was physically dependent. He couldn't just walk away from staff people who bored or irritated him; they were his *legs*. And he couldn't ignore their attitudes.

"Undoubtedly he himself would have found you interesting to talk to; you would have enjoyed each other a great deal. But you see he was so surrounded, so insulated — and not always by the best possible people. Many were grabbing for personal power, angling for influence over the boss."

FDR, his widow insisted, was sympathetic to Jewry: "His greatest compliment to anyone was, 'He has a Jewish head.' "

"Yes — that's why the Jews trusted him — and so many wound up in gas chambers."

After Fanny's sharp retort, the subject was dropped. It did not come up again between the two women for several months, by which time Mrs. Roosevelt was actively pressing her husband's successor to aid Jewish refugees.

Fanny returned to the United States in early February, Mrs. Roosevelt a few weeks afterward. Several exchanges by letter concluded with word from the president's widow that she would be back in Manhattan by late April: "Then I would so much like to see you. Perhaps you will come to tea some afternoon?"

Fanny came on April 29 to Mrs. Roosevelt's cluttered little apartment overlooking Washington Square. Her hostess arrived late and in a pleasurable flutter. She had been riding down by subway from the temporary UN headquarters at Hunter College in the Bronx —

"The rush-hour subway, on a clammy afternoon like this? Why didn't you take a taxi?"

"My dear Fanny, do you realize how much a taxi from the Bronx costs?" She resumed her story. There she was, hanging onto a strap in the crowded, steamy express when a fellow voyager looked up from his newspaper and recognized her. "Until that moment I had been just another old lady in the jostling crowd, trying to stay on my feet and catch a breath of air. The instant he called out my name and offered me his seat, the whole car came to life. A path opened up for me like the Red Sea parting; everybody gathered around. It made me feel so good that people remembered Franklin!"

Two weeks later Fanny was at Hyde Park for lunch and a visit to the Wiltwyck School for Boys. Wiltwyck, an interracial center for troubled youngsters under the age of eleven, stood directly across the Hudson at Esopus, New York. The drive was short, but as executed by Mrs. Roosevelt in her Lincoln, harrowing. Fanny, herself not the most adept of drivers, flinched as her hostess groped between the gas and brake pedals.

En route, Mrs. Roosevelt expressed her chagrin at being unable to do more financially for Wiltwyck: "You're a lawyer, you know about estates.

If Doc had taken better care of Franklin's affairs, my situation would be different."

Arriving at the school, Mrs. Roosevelt was instantly surrounded by a dozen small residents, mostly black. Every one of them was clamoring for her attention — and, Fanny noticed, every one of them got it. The former first lady addressed each boy by name, bestowing a word of praise here, a smile of recognition there.

Then she led Fanny through rickety halls into the main dormitory. Bedding was in wild disarray. One corner was a jumble of old baseball gloves, leftover bicycle parts and discarded clothes. From the lavatory beyond came a powerful stench of small boys in their most casual manifestations.

Mrs. Roosevelt noticed Fanny's dismay. "We have a hard time getting help from Harlem. Nobody wants to look after deprived problem children; it's pleasanter to work in the sunny kitchens of the wealthy. Actually, this doesn't smell any different from a dormitory at an exclusive boarding school. Little boys are all alike."

She went to a closet and took out cleaning equipment: pail, mop, scrub brush. Fanny, at her elbow, inquired if she could help.

"My dear, it looks to me as if you're about to throw up. But you can give me a hand changing these sheets. I'll take care of the rest."

Together they replaced several soiled bedsheets. Then the president's widow moved on into the lavatory where, dropping to her hands and knees, she methodically scrubbed the floor.

It was a scene Fanny would never forget, "an act of humility, responsibility, love. There, in that washroom for forgotten little boys, I felt in the presence of greatness."

Fanny translated her admiration into action. Within four days her friend Douglas Black, vice-president and general counsel of Doubleday, sent a package of books to Wiltwyck. Similar offers came from other of Fanny's friends: Jack Kapp, president of Decca Records; Harry Brandt, the theater magnate; and David Marx, who with his brother Louis operated one of the country's largest toy manufacturing concerns. Fanny went with Mrs. Roosevelt to make the toy selection. Each time the older woman hesitated diffidently before some spectacular item, Fanny told the clerk, "Throw it in."

As they departed, assured of a wagonload that would delight Wiltwyck, Fanny observed, "It's a good thing for the kids that you look me along."

Mrs. Roosevelt smiled. "It's a good thing for the boys that I met you in London."

Some months afterward she telephoned to suggest a neighborly visit; she had just rented the garden apartment and first floor in a town house on East Sixty-second Street off Lexington Avenue.

Fanny found her lunching in the downstairs kitchen. Her living room–office was upstairs in the back, overlooking the garden. "My grandson Buzzy is my secretary," she told Fanny "It gives him a job and, I hope, some training in the idea of public service." She indicated a convertible sofa. "He's allowed to sleep here overnight so long as he has things back in order by nine A.M. so I can start work."

Fanny took a step toward the large room adjoining.

"Oh, don't go there," Mrs. Roosevelt cautioned. "That's my maid's room. You have to provide comfortable quarters for your help."

Her own room was a narrow cubicle off the hall, barely big enough for a cot, bedtable and dresser. A wall shelf running the length of the bed was covered with photographs. Several showed the Roosevelt children as youngsters. All the rest were of FDR: as a boy, as governor and president, as a young sailor, as a baby. Some Fanny had seen at Claridge's, others at Washington Square; this seemed a complete montage of the late president's life.

Mrs. Roosevelt saw her staring. "Franklin's face is the first thing that greets me in the morning," she said. "And the last thing I look at before going to sleep." Her voice quavered slightly. "He was a great man, Fanny. A man like that, you never have completely to yourself. You must share him with the world." Suddenly she was crying.

Fanny felt no embarrassment, only compassion: "I was crying with her."

She saw Mrs. Roosevelt once again, when the president's widow paid a warm, reminiscence-filled visit to Fanny's home on East Sixty-fourth Street. For Fanny, Eleanor Roosevelt would always remain "a model of intelligence and simplicity, altogether the most wonderful human being it has been my privilege to know."

A major item engaging the delegates to the Preparatory Commission in London, including both Adlai Stevenson and Mrs. Roosevelt, was the selection of a headquarters site for the UN. Fanny too had a hand in what would become an exceedingly tangled, if not indecipherable, chapter in international history.

The initial struggle over location was between pro-Europe forces and those favoring the United States. The Europe bloc, led by France, encountered unexpected trouble rallying support from the other big powers. Russia was still smarting over its ouster in 1939 from the Geneva-based League of Nations. Britain, heavily dependent on postwar aid from America, looked toward Washington — which decorously abstained.

That put the issue up to Wellington Koo, who came down firmly against the Continent. "It would be a graveyard for a new world body," he told Fanny. "In all my years with the League, very little happened; and when it did, nobody cared." His choice was San Francisco, a window onto Asia, where "the next round in history" would occur.

By December the French had given up. A concerted drive was made for San Francisco; when it failed by two votes, other American cities were emboldened to enter the bidding. Twenty-two cities, from Oahu to

Virginia, rushed spokesmen to the scene; New York was the conspicuous exception.

Wellington Koo found all this high-powered salesmanship enervating. He turned over chairmanship of the Situs Committee to Roberto MacEachan of Uruguay to minimize big-power maneuvering, and asked Fanny to handle the tide of visitors.

After two weeks, she met with Dr. Koo and Mrs. Roosevelt to compare notes. The president's widow did not like the images of violence associated with Chicago. Fanny was equally dissatisfied with Princeton: "It's academic, remote, too detached from the center of things." Nobody had any real enthusiasm for Boston or Philadelphia.

"Which brings us back to San Francisco," smiled Koo. "Closer to Asia, where the future lies."

"But the West Coast doesn't have New York's communication facilities," Fanny insisted. More and more her mind kept returning to her hometown; partly, she was willing to concede, out of loyalty, but also from the nagging conviction that it could match and surpass anything available elsewhere. New York was as cosmopolitan as San Francisco, as culturally aware as Boston, had more hotels than Philadelphia, milder weather than Chicago. And with Palestine looming high on the UN agenda, what better ambience for the struggle of the Jews toward statehood?

Koo had the last word. "There is no space in New York," he pointed out. "You're talking about an overcrowded city."

Browsing through the Paris *Herald* shortly before Christmas, Fanny ran across a news item that snapped everything into place. William Zeckendorf, the realtor-entrepreneur, had acquired some ten acres of land in the rundown slaughterhouse-warehouse district along the East River above Forty-second Street. He intended to build there a "Dream City" of mighty towers and sweeping plazas, with a marina and an air terminal.

Fanny knew the terrain well. Years before she had bought Tudor City bonds from Fred F. French, whose hopes along similarly grandiose lines had fallen afoul of the market crash. This strip of real estate, she decided, was the answer to the UN's problem.

Bill O'Dwyer had won his race for mayor, but had not yet moved into City Hall. Fanny placed a call to his friend Eddie Rosen in New York, and half an hour later was talking to the mayor-elect: "Bill, every city in America has been besieging us for the UN site; it's *got* to be worth something if so many people want it! I've just been reading about the Zeckendorf deal on the East River. Why don't you go after some public-spirited citizen or foundation, like Ford or Rockefeller, to buy up the land and donate it to the United Nations? With a location like that, in the heart of the American communications complex, the world will *have* to pay attention to the United Nations. And you'll be administering the capital of the world!"

255

O'Dwyer was politely grateful; Fanny was never sure how much she had caught his imagination.

Months passed. The American government came down off the fence and officially put its weight behind San Francisco, only to run into the threat of a Soviet boycott; California was too far away. A campaign for the Westchester-Greenwich area foundered on bitter local opposition. Privately, Fanny continued to argue for Manhattan in talks with civic leaders like Bernard Baruch; but Philadelphia, as the site engendering least resistance, seemed destined to back into the prize.

Meanwhile, through the summer of 1946 Zeckendorf had bought up eight more waterfront acres. Evidently the swirl of debate had been reaching him; he began toying with the idea of the UN among others, as a prospective buyer.

Suddenly, early in December he offered his parcel to the city at "any price" they could pay. Telephones buzzed, limousines raced up to the Rockefeller estate in Tarrytown, and within the week John D. Rockefeller, Jr., had put up $8,500,000, thus providing Zeckendorf with a profit of $2,000,000 and the UN with a home.

In later years, and in her most cheerfully extravagant moments, Fanny liked to claim that she "brought the UN to New York." Clearly that is hyperbole; but just as clear is her persistent influence on the chain of events leading up to the decision. She was first to urge upon O'Dwyer the desirability of the East River site, and by her constant championing of Manhattan and her lukewarm response to rival applications she helped keep the way open for the last-minute intervention of the Zeckendorf-Rockefeller forces. Her mock lament about bringing the UN to the city, only to wind up with "a rent hike and no bus seat" for herself, had at least a trace of truth to it.

Less subject to argument was her contribution to the Chinese. She had functioned as counselor, catalyst and intermediary, with a verve that converted the normally reticent Wellington Koo into an admiring tubthumper — "my Eddie Goulding on the international level." The sizable check presented for her services she had turned over to Soochow University to launch the construction of a women's dormitory; she did not think a prosperous lawyer should be paid for the privilege of helping to organize a new world order.

Now the United Nations was in business, and its first business would be Palestine. Fanny had never lost sight of her mother's original motive in urging her to align herself with Wellington Koo. The better era yearned for by humanity could not be built upon the ruined hopes of the Jews.

She had amassed substantial credits in a dozen chancelleries. It was time to cash in her chips.

Chapter 11

THE JEWISH HOMELAND had been high on Fanny's priority list long before it reached the agenda of the United Nations. From the moment she financed the Palestine-bound romance of Moshe Goldfeld and his bride in Galicia a decade earlier, she was never far removed from the settlers or their dream. Her first act on arriving in London after the war was to pluck Basia Zuckerkandel, the sole survivor of the holocaust on her father's side, out of a DP camp in Heidenheim. She then sent Basia and Basia's husband, John Horn, to Palestine after lining up a job for him as an accountant with the skeleton government.

Earlier, at the UN charter sessions in San Francisco, she had made the most of her association with the Chinese delegation to plunge deep into the Zionist issue. Among the many nongovernmental organizations seeking a voice in the deliberations were Jewish groups ranging from militant nationalists to bitterly anti-Zionist assimilationists. Wellington Koo, as dean of the experts on trusteeship, was their natural focus.

Koo quickly found himself lost in the labyrinth of conflicting claims. When Fanny suggested that she take over the lobbyists, he was delighted to step aside.

The most heavily financed group was the American Council for Judaism — wealthy Reform Jews eager to disassociate themselves from any campaign for a Jewish homeland. "We are nonhyphenated Americans," they proclaimed. "Judaism is only a religion. Our children must grow up as integrated Americans."

At the other pole was the Hebrew Committee for National Liberation, dedicated to pushing immigration by any means and bristling for battle. The HCNL people, who had the fiery support of Fanny's friend Louis Bromfield, were an embarrassment to her. She understood their feelings and had even looked the other way when her brother David sent them money from office funds; but she was deeply disturbed by terrorism.

The bulk of American Jewry, eager for an end to the DP nightmare, stood at neither extreme but behind the middle-Zionist coalition, whose aims were twofold: to mount immediate and irresistible political pressure against the British closed-door policy in Palestine and to ensure that Jewish rights to ultimate statehood would be preserved in any new United Nations mandate.

Their chief spokesman at San Francisco was Rabbi Stephen S. Wise: tall, grave, gentle, an outstanding champion of liberal and intellectual causes. When he knocked at Fanny's door to announce his mission, she said: "You need no introduction here, Dr. Wise. I've been hearing about you from my father since I was a little girl."

Wise was accompanied by a stocky, heavy-featured man who promptly took over the conversation. "We didn't come here to talk about personal matters," he told Fanny brusquely. That was her first contact with Nahum Goldmann, president of the World Jewish Congress. She reacted instinctively: "with instant dislike." Future meetings did nothing to assuage her feelings.

The two Jewish leaders were counting on the United Nations to coax out of Britain a more sympathetic stand on the DPs. So was Fanny, she assured them. It was not until she arrived in London late in 1945 that she became aware of the widening chasm between Zionist aspirations and the policy of the British Empire.

In the face of an appeal by President Truman for the admission to Palestine of 100,000 refugees, Foreign Minister Ernest Bevin on November 23 bluntly announced what amounted to a reaffirmation of the 1939 White Paper, set up to assure minority status for the Jews in the Holy Land by steadily cutting down immigration. His Majesty's government had a "dual obligation," to Arabs as well as Jews; anyway, Palestine could not possibly absorb the hundreds of thousands of refugees. Some would have to be resettled in Europe.

American critics, led by Senator Owen Brewster of Maine, pounced upon the statement as a transparent excuse for maintaining Middle East colonialism. The British reacted angrily, their testiness aggravated by their acute economic dependence on the United States. America's righteous congressmen, they retorted, had done little to relax their own immigration quotas in favor of DPs.

Fanny went to lunch with Francis Williams at No. 10 Downing Street, where the atmosphere was not encouraging. Bevin sat in surly silence. The foreign minister was very touchy, she was told, about what he considered "unfair Zionist attacks." Other sources in Whitehall spoke of a definite antipathy by Bevin toward Jews, supposedly based on an unfortunate romantic experience in his youth.

Fanny mentioned her concern to Wellington Koo. A few days later, without fanfare, he brought her together at a Chinese Embassy dinner with F. W. Rickett, an Englishman enjoying unparalleled contacts in the Arab world.

Bill Rickett flung off a scent of emirs, oil millions, and E. Phillips Oppenheim intrigue. Ruddy-cheeked and impeccably formal of dress, with curly iron-gray hair, he had masterminded the carving-out of "independent" states in the Middle East after World War I and was currently, according to whispered word from Harry Hussey, trying to secure oil-drilling rights in China.

With a few sharp questions, he established that Fanny had access to such key figures in Jewry as Dr. Stephen Wise. "The opportunity is here," he told her, "for a vast renaissance of the Middle East, combining local raw materials and manpower with Jewish intellect and organizational ability. Either Jews and Arabs will merge their resources for their common benefit, or unrest will sweep the area and the Soviet Union alone will reap the harvest."

Fanny listened, spellbound: "It takes something to keep me quiet. But this man's tales of Levantine adventure, and his pleas for imaginative leadership, struck a new note."

Rickett followed through a week later by presenting "my cousin Abdullah, prince of Transjordan — I'm going to make him king," which he did soon after. Fanny found Abdullah gracious, charming, and — to her astonishment — inexhaustibly articulate about the virtues of the Jewish people. Bowing in farewell after their luncheon at the Ritz, Abdullah expressed hope that he would before long be able to "welcome you to the Jewish Homeland."

This seemed to Fanny a fairly promising start toward rapprochement. But a few days later a noisome incident brought Anglo-Jewish relations to a new impasse.

Lieutenant General Sir Frederick Edgworth Morgan was Hollywood's vision of a senior British army commander: tall, limber, with lively blue eyes, a neatly trimmed moustache and a square forthright jaw.

A divisional commander until he became chief of staff to General Eisenhower in preparing the Normandy invasion, he was credited with personally winning over President Roosevelt to the plan. He held the Distinguished Service Medal and Croix de Guerre as well as his own country's highest decorations.

Late in 1945 General Morgan was appointed chief of the displaced persons operation in Germany for UNRRA, the United Nations Relief and Rehabilitation Administration. UNRRA, established as a stopgap humanitarian expedient, was soon caught up in a tangle of political issues, and Morgan fell heir to a complex situation for which he was unprepared by background or training.

Of the many problems competing for the world's attention after the defeat of Hitler, possibly the most urgent was the dire necessity felt by the surviving Jews of Eastern Europe, and especially Poland, to escape from the environment of hatred and slaughter which had fed millions of their compatriots to Hitler's gas ovens.

For more than five decades, Zionist groups in the area had been exhorting a return to the Jewish Homeland in Palestine. Never before, however, had their cry fallen on such receptive ears. For many Jewish survivors, such a restoration to Zion was the one unblemished ideal remaining in a world of nightmare.

During the war, the Zionist committees in Poland and the Ukraine had become rallying points for resistance to the Nazis. Now they reached out to thousands of their dispossessed brethren, offering them clothes, passports, money to tide them over, and an underground escape route to the Holy Land.

Jewish survivors, regardless of personal economic circumstance or previous Zionist affiliation, lined up eagerly for the return. As instant "Greeks," they were passed along a silent chain of sympathizers. Czech trains provided free passage to the German frontier, where they crossed into the army-administered United States Zone. Here they were taken over by UNRRA, with an assist from the highly organized Central Committee of Liberated Jews in Bavaria. Some were sent to Munich, others to special infiltree camps. A last journey southward took them to French Mediterranean ports for boat passage to Palestine.

Such a massive traffic could scarcely be hidden. The American Zone, already bulging with 400,000 internees, every day made room for another one hundred or two hundred Polish Jews. The status of these fugitives from Polish anti-Semitism was cloudy; having withdrawn since V-E Day from the aegis of a recognized government, they were officially adjudged by the occupation authorities to be "not DPs but voluntary exiles." So far, some ten thousand such "volunteers" had arrived. American military men estimated that sixty thousand more were awaiting transport in Poland, plus a backlog of a quarter of a million in Russian-seized territory east of the Curzon Line.

Direct responsibility for housing and feeding the infiltrees was in the hands of UNRRA. Lower-echelon officials of the agency shook their heads, initialed memos, and passed the buck up the line.

For General Morgan, the immigration of "illegals" from Poland, while in itself a complication, was of more importance as an index to a broader problem: the ostrichlike attitude toward UNRRA displayed by its multinational sponsors. With the agency scheduled to pass into limbo before the end of 1946, no successor body was even being discussed. Unless action was taken soon, a hard core numbering hundreds of thousands of helpless refugees would be dumped into an indifferent world.

Morgan decided to convey his misgivings to the people of the United Nations. The obvious channel was through the corps of foreign correspondents stationed at American Zone headquarters in Frankfurt. He called in his public relations officer, Brooklyn-born Leo Jay Margolin.

Together, Morgan and Margolin drew up a formal release emphasizing the general's concern over what he regarded as international foot-dragging.

On the morning of January 2, General Morgan met with a dozen correspondents, mostly American, at the Park Hotel. He read aloud from the release, interpolating an occasional amplification, and at the end offered to clarify any uncertainties. One correspondent posed a question, another joined in, and soon a spirited general conversation was under way, with the newspaper people voicing their own opinions as well as putting queries.

Morgan, unfamiliar with press conferences, unpracticed in the politician's ploy of muffling a "good quote" in guarded circumlocutions, spoke his mind candidly for more than half an hour.

He did, however, several times decline politely to give an opinion on where the Jews flowing in from Poland should ultimately be settled; that was a political decision, like the disposition of Baltic nationals.

One of his interlocutors persisted. Had General Morgan himself seen any of these Polish survivors?

Yes, he had — although only a small and perhaps not representative number observed in passing on visits to Berlin.

What did they look like?

Morgan shrugged. "They looked like people — not very different from you and me."

There was a stir in the room.

But weren't all these voyagers virtual human scarecrows, someone wanted to know?

Not necessarily, replied Morgan; at least not from Allied intelligence reports and from the glimpse or two he had had himself.

Ten minutes later, after ranging widely over other terrain, Morgan was steered back to the subject. He expressed puzzlement that some of the incoming Polish Jews seemed amply supplied with clothes, food and money.

Did that intimate a concerted plan to spirit them across Europe to a prearranged destination in Palestine?

The general pondered a moment. It was difficult, he said slowly, in the face of their seemingly synchronized stories, to conclude otherwise. But, he went on, why shouldn't they seek a friendly haven? "I know that if I were a Jew I wouldn't care to remain in Europe at this time." Anyway, he emphasized, the key question was not how much the Jews were helping each other, but whether the international community was ready to shoulder its responsibilities.

So, in broad outline, went the press conference. No recording or stenographic transcript was made, but that is the best recollection of those who were present.

It was not precisely the story that burst across the world's breakfast

261

tables the next morning. The New York *Times* and scores of other papers carried the Associated Press account, according to which General Morgan saw in the flood of Jews pouring into the American Zone a "well-organized, positive plan to get out of Europe," evidently sponsored by an "unknown secret Jewish organization." The ostensible DPs had been portrayed by the general as a jolly lot: "well dressed, well fed, rosy-cheeked and with plenty of money."

Buried far down in the text was the actual theme of the conference: Morgan's plea for a responsible long-range program.

The New York *Herald Tribune* story by Carl Levin was better balanced, leading off with Morgan's earnest warning to the world, before taking up the issue of the Polish migration. However, the headline-writer on Levin's copy desk chose to accent the "Jewish angle": "Briton Assails Polish Jews for 'Second Exodus,'" his large-type announcement blared. "Gen. Morgan Has 'Hunch' Migration Is Planned." Only the tail end of the half-column front-page headline made grudging mention of the correspondent's lead: "Sees Allies Passing Buck."

This pattern, with minor variations, was followed by other major wire services and newspapers. As the account was warmed over with a "new lead" for afternoon editions, it acquired flavorsome trimmings. Morgan was described as attributing a "vast plot" to some unknown but sinister "world organization of Jews." A cartoon caption in the newspaper *PM* asserted: "Morgan Charges Jewish World Conspiracy."

The story struck the Jewish community like a match tossed into an oil tank. The flames shot high and wide, totally obscuring the original event and all but consuming General Morgan.

"Sheer Nazism," roared the World Jewish Congress.

Eddie Cantor, the entertainer, blazoned in newspaper ads his resentment of "this shameful attack upon a defenseless people." He assured General Morgan that "the remnants of Jewry have survived Hitler, and they will with our sympathy and support survive you."

Bitter complaints poured into the Washington office of Herbert Lehman, the director general of UNRRA and a former governor of New York. On January 4 it was reported from London that Lehman had demanded Morgan's resignation.

The general declined to quit. The "Jewish fraction" of his comment, he insisted, had been exploited to distort the whole. Far from being an enemy of the survivors, he was determined to obtain for them "more than sympathy and temporary shelter."

A New York *Times* editorial on January 5 condemned Morgan as "heartless," but already from its own correspondents there were stirrings of a different view. Kathleen McLaughlin reported from Frankfurt that Morgan's UNRRA staff, who included many Jews in high positions, were "warm admirers" of their chief. They credited him with repeated personal interventions on behalf of the refugees, and would regard his departure as "a tragic loss." A *Times* dispatch from Eastern Europe by

Raymond Daniell confirmed the existence in Poland of vigorous Zionist underground committees.

Two days later, a *Times* story credited to the North American Newspaper Alliance (NANA) flung another bucket of water against the tide. Its author, a Jewish newspaperman who had attended the Morgan conference, declared flatly that "unguarded remarks, taken out of context," had been "wildly interpreted and elaborated upon"; as a result, "Sir Frederick's well-reasoned original thesis" was virtually blotted out and he was being "pilloried."

British newspaper opinion, at first shocked and dismayed, began swinging toward Morgan. At Whitehall there had never been any question about siding with a national hero who was also a popular figure around Mayfair. As days passed without any resolution of Morgan's status, smoldering resentment in government circles gathered force, reaching its peak with the publication of a full-page advertisement in the New York *Times* on January 15, under the imprint of the American League for a Free Palestine, attacking Morgan as a latter-day Goebbels reflecting the views of Nazi-minded superiors.

The morning after it appeared, Fanny had a call from her friend Francis Williams in the Foreign Office. Williams knew of her deep emotional involvement in the refugee issue. "Fanny," he told her, "these ads are causing a very bad reaction here. People feel that Lehman is literally firing from the hip in trying to get rid of General Morgan, out of fear of Zionist pressure. It doesn't help a bit that Lehman is Jewish. I'm very concerned about the negative repercussions on our Palestine policy. Perhaps you ought to come around to Downing Street today for lunch."

In the cabinet dining room, Fanny saw Foreign Minister Ernest Bevin, bulky and frowning, seated alone. "He's really furious," observed Williams, "that Morgan's boxes [trunks] have been ordered shipped back to London without even, as Bevin says, the decency of a hearing."

For a further appraisal of Bevin's frame of mind, Fanny had the word of Clement Attlee. The prime minister, a friend from San Francisco days, told her that Bevin was incensed to the point of bypassing normal cabinet procedures: "You see, under our system — unlike yours — each minister runs his own bailiwick, with no overlapping authority like that of your president. So Palestine would be strictly the responsibility of the colonial secretary, Arthur Creech Jones. But Ernie can't keep his hands off it. He's so outraged he's telling people he'll never let another Jew into the country."

There was more of the same, from other officials. As Fanny summed it up in a letter to her two brothers: "The Foreign Office people were sighing that the Jews were crucifying one of their best men, but that under the circumstances they would have to give in. That meant the Jews would get it in another way. The British were bitter. Who would suffer — Eddie Cantor and Walter Winchell, tearing herrings in Lindy's?

Or the poor Jews of the world, thousands in China and elsewhere who need the Foreign Office's help — to say nothing of the Palestine situation!"

Fanny left Downing Street much distressed. Returning to Claridge's late in the afternoon, she found a message to call the special operator at the War Office.

The operator had been holding open a military line from Frankfurt for nearly two hours. Who was trying to reach Fanny? Why, one of the senior war correspondents. "He said just to tell you it was 'Harvey' — you would know."

She did indeed. Harvey was the Canadian-Jewish correspondent for NANA who had come forward so strongly in General Morgan's defense. Tall and wiry, with a lupine attractiveness, he had had a wartime flirtation with Gertrude Lawrence, through whom Fanny had met him. She was not eager to renew the relationship; Harvey had aroused feelings of maternalism and vulnerability in her, and then left them hanging. But if he had more to say about the Morgan case . . .

He had word that assumed instant priority. In strained, emotion-laden tones, Harvey informed her that General Morgan had been ordered to leave Germany by 8 P.M. the next day. She had to do something before a terrible injustice was made final — with incalculable consequences for world Jewry. "It just won't wash in London, Fanny — sending home in disgrace, on such flimsy grounds, a man who was hailed by Churchill in Parliament for liberating half of Europe!"

"I'm inclined to agree with you. Would it be possible to talk directly with General Morgan myself?"

There was a pause, and a cool British voice came onto the line: "Morgan speaking."

The general continued speaking, calmly and to the point, as Fanny pressed questions upon him. After twenty minutes, she said: "General Morgan, I'm convinced you're telling the truth. But that isn't enough to make a case legally. We need facts on paper, depositions."

"How can all that be managed in twenty-four hours?"

"I'll have to come there."

"This is occupied territory, Miss Holtzmann. I'm in no position to invite you. And I'm afraid you'll find civilian visitors aren't encouraged."

"If there's a plane flying there, I'll be on it."

She put in a call to Adlai Stevenson: "Adlai, I've got to hitchhike a ride to Frankfurt, to see if I can line up witnesses for General Morgan. Can you get me aboard an army plane?"

"They're pretty sticky. But I'll see what I can do."

Fanny packed an overnight bag. As she was fishing out a map of Germany, Harry Hussey came to the door. She told him of General Morgan's imminent dismissal.

Hussey shook his head somberly. "This will do great harm to America. There'll be a wave of hysteria here."

The telephone rang. "Yes, Adlai?"

"I went all the way to the top, Fanny — General McNarney, commander of the American Zone. His answer was, and I quote: 'What? All this and Holtzmann too? I've got a war on my hands. I want no part of her in the American Zone!' "

"Maybe," suggested Hussey, "your friend down the hall can help. Mrs. Roosevelt."

They found Mrs. Roosevelt finishing up her column. Could she possibly use her influence at the embassy to get Fanny transport?

"What influence?" The president's widow turned her eyes on Fanny and, suddenly an old lady without defenses, burst into tears. "I haven't any power. There's a new president in office. I'm not first lady any more!"

Back in her own suite, Fanny reflected aloud: "All of Germany isn't under American control, Harry. What about the British Zone? How far is that from Frankfurt?"

"At the nearest point, very close."

It was after eight o'clock. She called Francis Williams at home.

"We're as disturbed as you are, Fanny. But what you're proposing would be very irregular. The War Office might be willing to go along, out of regard for Freddie. But if word ever got out —"

"Who has to know?"

"Would you travel by bomber?"

"Why not?"

A little before ten, Williams called back. He had made arrangements for a secret departure via RAF bomber. No, not even Hussey could go with her to the airport. Williams would have the details in a few minutes.

Hurriedly, Fanny drafted a cable to Governor Lehman in Washington, requesting him to hold the Morgan decision in abeyance until she could present "first-hand report not hearsay." Otherwise, "important international leaders here" shared her fear of a "grave injustice."

Williams was on the line again. A staff car was coming by to pick her up at 10:45. Her flight would be leaving at midnight, with a scheduled arrival time in Germany of 3 A.M. —"depending, of course, on the weather."

Bombers, Hussey warned her, had no sleeping sections. Or central heating à la Claridge's. A light rain was splattering against the windows. He advised warm furs — not mink, but beaver.

At five minutes past midnight the two-engined British Dakota rose from the landing strip north of London, a single pilot at the controls and one small, female passenger huddled in the depths of her beaverskin on the floor of the fuselage. The rain had changed to a violent hailstorm; lightning ripped through sodden black skies. The light craft bounced, swayed and shuddered in the wind; Fanny was too chilled to be frightened.

Four hours passed, and still the engines droned on. Twice the pilot dropped altitude, only to veer up sharply again; obviously he was having difficulty landing. Just before 5 A.M. a flare appeared in the blackness below, and the bomber slipped downward. This time it touched ground and stayed.

As Fanny — cold, hungry and shaken — was being helped down by the pilot, a huge figure loomed before her in the rain, rifle poking out of his dripping oilskin. "Your travel orders, ma'am?" The sentry extended a hand.

Fanny had no travel orders, movement papers or other official paraphernalia. But she did have presence of mind. "Oh, my papers," she wailed. "In my rush to get to General Morgan, I must have left them in my cloth coat!"

The sentry hesitated. At that moment, headlights appeared in the distance. A large black Cadillac rolled into view, and a tall spruce officer stepped out. Fanny fell weeping into the arms of General Sir Frederick Edgworth Morgan, who had been alerted to her trip by Francis Williams.

It was daylight when they reached the magnificent castle in Arolsen that served as Morgan's headquarters and residence. On the drive from the airport Fanny had already been sounding out Morgan on his interests and general philosophy, and reached her own appraisal. As she later wrote to her brothers, "The more we talked, the greater became my conviction that it would be a grave tragedy for the Jews to lose him."

She took out her notebook. Sleep, she explained to the general, could be caught up with some other time; meanwhile her "private internal engine" would see her through.

It did not take her long to set down Morgan's story ("since the age of ten I knew how to get an affidavit"). Supporting statements from witnesses might be harder to come by.

They put in a call to United States headquarters in Frankfurt. The commanding general there was out hunting, but the officer-in-charge was the genial sportsman-diplomat Tony Biddle, who had been so helpful to Fanny at Warsaw in 1939. Told of her mission, he cried: "Fantastic. Fanny-tastic! Our friend Jimmy Walker in his heyday would have given anything to be in on this. Come on over."

General Morgan drove with Fanny to the American Zone border: "If I go into Frankfurt with you, it will look self-serving. Good luck, my dear." He put out his hand: "And whatever happens . . . thank you."

Fanny was alone amid the rubble of Frankfurt. Only a few buildings stood intact, frozen sentinels in the late-afternoon gloom. She trudged across the street to the U.S. military offices in the Carlton Hotel.

Tony Biddle leaped up from his desk with a smile that restored her morale. "Fanny! How wonderful to see you. We've got a lot of news to catch up on."

"Not now, Tony. Can you get your press people over here — all those who were at General Morgan's original conference?"

"It'll mean breaking up their poker game — and maybe even postponing tonight's cocktail party." Biddle grinned. "But I'll see what I can do."

As he was on the telephone to the Park Hotel press room, Leo Margolin came in: big, blond, with smiling green eyes behind metal-framed glasses. "You must be Fanny Holtzmann," he said, "and am I glad to see you!

"This situation is crazy. Morgan is surrounded by Jews on his staff here, and we all worship him. Everybody knows he's been bypassing army orders for repatriation in hundreds of hardship cases — sticking his neck out for people that nobody else gives a damn about!"

The correspondents were filing in: men from the three American wire services, Reuters of London, Agence France-Presse, and several individual newspapers including *The Times* of London, the *Christian Science Monitor* and the Chicago *Daily News*. There was one woman: small, efficient Kathleen McLaughlin of the New York *Times*. Harvey, with his drooping melodrama-villain's moustache, strolled in last, ostentatiously careful not to recognize Fanny.

Biddle presented Fanny as a prominent American attorney, attached to the Chinese delegation in London, who would be speaking "off the record and to the point." Fanny got to her feet.

She was Jewish, she told the reporters, and had flown to Frankfurt through an all-night storm to perform what her people called a *mitzva*: "I don't know any exact equivalent in English. You might say it's a good deed known to the Almighty, even if unrecorded on earth.

"I'm here because I refuse to let a decent man be sacrificed to a moment's hysteria, simply because innocent remarks were misinterpreted. I know well some of the misinterpreters. Louis Bromfield is one of my most beloved friends. I doubt that he was ever in a Jewish home before he came to mine. It was my father, a pioneer Zionist, who fired Louis's imagination about Palestine, to the degree where his well-meaning zeal has now swept away his good judgment.

"Exactly what General Morgan said to you in his informal comments earlier this month we shall never know; no transcript was made. But what he meant to convey, I am convinced after hours of talking with him, was that the few DPs he saw in Berlin had apparently been well looked after. They were not cartoon freaks or undesirables.

"He swears he made no charges of a 'Jewish world conspiracy,' or said anything else remotely anti-Semitic. If that is true, he has been condemned without a hearing. That is a grossly un-American procedure.

"I intend to speak with Governor Lehman within the hour. If I can read to him supporting affidavits from the newspaper people who were on the scene, I'm sure I can persuade him to reverse his order of dismissal. Will you help?"

Kathleen McLaughlin stood up. "Will you take down our statements?"

"If I could type, I would never have become a lawyer!"

"We've got to round up some machines," said Harvey. With General Biddle and Leo Margolin, he started for the door.

The tiny open elevator worked overtime as the three ransacked the building for operable typewriters. Within twenty minutes Fanny had the first of a growing pile of affidavits.

Kathleen McLaughlin attested that General Morgan had made every effort to focus the attention of the correspondents on the need for UNRRA's activities to be carried forward in the future by "some other agency, possibly the Quakers or the Red Cross." He had tried to steer clear of political issues. No correspondent departed "with the slightest feeling that General Morgan cherished any anti-Semitic sentiment whatever." On the contrary, "he made very clear in indirect remarks" his sympathies for European Jewry.

John B. McDermott of the United Press declared that a "distorted picture of General Morgan" had been created by "many news commentators and headline writers who had not attended the conference but obtained their information secondhand." Morgan was emphatically not anti-Semitic but was "a straight shooter, a sincere man working his heart out at one of Europe's most difficult jobs."

Biddle's secretary had UNRRA-Washington on the line. Would Miss Holtzmann speak with Governor Lehman's deputy?

She certainly would not, Fanny made clear. She wanted the director general himself.

Coming onto the phone, Lehman ran into a blast of invective that must have seared his ears thirty-five hundred miles away. Fanny began with a disclaimer of any formal association with Morgan, who had been forbidden to discuss his case: "I am acting on my own, because of the dangerous situation into which we Jews have been thrust by you."

Then she let loose the frustrations of the past fortnight. Lehman was a traitor to his people, Fanny shouted, a spineless creature yielding to the likes of Walter Winchell; at best, an ignoramus unaware that his actions had international repercussions: "You are a Jew, but you've never known what it is to suffer as a Jew! You were elected by the Jews because you were a Jew, but you are a rich Jew. How dare you take the rescuer of those who survived the death camps and, without any hearing, send him home in disgrace? Don't you realize the hostility you are provoking in Downing Street, and the halls of the United Nations — the ammunition you are providing to those who talk of Jewish ruthlessness in high places?

"Let me give you the *facts* about General Morgan." She read several excerpts from the correspondents' affidavits. "Does *that* sound like the scoundrel who's being compared in New York to Hitler — and being fired from Washington without an opportunity to present his case?"

Lehman's response was meek: "What do you suggest we do, Miss Holtzmann?"

"First of all, retract his dismissal. Then, send for the general and give him a fair hearing."

"All right. We'll hold off everything until we've talked with him and examined your affidavits."

"They'll go out by courier"— she looked at Tony Biddle, who nodded — "tonight. Meanwhile, issue instructions that General Morgan is not to leave Germany."

"I'll do that."

Fanny fell back in her chair, exhausted. Biddle sent out for sandwiches and coffee, then put her on an American plane to London.

The next morning she was awakened by a call from Adlai Stevenson: Biddle had telephoned him at the embassy to report that Governor Lehman had followed through as promised, suspending the order for Morgan's dismissal until further notice.

The telephone rang again. It was Frances Williams, brimming over with relief: "The P.M. wants to thank you in person."

She was having tea the following afternoon with Clement Attlee when Bevin came over and sat down beside her: "Let me add my own appreciation. It was really ridiculous for the Jews to crucify Freddie Morgan. Nobody has done more for their brothers in Europe. I felt very strongly about it."

"So I heard. 'Not one more Jew into Palestine!' "

"Ah, that was rhetoric, you understand. Actually, my heart goes out to all those homeless people — no place to live, their families destroyed. Don't think it isn't on my mind. I can't sleep nights, my wife will tell you. I just can't see any good solution."

"That will take time and patience. The important thing for all of us is not to act hastily, not to slam doors. That, if I may presume to say so, is wrong — whether it's done by the director general of UNRRA or the British foreign secretary."

Bevin smiled broadly. "I see where you get your reputation. Very well: the 'quiet' sign will go up here. But I can't speak for the future. If something isn't done to muzzle agitators like that Ben Hecht fellow —"

"Splinter groups, Mr. Bevin. They don't speak for American Jewry."

"Who *does*? From where I sit, it's very hard to say."

"If I put the right people in touch with you, will you deal with them?"

Bevin looked at her shrewdly, standing up: "That's my job, now, isn't it?"

General Morgan flew to the United States for "consultations" on January 26, conferring with Lehman the next day at the former governor's Park Avenue apartment and then accompanying him to Washington. On the thirtieth, Lehman announced that after "long and searching talks" the general had been restored to office.

Appropriate salaams were exchanged: the director general said he was convinced Morgan had not intended to impute "sinister motives" to anyone; Morgan acknowledged that certain of his comments might have laid him open to charges of a racial bias that he absolutely did not entertain.

The general went back to his castle at Arolsen and stayed there until August, when he leaped, fell, or was pushed out of his post by the new UNRRA chief, Fiorello La Guardia. This time there was no great scandal; only mutual distaste.

There was a piquant aftermath to General Morgan's visit with Governor Lehman. The general's stay in America overlapped by one day Fanny's return home from Europe. He stopped off to express his gratitude in New York, where Fanny took him to see Gertrude Lawrence in *Pygmalion*. Before leaving for the airport, he handed her a letter of introduction to "my best friend in this country." It was addressed to Dwight D. Eisenhower at the Pentagon.

On her next trip to Washington, Fanny telephoned Eisenhower's office. A cheery voice told her to "come right over, we've heard all about you." A few minutes later she was being greeted in person by Colonel Robert L. Schulz, aide-de-camp to the chief of staff.

Schulz ushered her into an enormous sun-filled room. There, standing at a window, was America's leading military hero —"somehow bigger and warmer than in his pictures."

The general strode toward her, arms outstretched: "So this is Freddie's savior, the great Fanny Holtzmann!"

"I did what I could."

"You did what nobody else could! And you staved off a terrible tragedy. I hope you won't think I'm being forward, Miss Holtzmann, but I'd like to embrace you."

"It would be an honor," Fanny murmured.

She felt muscular arms closing around her, lips brushing her cheek. Eisenhower drew back, still holding her lightly: "You know, you literally saved a life. I talked to Tony Biddle about it. We both agreed that Freddie never would have gone back to Whitehall. He would have blown his brains out."

Fanny shuddered.

"The idea of branding Freddie Morgan as a bigot! He's a compassionate man, incapable of hating anyone." Eisenhower's eyes were moist. "How can I — how can any of his friends — thank you enough?"

At the sight of his emotion, Fanny's controls collapsed. "For *you*, the greatest hero of my people since Moses — the man who delivered my fellow-Jews from Hitler — to be thanking *me*!" She broke into tears herself.

An urbane, intelligent-looking man with a humorous glint in his eye appeared in the doorway. "Come in, Beetle," said Eisenhower. He presented Lieutenant General Walter Bedell Smith, who needed no briefing on the Morgan affair. The chief of staff turned back to Fanny: "I'm so glad it was a Jewish girl who came to Freddie's rescue."

"I think we should drink to that," said Bedell Smith.

Colonel Schulz opened a liquor cabinet. "Scotch or bourbon?", he asked Fanny.

Fanny smiled, dabbing at her eyes: "General Morgan told me all about that — how he learned to like American bourbon during the planning of the Normandy invasion, while General Eisenhower was being converted to scotch."

"That," said Bedell Smith solemnly, "is the secret of a successful collaboration."

"With apologies all around," said Fanny, "I'll stick to ginger ale, please."

She raised her glass: "To all our brave commanders."

Ike squinted down at her, amused: "And determined ladies."

Fanny's intervention in the Morgan-UNRRA imbroglio had at least forestalled an immediate ugly showdown between Briton and Jew, and kept open avenues of possible rapprochement. For the next eighteen months she was to be running back and forth between the antagonists. No effort of her life was more tenacious — or more ultimately frustrating. However, although she could not head off the collision, she was able profoundly to affect its outcome.

Her first move on returning to New York, buoyed by the praises of Downing Street, was to look up Rabbi Stephen Wise — only to find that Wise no longer held the Zionist reins in America. Jewish organizations, impatient over Wise's long and fruitless commitment to Franklin D. Roosevelt, had lined up instead behind his younger and more militant rival, Rabbi Abba Hillel Silver of Cleveland: Republican, fiery of speech, steely of resolution.

When Fanny telephoned the Jewish Agency and the American Jewish Conference, she could not even penetrate the outer ring of secretaries: "Everybody, it seemed, had a father who was a 'pioneer Zionist'; I hadn't so much as membership in Hadassah to give me status." Finally she reached a Miss Ettinger who had worked in a law office and knew something of Fanny's exploits. She directed Fanny to Harry Shapiro at the newly consolidated Zionist Emergency Council.

Shapiro was brusque and irritable on the telephone. He had "a big job here," he informed Fanny. He seemed surprised to find her still on the line. Oh, very well, he would send "one of my people" to her office.

A slight, bookish young man arrived, announcing himself as Harold Manson, publicity specialist and an aide to Rabbi Silver. Manson skimmed through a few letters to Fanny from Wellington Koo and British officials, gaped at the famous faces whose photographs lined the walls, and "came out of his Yeshiva-boy torpor."

Could he telephone Dr. Silver direct in Cleveland?

Silver flew in from Ohio that night. The next morning, flanked by Shapiro and Manson, he came to East Sixty-fourth Street, a massive, imposing figure of a man rolling forth sonorous phrases from a deep chest. His rotund delivery recalled to Fanny Shakespearean evenings in London; the thick black brows above his steel-rimmed spectacles reminded her of that other orator, John L. Lewis.

With Silver at her side, she placed a call to Francis Williams at Whitehall "double four double three." The special advisor to the prime minister of England —"Attlee's Kissinger," as Fanny later called him — came on the line, good-humored and obviously on very cordial terms with Fanny. She introduced him to Rabbi Silver over the telephone and briefly discussed possible procedures for setting up private British-Zionist talks.

There was no further question of her credentials with American Jewry.

Like her Mark Hopkins suite at San Francisco, Fanny's home became a diplomatic clearinghouse, this time for informal exchanges between British officialdom and American Jewry. Both sides welcomed the contact: the Jews because they had no other pipeline to Whitehall, the British because the bad publicity accruing to them on the Palestine issue was affecting their prospects for a huge American loan. At a moment when the two parties would confide almost nothing to each other, they would confide almost totally in Fanny.

Through Francis Williams, the Foreign Office sent to East Sixty-fourth Street the British Information Service chief in New York, then members of the embassy staff from Washington and finally the ambassador himself; later they were joined by cabinet specialists from the Middle East. For the Jews, Rabbi Silver was the recognized spokesman behind whom all factions gathered. The talks inched forward.

Unhappily, the negotiators were not operating in a clear field. On April 30, 1946, the British-sponsored Anglo-American Committee on Palestine made its report. Its major recommendation — immediate admission of 100,000 DPs — was quickly rejected by Whitehall.

Reaction in Tel Aviv was ominous. Clashes between British soldiers and underground Jewish forces, intermittent since the sabotaging of troop railway movements the previous autumn, increased in scale and violence, culminating on July 22 in the dynamiting of British headquarters at the King David Hotel in Jerusalem. Losses among personnel were heavy. The embittered British commander, Lieutenant General Sir Evelyn Barker, issued a nonfraternization order to his troops and branded the entire Jewish community as "accomplices in the guilt," whom his soldiers would be "punishing in a way that the race dislikes as much as any by striking at their pockets."

Soon after these incendiary words came the Bevin-approved formula for "solution" of the Palestine problem. Issued under the imprint of the joint London-Washington "Cabinet Committee," this foresaw creation of a "unitary state" split into autonomous Arab and Jewish zones under a British high commissioner. The Jewish national home, envisaged in 1920 as embracing forty-four thousand square miles and already reduced to ten thousand, would be shorn of the Negev desert and cut down to fifteen hundred square miles.

A storm of indignation, much of it non-Jewish, swept across America denouncing the so-called Morrison-Grady plan.

Fanny was outraged, especially by the attitude of General Barker. Much as she valued the approval of her British friends, she would not trade away her convictions for it. In a long letter to Francis Williams, she demanded the ouster of "that rat Barker." She was equally vehement on the subject with other highly placed Britons, to the point where the ambassador in Washington, Lord Inverchapel, cautioned her to "ponder your prose."

Yet, conversely, she would not give up on her attempts at mediation. Britain was the land that had welcomed her as a young girl, showered her with attentions, and been the scene of her greatest legal triumph. She had coped before with "impossible" situations; if anything, the challenge whetted her appetite.

Meanwhile, the pressure from the DP camps was exploding all over the Mediterranean. Shiploads of desperate "illegals" were being turned back at the gates of Palestine, sometimes brutally. President Truman and presidential candidate Thomas E. Dewey were joining the cries for admission of at least 100,000 — and being met with frosty silence.

Fanny asked Bill Ormerod to dinner. Dapper and suave, Major Cyril Berkeley Ormerod brought to his job as director of the British Information Service a BBC accent, an RAF moustache and a Piccadilly verve. He also had more subtle equipment: a wide-ranging receptivity to other people's viewpoints that endeared him to the New York intellectual community — and to Fanny. She and Ormerod, as fellow seekers of compromise on Palestine, had fallen into a natural alliance.

Fanny set forth her thesis: matters were approaching a point of no return. Nothing less than a meeting at the top might arrest their course. Ernest Bevin was coming to America in November for a meeting of the Council of Foreign Ministers. If Fanny could deliver Rabbi Silver for a secret parley, would Ormerod undertake to produce Bevin?

The major readily agreed. For several weeks cautious, confidential messages were exchanged. Early in December, after Bevin had been booed roundly in an appearance at the New York Polo Grounds, he met twice with Dr. Silver at the Waldorf-Astoria Hotel. Emerging from the second conference, Dr. Silver was in visible good humor. Bevin too was smiling as the pair encountered Fanny and Bill Ormerod in the lobby. "I hope you people appreciate," Bevin told Fanny, "that we English remember our friends."

For the next several weeks, strenuous efforts were made to expand the wedge opened up at the Waldorf-Astoria. The British had been trying to set up since October, and repeatedly postponing, an Arab-Jewish round table conference in London. With Dr. Silver now off to Basle for the Twenty-second World Zionist Congress, key proposals were funneled through Fanny. On December 12 she wired Lord Inverchapel in Washington: "Unless your people get encouraging word to Dr. Silver that the Morrison-Grady plan will be scrapped there is definitely no chance of Zionists' acceptance of invitation to attend the London conference."

Inverchapel, who through Fanny had been brought into cordial relations with Silver, promptly replied that Major Ormerod had been instructed to let her know in full detail just how far the British were willing to modify their position.

A new flurry of conferences, cables and overseas telephone calls was topped off by a 160-word night letter from Fanny to Francis Williams at Downing Street: "Conferred with Silver today. At Inverchapel's request and to prove good faith he appealed to Palestine Jewry to declare truce pending discussions, and denounced terrorism. Silver stated Zionists would attend conference if Britain assures them they concur with United States policy for viable Jewish State in adequate area, details of which can be discussed at London conference. If however Britain unable to comply with this request only other formula is to start moving refugees from Displaced Persons camps by sending immediately three or four boatloads to Palestine."

Fanny added her own observation that such a humanitarian gesture would get wide coverage from American newsreels; she would be enabled also to curtail "inflammatory advertisements." If on the other hand, Silver were totally rebuffed and martial law imposed in Palestine, "I dread consequences. Can only be construed war."

As the year ended, Inverchapel wrote to Fanny, "I must appreciate the immense trouble you are taking on our behalf." And Bill Ormerod, in a fervent handwritten letter accompanying his Christmas gift, paid tribute to her "magnificent efforts, the great part you have played and undoubtedly will continue to play" toward the achievement of peace on earth.

On January 9 Ormerod noted tersely, "We are very near the zero hour." A day later it was evident that the hour had passed. A glum letter from Fanny to Ernest Bevin's physician made oblique reference to recommendations agreed upon in New York but "probably not upheld in London."

Thereafter things went steadily downhill. In February the Jewish Agency executive in London angrily rejected a new and unpublicized British proposal to admit four thousand Jews a month for two years, after which the high commissioner would bar the gates. At the end of five years, Palestine would become an independent state with its Jewish population a permanent minority.

Harold Beeley, the Arabist said to be guiding Bevin's Middle East policy, told Fanny: "The Jews could never make a go of it in their own state. They would destroy themselves by their black-marketing." And the British consul general in Los Angeles made a speech chastising American Jews as "impudent trouble-makers."

Almost by reflex, Fanny kept trying to bank the fires. While strongly protesting the Los Angeles speech, she headed off a picketing demonstration planned against Lord Inverchapel in New Haven. But her patience was waning. In the spring and summer of 1947 she turned her pleas toward her wartime associate John Foster, now a Tory MP closely allied with Winston Churchill.

"I am afraid," Foster responded on August 14, "the Jewish situation in Palestine has been the result of a tragic muddle on the part of our Government. If the Labour Government had accepted the recommendations of the unanimous Anglo-American Commission all this would have been avoided."

With Anglo-Jewish clashes increasing in Palestine and at sea, Fanny made one last approach to Francis Williams. Information had reached the Zionists that the British colonial secretary, Arthur Creech Jones, was far more sympathetic to their cause than Ernest Bevin was; Jones had been pressing the cabinet for immediate admission of DPs to Palestine, regardless of political consequences. Would Prime Minister Attlee send Jones to New York to talk privately with Rabbi Silver?

"We might — if it weren't for your press people. Mr. Attlee doesn't care for those New York headlines: 'British Official Comes Crawling to Jewish Leaders.' "

"Do as I say and there won't be any headlines. Put him on a commercial flight —'A. Jones, Tourist Class'— and when he arrives in New York, have him take a taxi directly to my home. Dr. Silver will be there."

Jones came in late the following afternoon. He had exactly the mild unobtrusive Civil Service personality suggested by his Dickensian name. But Fanny "saw compassion in his face," and was momentarily heartened. She seated him and Silver in opposite chairs before the fireplace, and stayed just long enough to hear the rabbi, with declamatory flourish, embark upon Britain's long history of hospitality to the Jews: during the Spanish Inquisition, and later in the time of Cromwell . . .

Jenkie, peering in an hour later, saw the two gentlemen deep in conversation. She served them steaks and salad on trays. The discussion continued until nine in the evening; Fanny permitted her hopes to soar.

But whatever rapport was established could not survive the onslaught of the Foreign Office Arabists. On September 26, Jones formally advised the General Assembly of the United Nations that, in the absence of any settlement on Palestine, his government intended to withdraw both armed forces and administration. A confidential memo to British officials ten days later, passed along to Fanny by Bill Ormerod for use "with your usual discretion," reiterated that, whether Americans believed the announcement or not, it had been issued in dead earnest. Great Britain, having "administered" Palestine to the brink of disaster, was tossing back the whole hideous tangle upon an overburdened world.

Fanny received the news with mixed feelings. Although it meant the failure of her efforts at mediation, at least she need no longer tie herself in knots trying to serve two masters. She had done her best to save her British friends from their own folly; now she could dedicate herself unreservedly to the goal that had first prompted her enlistment with Wellington Koo, the drive for Jewish statehood.

The final proving ground would be the General Assembly of the United Nations. On August 31, 1947, the UN Special Committee on Palestine had recommended partition of the country into separate Arab and Jewish areas independent of British rule.

The Zionists were as eager for the test-by-ballot as they were ill equipped for it. They were a diverse crew of Americans, Palestinians and Commonwealth Jews who had no cohesive, firmly led diplomatic corps, no experience in the jockeying of international conferences. Fanny by contrast was a veteran of the big-power skirmishes at San Francisco and London, a mysterious figure whose telephone lines apparently reached everywhere. The Jewish Agency delegation to Lake Success didn't quite know what they wanted Fanny to do for them, but they wanted to be sure she was on hand to do it.

Implementation of the UNSCOP partition plan would require a two-thirds majority vote of the fifty-six-member General Assembly. A dozen votes were considered lost in advance: those of the seven Arab states, their neighbors Turkey, Greece, Afghanistan and Pakistan, and Cuba. India too was considered an exceedingly dubious prospect. With only six more supporters, the Arabs would be out of reach.

The Zionists, conversely, needed a minimum of twenty-six affirmative votes — *if* they could persuade the seventeen other countries to abstain. They had backing in Western Europe, the Soviet-dominated areas, and most of the English-speaking world. What they did not have was a strong position in Catholic Latin America, where the future of Jerusalem had been at times a touchy issue. The twenty votes south of the border loomed as pivotal. Apart from a few staunch liberals like Enrique Fabregat of Uruguay, the Latins seemed to be looking toward the Big Five for a clue.

Under these circumstances, Fanny's first self-selected target was Wellington Koo. Given China's large Moslem population, and minuscule number of Jews, no one had any illusions that the Chinese would come out in favor of a Jewish state. But Fanny did have hopes of coaxing them into a neutral stance that would have a profound psychological effect on other delegations.

As far back as March she had written Dr. Koo an eight-page letter carefully tracing the origins of the Zionist movement, its endorsement by the United States Congress in 1922, and its special urgency since the Nazi holocaust. The British Labour Government, she argued, was cynically betraying its mandate. As for the Arabs, "theirs is a case of having much and wanting more, while the Jews have nothing and seek only the little that is granted to every people on earth."

In October she went to lunch with Koo at the Hotel Pierre, where she had had the Chinese delegation installed through the good offices of Eddie Goulding. She brought along for forensic reinforcement her elder brother Jack.

Koo listened sympathetically —"I myself would like to see a Jewish state"— then explained his problem. The Moslems of Chinese Turkestan, exposed to Russia along a lengthy border, were being courted and armed by the Soviets; Nanking did not wish to offend them. In addition, Mao Tse-tung, the Chinese Communist leader, was flatly anti-Zionist; with millions of Moslems in his own back yard, he intended to cultivate the Arab countries and spread his influence in the Middle East. Mao was currently being regarded benignly in Washington; the Chinese Nationalists, their future uncertain, hesitated to rock the boat on what was for them a secondary issue.

Finally, Foreign Minister Hollington Tong had been detecting a distinctly anti-Zionist attitude in the State Department, despite President Truman's public stand to the contrary. If the Americans themselves were privately hostile, why should the faraway Chinese stick their necks out?

Nevertheless, Koo faced Fanny gravely: "You have been very helpful to us, and asked nothing in return. I shall do everything in my power."

Fanny came away from the meeting feeling that there was still a chance with China — but much concerned over Koo's observations on the State Department. Already, Warren Austin, leader of the American delegation, had been heard complaining after a corridor conference that his hands were "full of Jewish perspiration."

The same note of skepticism about the official American position was sounded by Mme. Vijaya Pandit, head of the Indian delegation. Foraging desperately for votes in early November, Fanny contrived a meeting with her. Mrs. Pandit turned out to be Holtzmann-proof, unswayed by Fanny's proposal of a switch to the Zionists in exchange for support in Washington of India against Pakistan; the plan was too iffy.

Besides: "Why is your own delegation sabotaging the Zionists?"

Fanny made a breakfast date with the ever-knowledgeable Adlai Stevenson, who had been promoted from special adviser to alternate on the United States delegation. By some quirk, Stevenson had never grasped the depth of her involvement in the Palestine question. She could generally count on him to pass along the latest development in the American camp, more or less as one mildly interested bystander to another.

*United Nations lounge, 1947: Fanny joins Moshe Sharett, future prime
minister of Israel, in presenting the case for a Jewish state to a delegate
from China*

His own views on the subject seemed to blow hot and cold, for reasons
that would not be clear to Fanny until nearly a decade later. His early
years had manifested hints of prejudice; Stevenson's letters from law
school referred to "the semitic element" and "the race," and told how he
had "jewed down" a book dealer. Involvement in Chicago politics,
where many Jews were active, had apparently softened his views; at the
preparatory meetings of the UN, he seemed receptive to Zionist
aspirations.

Now Fanny confronted him with the reports of State Department slug-
gishness, if not worse, on the partition vote.

Stevenson made a heated denial. True, he conceded, there was a sense
of "defeatism" spreading in some quarters, but not through any failing
on the part of the delegation. He promised to look into the mystery
further.

Early the next morning he telephoned: "It's Jim Forrestal [the secretary of defense] at the Pentagon, Fanny. He's determined to keep the Jews

out of the Middle East. And he's making inroads among the Latin Americans."

"What's he doing — telling them to back the Arabs?"

"Nothing as crude as that. After all, the United States is officially pro-Zionist. He's simply passing word along that no one should take too seriously the public statements of a president under domestic political pressure. A wink and a slap on the shoulder do the rest." Stevenson paused. "Forrestal carries a lot of weight, Fanny. I'm afraid your friends aren't going to get their state, ever."

Mid-November came, and the lobbying went into high gear. Every morning, as delegates and advisers bundled up for the long chilly ride out to Long Island, Fanny had her choice of four cars: Chinese, British, American or Zionist. She tried to rotate her schedule among the first three in a fashion that would provide maximum information to the fourth.

Most of her reports were delivered in the Jewish Agency limousine, since few places were free from eavesdropping: "Everybody was bugging everybody else. I felt like Mata Hari Holtzmann." The Zionist delegates were a tense, uneasy lot, worried about the outcome of their mission, split by differences in tactics and personality. Fanny sensed the familiar ambience of "a Jewish wedding, where the new in-laws turn up their noses at each other." There was a perennial wrangle about whether the car windows should be kept open, with Moshe Shertok (later Sharett), Ben-Gurion's representative, protesting that he would catch pneumonia.

Shertok was a small soft-voiced man with dark restless eyes, and something of Chaplin in his toothbrush moustache and quick nervous movements. He was flanked by two very clever young aides: slender, scholarly Eliahu Epstein (later Eylat) and the enormously polished, beautifully articulate Abba Eban.

Far less attractive in Fanny's eyes was Nahum Goldmann, whom she had found bumptious in San Francisco; he was no less aggressive in New York. It was on account of Goldmann that her attention was drawn to a woman delegate, Golda Meir: "She was the only one who stood up to him. He tried to dismiss her as a mere female, a lady socialist no less, who could not match his fancy wardrobe or his international standing — and she just wouldn't take it.

"Then I began to notice that she had something besides spirit. Every time Golda opened her mouth to speak, she made sense. She was the one who always broke up the squabbles in the delegation, like a capable Milwaukee schoolmarm shushing a roomful of unruly boys: 'Come on, now, behave, we're coming into Lake Success!' "

Another woman in the group earned Fanny's respect: "Until I met Rose Halprin, I had assumed Hadassah ladies were like the ineffectual Helen Hokinson clubwomen in *The New Yorker*, a standing joke. Rose was as clear-minded as Golda, but in a more feminine, floppy-hatted way." (The appreciation was mutual. A quarter of a century later, Rose recalled Fanny's "incredible tenacity. So few people have it. And she did it with tact; she persisted gently, like waves lapping steadily against a shore, until she got what she wanted.")

Ben-Gurion came to the UN, and Shertok presented Fanny to him excitedly: "This is the Chinese lady lawyer, B.G. — believe it or not!"

"I am *not* Oriental," Fanny corrected him. " 'Holtzmann'; how do you say that in Chinese? My father was a correspondent for Herzl in Brooklyn before you were born!"

Ben-Gurion's presence raised the tension level in the delegation: "Everybody froze up when he arrived. He quarreled with all of them except Rose Halprin and me. I was a newcomer to the inner circle, not part of their factionalism." With Fanny, Ben-Gurion confined himself to sharp, direct questions regarding the American and British positions.

What Fanny had to report, especially the Stevenson information about Forrestal, was not comforting. The Latin delegations, whether in response to American sabotage, Arab oil money, or both, were in a state of turmoil. Some openly invited bribes; others stood so firmly upon their integrity that they turned aside even the offer of a drink.

In the swirl of delegates, buttonhole-grabbers and reporters milling through the delegates' lounge, contretemps were inevitable. As Fanny said, "I could always spot a Chinese, but it wasn't so easy to tell the Arabs from the Jews. Except for a few Arabs who wore Bedouin robes, their delegates looked like Jewish businessmen."

One afternoon she came up to a thin, dark-faced man dressed in the standard UN ensemble of white shirt, blue tie and conservative gray suit: "He looked familiar; I assumed he was one of Silver's boys."

"I have an urgent message for Dr. Silver," she told him. "From Fanny Holtzmann. I want him to get to work immediately on one of the delegates." Fanny mentioned a man from a Central American state.

"But I just paid him off, myself!"

"Then why should he get word to me —" Fanny stopped. "You're a Jew, aren't you?"

"Most certainly not. I hate Jews." The man grimaced. "Not that I would trust my fellow Arabs, either. The leader of my delegation probably split our payoff with your Latin friend — who is now trying to collect from your side."

There were other surprises. Andrei Gromyko of the Soviet Union threw his weight behind the Zionist campaigning. A Jewish state could be the salvation of the Middle East, he told Fanny; the Jews had made a big contribution wherever they settled: "It's about time the oil imperialists got out. Why should they, just because they throw a rod into the ground and strike oil, dictate the policies of millions? Oil should be made available to the whole world."

Late in November, bad news broke: the French delegation, supposedly pledged to the Zionists, was wavering. As a result, the picture in volatile Latin America had darkened. A quick check disclosed that with the final balloting only a few days off, the Jewish state remained four votes short of the required two-thirds majority.

The atmosphere in the Jewish Agency limousine was gloomy. "If only," a voice in the back grumbled, "Walter White hadn't butted in. We might have a chance with Liberia."

Fanny perked up. "Liberia? What's the story there?"

The Negro republic in West Africa, she was told, had been considered susceptible to the influence of the Firestone Rubber people, who had enormous holdings there. But the Liberian delegation at the UN had been "infected" by the "white colonialist" argument against Zionism put forward by White, head of the National Association for the Advancement of Colored People, and UN official Ralph J. Bunche.

"Firestone Rubber — that's Harvey Firestone. Quick — get me to a telephone."

Harvey Firestone had ranked high in the delegation of rubber experts sailing under special State Department authority aboard the ship on which Fanny had traveled to London for the UN Preparatory Commission meetings two years earlier. Like his colleagues, he had been dazzled by the show-business aura attending her departure, to which Gertrude Lawrence and Noel Coward largely contributed; at his urging Fanny had been elected an honorary citizen of his hometown, Akron, Ohio.

Firestone came onto the telephone in great good humor: "Hello, Fanny! What can I do for you?"

She told him, bluntly.

"Well," Firestone said slowly, "we have a concession on rubber rights in Liberia — but we make it a point not to interfere in their politics. And you know, there are no Jews in the country."

"I'm told the government there has a lot of respect for your local representative."

"Byron Larabee? Yes, that's true."

"If there was some way I could have a word with him, on a purely personal basis — it's important to my people, Harvey."

A long, agonizing pause. Then, "Sit tight, Fanny."

Two days later Byron H. Larabee was in Fanny's living room (he had been brought by Firestone's private plane). The only other person present was Marvin Lowenthal, the art critic, historian, and writer-in-residence at Brandeis University.

Lowenthal sketched for Larabee the benefits that the underdeveloped nations of Africa could derive from the presence nearby of a dynamic, progressive Jewish state, willing to offer guidance in medicine, agriculture, technology. "Apart from the matter of simple justice," added Fanny. "Six million Jews were slaughtered for no crime whatever. Isn't it fair that the survivors have a chance?"

The next morning, Liberia quietly announced for the Jewish state. It was a welcome victory, but there was a bigger one ahead. As Fanny arrived for lunch at the delegates' dining room, she was greeted by a smiling Fabregat of Uruguay: "China has decided to abstain." Wellington Koo, true to his pledge, had intervened personally with Chiang Kai-shek and been given the go-ahead. Later the same day, word came that France would support the Jewish state after all.

Paraguay and Peru tumbled into the Zionists' "aye" column. With the issue no longer in doubt, the rest of Latin America hastened aboard the bandwagon. When the official tally was taken on November 29, 1947, fourteen states south of the border voted in favor of partition; the other six, like Wellington Koo, registered a life-saving neutrality. The UNSCOP plan was approved by 33 votes to 13, with 10 abstentions.

Fanny neither received nor sought any public recognition for her contribution. She did, however, get an unusual letter a few days later from Rabbi Silver. Dated December 2, it was "addressed to a very remarkable lady who has been a tower of strength to our movement in the past crucial months.

"The selflessness and devotion with which you have applied yourself to the task of winning friends for our cause among the nations of the world have produced gratifying results. You should be happy in the knowledge that you achieved much in this bitter struggle — and have played a prominent part in the accomplishment of an historic task."

Forrestal and his cohorts had been defeated, but not routed. Rallying the support of powerful oil and industrial interests, the defense secretary was able to enlist Senator Arthur H. Vandenberg of Michigan, head of the Senate Foreign Relations Committee. Vandenberg began urging on President Truman a "nonpartisan" policy in the embattled Middle East, exactly like the "nonintervention" in Spain, which had left the Loyalists there at the mercy of Franco and Hitler.

The ideal pro-Zionist counterweight to the midwestern Vandenberg was his Republican rival, Senator Robert H. Taft. Liaison with Taft had been maintained chiefly through his fellow Ohioan, Rabbi Silver. Fanny too, however, had known Taft through Ham Fish since the late thirties. Now, with Silver away in Europe, Fanny received a telegram in Beverly Hills from the Zionist Emergency Council urging her to cut short her business there and pursue the Taft contact again. She took the first available transport east and went directly to Taft's office.

The senator sat slumped over his desk, his head buried in his arms. As Fanny was ushered in, he let loose a loud and not especially senatorial belch. He quickly apologized.

"You should do that in public," Fanny smiled. "It shows you're human."

The plain, stern features relaxed. Taft was feeling miserable, he confessed; things were not going well.

"I'll trade *tsouris* with you."

" '*Tsouris*?' What's that?"

"Basic Yiddish for 'trouble.' "

Taft explained that with reelection coming up in 1948, he was taking a terrible editorial battering from the Toledo *Blade*, which had lately been acquired by the Philadelphia publisher J. David Stern.

"I'll get Stern off your back — if you'll get Arthur Vandenberg off ours."

Fanny outlined her mission. The pact was struck, both parties honored it, and the Vandenberg proposals in the Senate collapsed.

Still Forrestal did not give up. He turned his attention to President Truman, who although basically sympathetic to Jewry and suspicious of Arabists in the State Department had lately become sensitive to what he considered excessive Zionist prodding.

The American tone at the UN began to change. Arab rioting, declared Warren Austin, demonstrated that the partition plan was unenforceable. The Negev desert should be amputated from the unborn Jewish state.

On March 18, driving out to Lake Success in the State Department limousine, Fanny was calmly informed by Adlai Stevenson that Forrestal had finally won out: "Now we know where we're going. The partition plan is being scrapped." Two days later Austin formally requested a Special Assembly to "reconsider trusteeship" as a solution.

At this point Eleanor Roosevelt stepped in, with the third and angriest of a series of letters protesting the Forrestal-Truman Middle East policy. Mrs. Roosevelt was a veteran member of the United States delegation and chairman of the UN Human Rights Commission. This time she offered to resign.

Her ultimatum was a curious climax to a relationship with Jewry that had begun, like Adlai Stevenson's, on a note of conventional prejudice. When she arrived in Washington, Mrs. Roosevelt had been annoyed by the "very Jew" mannerisms of Justice Felix Frankfurter; "the race," she observed in a letter, had nerves of iron and tentacles of steel. But before World War II she had quit the Colony Club because it would not admit Elinor Morgenthau, and she was defending Jewish clannishness as a reaction to Gentile oppression. In London she told Fanny, "From the time I began to work in the ghettos, the time of my emergence as a human being, all my mentors were Jewish." She did not want in England to be "publicly vociferous" about her support for a Jewish state lest she endanger the bipartisan coloration of the United States delegation. However, when Fanny visited her the following April on Washington Square, and they discussed the sinking of a refugee ship off Turkey, she agreed to put her objections in writing to the White House.

There were more letters from Mrs. Roosevelt to the President in 1948, protesting Forrestal's opposition to a United Nations police force in Palestine and his insistence that American volunteers fighting for the Jewish state should be deprived at once of citizenship.

At Mrs. Roosevelt's flat threat to resign, Truman backed off from trusteeship to a cloudy ambivalence that lingered until mid-May. When

Ben-Gurion proclaimed the founding of Israel, the president abruptly threw aside the counsels of the Pentagon and the State Department and welcomed the new democracy.

It was not until more than a year later that Fanny had her first glimpse of the new Jewish state. She was in London on business for Charles Cochran, who had recently been knighted. As she was riding in a taxi past Manchester Square she saw Eliahu Eylat, the Israeli ambassador to the Court of St. James's, emerging from his legation building. She called out to him, and there was a brief, hectic sidewalk conversation punctuated by honking horns. It ended with Eylat suggesting that she join him on an El Al flight to Tel Aviv two days later; his secretary would arrange details.

That evening Fanny was on the platform at a London meeting of the Women's International Zionist Organization, as guest of the president, Rebecca Sieff of the Marks and Spencer mercantile empire. Fanny was wrapped in luxurious mink purchased reluctantly from Hattie Carnegie a month before under the goading of Gertrude Lawrence and Fanny's brother David. A newcomer to the costly fur, Fanny felt conspicuous and rather uncomfortable, especially in view of the austerity conditions still prevailing in England.

The English ladies, however, ogled the garment in admiration. "That mink would fetch thousands here," one remarked.

Fanny stood up and flung the coat off. "Good. I'm leaving for Tel Aviv Thursday. The coat is up for auction — full proceeds to Israel."

The mink brought $6,500.

The sequel to the story appeared two weeks later in the Boston *Post*. Grace Davidson, a staff correspondent who was touring Israel, met Fanny at the Jerusalem home of Gershon Agron, publisher of the *Palestine Post*. The February winds were cold and blustery. All through the evening the publisher, with many a gesture toward the bare Judean Hills, kept teasing Fanny about her departed mink.

The "dynamic Miss Holtzmann," according to the correspondent, responded to Agron's jibes cheerfully: "I have never been so warm in my life. This morning I visited a tent camp housing sixteen thousand immigrants. Seeing their plight and the courage with which they met it, how could I be cold?"

Fanny's deepest pleasure in Israel came from seeing the ex-Galician cousins whom she had dispatched to a new life in the Holy Land.

One of the couples whose transplanting to Tel Aviv she had financed and facilitated, the John Horns, were the parents of a healthy infant boy, William Moshe, who before his twentieth birthday was to capture a nest of Syrian gunners on the Galilee plateau.

Moshe Goldfeld, the erstwhile accounting student, had fought bravely in the Jewish Brigade of the British army during World War II, and now held the rank of major in the Israeli army. When Fanny greeted the buxom Mrs. Goldfeld by her German name, Regina, Moshe held up his hand in mock protest: "You must not insult my wife, dear Fanny. We are in our own land now, and her name is *Rivka* [Hebrew for Rebecca]. I fought for that!"

The pair had a brood of vigorous sabra children, who had been brought up on the legend of Cousin Fanny Holtzmann from America, to whom, their parents instructed them, they literally owed their lives. As the family gathered around the supper table, Moshe soberly introduced the visitor as "God's messenger on earth." Fanny felt awed eyes upon her. "Each one of them looked at me as if convinced I had descended directly from Heaven, like some Biblical angel. No material windfall could have made me feel so rich. Perhaps, I thought to myself, God did not mean me to be a mother and bring forth children; but He has been good to me. I have been privileged to give."

Giving was never a problem for Fanny. She topped off her services to Israel by obtaining hangar space at Idlewild (now Kennedy) airport for El Al, the state's fledgling airline.

Getting what she needed for herself was another matter. In the postwar years Harvey, the lanky Canadian newspaperman who had been active in the Morgan affair, turned his attentions from Gertrude Lawrence to Fanny.

Among his colleagues, Harvey was not regarded as a lovable character. Fiercely ambitious and rigidly self-centered, he referred to a little-known book he had written as a "collector's item." He was notoriously unconvivial, especially when the waiter brought the check around.

None of these endearing qualities evidently registered with Fanny. She saw only the Rudolf Rassendyl moustache with a pipe beneath, the dashing trenchcoat, and, hovering somewhere in the shadows, the ghost of a defeated Gertrude Lawrence. Fanny could be counselor to international statesmen and confidante to the great; she could display an earthy wisdom in guiding the personal lives of her client. But for herself, she remained as vulnerable as a child.

Maturing handsomely in the 1940's, with a soft mellowing of features that does not always accompany the middle years, Fanny still had the looks and fire to attract men — and still lacked, alas, the guile to handle them. In this one area she was short on experience, and on the confidence her achievements had imparted elsewhere. Ill at ease in a courting situation, she tended to fall back on name-dropping or to adopt a transparent coyness. Unequipped with the weapons of seduction, she could draw only upon the resources that had brought success in her career: directness, tenacity, aggressive imagination.

At the start, that was enough to intrigue Harvey. In September of 1945, soon after their meeting, Fanny was introducing him in a letter to Lady Cromer as "a very dear friend of mine." Before long, she was reaching out to Harvey quite openly in her need.

To Harvey, the reaching-out must have felt more like moving-in. He was the classical wandering Casanova, never married, insulated against intense involvement by a long attachment to his widowed mother.

The dauntless correspondent beat a hasty retreat.

And yet — Fanny was an exciting, influential woman. He came back. His oscillations of mood left Fanny restless and upset.

When they came into contact again over the Morgan affair, Fanny wrote to her two brothers: "Well, the last thing I wanted was to get mixed up with Harvey again, but you know me — how I cannot rest until a wrong is righted.

"As for Harvey, you will be interested and no doubt relieved that the trip had the effect of riveting my decision to mark 'Finis' to that friendship. It just does not fit into the pattern. Harvey has been useful — the Morgan matter would have collapsed without him — but that is all. I did not even have him wait to see me off on the plane [at Frankfurt]. He goes his way, I mine. He won't ever phone me again, he knows that."

But evidently her decision was not that clear-cut, because a few weeks later, on February 14, 1946, General Morgan was writing to her, after a report on his warm reception by Ernest Bevin: "To get back to the things that really interest you. As soon as I got back I tried to ring Harvey but I find he is in England. They told me he is coming back shortly to Germany and I have let it be known that I want to see him just as soon as he does so. I have a good deal to talk to him about." Did Morgan intend to play the stern Dutch uncle, rebuking his correspondent friend for trifling with Fanny's affections?

A postscript by hand added: "Harvey is back and has rung me. He will have your note and pills on Sunday."

Harvey returned to America that summer, with plans in his head for a novel about the Normandy invasion. He called Fanny, received a guarded invitation to dinner, and uncorked the outlines of his plot. Before the evening was over she had been in touch with a publishing house and was suggesting a new name for his heroine.

Since the days of *Fury* with Eddie Goulding she had been especially susceptible to authors in the throes of creation. As with Goulding and Stanley, once again she was involved with a writer whose work-in-progress she made her own. Any connection between her literary enthusiasm and marital yearnings was no concern of Harvey's; he was glad to accept her help without exploring its motivation too closely.

A letter from Fanny to General Morgan on September 9 opened on a note of virtual domesticity: "Harvey and I were sitting quietly sipping our after-dinner coffee last night . . ."

Morgan, responding to the "good news of your reunion" with Harvey, commented dryly: "And after all you have said about him too."

To Lady Cromer, Fanny wrote on the last day of 1946 that Harvey's novel would "head the publisher's list when it comes out in June." As a sometime author, her ladyship could understand "what Harvey is going through these days." But not alone: "We have high hopes." "*We*" were keeping fingers crossed for a book-club selection.

There was one more high-spirited letter to Morgan on January 30, assuring him that if he came to New York Fanny would "ask our friend Harvey to tear himself away from his beloved typewriter where he is now working on the last stage of his novel, to greet you." A reply from Morgan in early March expressed pleasure that "you and Harvey are apparently back on the level again."

And then — with Harvey's book presumably on the presses — silence.

The next reference to the subject came in a long seriocomic letter to Fanny on April 23 from Frank Scully: "My agent," ruminated Frank, "lacks what you have. I lack it too. But I thank God somebody has it. You can join me in this.

"You don't have a lot of other things. Why? Well, because you can't have everything . . .

"If by now I don't know your camera angles I never will. But I think I do. I think I know what makes you tick and what you would want more than anything else in the world and the reason for your sublimations and the drive behind them and if they come off, fine, and if they don't, okay too. C'est la vie. C'est la guerre. By my book you've given more than you've got and you've got plenty.

"As for your private life, as the phrase goes, tell David to put it in the grist mill. Let Gertie play it. Make another million and use it to give Palestine back to a beautiful people. I assure you it's a better play than it was a love story."

Fanny's anguish must have lingered in her friend's mind. Two months later Scully wrote again: "I suppose time has healed your wounds or opened them anew, and as you know there isn't much one can do about other people's affairs, except to listen. You know better than we do that you can't change human nature, and in this case you're so human as to make the angels weep. The guy isn't worth it, but what guy is?"

Fanny was never one to dawdle over rhetorical questions. Perhaps she was not destined for matrimonial ecstasy. The world held other possibilities.

Book Three

Chapter 12

AT THE PEAK of her professional career, Fanny made a right-angle turn into a new arena. After twenty-five years of guiding artists, she became one.

Toward the end of the war, she had at the urging of Gertrude Lawrence invested in a painting kit for her mother: "If Grandma Moses can do it, so can you!" But Theresa, although adept at needlework, declined to be pushed. So day after day the kit lay neglected in the hall closet, a constant reminder of Fanny's improvidence.

One afternoon a black dressing gown of Theresa's came back from the cleaner with its red-rose ornamentation badly faded. Experimentally, Fanny mixed a few colors from the kit and painted the roses back in. The next morning, her old friend Lucy Schneeberg had a telephone call: "Lucy, I'm going to take art lessons."

"Art lessons? Running a law office and the United Nations is *nicht genug* [not enough]?"

"I have to, Lucy. I'm stuck with all this beautiful equipment I bought for Mama. You know how I feel about wasting anything."

Fanny was totally innocent of art history or painting techniques. She had scarcely been in a museum except for obligatory tours of the Louvre, the Tate Galley in London, and the Prado in Madrid.

After enrolling in an East Side "art academy," she quickly discovered that conventional routes to painting were closed to her. She had no patience with plumb lines, careful measurements, the laborious mechanics of drawing. It was beyond her powers to reproduce in reasonable facsimile the fruit bowls or plump torsos set before the class; nor could she copy accurately a landscape sketched by Constable.

What she did submit for inspection scandalized her teacher: "Where did you get that ridiculous cow? And the storm clouds across the sky?

Quite impossible, Miss Holtzmann. You must learn to set down exactly what is before you." Anything else, the instructor implied, was a form of wicked cheating. Fanny, a perennial occupant of the last-row-last-seat in Brooklyn, felt thrust back thirty years.

In despair, she turned to Aaron Berkman. Aaron was the family's professional artist. He had studied in Paris in the twenties, served as art critic of the H. L. Mencken–George Jean Nathan *American Mercury*, and was directing a battery of instructors at the Ninety-second Street YMHA.

Aaron understood at once that Fanny could never respond to a close-order drill approach. He set out instead to convey the nature of painting —"it's an artifice, a framework for personal expression"— and to impart a few basics about art materials, the potentials and limitations of paint, brush and canvas.

The forms and colors of reality, he explained, should be a source not of enslavement but of stimulation to the painter. But before she could build upon them effectively she had to perceive their relationships better: the depth of a shadow, the thin trail of a cloud above the horizon. Aaron, as Fanny put it, gave her "another pair of eyes." And along with sharper perception came the courage to make her own experiments.

Just off the pantry at Sixty-fourth Street was a little-used maid's room, a catch-all for spare furniture and household articles. Fanny moved out the sofa occupying much of the six-by-eight cubicle and moved in an easel. She installed a shelf for canvases along the right-hand wall, and below it a rack to hold her tubes of pigment. On a table adjoining the sink at her left she scattered a few brushes. She had her "studio."

Belatedly she realized that the lone window looking out on a narrow courtyard provided little illumination. So she brought in a lamp from her bedroom, and later replaced it with an overhead neon. Of the painterly nuances regarding studio light, the usual insistence on a window or skylight facing north, she knew nothing. Years afterward, when a man from the Metropolitan Museum of Art inquired respectfully what kind of light she used, she replied, "Electric!"

Here, in the pale hours of dawn, Fanny began to paint. For a few weeks, at Aaron Berkman's suggestion, she kept a vaseful of flowers at hand as a kind of pilot light for her creative fires. What usually emerged on her canvas, a torrent of brilliant hues and outsize petals, was closer to the effusions of a tropical rain forest than to any visible model.

Gradually she discarded the vase and gave herself over completely to memory and imagination. Rising at 6 A.M., she would shuffle from bed into the studio and commence her "spirit-writing" with the brush: "It never felt like an act of conscious will, but more like the release of forces beyond my control. I could swear my hand was being guided by a *dybbuk*" (an unquiet spirit of Chasidic legend that inhabits and "possesses" human bodies).

The *dybbuk* created naked tree limbs, twisting in anguish toward a sullen sky. Or it might turn sudden handsprings of gaiety, splashing springtime yellows and greens across the playgrounds of Central Park. It was no respecter of seasons; on a chill January morning it might choose to remember the crowded beach at Coney Island; in summer it liked to paint snowscapes. One of its most haunting efforts, spun out rapidly during a steamy July, portrayed a skating scene in Central Park, all icy-blue reflections under a brooding gray sky. So powerful was the painting's evocation of the season — stark lonely trees, frozen lake, huddled skaters half lost in a snowbank — that a viewer would instinctively fold his arms to ward off the chill.

These unscheduled, unorthodox creations were exciting to Fanny, but also vaguely embarrassing. Why couldn't she paint from models, like other people? On a visit to Gertrude Lawrence at the Cape, she took along her colors. The two tramped out into the country, where Gertrude complacently sketched cranberry bogs nuzzled against the sea. Fanny could produce nothing.

Perhaps what she needed was a more exotic setting. Gathering up her sister Clara and a young niece, she headed for the spa of San José Purua in Mexico.

It was August, and the surrounding countryside could not have been more picturesque: a medley of towering mountains and sunny pueblos, bright shawls and burros.

But not so much as a sombrero could she capture on canvas. Disgusted, Fanny picked up her portable easel from the verandah and wandered down to a clearing half a mile north of the hotel. There, overlooking a ravine, she began to paint. Not, of course, the ravine. In the blazing sun, she conjured up a snow scene.

She became aware of having company. "Very strong, Harry," said a cool female voice. "No tricks, but a definite personal statement."

"You're right," a man replied. "Fantastic sense of atmosphere — I can feel the wind whipping around my face. I'll take it."

Fanny whirled around, seized with panic. Never before had her unfinished work been exposed to a stranger's gaze: "It was like being caught naked."

She found herself facing a little, vibrant woman accompanied by a stocky blond man. The man's garb was self-consciously negligent, Fifth Avenue Bohemian; his blue eyes, however, were warm, direct, instantly appealing.

The two introduced themselves as Nettie King and Harry Abrams. Evidently they were involved in art publishing, and had assumed that she too was a professional. She quickly disabused them: "I paint for fun, not commerce. I'm scarcely even a dabbler. My sister Bertha is the only one who will give me wall space."

"Nevertheless," persisted Abrams in his soft, coaxing voice, "you are extremely talented. You must come to my suite this evening for cocktails."

"I never drink, but I'll come." She added that she was a lawyer.

Abrams smiled gently: "I'll give you orange juice — and I'll get a copy of the *Law Journal*."

From mutual friends at the spa hotel, Fanny learned more about her interlocutors. Harry N. Abrams was a self-educated man from her own native Brownsville, and a cofounder of the Book-of-the-Month Club. He had expanded into art publishing, where his superbly reproduced illustrations were credited with broadening the appeal of the masters and refining popular taste; he was also noted for a low-key persuasiveness that, as Fanny observed, "made writers want to write for him, and painters want to paint."

Nettie King, comely and magnetic, had roamed through the art world since her teens, an energizing influence in a half-dozen countries. With her husband, the painter and wit Alexander King, she had been part of the aesthetic ferment of the twenties, the midwest-to-Paris era of Fitzgerald, Hemingway and Gertrude Stein. She had been agent for many of the great figures of French painting.

At the cocktail party, Fanny discovered that Nettie was on equally intimate terms with the giants of the Mexican scene. That weekend she took Fanny to the home of Siqueiros, where Diego Rivera and Covarrubias dropped in later for after-dinner coffee. Fanny "knew nothing of their work — how on earth would I know? When Rivera admired my snow scene, I thought he was being polite, like a mother raving over the pictures brought home by a kindergarten child."

Nettie King and Harry Abrams, under the imprint of the Gallery Artists Company, were in the midst of assembling reproduction rights to a series of old masters which would be bracketed with works by well-known moderns and a few "famous people who paint," and marketed as a Christmas card line. Nettie, as editor-in-charge, wanted to see what Fanny had hanging on her walls at home in New York.

Fall came, and Nettie had her chance. Twenty-five years later her impressions were still fresh: "I was confronted by an extraordinary native gift . . . raw and undisciplined, but absolutely arresting. Here, among the dozens of painters involved in the fads of the forties — neon lights, collages, reduction-to-minimum — was someone dealing in a totally personal way of expression, simply putting down what she saw and felt. Her canvases weren't controlled, polished, but whatever the subject — city scenes, still lifes, portraits — they had great power, always refined by a touch of delicacy and tenderness somewhere, something very feminine. It was the kind of work I like to buy not as an 'investment' but just for the hell of it, for the private pleasure of owning it."

It was also the kind of work the Gallery Artists were looking for. They already had rights to reproduce Picasso, Cézanne and van Gogh along with Grandma Moses, Salvador Dali and the leading Impressionists; they were eager for a contract with Winston Churchill.

Fanny hesitated, conscious in advance of her brother Jack's disapproval. What of her dignity as a member of the bar?

"You'll be listed alphabetically," Nettie told her —"right after El Greco. How dignified can you get?"

Fanny signed a three-year agreement turning over copyrights in exchange for royalties.

Early in 1948, Harry Abrams sold his entire Gallery Artists catalogue to the Hall brothers, whose Hallmark Cards dominated the greeting-card field. One midnight Fanny was awakened by a call from Abrams: "You know that painting in your dining room, the Central Park skating scene?"

Drowsily, "Yes?"

"J. C. Hall is here — the president of the company. I offered him any painting in my collection. You know what he wants? 'The original of that Fanny Holtzmann card.' We're coming right over."

Abrams lived a few blocks away. Fanny barely had time to comb her hair and put on a dressing gown before her visitors were at the door.

Hall stood before the painting lovingly, marveling aloud at the somber winter sky, the lively colors and swirling movement of the skaters.

"What?" whispered Fanny to Abrams. "Is it really so good?"

"It's great," pronounced Hall. "I'll pay anything you want for it."

"If it's that good," Fanny replied, "why should I part with it? I'll keep it for myself."

Hall was clearly disappointed, but took her refusal graciously. He used the skating scene in 1948 as his own personal Christmas card, observing in a note to Fanny: "I have said from the start that your skating subjects were ranked right near the top of the things produced by the Gallery Artists and transferred to us."

All together, Hallmark purchased reproduction rights to three of Fanny's canvases, including a sunnier, more crowded version of the skating pond and a winter street scene.

Even her brother Jack was mollified, although not to the point of sending out Fanny Holtzmann Christmas cards: "He complained they were too expensive. So did my sisters. I could impress everybody but my own family. Every Christmas the mail would come in — featuring my competitors. It made me furious."

Fanny also felt vaguely fraudulent at being classed with the masters. She needed more training.

And so, inquiring at galleries and art supply shops, she stumbled onto "the Baron." His name was Landau, and he was very European: pink-cheeked, portly, completely bald. A close friend of the German poet Rainer Maria Rilke, Baron Landau had studied with Henri Matisse in Paris.

But he did not see it as his mission to convert Fanny to French modernism — or anything else. "I can give you some technique," he told her, "but you'll never be an Ingres. It doesn't matter. What you have is more important than draftsmanship: the inner eye. Just cultivate that. Tricks are for calendar painters."

Landau would drift in around noon, after Fanny had been working for five or six hours, to review her handling of figures and perspective. Sometimes he interposed a deft brushstroke to demonstrate how drawing was a problem of form that could be integrated into painting. More often he talked to her of art history, and why one strong personal statement was worth a dozen academically executed banalities.

Thus encouraged, Fanny returned to Mexico. This time she brought back memories that flowered in her maid's room–studio into large, brilliant canvases soaked with local flavor and sunshine. An assistant curator at the Metropolitan Museum of Art, sent by Harry Abrams, was charmed by a study of a dozing peon; he wanted to display it, along with an oil of Times Square in the rain.

She demurred, fearful that her work would wind up in storage, unseen.

When several of her pictures did go on display, it was at the stately Leicester Galleries in London: far enough away to be forgotten if the response was indifferent, prestigious enough to be cited proudly in event of a triumph. The instrument of her acceptance there was that tireless ninety-three-year-old man for all arts, George Bernard Shaw, who was pleasantly amazed upon being shown color slides of her work and recommended to the gallery directors that they bring over the originals. Fanny sent a half-dozen "Moods of the City": sun-bathers on a tenement roof, Times Square by night, the beach at Coney Island, Central Park flashing with skate blades in winter and swarming in summer with children, balloons and greenery.

On June 20, 1949, Oliver Brown replied for the gallery: "We have looked at your paintings and taken a great interest in them. They all have a great deal of character." He wanted to include several canvases in his annual "Artists of Fame and Promise," a two-installment summer exhibition "which always attracts a great crowd and interest in London."

Fanny's pictures went on view a month later. As with the Hallmark Gallery collection, she was in respectable company: Edgar Degas, Raoul Dufy, Augustus and Gwen John, Walter Sickert. She was the only American shown.

Fanny's success was immediate and emphatic. Two days after the opening James Laver, curator of the Victoria and Albert Museum, congratulated her by letter: "I was really most impressed. You have an extraordinary gift of suggesting movement, and are improving all the time." The *Evening Standard* ran a full-page feature on "Moods of the City." And — accolade of accolades — several friends reported that Mrs. Winston Churchill had been seen standing for a long, long time, obviously enthralled, before the winter skating scene.

For the next several years Fanny rose at six in the morning and painted until eight-thirty or nine. If she lingered beyond that, she kept in touch with her office by telephone from the adjoining kitchen. The jovial Jenkie was frequently an interested onlooker; in fact, sometimes she had to be restrained from getting into the act.

It was David, now raised to senior partnership in Holtzmann and Holtzmann, who made this casual regime possible. With him on hand, the office was crisis-proof. Besides, Fanny claimed that her sessions at the easel were actually an asset to her law practice: "I can go into my little cubicle with a legal problem, putter around with my colors for an hour, and come out with the answer."

During this period she turned to portraiture, starting with her sister Bertha and virtually running the gamut of the family. Few of her "sitters" actually sat; seeking what Whistler called an "aroma" of personality rather than a camera likeness, Fanny preferred to work from memory.

In 1953 she donated three pictures to a giant exhibition in Beverly Hills on behalf of Women's ORT, the Organization for Rehabilitation and Training. All were sold in the opening minutes. A similar gift benefited the Kibbutz Scholarship Fund of Hashomer Natzair, the Zionist Youth Organization. Twice she sent paintings to the annual exhibition of the California State Bar Association, and won prize ribbons there.

One painting, perhaps her best, she could not send anywhere. The original Central Park skating scene so admired by J. C. Hall had been given by Fanny in 1952 to the singer Hildegarde and her manager Anna Sosenko, who were then sharing an apartment and a magnificent art collection. When Hildegarde and Anna decided to go their separate ways, their paintings were auctioned off at the Parke-Bernet.

"My painting wound up in a collector's hands. I couldn't afford to buy it."

Fanny's excursion into art had repercussions among her clients: some comic, some exhilarating — and in one case, near-tragic. "The first thing that happened was that my office began to look like an art gallery. Everybody had to get into the act. Gertrude Lawrence sent her best finger-painting down from the Cape, Noel Coward brought two large oils, Clifton Webb shipped a canvas from California, even Jack Buchanan contributed a seascape. I didn't have wall space to hang them all. It was very embarrassing."

David suggested that their future retainers should specify "legal services only. This does not entitle you to space in the Bar Building for your artistic efforts."

In 1952, Laurence Olivier and Vivien Leigh were temporary occupants of the Richard Aldrich–Gertrude Lawrence flat on West Fifty-fourth Street. The two British stars, having dropped in to see Fanny, broke into raptures about her paintings. She gave them two: a blazing still life of lilacs and chrysanthemums, overflowing the canvas in a wild profusion of color; and a Christmas scene of a woman coming down the steps of a snow-covered brownstone bearing a wreath and holiday packages. When the Oliviers parted, Vivien insisted on retaining custody of Fanny's pictures.

An unexpected bonus from Fanny's art was a deeper intimacy with Noel Coward. He had been turning out oils for years — discreet, meticulous, almost painfully correct — and rather fancied himself as a serious painter. After a visit to East Sixty-fourth Street, he pronounced Fanny "at least four times as good as I am."

He began haunting her office and her apartment, eager to exchange canvases and painterly confidences. It was as if by embracing fine art she had won passage to his innermost core.

Together, at Coward's prodding, they trudged through the Metropolitan Museum of Art, where he analyzed the methods of the old masters. These discussions discomfited Fanny — she had no talent for dissecting or copying — and she was relieved when his friend Edward Molyneux, the designer and connoisseur, told him Fanny did not need academy rules.

But there were occasions when Coward spoke of other matters, and Fanny found his talk consistently engrossing: "His mind ranged over everything, throwing off sharp, lively insights."

With constant contact, there developed a lawyer-client closeness surpassing anything Fanny had known before. Even with Gertrude Lawrence, a certain reserve had been maintained on both sides; the sisterly banter had never crossed mutually recognized borders. With Coward, Fanny not only laughed a good deal but quarreled freely: "We had no compunctions about slapping each other down. We both enjoyed watching people, and we had our private sign language of shrugs and glances for sharing reactions.

"Noel had an insatiable curiosity — everything intrigued him — and another quality that I've seen only in my sister Stella and myself: whatever crossed his path was stamped on his memory. Because Noel and I operated in much the same way — soaking up everything around us, learning from people, not books — he became the only client who ever really knew me."

Conversely, Fanny grew to know Coward: his childlike delight at parties in his honor, his intense attachment to those in his personal circle. Particularly impressive to her, after her experience with the backbiting of Broadway and Hollywood, was his devotion to his colleagues in the theater: "He was considerate of everyone — generous to his fellow stars, protective of the lowliest member of the cast. Once I made a mildly disparaging remark about a dancer in the chorus. He lashed out at me, like a monarch defending an unarmed subject.

"And he took such joy in helping people! I watched him and Gertrude breaking in Graham Payne, who was to star on the road with her in

Tonight at 8:30. The patience they displayed, the deft collaboration — they wound up making Graham feel he was more important than Noel's dialogue."

Gertrude and Coward were of course a celebrated duet, inseparable since dancing-school days. Only once was Fanny aware of a discordant note between them. After publication in America of Gertrude's auto-biographical *A Star Danced* in 1945, Noel was indignant. He complained in London that she was invading his author's bailiwick.

"Sibling rivalry," Fanny explained to Adlai Stevenson. It was despite Noel, rather than with his help, that she obtained a British publisher for the book and a six-figure advance for movie rights.

Noel's predilection for the company of men created no awkward-ness for Fanny. By this time she took such idiosyncrasies in stride. Life was more complex than the storybook idylls of her childhood.

Human beings were cut to a wide range of patterns; what was "devia-tion" for one could be fulfillment for another. She even evolved a theory about the mothers of homosexual men: "They thrive on their sons' affairs. Whereas a wife or girl friend would be a threatening rival, a male friend becomes like a docile daughter-in-law, an addition to Mama's entourage."

During the New York run of *Private Lives,* Fanny wandered backstage one evening before curtain time. She found Noel weeping bitterly in his dressing room, insisting to Gertrude Lawrence and the stage manager that "someone else must go on." His protégé of the moment, a handsome juvenile he had steered to stardom, was leaving him for — of all things — an *actress*!

Gertrude put a hand on his arm soothingly: "Don't take it so hard, darling. After all — it was only a friendship."

Coward drew back reproachfully. "How *can* you, Gertrude! After all you went through with your love for Philip Astley, I would have expected greater understanding from *you*!"

But a few seconds after the curtain went up he was onstage and on his toes, the ineffably polished Elyot Chase of *Private Lives.*

Noel Coward had his first taste of the New York Jewish milieu in the 1920's. From Fanny's observation, he could never get enough of it.

He was introduced by Jed Harris, the flamboyant theater director, to mushroom-and-barley soup at Ratner's on the lower East Side, and then to the drolleries of Molly Picon at the nearby Yiddish Theater.

But it was the pungency of Yiddish itself — its wry, untranslatable humor — that Coward relished most. Whenever Fanny dropped a frag-ment of earthy dialect into the conversation, he jotted it down. The prize expression on his list was acquired on an auto junket into Mexico in 1949 — almost at the cost of wrecking the trip itself.

He was on the West Coast to superintend the opening of *Tonight at 8:30,* in which the English actor Graham Payne was appearing opposite

Gertrude Lawrence. The play went very well, and was promptly booked for a long run. However, in order to stay on in America as a salary earner, Payne would have to obtain the appropriate nonimmigrant visa.

Fanny flew out from New York to arrange matters. The quickest procedure, she decided, would be for Payne to cross the Mexican border below San Diego and make the necessary application from Tijuana. She and Noel would go along and take their painting kits.

The trio set out from Beverly Hills on a sunny September dawn with Coward at the wheel. He hated driving, but he hated even more Fanny's casual approach to the perils of the highway; and Graham was not yet fully awake.

They spun southward, spirits rising in the dry, flower-scented air. As they emerged onto the open road and left the sprawl of Los Angeles behind, a huge white building loomed to the left, mail trucks clustered around its entrance.

Fanny let out a scream. "Oh my God, Noel! Your famous lawyer is a *shlemiel!* All the way from New York, and I forgot to get you an income tax clearance. You must turn off, right away."

"Where to — the irrigation ditch?"

"The Federal Building, up ahead. That's what reminded me." Aliens, she explained, could not leave the country without proof that they had paid their income taxes. If she had given it a moment's thought, she would have made arrangements through the Internal Revenue Service people in New York —"but who ever bothers with details?" Now, it was too late to invoke the aid of influential Californians like Louis B. Mayer; she would have to tackle the local bureaucracy on her own.

Trailed by the two Englishmen, she entered the building and walked up to the guard: "Who's in charge of aliens?"

"Mr. Morley, over at the window."

Fanny saw seated at a large desk a small man with horn-rimmed glasses. His birdlike profile was a replica of Joe Hochman's. The comfortable bulge around his middle suggested corned-beef sandwiches at Lindy's. Morley?

She approached politely. "Good morning, sir. Are you a native son?"

"I love California," came the hoarse reply, "but a native I'm not!"

"You sound as though you might be a *landsman* of mine."

Morley looked up. "You come from New York, too?"

"Where else? Don't tell me you're from Brownsville?"

"Not me. I'm pure Sheriff Street."

"On the lower East Side? My father taught there. Oy — you don't know what a pleasure it is to meet a *landsman!*"

"Thirty-five years I haven't been back." He echoed her sigh: "Oy . . ."

They smiled, exchanging silent memories.

Morley noticed Noel hovering anxiously in the background, trying to follow their conversation. "*Wer ist der goy* [who is the Gentile]"?, he asked in a lowered voice.

"A client from England." She presented her card. "We have some business to take care of across the border."

"Does he make a lot of money?"

"Money? He makes *wasser auf kasha*."

" '*Wasser —*' " Morley threw up his hands ecstatically. "This is music to my ears. Here in California nobody knows from such sayings."

Noel edged closer. He could not bear being left out, especially with juicy Yiddishisms being tossed around. "What's this about water?" he demanded.

"Just an expression," Morley told him. "Regarding your earnings."

"Oh, I can provide any information —"

Fanny jabbed him in the ribs. "Shut up, Noel," she murmured. "Let me handle this."

"But I'm only trying to help the man."

Fanny lost her temper. "*Es will ihm helfen vi a toten bankes*," she exploded at the bewildered playwright.

Morley leaned back in his chair, roaring with delight. "Beautiful, beautiful. My grandfather used to say that."

"Mine, too."

The immigration man reached for his tax clearance forms, still chuckling. He scribbled away while Fanny admonished Noel to silence. A few perfunctory questions, and the signed papers were in Fanny's hands.

The moment they were outside, Noel pounced. "I don't mind your stepping on my lines, but I do resent being cheated of a Yiddish lesson. What's this about '*wasser auf kasha*'?"

Kasha, Fanny explained, was a staple of the East European poor. A peasant whose fortune consisted of "water for his kasha" was just about struggling along at the subsistence level.

"Very clever," nodded Coward. "What about the other line — the one that nearly knocked him out of his chair?"

"That's a bit more complicated. Do you know about cupping — placing cups on the body to draw out a fever?"

"Of course. They still do it in France."

"Well, the expression I used means 'It will help him the way cupping helps a corpse.' "

Coward made her repeat the original Yiddish, and carefully pronounced the words after her. For years to come, he lost no opportunity to inject the remark into his conversation, delivering it with a clipped Mayfair elegance that savored and quite transformed each guttural syllable.

After Coward's wartime successes — *Blithe Spirit*, the films *Brief Encounter* and *In Which We Serve* — his career took a severe dip. The musical *Pacific 1860* siphoned off a good deal of his own money; *Quadrille*, written for Alfred Lunt and Lynn Fontanne, was tepidly received.

In 1955 the Desert Inn at Las Vegas offered him $40,000 a week for a personal appearance. Fanny opposed the move as undignified. David, fingering Coward's unpaid bills, retorted that it was no more so than Monte Carlo.

"Besides, Las Vegas is a cemetery for performers."

Noel had the final word: "Then I shall rise like Lazarus from the dead." He flew out to Nevada alone.

Although he could not read music, and his singing voice wobbled, Coward had a knack of inducing instant nostalgia with rueful ballads like "I'll See You Again." His rhythm tunes, graced with irreverent lyrics and delivered with brittle charm, entertained even in quarters where they were not entirely intelligible.

Late in the evening of his opening, Fanny had a telephone call: "These people are the most fun of any audience in the world. You must come at once."

Frank Scully was in New York, bouncing back from his latest hospital adventures with a new book. Would the ace columnist for *Variety*, on his way home to Palm Springs, care to stop in with Fanny and catch Noel Coward's act at Las Vegas?

He certainly would. Frank had covered a Coward appearance at a London cabaret years before, and still remembered some of the author's nimble rhymes. With Fanny's sister Stella, they boarded a plane.

All of Las Vegas converged that evening on the Desert Inn. To Fanny's enormous pleasure, she discovered they had come not to honor Noel Coward, the eminent playwight, but to pay homage to their beloved Frank Scully, Knight of St. Gregory the Great, president of the Hollywood Humane Society, and incorruptible tribune of show business.

Frank was introduced from the stage and asked to say a few words. He devoted them to Noel: "the greatest talent alive today; what he knows, you'll never pick up at the Yale Drama School."

Noel obliged with "Don't Put Your Daughter on the Stage, Mrs. Worthington." The audience, although struggling with his accent and not grasping half his allusions, refused to let him go.

Fanny's contact with Noel Coward went into a long hibernation after his triumph at Las Vegas. The playwright entered upon a less creative, if still gratifying phase of television appearances, interviews, and revivals of his old stage successes; Fanny embarked on new directions of her own.

Another factor separating them was Coward's erratic health. His one liability as a traveling companion, in Fanny's eyes, had always been his hypochondria: "He carried along a satchel full of drugs, wherever he went, and was constantly muttering, 'I feel a cold coming on.'" Ultimately, the imagined fragility became a fact. Plagued by phlebitis, Coward took refuge for a time behind an attentive entourage who screened him off lovingly from the outside world.

Among Fanny's friends and clients, none took a keener interest in her emergence as a painter than Clifton Webb. Clifton had been wielding the brush himself intermittently for nearly fifty years, ever since he had sat for and been the pupil of the American portraitist Robert Henri. Henri had predicted a great future in painting for him.

But Mabelle Webb had other plans, so the youthful artist was side-tracked first to light opera and then to ballroom dancing. But he had never completely abandoned his easel or forgotten the painter's forecast.

The Webb reputation had been in decline for a decade after Clifton hit his Broadway zenith in *Flying Colors* and *As Thousands Cheer*. Appearing largely in road-company revivals, the long-limbed dancer had drifted out of Fanny's sight.

In the late forties, just when Fanny was deep in her new enthusiasm, Clifton was pitched back into the Holtzmann and Holtzmann fold by a turn for the better in his Hollywood fortunes. With the release by Twentieth Century–Fox of *Laura* and *The Razor's Edge*, he was suddenly a new movie star, a dramatic actor, to millions who had never heard of him as a song-and-dance matinée idol. Producers and agents courted him; Garbo invited him to lunch.

Clifton panicked. The change was more than he could handle; his mother, capricious and domineering, only aggravated the situation.

Clifton got on the telephone to Fanny. Could she come at once?

Five hours later, Fanny was winging westward. Commercial air travel had added a welcome string to her bow. Thanks to a phenomenal memory, she could carry her practice virtually in her head. She had no tremors about flying: in the late 1920's she had gone up for a wild loop-the-loop on a fairground glider. To fill in any idle moments that might occur on her rescue mission to Clifton, she took along a slim kit of paints and brushes.

The actor was enchanted. Surely Fanny knew of his Robert Henri days? She took a suite at the nearby Beverly Hills Hotel, and for the better part of a week the trio had a merry reunion. Business was thrust aside while Clifton watched Fanny mix her pigments.

Then he unburdened himself. He wanted guidance on how to get his contract at the studio revised upward. He also needed assistance with his business investments; somehow, his earnings always seemed to trickle through his fingers.

Mostly, he needed a new agent. The Music Corporation of America was competent, upright —"but with MCA it's like going to a bank, there's no personal touch." He wanted someone who would gossip with him on the telephone, and pop right over if he was lonely; someone to counteract the tyranny of Mabelle (his resentment of his mother did not surface often, but once, walking through Central Park with Fanny, he had stopped to watch some youngsters at a batting cage, and remarked bitterly, "*I* never had a chance to play baseball") .

Did he have anyone in particular in mind?

"Yes. Charlie Feldman." Feldman, a former lawyer with Gable-esque moustache and shoulders, was a henchman of Darryl Zanuck's.

"I don't know, Clifton. He's awfully close to your boss."

"That's just it. He can get me a better contract."

"But when the chips are down, you can't be sure which side he'll be on. And in the meantime, you're cut off from everybody but Zanuck."

Clifton grimaced. "It's all right for you to talk, Fanny. You can go back east to civilization — but I have to live among these people!"

"If that's what you want —" Fanny shrugged. She would handle MCA for him.

She was on excellent terms with the agency's president, Jules Stein, who had several times been to her home; something equitable could be worked out in New York. However, the agency's back was up about poaching, and understandably —"too many of their stars have been snatched away." So she would have to proceed without rush or fanfare. In the meantime, Feldman could start quietly drawing up the terms for Clifton's new contract.

Fanny returned to New York buoyed by her old friend's ardent blessing. She had promised to send one or two of the completed canvases in her studio; when she could not arrange crating immediately, an impatient letter from Clifton demanded, "When in hell are those Holtzmann masterpieces arriving?"

The pictures went out — a tenement scene and a vegetable still life — eliciting a prompt and exuberant response from Mabelle addressed to "Fanny Rembrandt."

Fanny was touched — her own family had not been nearly so encouraging. She went into her little studio and, from memory, did portraits of the Webbs: Clifton weary and vulnerable behind his haughty mask, Mabelle as mindless and appealing in her furs as a Toulouse-Lautrec cabaret girl.

When the portraits reached California, it was the turn of the Beverly Hills household to be moved. Clifton telephoned to say that, contemplating Fanny's "splendid achievements," he was much tempted to return to the brush himself.

The temptation was converted to determination in the following month, when Fanny reported her accession to the ranks of Hallmark. Clifton received the news with joy — mingled, a moment later, with other feelings. He, after all, was a trained painter. If Hallmark was looking for talent among the famous . . .

Fanny heartily agreed. Upon Clifton's pledge to resume painting, she sent a note of warm recommendation to J. C. Hall.

The greeting card publisher assigned one of his West Coast artists, Vivian Smith, to review Clifton's work. She passed favorable judgment, and in October of 1948 Fanny had the pleasant task of checking over a contract between her friend Clifton Webb and her art publisher, Hallmark.

Nor was his other contract, as a film star, lying idle. After several months of spadework, Fanny arranged a meeting at her home in New

York between MCA's top executives and a lawyer sent out from Charlie Feldman's office. She acted as arbiter to bring about an agreement releasing Clifton from his commitment to MCA. Now, thanks to Fanny, he was free to accept the more lucrative terms worked out by Feldman with Darryl Zanuck.

Clifton was brimming over with gratitude — to the point where he wanted his business relationship with Fanny regularized. No longer, he insisted by long-distance telephone, should there be occasional payments for occasional services; nothing less than an annual retainer would do, as with her other big stars. "I want to feel I can consult you any time, without Mabelle saying 'Don't call Fanny, it will cost you money.' "

"Have you ever had a bill from me, Clifton?"

"No, but . . . I'll be easier in my mind this way."

The retainer was set at $25,000.

The arrangement had scarcely been reduced to writing and deposited in Fanny's files when a registered letter arrived at the Bar Building from Beverly Hills. Clifton was very sorry, and grateful for all she had done, but he wished to cancel the retainer. He felt his affairs could be handled better by an attorney who would be constantly on the scene, not based three thousand miles away. Would she please send all relevant papers to the legal department at Charles K. Feldman's office.

Fanny waited until early evening, Hollywood time, then placed a call to Crestview 6-0759. Mabelle answered the telephone, and a moment later Clifton came onto the extension.

"This is Fanny in New York. I have your letter, Clifton — but I don't understand."

"There's nothing to understand. I simply changed my mind."

"He's decided to be practical," interjected Mabelle. "We don't need lawyers all over the country."

Something in her voice, a certain shrill tension, told Fanny there was more to the story. "But the idea for the retainer came from Clifton," she pointed out, "scarcely a month ago. I can't believe he would just drop it out of the blue. Have I failed you as a lawyer in any way?"

No, not at all, Clifton assured her hastily. It was — well, something else . . .

He left it to Mabelle to spit out the charge: "It was what you did to Clifton at Hallmark!"

Now everybody began talking at once, and it was some moments before Fanny could sift out the essential fact: Hallmark had apparently advised Clifton during the previous week of a decision not to go ahead with the plans to use his paintings.

Fanny was shocked. "What excuse did they give?"

"Excuse?" rasped Mabelle. "You ought to know — you put them up to it!"

"Why on earth would I do that? I was the one who recommended Clifton to J. C. Hall."

"He didn't need your recommendation. My boy was a big painter before you ever picked up a brush. As for why you did it — isn't that obvious? You didn't want the competition. You were afraid you'd be overshadowed."

"That's ridiculous, Mabelle! Nobody was happier than I to see Clifton come onto the list."

"You were so happy you had him chopped right off. But the name Fanny Holtzmann, I notice, is up high in the ad — right next to El Greco."

"That was an alphabetical accident —"

Clifton came back in: "A most remarkable accident, Fanny, you must admit. Just like their suddenly dropping me."

Fanny felt helpless, baffled; this was like trying to conduct a rational argument with two people in a madhouse. "But I'm not —" She felt the tears welling up. "I don't even consider myself in your class as a painter, Clifton. If I could paint with a fraction of your skill, do you think I'd have to put up with being your lawyer?"

"Our *ex*-lawyer," snapped Mabelle. "The retainer is off."

Tears gave way to outrage. "You can take your damned retainer and —"

Telephones slammed down, at both ends of the continent.

A week later Fanny received back the paintings she had done of Clifton and Mabelle — but not as she had painted them. Great streaks of black and red were smeared across the canvases.

In 1960, when Mabelle was ninety and critically ill, Fanny telephoned Clifton from New York. For several minutes they spoke of personal matters; nobody mentioned the ancient dispute.

On a visit to the coast a few years later, Fanny called again. Clifton was alone now, and she was staying as usual at the Beverly Hills Hotel, a five-minute walk away.

At the sound of her voice, Clifton broke into sobs. "Fanny, dear Fanny, I must see you."

"Whatever you say, Clifton." Fanny, no hoarder of emotion, began to weep as well. "I'd go anywhere in the world for you. You and Mabelle were the greatest friends I ever had."

"I'd give anything to have you come over, but I can't. I mustn't let you see me now. You wouldn't recognize me, Fanny. I'm an old, sick man . . ."

"That doesn't matter, Clifton."

"Ah, but it does, it does. I would rather have you remember me the way I was."

"To me you'll always be the same, Clifton. Young, and beautiful, and the most generous of friends."

Quiet sobs. "Can you ever forgive me, Fanny? That nonsense about

Hallmark? It was Charlie Feldman's lawyer who put us up to it, you know."

"What's to forgive? When you love a friend, you love him."

Fanny never saw Clifton again. But long after he died in 1966, his silver-framed photograph remained on her desk — the urbane, floating-on-moonbeams Clifton Webb of *Flying Colors*.

Painting was only the half of it. Fanny also sculpted, and with startling authority. She started under the private tutelage of Jacob Epstein. The man who sent her there, repeating his intervention with the Leicester Galleries, was George Bernard Shaw. He felt that Fanny's grasp of three-dimensional modeling in painting would be enhanced by work in Epstein's studio.

Jacob Epstein, born on the lower East Side of Manhattan to Jewish immigrants from Poland, was at sixty-seven one of the titans of the art world. After studying among the post-Impressionists in Paris, he had settled in London, where Winston Churchill had sat to him, as had Shaw, Albert Einstein, Paul Robeson, and Emperor Haile Selassie.

Like many an illustrious predecessor, Epstein was continuously embroiled with the Establishment. Throughout his endless scuffles with authority — over a nude grouping in the Strand for the British Medical Association, a harsh Christ bereft of angelic overtones, a squat unlovely Adam — his steadfast defender had been George Bernard Shaw.

A note to him from GBS therefore brought instant results. Fanny was invited to tea at the sculptor's studio, just across from the Winston Churchill house at Hyde Park Gate.

She found herself in a drafty, cavernous room crowded with stone blocks, hammers, chisels and unfinished statues. A rickety ladder reached up past enormous windows almost to the high ceiling. The busts surrounding her, in whatever stage of completion, had a common quality of rude vigor, of life bursting recklessly from the stone.

In the far corner, opposite a large old-fashioned stove, a proper British tea-table had been carefully laid: delicate China, massive silver, biscuits and jellies.

Epstein strode in. He was as rugged and individualistic as his work: a stocky, combative figure at once *toro* and *toreador*. His gestures, like his features, were broad and open; his wiry gray hair shot up as if in eternal protest.

He greeted Fanny briskly and waved her to the tea table. As he poured, he got down to business: had she come to sit for a portrait, or as a collector?

"Neither. I want to study with you."

Epstein put down his cup and stared. "You — *what?*"

Fanny repeated her mission.

"Goddamn! Do you think this is the Hebrew Educational Alliance?

I'm a sculptor, not a hack instructor. I don't teach anybody — and certainly not a beginner!"

"Mr. Shaw thought — and he discussed it with the Leicester Galleries —"

"So it's my bloody gallery, is it? They think that just because I'm having financial difficulties, I've sunk so low that I have to take in rich Americans . . ."

Epstein turned away, his elaborate tea party forgotten. Neither Fanny nor Shaw knew it, but they had stepped on a sensitive toe: the failure of the Slade School at Oxford, or any other major art institution in Britain, to welcome Epstein to its faculty.

Fanny gulped down a biscuit and flew out the door.

A year later, as Fanny was lunching at a Soho restaurant, Epstein suddenly turned up at her elbow: "Miss Holtzmann, I must see you. It's very urgent. Where are you staying?"

"The Savoy."

When she returned to the hotel at four o'clock there were two messages to call the sculptor. He sounded breathless: "Please, if anybody in the world can save me, it's you. Get me out of this scrape and — well, I haven't any money, but I'll do a bust of you. And I'll teach you — all you want."

They arranged to meet the next day at a restaurant on King's Road in Chelsea, the Bohemia of London. Epstein came in with Kitty, the statuesque brunette who had been his mistress-model for years. Still agitated, he blurted out in Yiddish: "Fanny, from Heaven you were sent to me!"

From Epstein's short, staccato phrases, Fanny pieced together his story. Decades earlier, in Paris, he had become friendly with Philip Sayers, a Jewish businessman visiting from Dublin. Sayers was fascinated by *la vie de bohème*, including the shapely ladies who streamed across the sculptor's threshold. "I gave him first choice," declared Epstein, "of all my rejects." Epstein in turn could count on a loan from his friend whenever there was a problem with rent or expensive materials.

As time passed, both men advanced in the world. Sayers' collection of early Epsteins became more valuable; his involvement in Epstein's career included putting up the mortgage money that financed the huge studio at Hyde Park Gate.

Now, without warning, Sayers had begun action to foreclose the house: "He started out as a patron of the arts — and ended up as a cold-blooded mortgagee. I won't have a roof over my head, Fanny. Or a place to work. Where will I store my sculptures? Unless you can do something, I see only one way out: to kill myself."

Fanny was puzzled. Was this strictly a money dispute? Between friends of thirty-odd years' standing, that didn't seem likely.

"Who knows? There could be personal reasons, jealousy . . ."

And that was about all Fanny could get out of him.

Reluctantly, she peered into the maelstrom of his private life. She learned that Epstein had had three illegitimate children by Kitty and at least one by an earlier model (the sculptor's indignant response: "I acknowledged the paternity of every child I ever had — so how could they be illegitimate?"). The children were all brought up, tenderly if erratically, by their father and Kitty. Currently there was a mild domestic crisis: a daughter was about to marry into the peerage. "How can we send out invitations, and brag about her catch," Kitty worried, "when we have no formal status ourselves?"

"Get married," counseled Fanny.

Kitty balked at such orthodoxy, finally yielding to Fanny's argument of "a sacrifice for your grandchildren."

All this was highly diverting — how many wedding ceremonies featured a bride and groom with three illegitimate children? — but it provided no clue to resolving the wrangle with Sayers. Fanny decided to ask the businessman down from Ireland for a talk.

He arrived two days later, a small, spry man wearing Savile Row pinstripes and an unmistakably prosperous air. His own story was bizarre enough: placed aboard an American-bound steamer from Russia as a young boy, he had instead been dumped ashore at an Irish port. He became a peddler, saved enough to open a general store, then expanded into real estate. Now, according to a Dublin newspaper clipping he displayed to Fanny at lunch, Philip Sayers held "a first mortgage on half of County Cork."

He also held a storehouse of pleasant memories. He had had access, he reminisced, as the friend and sponsor of many renowned artists, to the most beautiful models of Montparnasse; never, he bragged, had he been reduced to patronizing a public brothel.

Jacob Epstein? Ah, that was a sorrowful tale. "I was good to Epstein, the closest friend he ever had. I saw him through his marriage, his affair with his model Meam — she was the love of his life — and I was never tight-fisted with him."

Then what had happened? Sayers shook his head. In recent years the sculptor had become distant, unreasonable, even abusive. Sayers did not say so directly, but Fanny had the impression that Kitty was somehow involved in the estrangement, and that Sayers was punishing his former friend.

Would Sayers be open to a reconciliation, and to an equitable settlement regarding the house at Hyde Park Gate?

"Well now, if you could come up with a formula . . . I'm really fond of the old bastard, you know."

Meanwhile, Sayers agreed to put off the foreclosure.

Epstein could breathe again. Joyfully he plunged into his end of the bargain with Fanny. For the next three weeks she came to his studio for breakfast every morning at seven-thirty ("Kitty is getting jealous," he declared), and sat to the master for about an hour.

Then he stood her before a mound of clay and a metal armature and told her to go to work. Pulling up a chair, he threw in an occasional word of correction or encouragement: "Start with the broad proportions, Fanny — a particular shape. Then go to the most obvious features, almost as in caricature. The refinement comes last."

She had chosen to do the head of a child, working, as with her paintings, from imagination. Could he give her a clue or two, road signs for this unfamiliar journey?

"The ears," Epstein grunted. "Their lowest point should be at the same level as the bottom of the nose."

Over the days that followed, Fanny gradually absorbed his aesthetic and his technique. The ultimate goal was to penetrate beneath the surface to thought and feeling, à la Rembrandt. Form was important, but always in relation to forms in nature rather than as an abstraction.

Fanny took to the medium instinctively: the clay under her fingers felt as if she had been molding it for years. As Girls' High and Fordham Law School had demonstrated, she was either a wretched pupil or a brilliant one; and here she was doing something she enjoyed, under a recognized master who was also, when he wanted to be, an amusing raconteur. Epstein described how the coterie of Jewish faithful in the Impressionist movement would gather on the Day of Atonement around their leader, Camille Pissarro. "But you could never be sure about Modigliani. You know where those long-necked ladies of his came from? Hashish!"

A superbly aristocratic bronze, half covered in a corner, caught Fanny's eye. "A Greek princess," Epstein volunteered. "She offered me a very fancy commission. Just after I sent the head to the foundry, her lover deserted her. She took poison and died on the spot. There was no one to pay for the bust — and I still owe the foundry."

It was such a lugubrious tale, on all counts, that Fanny was moved to buy the piece: "At least it will reestablish your credit."

This kind of financial improvisation would soon be unnecessary, she assured the sculptor. Armed with an inventory of his work, she had been discussing with Philip Sayers an elaborate schedule of time payments backed by stone-and-bronze collateral. The Dubliner was coming to London in a matter of days.

He did, and Fanny brought the quarrelsome cronies together in a Soho dining place. "It was a bigger diplomatic coup than getting Bevin to sit down with Rabbi Silver. The two of them sniffed and growled and scratched like a couple of old tomcats — and the next thing I knew they were falling on each other's necks, overflowing with affection. When I left at 2 A.M. they were singing Yiddish folk songs together."

Thereafter, the talk at Hyde Park Gate returned from foreclosures to art. Epstein finished his bust of Fanny, and dispatched it to the foundry along with her check for sixty pounds.

To Fanny's chagrin, the bronze casting that came back displayed "a grinning idiot"; the mouth had been rendered unrecognizable.

"One of my models," Epstein told her, "must have altered it."

"But who?"

The sculptor shrugged. "Do I know who's jealous of my sitters this week? It's your fault, for looking so nice."

Of Fanny's own work in his studio, he was openly admiring: "You have a very large talent; Shaw was absolutely right." Epstein had no doubt that she could turn from law to sculpture without loss of prestige — but he wouldn't recommend it. If, on her return to the States, she decided to go ahead anyway, "Be prepared for a most unrewarding experience. Nobody will like what you do. You will make no friends, but lots of enemies.

"People will insult you, threaten to sue you for libel, screaming 'My husband doesn't look like that!' They will do everything but understand. Because the sculptor is not engaged in photography; his fingers are spelling out what he feels inside."

Profound philosophical decisions could wait. For the moment, Fanny tugged some canvases aside and set herself up for sculpture in the maid's room–studio. On her armature a head of Henry Holtzmann, eight years gone, took shape. Guided only by an old photo, Fanny produced a study that was a personification of the scholar-poet: eyes as dreamy and far-seeing as Swinburne's, neat moustache above the rounded chin and generous mouth.

Pleased by her success, Fanny sent the plaster cast all the way to Italy for reproduction. The finished bronze went to the American Fund for Israel Institutions, for display in a Tel Aviv museum; a set of photographs was mailed to George Bernard Shaw.

Other heads spun out of the tiny atelier, mostly done from memory without benefit of sitter: Epstein's daughter Esther, heavy-lipped and brooding; Fanny's mother and her brother Jack, each pinpointed in a fleeting attitude.

Twice she worked from live models. Jenkie, the imperfect housekeeper, was blessed with perfect bone structure; Fanny coaxed her into a chair long enough to capture the Grecian nose, columned neck, high cheekbones that melted into delicate hollows.

Her other sitter was Jenkie's idol, Gertrude Lawrence, who yielded a bust of unusual sensitivity. As with Fanny's painting of Clifton Webb, the clay portrait of the performer was softer, more troubled than the effulgent public image.

Over the next few years Fanny stayed in touch with Epstein, occasionally sending him a well-heeled sitter like Mrs. Samuel Bronfman of the

Seagram Distillers empire. On a visit to London in 1951, she decided that the sculptor deserved to be knighted.

Official dispenser of British honors was the treasurer of Buckingham Palace, Lieutenant General Sir Frederick Browning. As the husband of the distinguished author Daphne du Maurier, "Boy" Browning was a familiar of the London literary-theatrical scene. Fanny went to him directly.

Jacob Epstein, she pointed out, was a seminal figure in art, a sculptor of international repute. Past seventy, he was now living in decorous domesticity, a credit to his adopted home. "Frankly, Boy, some people in America are wondering if royal recognition has been withheld because his name is Jacob."

No indeed, Browning assured her. However, it was the custom for any such move to be initiated by an artist's peers, the people in his own or related fields.

Fanny raised a skeptical eyebrow — and her good right arm. Whirling around London, she bludgeoned and cajoled gallery directors, critics, collectors.

On a visit to Downing Street, she murmured that the absence of a knighthood for such a distinguished artist was causing whispers in America, where much sensitivity lingered in the wake of the Nazi slaughters. Could the bypassing of Epstein be a hangover from the leanings of the notorious Cliveden set?

At the home of Sir Louis Sterling, the Victor Records magnate, she buttonholed a Labour MP of Jewish extraction: "A knighthood for Epstein would have a smoothing effect on Anglo-American relations."

"But he's such an unpleasant fellow personally!"

"By that yardstick, you'd have to disqualify half the peerage."

"Besides, he's not very popular in the Jewish community."

"Make him a knight and he will be."

Fanny dropped the seed everywhere, teasing and nagging with her celebrated persistence. By 1953 she was advised from Downing Street to have patience; "things are coming along nicely." The following year Epstein had his knighthood.

By that time, Fanny had stopped sculpting herself. She had discovered that for her, sculpture, unlike painting, could not be pursued as an avocation, a sideline: "Once I start, it takes over my life — there's no room for law or anything else. It's like the drunk who goes out of control the moment he touches a drop. So, again like the drunk, I had to made a total break."

Her career in clay was closed out formally fifteen years later with a special display at the annual art exhibition of the New York Bar Association. Highlight of the show, dominating the gallery set apart for sculpture, was a group of seven heads by Fanny.

Six of the subjects were intimates or members of her family; in only one case did she wander outside her immediate circle. But when she did it was to achieve a bronze so commanding, so alive with humor and goodwill that its gratified subject personally chose it for showing at the Philadelphia Museum.

The subject was something of an artist himself, who was to play affable host to Fanny through his days in the White House: Dwight D. Eisenhower.

Chapter 13

*T*HE 1952 presidential campaign confronted Fanny with a pleasant dilemma. Three of her favorite people were seeking the nation's highest office. Senator Robert H. Taft held a clear advantage in political experience. But Adlai Stevenson had shared with her the birth struggles of the UN; and Dwight D. Eisenhower was the model for her most successful sculpture.

Fanny's bust of General Eisenhower grew out of their second meeting, late in 1948, after he had retired to assume the presidency of Columbia University.

From her first visit with him at the Pentagon, in the emotional afterglow of the Morgan affair, Fanny had carried away only a vague impression of solidity and warmth. In the interim, however, she had worked in Epstein's studio; now she was viewing the world, and especially human features, with a heightened awareness of mass and plane.

On entering Eisenhower's office at the university, she was struck by his "good strong head": clean-lined, bold-featured, well proportioned. The broad brow, topped by a few wispy hairs, reminded her of her father. Something else evoked echoes of Henry Holtzmann: an aura of gentle detachment. "It was difficult," as she put it later, "even grotesque, to associate General Eisenhower with the brutalities of war, with giving orders for killing. He was the kind of man you would think of as being happiest bending over a rosebush."

Fanny had brought along color slides of several paintings. While Ike studied the slides, she studied him. That night in the studio she began translating her observations into clay.

The bust that took shape under her fingers had a marvelous simplicity. Here was the Eisenhower she had enthusiastically described in a letter

Fanny turns to sculpture: Ike

to Freddie Morgan: "human, wise, kindly"— a calm statesmanlike leader with brow slightly furrowed and lips firmly compressed, yet bearing a hint of the famous smile. If there were overtones of George Washington, the pledge of allegiance and the Battle Hymn of the Republic, that was entirely intentional. Fanny had nursed a streak of hero worship since *Ivanhoe* days: "The way most people idolized my movie-star clients, I idolized the great figures in American history."

The added dimension was not lost on the general. Contemplating a celluloid transparency brought to his desk by a mutual friend, the ubiquitous Tony Biddle, Ike grinned his pleasure: "I like it, Tony. That wrinkled brow makes me look like a heavy thinker, an intellectual."

When the Philadelphia Museum of Art later approached Eisenhower about exhibiting the bust, he gave his hearty approval. It was featured in a special exhibition of works by "distinguished" nonprofessionals. A note of appreciation to Fanny from E. M. Benson, chief of education at the museum, remarked on the widespread and admiring response to the Eisenhower portrait.

But it was as a fellow painter that Ike preferred to regard Fanny, a fellow painter who had won entry to the Hallmark Gallery. On her visit to Columbia — ostensibly to ease the passage of a young relative into law school there — Ike had brushed aside talk of international affairs and reached eagerly for her color slides. These dazzling still lifes: were they done outdoors?

This night scene of Times Square glistening in the rain: was it based on a photograph? Or a recollection?

"Neither. The *dybbuk* did it."

What really bowled Ike over was the Central Park skaters, already earmarked for greeting-card reproduction: "Phew! No wonder Hallmark grabbed it. Why, that sky quality alone . . ." How did she do it? He had to know. For years he'd been struggling to get just that misty blend of blue and green. "But I can never bring it off. Did you use some kind of soft brush?"

Fanny shook her head. "The fact is — it was an accident. There was this smudge I had to wipe off, so I grabbed the nearest thing at hand. It happened to be, er, bathroom tissue. And that's what created the blurry effect."

The general was amazed. "You mean — plain toilet paper?"

"Yes. But it won't work with the coarse kind. That wipes away the oil."

The great military commander and future president of the United States absorbed this intelligence carefully.

After Fanny's visit to Columbia, the general would from time to time, when musing over a bourbon with Tony Biddle, refer wistfully to her talent: "Oh, that Fanny Holtzmann! Never mind about her law practice. If I could paint a winter sky the way she does . . ."

It was through Biddle that their third and most spectacular meeting came about. In the spring of 1951, Fanny was in London on business for Gertrude Lawrence when she had a call from her brother Jack urging her to join him in Paris, where he was vacationing with his wife and sister-in-law. Jack had recently been named to the New York State Board of Regents.

Fanny packed an overnight bag and checked in at the hotel where Jack was staying, the Prince of Wales.

The next morning her telephone rang. It was Tony Biddle, who had seen her name while thumbing through the out-of-season "Arrivals" column in the Paris *Herald*. Biddle had been in Europe since February, when his boss, Eisenhower, had been summoned back into the army to head up defense planning for NATO, the North Atlantic Treaty Organization. The two generals were stationed at the Camp des Loges near Marly, some fifteen miles northwest of Paris.

"I'm sure Ike would love to see you," Tony bubbled. "We'll put on the dog, give you a military reception. How would you like that?"

"Who needs it, Tony? Me, you don't have to impress."

Then Fanny had a wicked inspiration. Why not give Jack something to brag about on his home terrain, and at the same time make him realize once and for all that he wasn't the only pebble on the Holtzmann beach? He was constantly rebuking her for "wild exaggerations" about her contacts among the famous. It was time for the Great Educator to be taught a lesson.

On second thought, she told Biddle, an official visit sounded like a nice idea. Only the invitation should be extended to her brother, Jacob L.: "Address him as 'Regent,' and tell him General Eisenhower wants to welcome him as a VIP. You'll send a car to pick up his party. That will stagger his in-laws; and I'll just happen along."

Biddle chortled; the prank appealed to him. He played out his part with flourish, and at dinner Jack proudly announced he was being honored at lunch the following day by General Eisenhower. His wife and her sister were unable to go; they were attending a memorial tribute to their late brother, Dr. Harry Plotz, at the Pasteur Institute. Fanny meekly volunteered to keep Jack company.

She had brought only a casual change of clothes from London, but the treasures of her designer friend, Captain Edward Molyneux, were at her disposal. His couturiers on the rue Royale selected a gleaming green-and-gray "model," took out a confining seam or two, and complemented the gown with a gay multicolored spring hat topped off by taffeta bows.

Jack, whose conservatism in dress bordered on the funereal, took one look and shuddered. How could he be seen in public with a woman dressed like that? At the very least, she would have to get rid of the "gaudy" hat.

All through the drive out from Paris, while their sergeant-chauffeur sat silently up front, he continued to drum away: She was a disgrace to their profession . . . lacking in self-respect . . . would be an eyesore among the military men in their quiet khaki. Fanny, who had rather looked forward to a trip alone with her big brother, was beginning to regret the whole thing.

Suddenly they were pulling into the town square at Marly, and Jack shot up in his seat. "My God!", he ejaculated. "Look what's here! Quick, Fanny — take off that damn hat!"

Two long rows of soldiers stood at attention, and beyond them a corps of staff officers in full regalia clustered around General Eisenhower: dress uniforms and battle ribbons as far as the eye could see. It was the kind of reception usually recorded by newsreels and reserved for heads of state.

Jack squared his shoulders and took a deep breath. "You see, Fanny, what it means to be a Regent of the State of New York? You people never recognize that."

The guards were approaching to help them out. "The hat!" Jack hissed. "Take the goddamn thing off."

"I will not!"

He glared, bringing to bear all the authority of his senior status in the family, and Fanny wilted. As she emerged from the car, she reached up to remove the offending headpiece, when suddenly Eisenhower stepped forward, extending his arms. He enfolded Fanny warmly, and the officers all broke ranks, with Biddle and others of long acquaintance embracing her in turn.

Ike turned apologetically to Fanny's brother: "Forgive this unconventional reception, Regent Holtzmann. I wasn't expecting to see your sister here . . . Let me assure you, it's a privilege to have you with us." He took Jack by the arm with a deference that dispelled any suspicions possibly brewing in the Regent's mind.

For the next two hours, Fanny reveled in the luncheon attentions of eighteen smartly turned out military men. She demanded a vote on her hat (overwhelmingly approved), and described how she had squeezed herself into the slinky Molyneux "model": "I couldn't breathe, I couldn't walk, and now I can't eat — but it's little enough sacrifice to make for the United States Army!" From Molyneux the talk turned to Noel Coward and Gertrude Lawrence, while the *salade niçoise* went untouched. The officers could get salad tomorrow.

Tony Biddle delivered a dramatic account of the Morgan affair, somewhat embellished with the passage of time: "Freddie was in despair; he had actually drafted a suicide note." Eisenhower nodded solemnly. What Fanny accomplished there, he agreed, on both the human and political planes, was beyond praise.

Fanny glanced over at Jack, who was listening intently; she caught a new respect in his eye. "My story was finally getting through to my brother — not from me, but from Ike Eisenhower."

After lunch, Eisenhower invited his guests into a private office where Jack, a potent figure in Republican national politics, questioned the NATO commander about Russian intentions, the strengths and weaknesses of the Western alliance, and decision-making in a democracy.

Jack's probing was acute, far-ranging, and, thanks to the theatrical flair that had emptied the corridors of the New York Supreme Court building every time he argued a case there, ultimately entertaining. As Tony Biddle later reported to Fanny, "Your distinguished brother made a tremendous hit here." In taking leave of the general, Jack grasped Eisenhower by the arm and exclaimed: "You should be a Republican! And you should be our president!"

Ike smiled enigmatically. But he didn't object.

Ultimately Jack was in the vanguard of GOP spokesmen negotiating with and campaigning for Ike. In reward, he was offered an ambassador-ship, but chose instead to secure his place in history as president of the Electoral College. It was his gavel that officially proclaimed the ascension to office of the Eisenhower-Nixon team.

Fanny was far less of an Eisenhower partisan. It was one thing to "like Ike," and quite another to entrust him with the most powerful office on earth. In 1946, after her first encounter with the "Moses of my people," she had reported back to Freddie Morgan that Ike "towered above them all" in Washington.

Later impressions were less cosmic: on social and economic issues, Fanny told friends, the general "ran out of dialogue"; lacking political background of his own, he tended to stand in awe of civilian advisers and might be manipulated by them.

Her own preference for the Republican nomination would have been Senator Robert A. Taft. Fanny felt that although Taft needed educating toward internationalism, essentially he was a man of erudition who could grow in office.

These waverings were abruptly settled by the Democratic riposte to the Eisenhower convention victory. The Democrats named Adlai Stevenson, her old San Francisco factotum, and Fanny toppled temporarily into the opposition camp: "Ike was a nice man, much more friendly and outgoing than Adlai; but Adlai — well, he was my boy."

She had watched Stevenson's rise with mild incredulity. A mere seven years before, he had been sitting in her office, a perpetually-on-leave Chicago lawyer, fretting over the dullness of his corporate practice. There had been some tentative talk in 1945 of his joining Holtzmann and Holtzmann, where the action revolved around more exciting cases and personalities.

In 1946, after completing his stint at the UN organization meetings in London, Stevenson stopped in again at the Bar Building to talk about his future. This time, however, Fanny had broached the matter to her younger brother and partner, David: "This fellow is perfect for us. You're always complaining that I'm running around Europe; well, he can take over a lot of chores there. He knows how I work, and he makes a very favorable impression."

David, after a cursory chat with Stevenson, did not agree. "He's awfully quiet, Fanny. Not much personality. What makes you think he'd be able to keep up with people like Eddie Goulding and Gertrude?"

"He's dependable, David. He'd never try to steal a client. And he has good manners."

"Maybe. But you'll spend half your time going to his rescue."

As it turned out, Stevenson had other plans anyway. He had definitely decided to go into politics in Illinois. Fanny was astonished, as much by the decision as by the authority with which it was announced. "Adlai had always shrugged off the 'combatant-politico' role as something that went against his temperament. And he had never, never spoken about himself with such conviction. Here was my good-natured fetch-and-carry guy talking about being the new U.S. senator from Illinois!"

Wasn't he aiming rather high, Fanny inquired?

"Not particularly."

"Are you in with the Democratic organization?"

"Well, there's a man named Arvey who runs it. I'm going to concentrate on him."

"Jake Arvey? From the South Side of Chicago?"

Stevenson threw up his hands. "Fanny — I have seen Gertrude Lawrence borrow your stockings, and the lord chamberlain of England pour your tea — but I can't believe your sphere of influence extends to the Twenty-fourth Ward in Chicago!"

"Why not?" Ten years earlier, Fanny had been invited to Rickmansworth, outside London, to help entertain a visiting alderman from the United States. Her host was the Chicago-born attorney Albert H. "Bob" Robbins; Bob's father, an Orthodox rabbi, had presided at the Bar Mitzva of the visitor — who was, of course, Jacob M. Arvey. Fanny remembered him well: a pleasant little man, no crude ward heeler but the kind of local attorney frequently encountered around the municipal courts. If a word to Arvey would do any good —

"I suspect it would — but not yet."

The following summer, rumblings of a Stevenson-for-senator campaign in Illinois reached New York breakfast tables. Fanny put in a call to Jake Arvey.

He came onto the telephone quickly: "Ah, my international friend! What can I do for you, counselor?"

"Get behind Adlai Stevenson." Fanny told of her association with the candidate. "He's honest, hard-working and well known among the foreign community. He'd be a real asset to the U.S. Senate."

"The job has been promised to Paul Douglas."

"Jake, I'm telling you this man could be sold to the voters. He's great political material. I'll vouch for him."

"You don't have to vouch for him. I know all about the man, more than you'll ever know. But there has to be the right opening . . . Wait a minute, wait a minute — somebody came up with a thought the other day . . . Tell me this, Fanny: what would you say to Stevenson for governor?"

"Governor? He'd be a natural. Very sound on organization and detail."

"Senator," Arvey went on as if talking to himself, "I can't make him. Paul Douglas is entitled. But governor, I can."

And that was the ticket announced from Springfield early in 1948 by the Democratic State Central Committee. Fanny telephoned Stevenson her congratulations, along with an offer of monetary support. It was declined with thanks, but she sent a check anyway.

She still thought of the candidate as a man without means. En route to

Hollywood in February, she telephoned the Stevensons during her train stopover in Chicago and was urged by Ellen Stevenson to spend the night with them there: "We're dying to hear your news. Ad and I will come in from Libertyville and we'll all stay at my mother's place."

Fanny, wincing at visions of a crowded little flat with people doubled up on daybeds and sofas, begged off.

It wasn't until the summer of 1948, as she splashed in the pool of a Mexican spa, that she learned how badly her sympathies for "poor Ad" were misplaced. Hughston McBain, president of Marshall Field, informed her that Ellen Stevenson was a Borden, heir to a vast mining fortune. And Adlai himself came from a family well entrenched in publishing and business. As for Ellen's "mother's place" in Chicago, from which Fanny had shrunk in fear that it would be a cramped hovel, that was "nothing less than palatial — one of the showplaces of the Middle West!"

So Adlai didn't need money — only votes.

Fanny wrote, suggesting that he seek appointment as presidential adviser on Palestine. Stevenson answered by return mail: it would be a sound move politically but all his time and energy were going into the gubernatorial campaign. "I am afraid my constant presence here would make the whole thing a little too transparent."

In November he won by a landslide.

Over the next few years, his reputation grew (paralleled, ironically, by the collapse of his marriage; the Stevensons were divorced in 1949). Fanny, instinctively separating herself from the favor seekers clustering around a successful politician, maintained only long-range contact. Twice she passed up invitations to the executive mansion; several times Stevenson recommended her to litigants in search of international counsel.

Early in 1952, Stevenson had his fateful summons to Washington from Harry Truman. A few days later, Fanny's telephone rang:

"Fanny, they want me to run for president. Truman says I can have the nomination. Should I take it?"

"Should you take it? But of course! That's marvelous, Adlai!"

"I don't know . . . I have all sorts of reservations. About the party. About myself . . ." He trailed off.

A remark made years before by Stevenson's wife during a moment of impatient anger came back to Fanny. "He's helpless, hopeless," Ellen had complained at the end of a heart-to-heart talk in New York. "He can't make up his mind what slot to stick the toothbrush in!"

Fanny filled the silence: "Do you need to be coaxed, Adlai? To take on the most challenging job in the world?"

"But they'll get into my divorce, Fanny, my personal life. I can't fight on that level."

"Remember your grandfather, Adlai. Your pride in the family tradition. Our country needs you."

"I guess I have trouble believing that."

Stevenson's "trouble" lingered until the very eve of nomination, when

Truman intervened personally to put his candidacy across. Fanny was advised of the climactic decision in a telephone call from Stevenson's secretary: "The governor wanted you to have the word directly, before you read about it in the newspapers."

From then on, Fanny was heavily involved in her friend's bid for the presidency. She made a substantial contribution of money, and raised a great deal more among her wealthy friends. She threw in policy suggestions, campaign ideas, critiques, typified by a long telegram to Springfield soon after Stevenson plunged into battle: "Studying your telecasts carefully and feel impact would be heightened if you displayed anger more freely. Eisenhower leans largely for television effect on belligerent manner which undeniably conveys strength. Suggest you remove gentlemanly gloves and fight back, because your public's interest is held by personal conflict rather than abstract ideas. Always remember your audience is same people who are conditioned by prizefights, ballgames and suspense plays. Today's society is geared to innumerable stimuli, so hit them hard Adlai and best of luck."

Whenever "the governor" campaigned in New York, Fanny traveled with his party. By running as an "independent," Stevenson kept himself at arm's length from the corruption-tainted Democratic national machine, but because he thereby also cut himself off from experienced guidance, planning was often haphazard.

A foray into Fanny's native Brooklyn was a fiasco. It began with the candidate himself languishing in a dental chair on the wrong side of the river while his campaign caravan rolled through the streets of Williamsburg: a troublesome incisor had finally broken off at lunch, and he had been rushed to the nearest waiting room for emergency repairs.

Fanny found herself riding in the forward car with her niece Betty Ann Holtzmann, Doris Fleeson of the *Daily News*, and a young Stevenson aide. The aide peered out at the sidewalks, brimming with bearded Chasidic Jews in the long coats and medieval *streimelach* (fur-trimmed black hats) of Eastern Europe. "Ha!" he cried. "The whole community has turned out to see us. We've got the Brooklyn vote in the bag!"

Fanny shook her head sadly. It had escaped the neophyte campaigner that the time was sunset on Friday, and the Chasidim streaming past were on their way either to or from Sabbath services; furthermore, ninety percent of them were immigrants ineligible to vote.

A more receptive throng was waiting at the Brooklyn Academy of Music, where Stevenson was finally delivered, tense and weary. He had been inadequately rested and poorly briefed. To an audience concerned about the beleaguered Jews in the Arab Middle East, he offered lofty generalities about the philosophy of good government.

Fanny squirmed, painfully aware that his words were sailing through the roof: "After a while, we were just praying that he would get offstage before that front tooth came unstuck again."

The Democratic campaign stumbled forward, and sometimes sideways, against a multitude of obstacles, not least of them the apathy of a glamour-struck electorate. Predictably, American voters chose the smiling "war hero" over the man vowing to "talk sense" to them.

Stevenson had not expected to win. But the scope of his rejection — he carried only nine states, all south of the Mason-Dixon line — was deeply disappointing.

Fanny telephoned him in Illinois, urging him not to lose heart. Eisenhower would be unable to hold the people: "I know the guy, Adlai. He's limited. Nothing exciting will come out of his administration."

"But there's nothing *against* him, either. And he'll never make an unpopular move that might antagonize the people."

"Conditions change, Adlai. This campaign was only a run-through, a tryout on the road. Build your contacts, travel abroad — prepare yourself for the next one."

Fanny turned back to her law practice. A court case would require her presence in London in a couple of months. Meanwhile David O. Selznick, former son-in-law of Louis Mayer, had a grievance against MGM. Some years before, $12,000,000 in debt after the financial disasters of *The Paradine Case* and *Portrait of Jennie*, Selznick had sold a batch of literary properties to the Culver City studio. Lately, according to Selznick, a story turned down in that transaction had resurfaced in slightly altered form as the basis for a profitable MGM movie.

Fanny was dubious. Infringement cases were always sticky. Suppose, she suggested to Selznick, that instead of asking for cash, she tried to get one of his old properties back?

"Terrific. That's the kind of thinking you don't get out of a lawbook, Fanny. See if they'll let go of *The Wings of the Dove*."

Fanny called her old adversary of *Rasputin* days, J. Robert Rubin, general counsel for MGM.

"What do you want, Fanny? Didn't you do enough to me?" Rubin had been spending several months a year in treatment at Duke University since his post-*Rasputin* heart attack.

"Let's have lunch tomorrow."

"Lunch? I have rice, without any seasoning!"

They met at the Algonquin, where Fanny explained that she had been retained by White and Case, a major Wall Street firm, to press Selznick's claim.

"It's ridiculous, Fanny. David has no claim."

"That's what you said in the Youssoupoff case. For Nick Schenck you have to play tough guy? For the stockholders, so you should get a big wreath when you die?"

Rubin looked unhappy. "I'm not a cash register, Fanny. Didn't you get enough out of me?"

"We're not looking for money. Just give David back a property he sold you a long time ago. With that, you'll have a full release."

"What property?"

"Does it matter, after sitting so long in dead storage? It's a novel by Henry James, *The Wings of the Dove*."

"I don't remember it."

"So how valuable can it be to you?"

Rubin shook his head wearily. "All right, Fanny. Take the book. Just let me live."

Because a new regime had just taken over at Culver City, the settlement had to be endorsed on the Coast. Fanny took a leisurely train trip west. Her papers signed, she continued on to San Francisco to attend an opening there by Victor Borge, an office client; she planned to fly back afterward to New York and then go on to England.

But in a San Francisco elevator she ran into Alfred Katz: bluff, mountainous, a perpetual wanderer of the world's byways who was engaged in promoting the appearances of opera divas and ballet stars. Katz was an old stand-by from the Anton Dolin–Alicia Markova days.

He pronounced her intended itinerary absurd: "Why go across the whole span of America, which you've seen so often, and then the Atlantic, which is as familiar to you as Times Square? For the same fare you can continue westward around the world, taking in the splendor of the Orient! The way to go to London, my dear Fanny, is via Hong Kong!"

"But I don't have my passport with me. Or money. Or clothes."

"Since when have such trivia deterred Fanny Holtzmann? You can drop in at Taiwan and see your friend the generalissimo."

A visit to Chiang Kai-shek she might resist; but a colossal bargain she could not. *"For the same fare . . ."*

She telephoned Lou Lurie, a local realtor friend of both L. B. Mayer and William Randolph Hearst; he telephoned a federal judge, and before noon the next day she had a passport. At the Bank of America, "Doc" Giannini's elder brother Amadeo, founder of the institution, greeted her with an embrace and a letter of credit for $10,000. For wardrobe and baggage she darted through the racks of the White House department store, and was back at her hotel by evening, ready for the trip to the airport.

As she was hurrying through her hotel lobby, she saw a familiar figure rushing past in the opposite direction. Simultaneously the man stopped, turned and stared.

"Fanny!"

"Adlai!"

"I've got a lot to tell you — but I can't talk now. Running for a plane."

"Me too."

"See you in a couple of months." He waved and disappeared.

He saw her much sooner than that. It turned out that both were booked on the same flight to Tokyo — the first leg for Stevenson of a round-the-world observation tour he was making with William McCormick Blair and William Attwood, an editor of *Look*.

For the opening hours of the trip, while Stevenson's companions dozed or read, Fanny sat chatting with him. In the special intimacy of an air journey, she acquired a new and disconcerting close-up of the Democratic standard-bearer: "For a while, when he first committed himself to politics, he had seemed forceful, sure of his direction. Now he appeared more than ever lonely and insecure, torn with inner turmoil, groping for a way to handle his personal relationships. I had the impression of a man who felt he had failed in his family life, and was restless, almost bored, with the role of politician."

Nonetheless, she pressed Stevenson into political discussion, emphasizing his special responsibility as spokesman for the globally-aware segment of the electorate. She was particularly eager for him to see the Middle East at first hand, and make his own judgment on the conflicting parties there.

Stevenson indicated a certain reserve on the subject. However, as they parted in Tokyo to pursue their separate schedules, he agreed to report his reactions in Belgrade, where their paths would cross again.

Fanny waited until Stevenson had left Formosa before she flew there to visit Chiang Kai-shek.

The generalissimo sent an imposing delegation, including General Moshe Cohen, to meet her plane, and received her with an English-speaking colonel, officially his "interpreter," at his side. Fanny was sure that in fact he understood every word she said.

She still had hopes of encouraging a Nationalist-Communist compromise. The generalissimo's reaction was brief but emphatic: "Communism is a very evil force. I went to Russia, worked and studied among them. No Communist can ever be trusted."

He asked if she could come to a reception at his home that weekend, when Madame would be back in Taipei.

"I would be honored. But that's when the Jewish Passover begins."

Chiang, an ardent Methodist, nodded. "I know — the Book of Exodus. And you would like to be with your own people."

On Friday morning she arrived at the Hong Kong airport. A small fleet of expensive cars was waiting. But the plump, curly-haired man who stepped down from a Daimler and hurried up to Fanny was from neither Twentieth Century nor Paramount nor MGM. "I am Kadoorie," he announced. "The Generalissimo sent word you were coming — and that you might be free to celebrate the Seder with our family. My house is at your disposal."

Lawrence Kadoorie's "house" was a magnificent palace on a peak overlooking Hong Kong Harbor, whose ferry lines and dock facilities had been largely owned by Kadoorie's grandfather. The family was among the wealthiest in world Jewry.

But more than by their priceless art collection, Fanny was struck by Kadoorie's philosophy of sharing. He had rescued and sustained countless refugees from the Chinese mainland. *"Kol Israel* [All Israel]," he told Fanny, "must aid our fellowman. It is our heritage and our privilege."

However, the task in Hong Kong, he added sadly, was beyond the political or organizational resources of any individual. It was a matter for international humanitarian action. No, he did not think it would be wise for Fanny to see the refugees; she would only be distressed.

So of course Fanny was up early the next morning looking for refugees. For four days she haunted their camps and colonies in the area, including a food kitchen in Portuguese Macao; then she sat down and wrote to John Alexander-Sinclair, a senior United Nations official long engaged in relief work:

"This is an angry letter because I have just returned from a visit to the Chinese refugee camps here and what I saw makes my blood boil. . . . When I think of the time I idealistically spend helping the builders of the International Refugee Organization . . . to have witnessed what I did at first hand makes one sick.

"I am turning to you, John, because it is *not* a matter of the Chinese or politics or alibis or excuses — it is a vitally important personal problem so far as I am concerned. I appeal to you as a friend to aid me in every possible way to alleviate the outrageous, unfair and inhuman way in which these refugees are existing. Until this is done I cannot sleep, eat or pursue my normal activities. Of course this is an emotional letter but then, you know me — everything I do springs from my emotions. . . .

"These refugees lived in what might be termed apologies for temporary mat tents — sans floor covering, beds or anything other than these mats — a fire broke out in the improvised sheds which had been constructed, and the poor people were driven out. . . . The place is overrun with starving sick women and children and gaunt men — I have been to the Camps in Germany and Middle Europe and I tell you, John, those places are like the Ritz compared to what is going on in Hong Kong and Macao . . .

"The Salvation Army, the Catholic Church and the Generalissimo's Relief Fund are limited. Please get busy at once and cut the red tape. There will have to be help from the IRO or UN — otherwise I will go after them and start such a rumpus that the very buildings on the East River will be in danger of toppling over. . . . I will stir up such a fuss that the H-Bomb will seem mild. I WANT THESE POOR CHINESE REFUGEES GIVEN AS MUCH CARE AS THE NAZIS IN THE EAST GERMAN SECTOR and the Japanese and the Arabs!"

According to John Alexander-Sinclair, although the situation in Hong Kong posed certain technical difficulties ("the General Assembly in its unwisdom" had restricted aid to those persons outside the jurisdiction of any government), Fanny's letter was directly responsible for the opening of an emergency bureau there by the UN high commissioner for refugees.

Fanny spent a number of days in India, which on the whole she found depressing, a land of brown hills and unsmiling people. By contrast, the Chinese and their cousins in Thailand seemed to have a capacity for rising above the crises of the moment; even in the hovels of Hong Kong she had encountered serenity and humor.

But the main lesson of her Asia travels was the essential similarity among peoples: "Kindness created an instant response everywhere."

For weeks Fanny had been looking forward to Adlai Stevenson's report on Israel. Although she knew he had never shared her intense emotional involvement with the Jewish state, she hoped that actual contact with the settlers would fire his idealism.

But when she appeared for their breakfast rendezvous at the Hotel Majestique in Belgrade, Stevenson was not there. Instead he sent Bill Blair, with instructions to reschedule the appointment for lunch the next day.

This time it was the headwaiter who intercepted her at the door. Mr. Stevenson had been called away to an official luncheon; however, his son Borden was at hand and would be happy to bring her up to date.

The young man was waiting at the table, rosy-faced and handsome. He had flown down from London to the Middle East, he told Fanny, to join his father on that crucial leg of the trip. It had been an "absolutely wonderful" experience. The Arabs were marvelous hosts, with a fascinating culture. As for the Israelis, they had not been so much fun. Evidently they had pressed their case with single-minded earnestness, to the point where Borden "couldn't wait to get out."

"Did your father have the same reaction?"

"Of course. After all, he's the one they were concentrating on."

No wonder Adlai had not been eager to meet her in Belgrade face to face! Apparently he had been subjected to a stiff dose of unvarnished Jewish intensity — and an equally rich brew of romantic Arab ceremonial. It was obvious which he preferred.

But there was more. The Stevenson predilection for Arab culture, Borden was pointing out, went back at least one generation: "Mother's aunt, Mary Borden, lived in Palestine as a journalist for years and knew all the leading families, like the Husseinis. Aunt Mary is married to General Spears."

Fanny needed no briefing on Major General Sir Edward Louis Spears. A celebrated Arabist, Spears served during World War II as Britain's first minister to the Republic of Syria and Lebanon; he was widely credited with conceiving and organizing the Arab League.

Fanny could see in the Spears connection a likely source of Stevenson's frequently voiced ambiguity about Israel. She was not prepared, however, for the 4,500-word report that appeared under the former candidate's by-line in *Look* magazine of August 11, 1953.

Ostensibly the article was an objective, evenly balanced analysis of the Middle East scene. Sounding a note of anxious hand-wringing, Stevenson deplored the hatred poisoning the area; he expressed worry for the future of an economically dependent Israel harassed by Arab blockade. Yet throughout ran the thread of a very different message: subtle praise for the embittered Arabs, and chiding of the Israelis as instigators of the tension.

In the Old City of Jerusalem, Stevenson wrote, his "moments of reverence" were shattered by descriptions of Israeli atrocities. Everywhere there was "fear of Israeli expansion" and "a sense of Arab brotherhood in the face of common peril." As for reports that the Arabs might be preparing to attack, "personally, I detected no such dark designs."

To Fanny, the report was revoltingly superficial. In reflecting obliquely the outlook of Radio Cairo — and neglecting to mention that Middle East passions had been fomented largely by its broadcasts — Stevenson was being either naive or malicious.

Nowhere in his article did he make any attempt, as a leader of the world's greatest democracy, at qualitative evaluation of the Middle East societies; nowhere was there a suggestion that the America of Washington and Lincoln had any kind of spiritual bond with the Israeli pioneers or any obligation to the miserable masses of the feudal Arab lands. Stevenson could deliver odes to "towering, majestic" Ibn Saud; but he had no eloquence for the Bedouin tribesman who, empty-bellied among His Majesty's Cadillacs and swimming pools, under ancient Islamic law risked loss of his right hand if he snatched up a loaf of bread.

Stevenson's Adlai-of-Arabia fever never subsided. During the Suez crisis of 1956, when combined Anglo-French-Israeli action threatened to topple Nasser from power, Fanny appealed to Stevenson to oppose American-Soviet intervention. He flatly refused. The Jews and the industrial West were ganging up, he declared, on helpless, peace-loving Nasser: "You never heard the Arab side, Fanny."

In 1964 many intellectuals felt betrayed when Stevenson, who had been appointed ambassador to the United Nations by President Johnson, warmly defended American policy in Vietnam. For Fanny, disillusion with the former Democratic standard-bearer had been fairly complete a decade earlier: the *Look* article confirmed an impression she had begun to develop in the air over Hawaii. "Until that time, I had attributed certain qualities to him — a penetrating mind, for one thing — but the man sitting beside me in that plane was all veneer. Something seemed to have been knocked out of him — or perhaps it was never there. The Stevenson who rubbernecked around the world was shallow, a dilettante lacking convictions. He was like an actor without a script."

She remained in touch with Stevenson sporadically until his death in

1965; a note from him in the sixties referred nostalgically to "many memories" of their "collaboration." But the old closeness was never restored.

In the fall of 1953, Fanny made her own report on her trip across Asia and Europe. Written at the request of Allen Dulles, then director of the CIA, for his private perusal, it sounded a warning on the "rapid decline" of American prestige overseas — less, Fanny claimed, as a result of Communist machinations than from the negative impact of American personnel and products.

By Fanny's account, civilian and military missions from the United States were breeding deep resentment by displays of neo-colonial arrogance, especially in poorer countries like Greece: "No Greek can park his car near 'our' Tamion Building in Athens; our PX at a main intersection offers a glorious array of merchandise — for sale to 'Authorized Americans Only.' Is this kind of extra-territoriality any better than the treaty ports which the United States renounced in 1943?" Throughout Europe, Fanny asserted, the PX system was "a focal point of black marketeering."

In Asia, she found even greater cause for concern. "The key fact in the Far East today is the hatred of the white man, especially white troops who come to kill Asiatics. The Russians have managed to sell themselves to most of the area as fellow Asiatics."

Easing the way for Communist penetration was the American practice of shipping across the Pacific "the shoddiest products of our civilization": slot machines, garish cosmetics, "comic" books, and, especially, crime-and-sex "exploitation" movies.

"Anti-Americanism abroad has been allowed to flourish unchallenged. A whole generation of children has imbibed it — along with the dried milk we supplied for their subsistence.

"The time has come," Fanny suggested, "to arouse the nations with constructive news from our country. In this cruel struggle, let us be represented by Tuskegee and Hampton Institute rather than by share-croppers and Harlem; by our life-giving research foundations as well as our atomic program; by our democratic town meetings and elections rather than by our criminal-political machines.

"Above all, let us strive to speak with deeds — and then make our deeds speak for themselves."

Her recommendation anticipated precisely the policy that Edward R. Murrow, who took over the United States Information Agency eight years later, tried to implement.

Twice during the Eisenhower administration, Fanny dropped in to see the general at the White House. He struck her as being a perennial stranger there, a fish out of water, "longing for the good old days of uncomplicated soldiering in Britain." Even his relaxation on the golf links, he complained, was interrupted by clamorous autograph-hunters; the English public had a nicer sense of privacy.

Eisenhower spoke wistfully of his days at Columbia. Although he had apparently never felt quite at home there either, contact with the academic community had expanded his horizons. He seemed terribly impressed when Dr. Arthur F. Burns, the former Columbia professor, spied Fanny through the open door and came in to greet her affectionately. Burns, who later became chairman of the Federal Reserve Board, was then reigning as the economics pundit of the White House.

Fanny's last contact with General Eisenhower had a strong whiskey flavor. In the late 1960's she was retained by Mrs. Clarence Shearn, the widow of an appellate division judge, to contest a large storage bill presented by a liquor warehouse. Fanny settled the case out of court. A few days later she was informed that Mrs. Shearn had vanished from sight, after leaving instructions that the liquor involved in the litigation should be delivered to Fanny in lieu of a fee.

Fanny, the most total of teetotalers, suddenly became the baffled inheritor of liquid treasure stored away by the judge twenty years before, on the morning after Pearl Harbor. To her rear delivery door came a quantity of champagne, nearly all of it gone bad, and dozens of cases of something called Old Bridgeport Rye.

She struggled in vain to get rid of the stuff. Her family wanted no part of it: the whiskey's name was unknown to them, and its mere four years of aging did not sound promising. A few bottles were disposed of to the building staff —"only the elevator men in the back; I couldn't insult the front men with such an obscure label." One case was accepted by the United Catholic Charities, and another by the Hebrew Home for the Aged. But that scarcely made a dent in Fanny's supply.

One evening, as she was brooding over the depressing tax prospects accruing from her "fee," Dr. John Staige Davis stopped in. Davis, a prominent society physician and bon vivant, gaped at the plain bottle on her liquor cart: "Where'd you ever get that, Fanny? It's a collector's item — hasn't been posted for years!"

The next day the doorbell started ringing: old friends who hadn't been around in months, new friends-of-friends on dubious errands. Obviously whiskey connoisseurs had passed around the word about what a clubman cousin of Hamilton Fish's pronounced "a sip to delight Ponce de León."

On Fanny's next trip to Europe, she packed a couple of bottles for General Morgan.

That left only Morgan's crony Eisenhower to take care of — a detail that was encompassed when Fanny found herself seated at a dinner party next to General Kevin McCann, an Eisenhower aide at the former president's farm in Gettysburg.

McCann came to East Sixty-fourth Street the next morning to pick up several bottles of Old Bridgeport. He reported back to Fanny that "Ike grabbed them all — including the one you gave me." The following week, a note from Ike himself confirmed the delivery and expressed gratitude for Fanny's thoughtfulness.

Fanny kept up the shipment arrangements all through Eisenhower's illness. She never saw the general again, but according to McCann, Ike's last days at Walter Reed Hospital were brightened by the "sip to delight Ponce de León."

Chapter 14

*N*EW HORIZONS BECKONED to Fanny constantly; yesterday's skills were never enough. In the early 1950's she signed up for private lessons in French and in the Mensedieck breathing exercises. On her swing around the globe, she startled the staff of the Imperial Hotel in Tokyo by practicing Chopin in the grand ballroom at eight in the morning.

With Central Park only a few steps away and an early-morning rink permit from Newbold Morris in hand, she turned to ice-skating, and was soon struggling through awkward figure-eights. Her prospects for Olympic stardom were summarily canceled by a stage mother who, upon learning Fanny's identity, came panting after her with pleas for an audition. Fanny tried to shake loose, lost her footing and crashed down on the ice, breaking her left wrist.

The blow was not softened by the discovery that, as a female, she was entitled to only half the $100 weekly normally collectible under her New York County Lawyers Association insurance plan, the assumption presumably being that women attorneys were lowlier specimens whose removal from circulation would have negligible financial consequences.

In fact, few lawyers anywhere could rival Fanny in earning power or in the prestige of her clients. Since the days of Mabelle Webb, her office roster had always included a few names from the Blue Book world of immense fortunes, Park Avenue duplexes and transient matrimony.

Doris Duke, seeking a divorce from Jimmy Cromwell, was advised by Fanny to move from New Jersey to Nevada, buy a home there, and register to vote before bringing suit. She did. Fanny never sent a bill to the richest woman in the world: "Frankly, I pitied her. She had to live in villas and night clubs, gregariously. She never had the anonymous fun of talking to her neighbor on the bus."

Gloria Vanderbilt, too, passed through the office portals — although differences in personal philosophy led to an amicable parting.

After World War II, William B. Leeds swung aboard. He was the colorful tin-plate heir who in pre-Depression days had gladdened the hearts of yacht manufacturers and tabloid editors. Coming into a fortune of $7,000,000 in boyhood, he had dispensed it copiously on speedboats, private airplanes, nonstop merrymaking and assorted philanthropies; he supported a leper colony in Tahiti and in 1940 donated an entire corps of forty ambulances to the hard-pressed British.

Leeds was steered to the Bar Building by Eddie Goulding, a sometime playmate, when the mining heir became the target of a damage suit by a showgirl who claimed she had been "injured for life" at one of the Leeds champagne parties. Fanny engaged a private detective who not only persuaded the beauty to drop the litigation but wound up making her his bride — a moviesque ending that delighted the quixotic millionaire.

In lieu of payment, Fanny proposed — and Leeds quickly accepted — a $25,000 annual retainer under which her office would take responsibility for handling his taxes, his investments, and his superb art collection. A few years before his death in 1972, one of his Rembrandts, *Portrait of a Man*, fetched $390,000 in auction at Sotheby's.

Fanny was fond of Bill Leeds, "a brilliant man but shy and unhappy. His tragedy was his money. It insulated him from the rest of mankind."

A less endearing eccentric who crossed Fanny's path was Helena Rubinstein. The cosmetician was a great rival of Elizabeth Arden, for whom David Holtzmann had performed legal services.

One Sunday afternoon in September, a newspaper friend from Boston telephoned Fanny to say he was in the Rubinstein apartment nearby, and that Fanny really ought to run over and see Madame's remarkable art collection. He added that there was also "a little business matter" that might be worth discussing.

Fanny tossed a light sweater around her shoulders and headed for the Rubinstein duplex at Park Avenue and Sixty-fifth Street, two blocks away. She was to be picked up there later by her sister Stella, who had been part of the Bar Building legal force since being widowed in 1951.

Led out by a butler onto the terrace, Fanny blinked in astonishment. The only person in sight was a stocky, elderly woman wrapped in a faded blue robe that more or less surrounded a flannel nightgown. The robe had seen better days, but not lately; its hem and collar were frayed, and there were eggstains on the sleeves. Could this be the world-famous arbiter of elegant grooming? Her hair, thought Fanny, looked as if it had been caught in a wind machine. With her work slippers and general air of neglect, she might have been the slovenly wife of a *shochet* (kosher slaughterer) in the backyard at Rohatyn after a long day.

Madame Rubinstein was staring with equal amazement at Fanny: her slight figure, casual clothes, the arms and neck innocent of jewelry.

"I can't believe this is the great Fanny Holtzmann," she said at last. "You might be anybody riding on the bus."

"I often am."

After some talk of painting and mutual friends in the theater, the old woman turned to the subject of the law. Fanny, sensing a brain-picking operation, kept her answers brief.

"The fact is, Miss Holtzmann, I have a problem."

"New York is full of lawyers."

"Not like you."

"Thank you — but we don't do commercial work."

"I happen to know your firm represented Elizabeth Arden."

"That was something my brother David handled. On a personal basis, not for the cosmetic company."

"So is this. It concerns me, individually. You see, I've worked hard in my life and made a lot of money. But when it comes to disposing of it — well, I have many relatives, but few people I can trust. I want to put together a will."

Fanny perked up. Maybe this was a bona fide inquiry.

Before the matter could be pursued, Stella breezed onto the terrace — as ever bright, generous, and where her roommate of Eastern Parkway days was concerned, magisterial. She was double-parked downstairs, and not about to risk a ticket.

Helena Rubinstein shuffled after Fanny to the door. "I'm really interested," she insisted. "I need your help, so that the government and the tax laws don't eat away my estate."

"I practice in the Bar Building. Come to my office."

Madame would not do that — but she wouldn't let go, either. Two days later she telephoned Fanny at home: "I really can't go out. And I see very few people. Please come to me for dinner tonight, alone."

Again she was waiting in her tattered robe, this time making wry contrast with the stately dining-room setting of lofty candelabra, heavy English silver and banked flowers. At the end of the meal, she carefully poured the unfinished wine in her goblet back into the bottle: "You're a regular person, you can understand. Why waste it?"

Even for Fanny, this was carrying frugality too far; once more she had the uneasy feeling that Madame was interested in pumping her for advice rather than in paying for it. However, as the old lady was now plunging into financial specifics, Fanny listened and made notes.

Over the next few weeks, Madame telephoned Fanny every day, chatting of world affairs, contract bridge, the achievements of her children and grandchildren. Meanwhile, Fanny spent several afternoons reviewing the cosmetician's problems with the Holtzmann and Holtzmann estate-tax consultant. She then turned over to Madame a number of recommendations for the "fragmentizing" of her future tax liabilities.

The next morning, the chummy telephone calls abruptly stopped.

Madame had become "temporarily unavailable." A bill for legal services brought no response.

Fanny was not in the habit of being outmaneuvered. On her next trip to London she summoned Madame's elder son, Roy Valentine, to Claridge's and laid her complaint before him. Her bill was paid.

At the core of Fanny's practice remained a handful of longtime associates, impossible to pinpoint as either "friend" or "client" because by now the categories hopelessly overlapped.

Eddie Goulding, with more talents (and more uncertainties) than he could deal with, was entering upon the last decade of a troubled life. Novelist and dramatist, composer-lyricist collecting royalties on such "standards" as "I Kiss Your Hand, Madame," screen director of *Grand Hotel, Dark Victory* and *Of Human Bondage*, Eddie had at long last attained the presumably perfect contract — one and a half million dollars for six comfortably spaced pictures — only to find Darryl Zanuck's vanity buried inside. Once again he turned in desperation to Fanny.

Over a twenty-five-year span, the pattern of their relationship had never really changed. Since being planted on the Coast by Fanny, Goulding had oscillated between nervous dependence and frantic rebellion. Fanny had been obliged to make a major rescue effort late in 1940. Despite Goulding's triumph with Bette Davis a year earlier in *Dark Victory*, his personal peccadilloes had brought him to the brink of ruin. Heavy drinking had laid him open to a bout of double pneumonia; recklessness at the poker table had left him without a penny. The ominous word was quietly making the rounds of the Hollywood front offices: Goulding was a "drunk," a bad boy best left to pickle in his own juices.

Goulding telephoned Fanny from Palm Springs — the usual tale, the usual penitent promises — and she hurried westward. At Burbank she sat down in the studio dining room with Jack Warner, Goulding's most recent boss:

"Tell me this, Jack: is he good?"

"The best, Fanny. A very big talent."

"Does your studio need big talents?"

"Of course — if they're under control."

"Did Eddie ever go on a bust during shooting?"

"Not yet. But with a *shikker*, there has to be a first time. And I don't want to be the fall guy."

"Look, Jack — you need Eddie, and I need you. I'll guarantee to straighten him out — if you'll help."

"I'm listening."

"The first thing we'd have to do is set his mind at ease. He's terrified of borrowing to meet his present obligations."

"What would it take?"

"Well, let's see — debts, family, household expenses — about fifty thousand would see him through. After that, I'll assume responsibility. With me, you've never seen him drunk."

"Let's go to my office, Fanny."

In ten minutes the check was written out, a loan without interest; within the week Goulding was back at work.

His gratitude was near-pathetic: "If you had done nothing but come out here at your own expense, it would have been enough; if you had simply gotten me the money — or talked Warner into putting me on a picture — but to do everything, and then refuse a fee —"

"In other words," Fanny summed up crisply, *"Dayenu!"*— a reference to the Passover chant in which Jews recite the many beneficences of the Lord, any one of which would have warranted eternal thankfulness.

The afterglow of her coup with Warner lasted until 1945, when Eddie wrote *The Ryan Girl* for Broadway. Fanny told him flatly that he was being hoodwinked by promoters; the play was dated and unworthy of production. If he insisted on going ahead, he'd better get himself another lawyer.

He did. *The Ryan Girl* ran for forty-eight performances.

At loose ends, Goulding was approached by Charles K. Feldman, the Zanuck satrap and lawyer–turned–ten percenter; Feldman had a picture for him at Twentieth Century–Fox. The picture turned out to be Somerset Maugham's *The Razor's Edge*. Eddie came up with a scintillating screen version, and he was riding high again.

Feldman — the same Feldman who two years later would woo Clifton Webb away from the MCA agency for Zanuck — followed up with a seductive offer. If Goulding would commit himself wholeheartedly to Twentieth Century–Fox, he could have the dream contract: six pictures to be made over a period of ten years, at a salary of $175,000 each. Payments, totaling $1,500,000, would be spread over fifteen years.

Cautiously, Goulding sounded Fanny out for an opinion.

He knew very well her misgivings about most agents, she responded. They were the Rasputins of Hollywood, with more influence over high-priced talent than any priest or psychiatrist. All too often they used that influence as barter to improve their own positions.

On the other hand, it was clear that Eddie needed somebody; he had never been self-sufficient. And Feldman's deal was attractive, at least in terms of assuring a comfortable future for Eddie, his mother and his sister.

True, there would be the hazard over his head of Zanuck's capricious despotism; Fanny would have liked to see a clause providing that in the absence of mutual agreement on an assignment, Eddie would be free to do a picture "off the lot." But no contract was perfect; good faith was the unwritten ingredient.

Fanny had real qualms about Zanuck. He had first come into her ken in the middle thirties, when as the brash young production boss of newly formed Twentieth Century–Fox, he had wanted one of her clients, the woman big-game hunter Osa Johnson, for a film. Zanuck, the son of midwestern Polish immigrants, had been respectful to the point of obsequiousness.

With Zanuck's rising power, reports filtered eastward of his mounting arrogance; the studio rapidly developed a one-man image. As Fanny saw it, he was "a frustrated writer and director whose only gift was in editing. He craved the limelight, and by asserting his primacy, made sure he got it.

"Like Harry Cohen at Columbia, he took pleasure in browbeating the truly creative people on the lot. As gentleman-poloist, he needed horses to dig his spurs into; as genius-executive, he made the same use of writers, directors and stars."

Zanuck regarded himself as the sole competent judge of how and where his actors should expend their efforts. He claimed the same omniscience with respect to directors. For two pictures, Eddie Goulding went along unprotestingly. His *Nightmare Alley*, a carnival-hypnotist melodrama starring Tyrone Power and Joan Blondell, was praised in the New York *Times* for its eerie, gripping atmosphere. Two years later, with *Everybody Does It*, he displayed an equally appealing comic flair. This was a tale of a cloddish business man (Paul Douglas), married to a would-be diva, who suddenly sprouts a booming baritone. "Good and gleesome farce," chuckled the critics. "An artfully crazy show."

But the film was a remake of a lightweight story already done passably ten years earlier. Goulding yearned for stronger stuff. He shook his head at a couple of routine gangster scripts. Then, with the ardor of an Americanophile who had just applied for citizenship, he turned down a story that he felt sensationalized small-town life in the United States.

Zanuck found this attitude irksome. Even though script-refusal rights were specified in the director's contract, who was Goulding to challenge a decree from Olympus? If Goulding would not do the stories assigned to him, he would get nothing at all.

Legally, the situation was a stand-off: Goulding was under no obligation to do bad stories; Zanuck couldn't be compelled to give him good ones. In the ensuing deadlock, however, it was Goulding who suffered. Although his pay checks continued to arrive, he was being kept off the screen. To underline his plight, Zanuck inflicted small humiliations: Goulding's special place on the parking lot, symbol of status in the studio hierarchy, was taken away.

Fanny, hearing at long range of Eddie's troubles, took every opportunity to slip in a word with Zanuck. But the baron of West Pico Boulevard, while deferential, refused to entertain the subject.

At the close of the forties, Fanny saw a possible way of softening Zanuck's stand. David Niven, originally a protégé of Eddie's, was being sought by Twentieth Century. However, he had been tied up by his agency, MCA, with Samuel Goldwyn for the next few years. Once again it was a question of negotiating a tactful transfer, this time from Goldwyn and MCA to Darryl Zanuck and his agent-henchman, Charlie Feldman. Fanny had done the trick for Clifton Webb; she was prepared to repeat it with Niven if that would be any help to Eddie.

The British star telephoned her from Beverly Hills: "I met you years ago in London, but I wasn't big enough for you professionally then . . ." He flew east to tell her his story. It sounded like a replay of Clifton Webb: MCA was efficient, but Charlie Feldman made him feel "more comfortable."

Legally, Fanny warned, he had no grounds for breaking the MCA contract. However, Lew Wasserman was a reasonable man; she would fly out and talk to him. There was no necessity for Niven to be out of pocket on the deal: "Charlie Feldman doesn't need money, so long as he has the prestige of bringing you to Zanuck."

The plan worked out perfectly — except that where Goulding was concerned, Zanuck remained unmoved. Months, then years, dragged by. Grimly, Goulding tried to occupy himself with projects for novels, plays, screen stories. Meanwhile, other directors were coming to the fore in Hollywood; Goulding, at the height of his creative powers, had no place to exercise them. At long last his morale began to sag.

Late in 1954, after five years of helplessly watching his name recede into the archives, he wrote to Charlie Feldman from Florida.

Goulding refused to believe that "when I signed the [Zanuck] contract I signed myself out of the business; that in this day and age a top producing company would rub a man out of an industry unless he were an enemy or there was a valid reason for destroying him. Even so, it's a brutal, inhuman punishment to very slowly deprive him of his pride and spirit."

He expressed puzzlement that in the face of his artistic and budgetary record, he was being "completely ignored" by every studio in Hollywood: "Who was out for me when I signed? Who is out for me now? If for the life of this contract I am not to work at a profession in which I have engaged all these years, I am finished." He begged for a chance to "make a picture for Darryl for nothing," rather than continue in his professional exile.

That same week, he sought advice from David Holtzmann: "I know I am sentenced not to direct while this contract is in existence. The agents are part of the conspiracy."

It was Fanny who took it upon herself to reply. She wrote Eddie that his torment was something that came sooner or later to everyone, "harder to endure in your case because one is older and mature people suffer more." But from it would come "a compassion that will be reflected in your work." Meanwhile, he should return to Hollywood, head high; the whole town sympathized with his struggle.

On a trip to London in 1955, Fanny ran into Ben Goetz, a cofounder of Twentieth Century–Fox, at the Savoy. With him was Lew Schreiber,

Zanuck's manager of studio operations. As a result of her urgent pleadings, Eddie Goulding was once again permitted to set foot on a sound stage. He responded with *Mister 880*, in which Edmund Gwenn played a whimsically larcenous old eccentric. It was welcomed as "a deft comedy, delightfully turned."

Fanny took heart. Perhaps she could still deliver Eddie from his purgatory and reverse one of the most personally frustrating situations of her career. She made sure that everybody at the Westwood lot saw the notices, and Goulding was rewarded the following year with a Ginger Rogers–Michael Rennie feature, *Teenage Rebel*. Critics scolded the studio for saddling a "delicate sensitive" film with such an inappropriate title, then went on to laud the director for his skillful pacing and consistent good taste. Despite the absence of promotion, the picture hit No. 8 in the national box-office listings.

Goulding was keenly conscious of his debt to Fanny. "You are wonderful," he wrote after she set up an appointment for him to see Joseph H. Moskowitz, an influential Twentieth Century vice-president. "I am very grateful, and love you very much."

The meeting with Moskowitz led to *Mardi Gras*, a Pat Boone–Gary Crosby musical described in the New York press as "a romp for the undergraduate set." Although it quickly racked up a No. 1 box-office rating — "conclusive proof," Fanny wired Moskowitz, "that you were not battling in vain for Eddie Goulding" — qualitatively it was a long, long way from the director's early-Garbo epic of *Love*.

In 1959 Fanny wrote to Jack Warner, reminding him of his generous loan to Goulding nearly twenty years before, and suggesting that Eddie would now be valuable as a producer as well as behind the camera: "What has long distinguished you has been your vision. Long before Hollywood caught up with you on the Thalberg Award you were in our book for the Holtzmann Award as one of the most decent and understanding fellows in any industry."

But before the matter could be pursued, Goulding was dead of a heart attack.

Fanny was deeply saddened. To her Goulding had shown nothing but his gentle, sunny side, frantically hiding the cankers beneath. She wept for the anguish that had been visited upon him and for the waste of an extraordinary talent. Nor could she put aside completely the thought of what might have been between them.

Still, she had the comfort of knowing she had coaxed and hammered her first real client into functioning despite bouts of alcoholism and despair, and had brought him to a commanding position in film, the medium that best matched his protean gifts.

The female counterpart of Eddie Goulding — in incandescence, improvidence, and long, close involvement with Fanny — was Gertrude Lawrence. Like Eddie, Gertrude had the chronic problem of finding a vehicle that would stretch her creative muscles — but with an important difference. Gertrude was under no bondage to a production organization. She didn't even have an agent. Instead, she enjoyed the concentrated attention of a trusted troika: Fanny, David, and her theater-wise husband, Richard Aldrich.

Soon after the war, Fanny coaxed loose *Pygmalion* for Gertrude from George Bernard Shaw, despite the savant's protest that it was a tattered old potboiler. Fanny argued back that he didn't know a potboiler from a classic; whereupon Gertrude demonstrated the point by touring in the play before packed houses all over the country. For two years she enjoyed the freedom of the road where, far from David Holtzmann's watchful eye, she could indulge in such extravagances as feeding fresh lobster to the seagulls on her hotel terrace in San Francisco.

Back in New York, Gertrude had her antennas up for a Broadway musical. She was offered *Love Life*, with music by Kurt Weill, book and lyrics by Alan Jay Lerner, whose *Brigadoon* had just completed an impressive run of 581 performances. The new show was another Lerner original, tracing the gradual failure of a marriage over a string of historical periods.

Gertrude shook her head: "Some nice tunes, but the book doesn't stand up. The Virgin Mary herself couldn't hold that show together."

Instead, she did a coast-to-coast tour in *Tonight at 8:30*; flew to London to open Daphne Du Maurier's *September Tide*; and late in 1949 deliberately deglamorized herself to play the role of Amanda, the faded southern belle, in the movie version of Tennessee Williams' *The Glass Menagerie*.

Suddenly she was at a dead end. There were no plays in sight, no story ideas, not even a promising revival. Fanny was intrigued by the notion of a biographical drama on Victoria Woodhull; but the script submitted fell short of her expectations, and her two male associates doubted that the country was ready for the woman-in-the-White-House theme.

Gertrude spoke of becoming a Christian Scientist, to invoke a property by prayer; Fanny pursued more mundane methods, beating the bushes among authors, agents and producers. The veteran moviemaker B. P. Schulberg, after a conference on a proposed television series, commented admiringly to David: "To see the sparks shooting from Fanny's mind is like nothing but nuclear fission."

Early in 1950, a book arrived in the mail from the William Morris Agency, representing its author, Margaret Landon. Fanny glanced at the title: *Anna and the King of Siam*. Her curiosity was piqued.

Reading, she very soon felt the tingle of discovery. Here, based on a little-known episode in late Victorian history, were two tremendous acting parts: the semibarbaric ruler of an exotic Oriental court and, even more enticing, the widowed English governess summoned to tutor the king's multitudinous offspring.

It was a role hand-made for Gertrude. Fanny telephoned her and sent the book. By the next morning both Gertrude and her husband were enthusiastic; nor was David Holtzmann disposed to cast a veto.

Fanny hurried down Madison Avenue, the names of composer-lyricist teams whirling through her mind. Crossing Sixty-third Street, she found herself abreast of Dorothy Hammerstein, who was hastening in the same direction. Dorothy waved a gloved hand: "Can't talk now, Fanny. On my way to Sammy's Deli to get a sour pickle for Ockie."

Ockie. But of course! What greater master of mellow sentiment and wry humor than Oscar Hammerstein II? And who could pour out melodies as tender as those of his partner, Richard Rodgers, the composer of *Oklahoma, Carousel* and *South Pacific*?

Fanny grabbed Dorothy's arm. "Look — if I send a book over, will you make sure Ockie gets to read it? It's a musical for the boys to do with Gertrude. Set in Siam."

Hammerstein's wife nodded vigorously, then disappeared with long strides southward. Late that afternoon, having obtained another copy of the book from William Morris, Fanny made delivery to the Hammerstein home in person.

Silence. Fanny, aware of strained relations and sometimes sluggish communication between the Hammerstein and Rodgers households, reconciled herself to patience.

Meanwhile, a complication came to light: Margaret Landon's novel had already been produced as a film by Twentieth Century–Fox, with Rex Harrison as the haughty monarch and Irene Dunne as Mrs. Leonowens, the original Anna. Fanny telephoned Joe Moskowitz, the studio's eastern vice-president in charge of production: "If I get you Gertrude Lawrence for a Broadway musical version, will you finance it?"

"Come have lunch with me and Skouras. You can get anything you want out of Spyros."

The first thing Fanny wanted was a private screening of the picture. She returned to her office to find a message from Oscar Hammerstein: "Dick likes it. Can we see the Fox picture?"

A second screening was arranged. It fired up the partners further. They didn't need movie-company money, Hammerstein told Fanny; they preferred to do the whole thing themselves. Skouras was amenable to a deal.

A few days later, the writing-production team invited Gertrude to lunch at Hammerstein's home on East Sixty-third Street. At Gertrude's insistence, the party was expanded to a foursome to include Fanny. Normally, Fanny steered clear of artistic conferences; "but this time, Gertrude said she wouldn't go without me."

The meeting lasted several hours. Story line, music and costumes were reconnoitered, with gathering excitement. Before the ladies left, the project was firmly under sail.

One detail still worried Gertrude: who would play the king? She had seen Yul Brynner in *Lute Song*, and been impressed with his forceful masculinity. At her urging, Fanny looked the actor over. She agreed that he was a first-rate professional and, equally important, a cultivated gentleman who would not engage in petty bouts of upstaging. Together, they mapped a plan for winning over the producers to their view.

It proved to be unnecessary. Oscar Hammerstein had already spotted Brynner and was "on the point of mentioning it to Dick."

By fall, the libretto was in hand and most of the songs were ready. Gertrude and Fanny, invited to a run-through, were thrilled by the rich texture of the ballads, especially "Hello, Young Lovers," written for Anna, and "Something Wonderful," which would be sung by Dorothy Sarnoff as the king's No. 1 wife.

Late in 1950 the costumes were ready. Soon after the new year, the show went into rehearsal. With war blazing in Korea, Dick Aldrich had been summoned back to naval duty at the Pentagon. Responsibility for looking after Gertrude fell upon the Holtzmanns.

And it was a responsibility. Anna was the most exacting role, both physically and emotionally, of the actress's long career. Weighted down by a steel hoop under layers of Victorian finery, Gertrude was obliged to rack up no less than four miles of walking at every performance. Her songs encompassed a lifetime of moods; her final scenes with Yul Brynner had to soar beyond musical comedy into poignant drama.

One of the charms of *The King and I* was its corps of grave-faced "Siamese" children, portrayed by Puerto Ricans. Unfortunately, seventeen boys and girls crowded into close quarters made an ideal breeding-ground for infection; and when a cold virus struck during the last week of rehearsals, it not only swept through the ranks of "Mrs. Anna's" pupils but latched onto the governess herself. When Gertrude entrained for initial tryouts in New Haven, she was running a temperature of 103 degrees.

David Holtzmann thought the out-of-town opening should be postponed and said so — precipitating the first of many rows with the producers over Gertrude's physical condition. Rodgers and Hammerstein took a skeptical view of her illness, hinting strongly that she was creating difficulties as a protest against being given too few songs. It was no secret, they conceded, that the production had not yet crystallized. Was Gertrude putting on an act to justify an imminent walkout?

Exasperated — Gertrude's professionalism was legendary — David told Rodgers: "Get hold of your brother — let's see what he says." Dr. Mortimer Rodgers was called, and he brought up from New York the famous ear and throat specialist Dr. Samuel Rosen. At a very considerable cost to Holtzmann and Holtzmann David's claim was confirmed: Gertrude Lawrence was not faking.

David reported back to Fanny that the producers were still sulking: "They're talking about closing the show." It was agreed that Fanny would come up for the Boston opening, and decide afterward whether Gertrude should pull out.

The critical reaction in New Haven had been lukewarm; in Boston, it was downright chilly. Clearly, there was "book" trouble, mainly in the first act.

After the opening, two dejected little groups gathered around supper tables in the Hotel Ritz. At the far end of the room sat Rodgers and Hammerstein, their families and their henchmen; a dozen tables away were the Lawrence-Holtzmann forces.

Gertrude was for once gloomy. She turned to her husband, who had flown up from Washington for a few hours: "I don't mind coping with the fatigue, Richard. But in all my years in the theater I've never seen such hostile management. How can I go on in such an atmosphere?"

Gingerly, communication was restored between the two camps. The author-producers, brooding on a sofa in the lobby, made room for Fanny and David. Fanny spoke softly but to the point: "I'm sorry to tell you this, Ockie, but the show just isn't ready. The first act doesn't catch fire."

Hammerstein was quick to defend himself. Certainly there were rough spots in the script, but he already had some cuts in mind; that's what tryouts were for.

"No, it's more than that. The audience is restless for the first half hour, shifting from one side of their seats to the other. They've come to see Gertrude Lawrence."

"What do you suggest?" put in Rodgers. "More songs for her?"

"I'll tell you what . . ." Fanny paused, remembering. "Nearly twenty years ago, I saw Gertrude open in a Cole Porter musical in Manchester. She had laryngitis, but she brought down the house without raising her voice. She just knelt on the apron before a closed curtain, while the stage was being dressed behind her, and practically whispered 'The Physician.' It was intimate, relaxed — and it stopped the show."

David Holtzmann frowned. "A new number? It's Monday, Fanny. The boys have to open in New York in a week."

"I can't believe Dick hasn't got something in the bottom of a trunk that can be salvaged."

Rodgers snorted. "You think it's as easy as that? A composer can dip down and come up with a hit?"

"Cole Porter did it with 'The Physician.' That was added to *Nymph Errant* at the very last minute."

"And you really believe," grumbled Hammerstein, "that lightning can strike twice."

"Gertrude *is* lightning. Give her a proper cloud background, and she'll come through."

Two days later, Oscar Hammerstein phoned the Bar Building from Boston. There was a triumphant bounce in his voice: "We've got the number, Fanny — an old tune of Dick's set to a new lyric! And it works. Even *you* will like it."

Fanny promptly checked with Gertrude.

"It's true, Fanny. We're still firming up the staging, so John [Van Druten, the director] would rather you stayed away from the dress rehearsal in New York. They don't want you to see it till it's perfect — at the opening."

That was good enough for Fanny.

At the premiere, seated beside Billy Rose, she practically held her breath until the scene in which "Mrs. Anna" introduces herself to her royal young charges. As Gertrude dropped to her knees to begin "Getting to Know You," Fanny could not restrain a whoop of recognition: this was exactly the posture from "The Physician."

The melody began, lilting and tender; a hush of enthrallment swept over the house. Fanny jabbed the bewildered Rose in the ribs: "We're in, Billy, we're in!"

When Gertrude finished, the audience was hers. Applause pealed out like thunder. A show that had been limping along hesitantly was lifted to full stride, never to slacken thereafter. *The King and I* was a hit.

Fanny left for Europe to put in several months catching up with clients' affairs there. When she returned, it was to confront a serious problem with Gertrude. The star's contract provided for no time off during the first year of the show's run. It did not square with the hard realities of her situation.

New York summers, notoriously sticky, were always a trial for northern-bred British performers. In *The King and I*, Gertrude had to contend not only with high temperatures — backstage, in the airless dressing rooms of the St. James, rarely below ninety-five — but with suffocating costumes.

Fanny went to the producers. A temporary closing, she suggested, would not only relieve her exhausted client but in the last analysis would benefit the show, since Gertrude carried so much of its burden on her slim shoulders.

Rodgers and Hammerstein were not persuaded. Why turn away sellout houses? Rodgers' brother, summoned again, reported that the star was suffering from nothing worse than laryngitis — perhaps, it was intimated, "Lawrence-itis."

Fanny managed through friends to arrange for air-conditioning the St. James dressing rooms, and to install Gertrude for several weeks in a cool, garden-scented town house.

August brought an offer for Gertrude to teach acting at Columbia University. The drain on her energies, Fanny decided, would be outweighed by the boost to her morale. For several months, the former waif from Golders Green reveled in her role of "professor."

But as the fall term came to an end, so apparently did her reserve. Two days before Christmas, Gertrude was stricken with pleurisy and taken to the hospital. For the first time, an understudy went on as "Mrs. Anna."

After eleven days, Gertrude returned to work — and within a month was hospitalized again with bronchitis. Her husband joined Fanny in urging her to quit. Her portrayal of Mrs. Anna had already been rewarded with a Tony, the New York theater's highest honor. But Gertrude now had her heart set on doing *The King and I* at the Drury Lane in London during the 1953 coronation season celebrating the accession of Elizabeth II.

To those around her, it was clear that determination would not be enough. In April, with Fanny overseas, David Holtzmann asked the producers to close the show for Holy Week. They demurred; it would be too expensive.

By May, Gertrude herself was gravely worried. "Physically and mentally," she wrote in a long letter to David, "I am worn out." Could he possibly persuade the producers to bring in Celeste Holm as her six-week replacement in June, rather than wait till her allotted vacation time in July?

David reached Fanny at the Rome airport, where she was about to board a plane for London. Instead she switched her booking to New York, and the next day, without stopping for sleep, took Gertrude's plea to Rodgers and Hammerstein over lunch.

Once again the answer was no. Gertrude would have to take her time off during the period specified in her contract.

Somehow Gertrude stumbled through the final weeks. In July she joined Richard Aldrich for a blissful holiday on the Cape, where he operated two summer theaters. On August 11 she returned to *The King and I*. That weekend saw a soggy blanket of heat settle over the city. As the curtain came down on Gertrude's Saturday matinée, she staggered a few steps toward her dressing room and collapsed. Hazel, her maid, heard the whispered confession of defeat: "I can't go on tonight. Call Miss Fanny."

Tests at the New York Hospital yielded a diagnosis of hepatitis. A few weeks of treatment, the doctors assured Richard Aldrich and Fanny, and she would be dismissed for a leisurely convalescence. Gertrude professed to be pleased by her clever timing: "Isn't it wonderful, Fan? Just right to catch the off-season rates in Florida. You must admit — after all these years, I've finally learned to economize!"

Absolute rest for the ailing star was decreed, so Richard returned for several days to the Cape. But Fanny, keeping vigil in the corridor, heard low moans from Gertrude's room.

She sent for more consultants. All insisted the patient was "improving."

On September 5, Gertrude asked to see her. "I don't think I'm going to get out of this place, Fan," she said quietly. "Don't tell Richard, but I have a feeling . . ."

The events of the next hour were later described by Fanny in a letter to Colonel Philip Astley, one of Gertrude's lifelong admirers. "It was

345

photographed as
"a Cape Cod housewife"

painted by Fanny as "Mrs. Anna"

uncanny. She asked me to go through every parcel and flower sent her, and told me what to say to each sender in thanking them for their kindnesses."

As Fanny gathered her notes and started for the door, Gertrude called after her: "See that Connie Carpenter steps into the play; she has waited so long for her chance. And that Yul gets star billing. He has earned it."

Aldrich, alerted by Fanny, hurried to his wife's side.

Late that night, Fanny's telephone rang. Gertrude sounded feeble, far away.

Was there anyone she would like to see?

"Well — yes. It would be nice to see Noel. That would make me happy."

Fanny called Coward at his flat in London, where it was early morning.

"This is terrible, Fanny! I'm directing the Lunts in *Quadrille*, and we have a dress rehearsal tonight. How can I be there — and in the theater here, at the same time?"

"I understand, Noel. And I'm sure Gertrude will."

Six hours later, Fanny was on the transatlantic telephone again, keeping a melancholy promise. "She's gone, Noel."

A pair of striking ironies attended Gertrude's passing. Her running battle with the *King and I* management had never been resolved, and on the morning she died a notice to attend an Actors Equity hearing still lay on David Holtzmann's desk. It was returnable on the day of her funeral.

And the issue of the New York *Times* — Sunday, September 7, 1952 — that on page one reported Gertrude's death, carried in its magazine section a handsome Lawrence painting executed by Fanny. The main illustration of a feature article on theatrical luminaries, it was a queenly, silken-gowned evocation of the star as Mrs. Anna, photographed over Fanny's mantelpiece and processed for reproduction weeks earlier. The *King and I* portrait, despite the efforts of many collectors, never left its place of honor above Fanny's fireplace.

Fanny was to paint Gertrude Lawrence just once again. On the night before the funeral, Fanny tossed sleeplessly in bed, episodes from their long association crowding through her mind. Particularly recurrent was the memory of Gertrude on holiday this past July, running through the open fields of the Cape in search of flowers for her breakfast table. Fanny had been reminded of a passage from her early classical studies, two lines from Virgil's *Bucolics*:

> For behold, the Nymphs bring to you
> Lilies, in their full baskets . . .

She had mentioned the verse to Gertrude, who had glowed with excitement: "What a lovely idea for a painting, Fan! One day you must do me like that!"

Fanny slipped out of bed. In the darkened apartment she groped her way to her studio. From three until nearly eight she worked with furious concentration, re-creating lush meadowlands under a bright morning sun. In the foreground, gathering lilies and cornflowers, stood Gertrude, hair swept back, wearing the simplest of pink frocks but exuding the radiance that had captivated millions.

"Lilia feront Nymphae" was begun and finished in that one session: a prime example, according to Fanny, of a visitation from her *dybbuk*. The painting afforded her some release from the trauma of Gertrude's death, but hardly a dismissal of it; Gertrude would always remain a significant force in her life.

Belatedly, Gertrude's doctors revealed the cause of her death as cancer: another irony, since much of her offstage energy had been expended in widespread volunteer work for anticancer organizations. Fanny and David promptly established the Gertrude Lawrence Foundation for research into the disease.

But Fanny felt that Gertrude deserved another, more personal kind of memorial, and in 1953 she hit upon it: a book of reminiscence by Gertrude's producer-husband, recounting the roller-coaster adventure of their life together. *Gertrude Lawrence As Mrs. A* was Fanny's concept, and in large part a product of her tireless persistence. It was she who urged Dick Aldrich to write the book, who prodded his memory about long-forgotten incidents and ferreted out Gertrude's scattered letters.

Fanny wrestled against Aldrich's New England reticence to bring out the charming interplay between his impetuous cockney bride and her Puritan mother-in-law. The result was a sparkling, warmly human narrative that gathered critical bouquets and book awards all over the country; it held top place on the best-seller lists for more than a year and repeated its success in a dozen foreign translations, including the Chinese.

The book also served a private purpose for Fanny. Throwing herself into it wholeheartedly, she created an outlet for the feelings of her mature years, a personal testimonial to the durability of love: not as Hollywood-tailored perfection, all moonbeams and roses, but as an adult sharing of imperfections, a mutual shield of understanding thrown up against loneliness. In urging upon Aldrich this emphasis, Fanny was demonstrating once again her capacity for faith in life and mankind, her refusal despite disappointments to reach for the anodynes of bitterness or cynicism. She was big enough to cheer for the carrousel even while conceding that she herself had missed the brass ring.

The success of *Mrs. A*, which originally appeared in a *Ladies' Home Journal* serialization in the summer of 1954, brought Fanny into the orbit of the Churchill family — not for the first time, but now at truly intimate range.

Among those yearning to play Gertrude in the inevitable dramatiza-

DEE KNAPP

A visit in 1954 to the New York offices of the Ladies' Home Journal,
which was serializing Gertrude Lawrence As Mrs. A

tion was Sarah Churchill, the actress-daughter of the prime minister. Red-haired and shapely, Sarah had already achieved mild celebrity as a film and television performer.

Adoration of Gertrude Lawrence was a Churchill shibboleth, laid down by the head of the clan. Sarah grew up identifying with the star in small personal ways; her favorite song was the Gershwin brothers' "Someone to Watch Over Me," long a Lawrence trademark.

Independent but shy, Sarah had some early tremors over Fanny's reputation as a forceful personality. Actual acquaintance quickly brought respect on her part and fondness on Fanny's: "She was really a beautiful character, absolutely without malice, responsive to beauty in any form. And her mind! She had wit, the turn of a phrase, just like her father; in fact, he always insisted it was a direct inheritance. Generally, women bore me; but I could listen to Sarah any time."

Fanny thought Sarah had the spirit and attractiveness to play Gertrude: "Sarah was blessed with the Churchill coloring, than which there is nothing lovelier. Nobody ever talks of the *beauty* of the Churchills."

Sarah had had a brief taste of the Lawrence role in a special tribute to the British star presented by Ed Sullivan; now Fanny sought to expand the identification through a full-scale television drama.

She went first to her friends at Hallmark, on whose network dramas Sarah had starred. When parleys there fell through, the project was taken to NBC, whose executives were interested — if certain conditions could be met. The most important one — that the cast should be buttressed with box-office names to ensure a national audience — aroused Sarah's indignation, and the talks ended.

Meanwhile, Fanny had embarked on a separate and more ambitious scheme. If American housewives gobbled up the story of Gertrude Lawrence, would they not thrill equally to the autobiography of Sarah Churchill?

Fanny brought her charge together with Bruce and Beatrice Gould, editors of the *Ladies' Home Journal*, who perceived the possibility at once. Sarah had great personal charm, Gould observed in a letter to Fanny, and considerable skill as a raconteur.

What he was talking about, Fanny explained to Sarah and her husband, Antony Beauchamp, might well translate commercially into $200,000 for the English-language serial rights alone. Lila Wallace of the *Reader's Digest* would pay separately and handsomely for abridgment rights. Even before book publication, Sarah would be assured of millions of readers, with consequent enhancement of her professional prestige and betterment of Anglo-American understanding.

However, as Fanny wrote to the couple, "Before Bruce Gould's suggestion can be considered, I know Sarah will first want to consult her parents and be guided by their wishes."

Late in October, Sarah and Antony Beauchamp left America for a visit home. A few weeks later Fanny joined them in London, just before the gathering of the Churchill clan at Chartwell in Kent to celebrate Sir Winston's eightieth birthday. Fanny, as Sarah's counselor and friend, was invited to come along. It would be her sixth meeting with Churchill, and the one she cherished most.

Their acquaintance dated back to 1935, when Fanny crossed the Atlantic on the *Normandie* with her brother David. David was an ardent Anglophile and a formidable legal scholar. His most cherished desire, he announced on docking, was to see the English Parliament at work. He was particularly fascinated by a rebellious Tory named Winston Churchill, who was out of power and out of favor, but not at all, in David's view, out of step with European reality, although with his anti-Nazi banners he marched virtually alone.

Fanny telephoned her leading friend in the government, Lord Cromer. The lord chamberlain hesitated. Yes, of course he knew Churchill; but he did not seem keen on setting up an appointment. His people felt that the man was on a "sticky wicket" with all this fuss about keeping the Germans out of the Rhineland. It was difficult enough to preserve the peace without alarmists stirring up trouble . . .

Fanny turned to Lord Hanworth, master of the rolls — in American terms, presiding justice of the Court of Appeal. Years earlier, as E. M. Pollock, he had entertained her at his home. Could he bring her brother to Winston Churchill?

Hanworth suggested luncheon with his fellow justices first. Two hours later, decked out in striped trousers and a gray topper from Moss Brothers in Soho, David strolled into the restaurant with a corps of justices similarly attired. Fanny, on his arm, was enormously proud.

She became prouder still as the conversation turned to fine points of discrepancy between English and American law: "David, unlike me, was a profound student of legal theory. He had a genius for absorbing information; he could digest a page at a glance."

The justices had met few Americans with a comparable knowledge of their landmark cases. Before the meal was over, David had an invitation to honorary membership in the English bar — and another to come to tea the following week with Winston Churchill. Earlier in the day, there would be seats reserved for him and Fanny in the House of Commons gallery from which they could hear Churchill address his fellow parliamentarians.

The reservations proved hardly necessary. The gallery was less than half full when they arrived; and most of the remaining spectators, like the MP's below, drifted off when Churchill rose to speak.

The great orator was not in the least impeded. Phrase after phrase roared from his throat with passionate vehemence. Hitler had to be stopped in his tracks, he warned, or the ensuing conflagration would engulf mankind. David was tremendously stirred.

Afterward Churchill, sharing tea with the American visitors in the House dining room, gave voice privately to his frustration. The government was charging merrily down the road to ruin, he declared, without a glance at the all-steel Juggernaut into which Hitler was converting the Third Reich.

David heartily agreed; the historical portents were clear. As they fell into animated discussion, Fanny sat back, listening. Political analysis was not her forte, and David was holding his own very nicely. What stood out in her mind later was that Hitler's anti-Semitism came into the conversation only secondarily, in the context of Nazi propaganda techniques; Churchill addressed her younger brother not as a Jew but as an informed American barrister.

Four years passed before Fanny saw Churchill again. In September of 1939, after her whirlwind efforts to extricate relatives and other imperiled Jews from the Continent, she crossed the channel back to England. The war predicted by Churchill had broken out on the first of the month with the German invasion of Poland; London, stripped of its women and children, was a deserted city.

Although Neville Chamberlain still occupied No. 10 Downing Street, other Conservatives were beginning to have second thoughts about his leadership. Lord Cromer conceded to Fanny: "We were foolish to take Winston so lightly. Your brother David was quite right about him."

Through Fanny's friend the duchess of Atholl, like Churchill a Tory dissenter from Chamberlain policies, another teatime meeting with him was arranged just before Fanny sailed for home. She found Churchill more restless and impatient than ever. When she mentioned the shoulder-shrugging she had recently encountered in Washington, he reacted strongly: "We're *all* being so stupid. My government keeps clinging to the illusion that this is some sort of 'phony war,' that Hitler is bluffing, and our Overseas Trade people are going to bring him into line with some clever deal. Lunacy!"

Churchill took pains to separate his views from those of the so-called "Red Duchess"; he made plain his loathing for Communism. Fanny had the impression that his feelings against Fascism as an ideology were not quite so intense; Spain's Franco seemed to evoke relatively mild distaste. It was the Hitler regime that bothered him: "We've given license to a madman, the worst in history, and he's ready to blow us all up — to wipe out civilization!"

Although by the following spring Churchill would come into office, he did not appear to be pleading or preparing for an assumption of power. His chief concern was that Fanny should take back to America the urgency of tooling up quickly and massively for war production: given the tools, Britain would do the job.

Fanny promised she would get his message across, noting her special involvement in the matter as a Jewess. This touched off a panegyric from Churchill about Jewish culture. "Where do I stay when I visit New York? With my friend Bernie Baruch!"

As a young man, Churchill said, he had been with the Liberal Party.

Jews, with their devotion to progress, were "always on that side." Whenever he had a Saturday speech scheduled at Manchester, he went up the night before to stay at the home of Neville Laski, the leader of the Jewish community there and the father of Harold Laski, the Labour Party theoretician. "I never ate so well anywhere, or enjoyed such stimulating talk. The Laskis' home was like my own."

Their Sabbath, however, was an agony for him. Neville Laski kept a rigorously Orthodox house, and although Churchill reveled in the prayers, the people, and the lively conversation, he could hardly stand the twenty-four-hour ban on smoking. Of course, he agreed, he could have slipped out into the garden with his cigar. "But I was their guest. I wouldn't desecrate their Sabbath."

Soon after the bombing of Pearl Harbor in December, 1941, Churchill came to America to confer with President Roosevelt. When a reception was held for him at Blair House, Fanny was among those invited. Mingling at the buffet with a group of British Embassy officials, she noticed a tall, striking, and visibly pregnant young woman in apparently heated colloquy with the guest of honor. Fanny turned in curiosity to John Foster, counselor at the embassy.

The girl was Jessica Mitford, Foster explained, sister of the dazzling "Aryan" beauty Diana Mitford who with Hitler's blessing had married the British Fascist leader, Sir Oswald Mosley. But Jessica, familiarly known as "Decca," had nothing in common with Diana except their uncommon physical splendor. She had run off in her late teens with Esmond Romilly, like her a young aristocrat with liberal leanings. Romilly had flown against the Nazi Stukas in Spain, then joined the Royal Canadian Air Force and had recently been killed in combat, leaving Decca a young widow with a child on the way.

Decca was related by marriage to the Churchill clan. Her late husband had been the son of Nellie Romilly, Clementine Churchill's sister. It was John Foster's guess that her vehement conversation with "Uncle" Winston revolved around an offer of financial aid: "She refuses to take a penny from the family. Says it would compromise her political principles."

Fanny made a mental note of stunning beauty combined with admirable integrity.

Three years later, amid the hurly-burly of the initial UN meetings at San Francisco, Fanny saw her again. Decca was a receptionist working for the Nation Associates, a group organized to ensure the ostracizing of Franco Spain by the new world body. Lilly Schultz, the New York editor, introduced the two women but warned Fanny not to say anything about knowing Decca's London relatives: "She lives here now with her second husband, a left-wing Jewish lawyer, and her little girl by Romilly. She's terribly independent."

Fanny caught a glimpse of Romilly's daughter, round-faced and golden-haired, when she and Lilly dropped Decca off at the child's nursery on their way to lunch. That glimpse prompted her first invitation to Chartwell.

"When I arrived in London for the UN charter sessions, word got around that I had seen Decca in San Francisco. One of the Churchill girls called to say that 'Aunt Nellie' was most anxious to have word about her grandchild; the baby was Esmond Romilly's only legacy. Would I come out to Chartwell for the weekend?"

Fanny took a train to Westerham on the Kent-Surrey border, where Churchill had bought a chunky peak-roofed mansion in 1922, set on high ground amid lush meadows and tall trees. Lady Churchill and her sister were waiting at the door. "I became a Very Important Person — not for my achievements at the bar, but because I brought personal news. Everybody, including Nellie's brother-in-law Winston, peppered me with questions — not about the war, not about the White House, but about Decca and her little Constancia. 'Did you really see the baby? What does she look like? Does she go to school yet? Where? Does Decca seem happy? What is her husband like?' They were starved for any scrap of news. I was hard put to stretch my few minutes of observation into a comprehensive report."

By the time of her next trip to the Churchills' country home, in 1949, Fanny had a new point of contact with the great man: painting. She had just been discovered by Nettie King and Hallmark; he, as an elder statesman presumably departed from major office, now had plenty of time for the canvases that had occupied him intermittently for twenty-odd years.

The ostensible purpose of Fanny's visit was to get for Gertrude Lawrence, long an ardent Churchill worshipper, an autographed copy of his slim volume *Painting as a Pastime*.

Fanny found her host in his garden apartment-studio a few steps down from the main entrance. The spacious, many-windowed atelier was "as orderly and antiseptic as a hospital operating room." It was the only painting area she had ever seen that was naked of dripping oil tubes, pigment-smeared easels or sprawling canvases. "He didn't even clean his own brushes; family and friends were on hand with a continuous supply of fresh ones."

Churchill was willing enough to inscribe a book for Gertrude, although he grumbled about her not coming around to collect it for herself.

The studio visit was disenchanting. "Painting a picture is like fighting a battle," Churchill had written in his book; and his canvases, especially the stiff, labored still lifes, looked it. Fanny was reminded of Noel Coward's work. The Mediterranean landscapes, with their cool, vivid blues and yellows, were better. But it was obvious that Churchill painted by the rules: John Ruskin plus a touch of Cézanne. "He had to have his subject directly before him. I wouldn't have dared to mention, as I did with Eisenhower, such unorthodox techniques as smudging with toilet paper." Nonetheless, she did mention to Churchill the Hallmark interest in "famous people who paint," and her own involvement with the greeting-card company.

Churchill had never heard of Hallmark, much less of its special Christmas line; but he wanted to know more. Did they pay well for their reproductions? And give the pictures wide circulation?

"All over the country," Fanny assured him. "Your name," she went on with a straight face, "could become a household word throughout America."

The old man chuckled. Yes, he would be pleased if she would put in a word about his work with J. C. Hall. Hall, notified by Fanny on her return to America, was equally pleased. He promptly sent over an aide to sign up Fanny's "discovery."

By 1954, many things had changed. Gertrude Lawrence had taken her place in the theatrical pantheon; Winston Churchill had his old job back at No. 10 Downing Street; his daughter Sarah was creating a name for herself as an actress in America.

The prospect of Sarah's appearing in the role of Gertrude was a dazzling one for the Churchills. The entire family, like most of the English aristocracy, was theater-struck; according to Fanny, in reaction to the circumscribed quality of upper-class English life. Not least afflicted with footlight fever was Sir Winston himself: Fanny remembered a story recounted to her years earlier by Boris Morros, the Hollywood producer, of Churchill's eagerness to serve as scenarist and technical adviser for a film on Napoleon.

Because of the family's long involvement in professional writing, the Churchills were keen also on promoting a literary career for Sarah; they had all read *Mrs. A* and were aware of Fanny's part in shaping it. She was therefore made welcome at what was otherwise a very private family celebration. Gathered at Chartwell to honor him and his wife Clementine on the weekend after his eightieth birthday were his son Randolph, the three Churchill daughters, and an assortment of in-laws, cousins and small fry.

First order of business between Fanny and the prime minister was some amiable jousting about their mutual "patron," Hallmark. Sir Winston let it be known that he had contracted with the greeting-card company for not only one or two pictures but "a whole line" of reproductions. Fanny riposted by showing him the original full-page ad from *Life* magazine, in which her name followed that of El Greco.

Churchill quickly scanned the list of gallery artists: Cézanne, Chastain, Dali . . . Where was Churchill, he demanded?

"Oh, that was from their pre-Churchill period," Fanny explained.

Mollified, Churchill turned to the subject of royalties. With evident pride, he fished some papers from his library desk: "But he didn't have to; he knew the figures by heart. It was obvious that he got a bigger kick out of being recognized as an artist than he did out of running the British Empire."

And how much, inquired Churchill blandly, had Fanny received from Hallmark this year?

Fanny pleaded no contest. "They charge too much for my snow scenes. At twenty-five cents apiece, my own family won't buy my cards. So why should the general public — especially when they can get a whole boxed set by Winston Churchill for a dollar?"

Sir Winston reacted warily to this mixed compliment; Fanny suspected that he "never forgave Hallmark" for not putting a top price on his work.

For the next two days, the senior Churchills and their flock chatted casually and intimately with Fanny around the fireplace or on strolls through the shaded grounds. They were remarkably free with their confidences: "they knew I was no gossip-mongering journalist, and they were anxious to help Sarah in any way they could."

From Lady Churchill in particular, Fanny gleaned some illuminating facts regarding the prime minister's early life: "Apparently writing was never for him just a gentlemanly avocation. He had a family to support, a big house to maintain at Hyde Park Gate, a country estate to be kept up. There was a constant scramble for money." Just as Churchill had followed his parents in writing and lecturing, so his journalist son Randolph was perpetuating the family tradition.

Lady Churchill herself was portrayed by other family members as a loving but strong-willed wife who never changed her Liberal Party affiliation; her husband emerged from their descriptions as a fanatically devoted family man, "positively un-English" in his tender treatment of his children: "They told me of an episode at the end of World War I that all but brought his life to a standstill. He had taken his brother Jack's children to the country along with his own to escape the bombing. They got their milk from a small herd of private cows; and when one of the animals came down with typhoid Churchill's youngest daughter, Marigold, was infected. She died before her third birthday."

It was only by a great effort of will that Churchill returned to public life. "Long afterward, when Clemmy had a late pregnancy, they prayed for a baby girl — and got one. Mary, now Lady Soames, turned out to be the only non-redhead in the family, and the comfort of their old age."

Of Churchill's deep affection for his grandchildren, Fanny had direct evidence. They clambered over him without restraint. Seated with Fanny in the library, Sir Winston gestured toward the russet-haired youngsters gamboling on the floor: "Look at them, like playful cocker spaniels. That's one legacy I have given them: their gay plumage."

From a business perspective, the visit was less rewarding. Fanny never was able to set up Gertrude Lawrence's life story as a vehicle for Sarah. The first film adaptation of the material, turned out by a well-known writing team at Paramount, leaned far too heavily on broad comedy to win Fanny's approval for production. Later, when the property was acquired and developed by Robert Wise of *The Sound of Music* fame, Fanny urged Sarah upon him for the lead. But Wise opted for Julie Andrews, then moviedom's top-ranking box-office attraction.

Fanny's counterproject of a book by Sarah fared no better. The actress had misgivings about shifting careers in midstream, and there were apparently questions raised within the family about the timing.

In Winston Churchill, Fanny had known the most celebrated Englishman of her era; but not, in her view, the most fascinating one. That accolade would have to be reserved for the bearded Anglo-Irishman who by his own admission was the world's greatest literary genius since Shakespeare.

Chapter 15

*G*EORGE BERNARD SHAW and Fanny were separated in years by nearly half a century; in politics, religion and philosophy by a good deal more. But their differences rarely had a serious chance against their common verve and humor.

There were also beguiling extras on both sides. Shaw had been an early and ardent feminist; he might scoff at popes and potentates, but hardly at a five-foot woman who in the *Rasputin* case had stood British jurisprudence on its stately ear. He in turn held a unique appeal for Fanny: he was an instant replay, complete with snowy beard and piercing blue-gray eyes, of her Zaida.

From the early 1930's, playwright and lawyer enjoyed a lively friendship. Shaw had something to say about everything — usually, according to Fanny, "something provocative and unsettling. He deliberately needled me, just to get me mad." The clash that ensued was relished by both, like a well-matched pair of seventeenth-century duelists, for its own sake.

Shaw also permitted Fanny to interpret for him the nuances of international copyright law. Although repeatedly dangling hints of an imminent retainer, the budget-conscious sage succeeded in getting a good deal of advice without ever paying for it.

Shaw came into Fanny's life, as had the Grand Duchess Xenia, through Frank Scully. Scully had been secretary and friend on the Riviera to Frank Harris, the Galway-born author-editor. When Harris died in 1931, he was in the process of writing a biography of Shaw, which Scully then completed.

Harris had left behind in Nice not only an incomplete manuscript but an insolvent widow. Nellie Harris was red-haired and blue-eyed, with a glazed-china complexion assiduously shielded from the Mediterranean sun. Unschooled in anything but looking decorative, she fluttered on the fringes of the Scully crowd.

When the Scullys departed for the United States soon after welcoming Fanny to the Riviera in the summer of 1933, Nellie Harris begged Fanny to leave the Grand Hotel and stay as a paying guest in her apartment. "I'm so lonesome, with Frank and Alice away. And it will help pay my rent." She painted a grim picture of her late husband's extravagance.

Fanny was touched ("She had nothing left but her beauty, and even that was giving her a hard fight"), so she moved in and during her brief stay picked up the food bills, too. As she was packing her bags for the return trip to England, Nellie requested one more favor: "Could you please speak to George Bernard Shaw for me in London?" Shaw, she explained, had always been fond of the Harrises. Harris had stood by him stubbornly when Shaw, in his early days as a theater critic, had had the audacity to find flaws in Shakespeare.

However, the Shaw biography had created a severe rift. According to Nellie, her husband had been too befogged by age and dissipation to finish the job. After Scully took over the manuscript and completed it, Shaw accused him of doctoring it with *Variety*-style wisecracks, then thwarting the efforts of the subject to restore a properly dignified tone.

Shaw had ended up furious at the whole Riviera menage. Nellie, caught up in the backwash of his resentment, had recently been cut off from his occasional remittances to her. "He's still angry at us all, Fanny. But perhaps if you could let him know how things are with me?"

Fanny agreed to try. She was curious, if largely uninformed, about Shaw. Her father, she remembered, had once come home from a Shaw play rumbling with indignation: the man was an anarchist — anti–God, anti–free enterprise!

She composed a brief, straightforward note reporting on her visit with Nellie. His friend's widow, she told Shaw, seemed awfully hard up and anxious for the playwright to get a first-hand description of her circumstances. She added that if Shaw was too busy to receive her over the few remaining days of her stay in London, she would understand. In any case, she had discharged her obligation. She was sure that any aid dispatched to Nellie would be much appreciated. She sent the note by hand to Shaw's flat in nearby Whitehall.

A few hours later her telephone rang. It was Shaw's secretary, Blanche Patch, violating custom to use the loathed instrument and compounding the departure by suggesting a visit without an appointment: "Why don't you just pop over?"

Miss Patch was a tall, spare woman in her middle fifties, with lank brown hair plastered down in a discreet marcel. Fanny felt immediately at home. "She was like all the lonely Victorian schoolteachers who used to come to our parlor in Brooklyn to discuss Fanny, the problem child. Behind that stiff exterior I sensed a starvation for human contact."

Fanny thanked Miss Patch for arranging the meeting: "I've heard about your efficiency in protecting Mr. Shaw from distraction."

The secretary's bleak features thawed a little. "He rarely sees people these days, but he liked your letter — the simplicity and directness of what you had to say."

Later Fanny learned there had been more to it than that. Blanche, an avid reader of the popular London press, had briefed Shaw on Fanny's exploits, which were previously unknown to him. As an avowed Socialist committed to total equality between the sexes, a playwright exploring the boundaries of Ibsen's "new woman," and an admirer of "advanced" American womanhood, he "had to find out," as Blanche put it, "what a female lawyer was like."

The secretary led Fanny down a passageway. "He's in a good mood. I'll walk you in."

Shaw was seated before a typewriter, hammering away with a briskness that belied his seventy-seven years. As Fanny came into the study, a spacious tidy room with a few watercolors on the walls, he rose to greet her, uncoiling a slender six-foot frame attired in gray tweeds.

Even more than with Blanche Patch, Fanny felt a sensation of instant recognition. The long face with its neatly trimmed white beard, the calm, erect bearing, and above all the keen humorous gaze, at once whimsical and penetrating . . .

Shaw caught her fascinated stare. "So you are pleased to meet the legendary sage?" His speech, light and melodious, was flavored with a distinct Irish brogue.

"More than you can imagine."

Shaw nodded approvingly. "You are thrilled to be in the presence."

"My eyes haven't had such a treat in years."

The playwright arched his neck. "Am I really so handsome? Or is it your deep admiration for my plays?"

"Neither. It's because you remind me of my grandfather."

Shaw was taken aback. "Ohhh?" He let out the interjection slowly, histrionically, in a kind of rising growl. "Your *grandfather*? In what way?"

"Your blue eyes . . . pink cheeks . . . white beard."

"Features common to Father Christmas — and every other old man of similar coloring!"

"Ah, but you look like a *witty* Father Christmas, and my grandfather was one of the most amusing people I've ever known. Also one of the most exasperating. I feel as if I want to kiss you — or kill you."

Shaw blinked. "What sort of wit did he have?"

"Very adaptable. He had a remark for every situation — usually so impudent, so outrageous, that his listeners were left speechless."

"Perhaps," suggested Shaw, "he studied my plays."

"He couldn't have. He never went to the English-language theater except when we got tickets for nothing. I doubt if he ever heard of you.

He was a holy man from Eastern Europe whose life was dedicated to the worship of God rather than secular matters."

Another drawn-out "Oh" of displeasure.

The dialogue, Fanny realized, was not going at all along prescribed lines. But she felt no inclination to retreat.

"What form did his wit take?" persisted Shaw.

"Well . . ." Fanny groped for an example. "There was this coffeehouse discussion in Brooklyn. A young law student — one of those bright, earnest types — was denouncing the American political system in favor of Socialism —"

"Very sensible," murmured Shaw.

"First, Zaida skewered him with logic. 'It was to escape the dogmas of Europe that your family came here,' he said. 'Now you attack the one government that lets you live in freedom. How, after all, did your parents come here? Not, I suspect with Christopher Columbus — but with a lot of other refugees in steerage.'

"The young man conceded the point. But he returned the challenge. 'And you, Rabbi Bornfeld — how did you get to America?'"

"Zaida looked around the table with that dangerous twinkle in his eye. 'Me?' he repeated innocently. 'Why, I just rolled up my trousers and waded across!'"

Shaw chuckled loudly. But enough of Zaida, he indicated. The author of *An Intelligent Woman's Guide to Socialism and Capitalism* wanted to know how Fanny felt about practicing law in a man's world. "Do you encounter difficulties?"

"No. I make it my business not to look conspicuous — my office in the Bar Building looks like any other legal office, not like a feminine boudoir. My staff are all men. I find that if I assume equality, clients and other lawyers accept me that way."

"Nobody tries to thrust you into an inferior position?"

"On the contrary — I've run into a surprising amount of chivalry. For instance, opposing lawyers never ask me to come to their offices; they come to mine."

"And how do you behave then? Are you ever tempted to flirt?"

"If I am, I put the temptation aside. In my office, I practice law."

Shaw reflected on that for a moment. "And what about other women? Do they come flocking to you as clients?"

"Not particularly. Mostly when men bring them."

Shaw seemed to be ticking off a checklist in his mind. "Do you wear a wig?"

"Why should I? My hair is healthy." Fanny explained that the practice among English barristers of donning a white wig for court appearances was not followed in America.

Shaw nodded. He seemed almost ready to hear about Nellie Harris. Then he remembered something. "Do you know Lawrence Langner?"

"Yes, and his wife Terry, too. The Theatre Guild has given a new dignity to Broadway. In fact, that's the main reason I wanted to meet you. My learned brother-in-law, Dr. Berkman, never misses a Guild production of Shaw. He says you are the greatest writer of the century."

"Indeed?" The thick white brows rose mockingly.

"He won't believe I've been here unless I bring back an autographed photo. Will you give me one?"

"We'll see, we'll see. First, tell me about Nellie."

Fanny did; and Shaw put a check in the mail to Harris's widow that same day.

Thereafter, Fanny saw Shaw at least once on every trip to England. Blanche Patch was happy to smooth the way. The spinster secretary was incorrigibly stagestruck, mesmerized by the theater and its people. Fanny obliged with luncheon-cum-matinée afternoons, climaxed by impetuous dashes backstage, where Ivor Novello, Gertrude Lawrence, Jack Buchanan and other reigning figures of the West End would peel off costumes and make-up before Blanche's disbelieving eyes.

Afterward, she would regale Shaw with accounts of these visits. He listened because he did not consider her imaginative enough to invent a lie. That, Shaw explained to Fanny, was in fact why Blanche had been kept on his payroll since 1920. Her workhorse predictability, the narrowness of her horizons, were for Shaw her greatest assets: "She's like a machine, Fanny — precisely what I recommend to you if you do creative work. She doesn't talk or get in the way or make suggestions; simply records what I want put down. She has no idea of the significance of what I'm doing.

"That means that when people try to pump her about me, all she can tell them is what I eat and when I send out the laundry. She gives them nothing because she has observed nothing."

It was a congenial arrangement. Shaw felt secure in his privacy; Blanche enjoyed the small attentions that came her way as the faithful Keeper of the Gates.

During the prewar years Fanny was invited often for tea, occasionally for lunch, always at Shaw's Whitehall flat. Shaw was married — but not perceptibly. Although Fanny caught a glimpse of Charlotte through a doorway now and then, there were no introductions. The lady of the house was in failing health and, Fanny felt, had reason to be less than overjoyed with Shaw's openly flirtatious ways. Notorious as a long-range cavalier who blossomed best when safely separated by geography, matrimonial status or age, he kept up a running chatter of gay-dog references to his guest's hat, her smile and her "intoxicating" brown eyes.

Conversational embellishment was necessary to a meal with Shaw. Unlike Fanny, the sage took no epicurean pleasure in eating. He regarded it as an irksome but unavoidable interruption of higher pursuits. His own vegetarian views were well known, but he did not, he insisted, force them on others.

With a shudder and a grimace, he would wave toward the lamb chop set down on Fanny's plate: "I prefer not to gorge myself on animal flesh; but I wouldn't deprive my cannibalistic guests of their private delights."

After such an "invitation," Fanny usually opted for her host's own menu of salad and fruits.

If Shaw was grudging about consuming food, he had no such qualms about discussing it. He talked to Fanny at great length about his theory of a foodless universe. He was convinced that one day people would get along on sunshine and oxygen, thus simplifying their lives and improving their efficiency.

He also discoursed on Socialism and the Soviet Union. Fanny had lately become embroiled in the *Rasputin* case, and he wanted to know her off-the-record impression of the Romanoffs.

Fanny told him what she had drawn out of the Grand Duchess Xenia and the others: the portrait of Czar Nicholas as a befuddled innocent, a "captive little boy" surrounded by intrigues beyond his comprehension. She mentioned Xenia's apparent shock upon learning of her country's savage anti-Semitic pogroms.

Shaw sniffed his disbelief. The Romanoffs were a pack of worthless decadents, he declared. The new Russia, where during the week of his seventy-fifth birthday he had been lionized and then ceremoniously received by Stalin, was busy cleansing itself of its terrible past. It was through Socialism that the world would be led to salvation.

The war years brought Fanny across Shaw's path in a more professional context. She had always delighted in setting up imaginative combinations of clients, friends and relatives: calling the attention of Hallmark to Clifton Webb and Winston Churchill, entrusting Hollywood-bound Sheilah Graham to the capable hands of Frank Scully, persuading Dolin and Markova that Alfred Katz — despite his lack of ballet background — would make a brilliant manager (he did). Now she envisioned a new match: Gertrude Lawrence, an actress constantly on the lookout for suitable vehicles, and Bernard Shaw, a playwright with a shelf full of properties.

As *Lady in the Dark* neared the end of its two-year run, Fanny recalled Shaw's *Pygmalion*, based on the legend of the Greek sculptor whose statue comes to life. The plotting was strong, Fanny felt, and the cockney flower girl turned glamour queen *was* Gertrude. Fanny had first read the play in 1939, just before returning to America; at lunch with Blanche Patch, she had enthused over its possibilities for her client.

"The old man won't let you do it," said Blanche. "He thinks it's dated and would hurt his reputation."

Gertrude too was dubious about *Pygmalion*. In wartime people didn't want highbrow drama. "They come to the theater for music, dancing — to forget their sorrows."

Then Fanny learned of a movie version, produced and directed by

Gabriel Pascal and released by MGM in 1938, when she was abroad on her refugee-rescue missions. Acting on a hunch, she persuaded Gertrude to join her at a special screening.

As they watched the unfolding of Shaw's witty fable, Fanny turned the hunch loose on her client: "Imagine this with music, Gee!"

The ingredients were all there, Gertrude had to admit, for a charming song-and-dance show.

"What's more, Gee, it isn't too highbrow at all! If an audience will listen to a *Lady in the Dark* singing about psychoanalysis, surely they won't mind her dancing with a grammarian. This can be the biggest musical of all time!"

Thirteen years of persistent effort were to pass before Fanny's judgment was confirmed with the opening of *My Fair Lady*.

In 1943, intuition told her that Shaw would not embrace the proposition. Reared as a student of grand opera, himself a pianist and trained singer, he held light music in light esteem. It might be years before he could be softened up to the idea of having his name associated with a musical comedy. Meanwhile, the first step would be to identify Gertrude with Eliza Doolittle in Shaw's mind, by having her do *Pygmalion* in America as a straight play.

She wrote to Shaw that Gertrude, "no longer the musical comedy actress of the old days" but an accomplished dramatic star, was finishing a successful run on Broadway: "Nothing would please me better than to advise her to appear in one of your plays," preferably as Eliza.

Back came Shaw's answer, scrawled with asperity at the bottom of Fanny's signature: "I know all about Miss Lawrence in her professional aspect. *Pygmalion* is worn to rags and filmed. But in any case I will not encourage any more revivals during the war, as the taxation is ruinous."

Fanny was not at all put off. A few months later she cabled asking permission for Gertrude to do a single half-hour broadcast of excerpts from Eliza's speeches.

"All right,' Shaw wired back. "Go ahead."

That tiny wedge was all Fanny needed. Shaw didn't know it, but an American production of *Pygmalion* was now inevitable. Fanny kept after him with gentle tenacity: through Blanche Patch, his British producers, mutual friends. Finally, in the fall of 1945, when the UN was making increasing demands on her time, she decided to press for a decision. She called Shaw by transatlantic telephone:

"Please, Mr. Shaw, you've got to help me. I'm booked on the *Queen Mary* to meet Dr. Koo in London — but I can't leave Gertrude here without a play.'"

"That is no concern of mine."

"But a better world *is* your concern. And how are we going to achieve it except by international cooperation?" Fanny softened her voice to a kittenish purr. "You're my only hope, Mr. Shaw. Be a darling. I shall love you always for it."

"I'll think about it."

The next morning his cabled authorization arrived. Three days later Fanny was aboard the *Queen Mary*.

Pygmalion was presented in New York by Theatre Incorporated, a nonprofit repertory company set up by Fanny with Richard Aldrich as managing director — thereby giving Gertrude's husband a graceful transition from naval uniform back to Broadway. From Times Square the play went on national tour, garnering crowded houses and critical cheers. On her return to America, Fanny shipped the reviews to Shaw.

He replied by postcard: "Why trouble to tell me old stories about Pygmalion the Potboiler? When has it ever failed in all these 33 years? What actress has ever failed in it? You seem to think it is a novelty. It is the stalest of subjects for me.

"All the same, your letters are welcome."

On the basis of this faint sanction, Fanny raised at last the question of a *Pygmalion* musical. Shaw reserved his answer until their next meeting after the war in England.

It was no, no and no. Stage musicals were anathema to him. He had spent years as a music critic and took his composers seriously. Besides, Gertrude could not even carry a proper operetta part; "she's a typical music-hall singer."

Shaw must have been astonished when nearly two years later, Fanny sent him an exultant cable. Her client Noel Coward was entranced with the idea of a musical *Pygmalion*; he was ready to undertake an adaptation and eager to provide the score.

Shaw answered by longhand, in thirty-nine crisp words:

"My dear Fanny
Stop cabling crazy nonsense.
What you need is a month's holiday.
Noel could not possibly interfere in my business.
My decision as to Pygmalion is final: let me hear no more about it."

To anyone else, this would have conveyed end-of-subject. To Fanny, it merely dictated a change of tactic.

Gabriel Pascal was a storybook Hungarian: dark, intense, an ex-gypsy, ex-army officer, ex-actor turned knockabout film producer. In the mid-1920's he encountered Shaw while swimming off the French Riviera, and delivered a stunning impromptu lecture on how the playwright's work should be transferred to the screen.

Ten years later he turned up at Shaw's flat in London with two and a half shillings in his hand, and asked for the film rights to *Pygmalion*. Shaw gave them to him.

This was no quixotic gesture. Two of Shaw's plays had been adapted to films in Hollywood during the 1930's, with what he considered disastrous results; he was determined that there would be no more "mangling" of his work by American commercialism. Pascal was blessedly European. Furthermore, careful inquiry convinced Shaw that the man was a film-maker of taste and competence, with a passion for perfection of detail surpassing that of the author himself.

The Shavian estimate was borne out by Pascal's film of *Pygmalion*, which won both Shaw's gratitude and an Academy Award.

Later film adaptations, however, were less successful. With *Major Barbara* and *Caesar and Cleopatra*, Pascal ran into problems of casting, financing and actors' unions, which were topped off by German bombs crashing around his sound stages. He was handicapped also by the vagaries of his sponsor. Shaw drafted his own contracts, scorning conventional clauses and insisting on 10 percent of the gross receipts for himself. He would never give Pascal a free hand in negotiating productions, but only an "option letter" certifying the Hungarian as Shaw's approved "artistic director."

By the latter part of the 1940's, studios in England and Hollywood were turning away from Pascal. But he still had the inside track — no matter how booby-trapped — to George Bernard Shaw. Obviously he was the man for Fanny to enlist.

Ben Goetz, the MGM chief in London, was glad to bring Fanny and Pascal together at Claridge's. Fanny then set up a meeting with the Hungarian and her friend Sir Charles Cochran, the British theatrical producer, and laid her plans on the table: a *Pygmalion* musical starring Gertrude Lawrence, to be presented at the Drury Lane in London and by Theatre Incorporated in New York, both productions in association with Gabriel Pascal.

Shaw's disciple was overjoyed. However, he was unable to raise money anywhere. To cap his miseries, he was stricken with cancer in 1949.

In the following year Shaw died, and Pascal was awarded the rights to *Pygmalion* and several other plays. By this time, however, Gertrude was tied up in *The King and I* — and no other star was interested.

In September of 1952, two weeks after Gertrude's death, Fanny encountered Alan Jay Lerner at a cocktail party. Lerner, bitter over the summertime closing of his *Paint Your Wagon*, told her he would never do another original musical. But if she knew of some presold subject, a book or a play —

Fanny told him the saga of *Pygmalion*.

On October 28, Lerner and Loewe signed to write the show for the Theatre Guild in association with Gabriel Pascal. More than three years later *My Fair Lady* opened its historic run at the Mark Hellinger.

Neither Pascal nor Fanny shared in the triumph. The director had died in the summer of 1954.

But the vicissitudes of launching a melodious Eliza Doolittle were only one facet of Fanny's continuous, exhilarating — and sometimes exasperating — relationship with George Bernard Shaw.

Early in World War II, Shaw had moved twenty-five miles out of blitz-battered London to his country retreat, a modest red-brick cottage in Ayot St. Lawrence, Hertfordshire. There he had become a widower in October 1943, when Charlotte died of a bone disease. And there Fanny visited him frequently, under relaxed, formality-free conditions, from 1945 until the end of his life.

On her first trip to the cottage Shaw ceremoniously displayed the modern "loo" he had had installed off the dim entrance hall. He pointed to the gleaming chain and painted seat. "You can boast to posterity," he declaimed, "that you sat on the same throne as the great Bernard Shaw."

Generally Fanny came on Saturday for lunch or tea; she dodged invitations to stay overnight because there was no central heating. Late afternoon was Shaw's preferred time for entertaining. He began his work-day at dawn, "when the body is fresh," pausing at midday for lunch and an hour's nap before returning to his study.

The real unwinding came with the break for afternoon tea. Braced by some herbal brew brought to his pink armchair beside the fireplace, Shaw would reach for his walking stick and go for a stroll with Fanny in the back garden, a checked cape thrown over his tweed ensemble of jacket and knickers. Usually the two stayed within the two-acre confines of the cottage grounds; on bright days they might walk past the red telephone booth opposite "Shaw's Corner" to a nearby church graveyard.

Their relationship moved to a more personal level when Fanny brought around Harvey, her war correspondent admirer, for Shaw's appraisal. Harvey stroked his moustache and spoke condescendingly for an hour about the Allied military leadership.

Shaw's reaction was decidedly negative. "My dear Fanny," he told her later, "that man wouldn't last a week with you. Women are all alike; they must all have their wartime romance."

He looked down at her, blue eyes glinting mischievously above the sharp nose. If she was really bent on matrimony, Shaw suggested, she could do much better without traveling half so far. Close at hand was a writer of real distinction, a wealthy widower entering his ninetieth year: himself!

The question came up of how Fanny was to address her elderly gallant. "Mr. Shaw" had such a commonplace ring. He was clearly not a "Bernie," like Bernard M. Baruch. "As for 'George'—"

"I don't like that. It was no choice of mine."

"What do your friends call you?"

"GBS."

So GBS he became to Fanny.

One rainy afternoon Shaw played and sang for Fanny at his old upright, his fingers still nimble and his voice firm. He owed his musical education, he told Fanny, to his mother's defiance of Victorian convention. Her devoted voice teacher, G. J. Lee, had lived openly in the Shaw home, the "other man" in what Shaw insisted was an innocent triangle; it was Lee who tutored him in harmony and opera. Shaw's actual father was a hopeless drunkard whose way of living the playwright emphatically despised and as emphatically rejected, thereby disproving, he asserted, the old saw about the sins of the fathers.

A few months later Fanny began painting, and brought a half-dozen slides to Ayot St. Lawrence. Shaw, who had been a London art critic, was startled. "Anybody who can paint like that," he declared, "I don't want for my lawyer." It was the first indication Fanny had that he was thinking of becoming a client.

Recovering his critical aplomb, Shaw offered some tips gleaned during his years as a museum and gallery buff. The secret of ensuring proper color values, he told Fanny, was to study a painting upside down. "That way you're not distracted by considerations of subject."

"But it's drawing, not color, that gives me trouble. I can't get proportions right."

"In that case you should work with clay. That forces you to observe spatial relationships."

Thus began Fanny's entanglement with Jacob Epstein. Her apprentice efforts in the sculptor's studio left Shaw flabbergasted: "This is even better than your painting!"

"Then you think I should go on with it?"

Shaw evidently assumed Fanny meant "go on" at the expense of her law career. He counseled against it. "Mind you, such a talent explodes upon the world very rarely. But you must be realistic in exercising it. Do not, I repeat, do *not* give up the practice of law. It will provide you with a steady income that will make it possible for you to work at your art."

Shaw did not care for tributes or ceremonials, in which category he put birthday celebrations. However, early in 1946, as he approached the ninety-year-mark, he told Fanny that just this once a party would be in order: "And I'm going to let you give it."

"Wonderful! I'll come back this summer."

"No — not in my house. In yours."

Shaw broadcast the news to his friends in America, and on July 26 a score of guests turned up at East Sixty-fourth Street. Among them were Gene Tunney, the retired heavyweight champion who had won Shaw's respect by challenging the authenticity of the author's prize-ring novel, *Cashel Byron's Profession*; Archibald Henderson, Shaw's authorized biographer; and a theatrical contingent that included Lawrence Langner, Gertrude Lawrence, Tallulah Bankhead and Moss Hart.

Fanny reported to Shaw that despite —"or perhaps because of"— the absence of the guest of honor, the party had been a great success. The celebrants read aloud excerpts from Shaw plays and vied with each other in saying nice things about their friend across the sea.

"They also"—she could not resist the Shavian dig—"told some truths."

Evidently in England as well the occasion did not go unnoticed. In a postcard to Fanny the following summer, Shaw pleaded:

"No more birthdays.

"My 90th would have killed any other man.

"Never mention them to me again if you love me."

As a leading spokesman for the gradualist Socialism of the Fabian Society, Shaw cultivated the public aura of a revolutionary. After a dozen meetings, Fanny wasn't so sure. She could not escape the suspicion that her host was "at heart a middle-class snob. He loved the lords and ladies Nancy Astor brought to him; he never got away from his white-collar childhood in Ireland."

Her skepticism was heightened when, back in the States, she saw the playwright's by-line sprawled across the front pages of the Hearst press. Although no expert in the tortuous ways of left-wing ideology, she did know that William Randolph Hearst, the Sunday afternoon philosopher of her Santa Monica days, was something less than a flaming Marxist. She called the paradox to Shaw's attention. Back came a bristling postcard:

"I do not write for the people intelligent and instructed enough to share my views, if any such exist in America or elsewhere, but to startle and wake up the readers of the H.P.

"W.R.H. is a personal friend, and a first rate paymaster."

Shaw the pundit pounced again when Fanny wrote late in 1946 mentioning her collaboration with Senator Robert H. Taft on behalf of an independent Jewish state.

Fanny's Republican friends, he asserted, bankrupt in domestic policy, were seeking to make capital of the crisis in the Middle East.

"No use trying that old game on me. Are you a Jewess? If so, by all means make the most of this foolishness; but do not bother me about it. If not, follow my lead; do your best to force a Fabian policy on both parties; and back up my nomination of Wallace as candidate for the succession to Roosevelt as president, whether as a democrat or as the leader of a new Labor Party.

"That is the only course that will really help the Zionists, who will have to be left, as the Irish were, to settle the question themselves by fire and sword if they cannot agree." The last four words were appended to the typed letter in longhand.

. Fanny could not, of course, let the reference to her race go unchallenged. On her next trip to England she took the sage to task: "What is this 'Are you a Jewess?' business?"

"It's a point I always try to establish, before parting with a license to one of my plays."

Fanny stared at him, dumbfounded. "Of all the childish, irrelevant issues to raise! For a man of your intelligence —"

"Intelligence has nothing to do with it. It's a matter of experience — of which I have had more than any other writer alive."

"Bigot! I can't believe it. You Irish are the worst in the world."

"And my experience has been," Shaw went on calmly, "that no Jewish manager has ever cheated me. Every time someone cheats me, I know he's a non-Jew." He smiled, enjoying her change of expression. "My dear Fanny, I admire Jews for their creativity as well as their honesty."

He was never to speak so well of his own forebears. Nor did he bother to mention that he had been appearing on Zionist lecture platforms since the beginning of the century.

In 1947 Fanny received a curious request. One of her favorite people, a self-made businessman close to the Holtzmann family, faced a problem beyond his judgmental resources: his son had been churning out reams of poetry, some of it published and praised. The father was uncertain whether the boy should be encouraged. "I don't want to be unfair," he told Fanny. "Maybe we're harboring a genius who should be allowed to go his own way or even be subsidized." She had many literary clients; would she ask one of them for an objective opinion?

The most famous critic Fanny knew was George Bernard Shaw. To Shaw went a batch of the neophyte's lyrics, along with an explanatory note. His answer came by return post:

"No sensible or prudent friend or relative can advise or encourage *anybody* to make a profession of poetry. If he (or she) cannot take that desperate step in spite of every discouragement and family opposition, the case is hopeless."

The verses she forwarded had, in his admittedly personal judgment, "a faint original lyric charm" but little distinction otherwise. "On the whole, if I were his father, I should advise him to write verses as a hobby, and to feed and clothe himself by peddling baked potatoes or something equally prosaic."

Separately, he wrote directly to the young poet:

"Please understand that the case put to me by Fanny was not whether your poems will live, a question which no mortal can decide, but whether you can live by them if you make their production your bread-winning profession.

"My answer is NO.

"I am giving you my best prosaic business advice, and my kindliest. I am not pontificating about your chances of being remembered when Homer is forgotten, nor indulging my quite imaginary reputation (invented by journalists who have no time to read what I write) for gratuitous offensiveness and hurting other people's feelings, nor preventing you from writing verses to your heart's content in your spare time all your life, if only as an unremunerative hobby. They may last as long as Lamartine's. He, too, was a specialist in melancholy . . ."

On the subject of fellow authors, Fanny could never tell which way Shaw would jump. Once she wrote to bewail the plight of a friend, a noted essayist, who despite a distressing illness was being hounded for the return of an advance by his publisher. The publisher was represented by Benjamin Stern, a veteran attorney whose firm had handled some of Shaw's affairs in America. Would the playwright intercede in the matter on compassionate grounds?

His answer all but blasted Fanny out of her chair. She was a lawyer, he reminded her, not a doctor, and as such could give no testimony as to the alleged "frailty and sensitiveness" of her client, "unless you can produce a doctor's certificate that a definite illness prevented him from fulfilling the contract on which he obtained an advance and spent it without doing what he was paid for." No moral sensitiveness could be claimed for a man guilty of this "grossly dishonest act."

Even if the author had "taken the precaution to make the money non-returnable," scolded Shaw, honesty would oblige him to give it back if he did not do the work. "You should tell your client that he has no case and ought to be in a gaol like any defaulting greengrocer. That will make him sit up and make him take his business obligations seriously if anything will."

Shaw went on to confirm that Benjamin Stern was his attorney in New York, "as you should be if he did not exist. All you can do is to say 'Mr. Stern: my client has not a leg to stand on. But you know what authors are, full of artistic scruples, and utterly conscienceless about money and women. Every publisher knows this just as well; and when they make advances . . . they know they have no real security except the author's desire to have his work published and get some more money by it.' "

Fanny should ask Stern not to press the case, Shaw recommended, and pledge in return that she would urge her client to fulfill his obligations.

Having delivered his stage directions and full dialogue, Shaw scampered offstage with a typical about-face: "Forgive my habit of advising my legal advisers."

Shaw's rectitude was not as unrelenting as it seemed. In 1947 an aesthetic young aide used his name to perpetrate an outright swindle, and Fanny offered to have the case prosecuted through barrister friends.

"No," said Shaw, "don't. He must have needed money very badly to do what he did. I don't want to hurt him."

"The Old Testament says, 'Thou shalt not steal.' "

"What comes first with you," retorted Shaw, "God or man?"

He was equally capable of reversing his harsh stand on the writing tribe. Noel Coward was by Shaw's yardstick a minor playwright, part of a declining era in the theater. Yet when Coward faced charges of violating government currency regulations early in the war, Shaw rushed to his defense. This time he saw himself on the side of a creative artist resisting government persecution. Out of the blue, Coward had a telegram from Ayot St. Lawrence urging him to stick to his guns.

Incidents like these, and Shaw's kindness to people in need, convinced Fanny that his grumpy manner was a pose. "You're like a hard-boiled egg with soft insides," she teased.

Shaw did not deny it. But he cautioned Fanny not to spread such tales. Evidently he feared he would be besieged by petitioners.

Shaw's letter about the "defaulting" author, written at the end of 1947, signaled a new phase in his relationship with Fanny. It referred to her as his legal adviser who would be representing him in America if he were not already committed to Benjamin Stern. And it closed with the reminder that he was now "so old," ninety-one, as to "forget everything in five minutes."

The allusion to his age reflected a growing concern with the disposition of his estate. For all his bluster — as Fanny put it, "He knew more law than any lawyer, and readily said so"— Shaw was not really well versed in the intricacies of international copyright.

His contact with Benjamin Stern was limited; Stern was himself advanced in years, ill, and three thousand miles away. Fanny, by contrast, came to England frequently on other business, and was an acknowledged authority on the protection of authors' interests.

It was tacitly understood on her side that she would never suggest supplanting Stern, who had been one of her benefactors early in her career; it was equally plain as far as Shaw was concerned that if Stern died before he did, he would switch his business to Holtzmann and Holtzmann.

Meanwhile, he did not hesitate to question Fanny about anything that came into his head — or to exercise his usual self-indulgence about dismissing her opinions on the spot. He regarded himself, according to Fanny, as "the world's greatest expert on everything. The result was that he felt free to seek advice, probing down to the most minute detail — and then equally free to disregard it. It was impossible to guide him. It was also very hard not to be hurt by him. His rudeness sometimes brought me to the brink of tears."

Shaw's arrogance, Fanny felt, stemmed in part from his experience with his London solicitor, a former public stenographer whom he was accustomed to treat as a browbeaten amanuensis. Together the pair had drafted a will, which Shaw wanted reviewed.

Fanny glanced at it and shook her head. "This isn't worth the paper it's written on."

"It's of some use, isn't it?"

"As bathroom stationery, perhaps — if the paper were softer!"

Most of their exchanges were similarly brief and caustic. Shaw would register some sort of complaint: "You said in your letter that I had only to delete the second paragraph —"

"No, I didn't. I said that under *our* copyright law, and American practice, renewal is necessary after twenty-eight years."

"Bosh! That doesn't make sense."

Somewhere around this point, Fanny's temper would go out the window. "Do you know that fifty percent of your work is not properly registered in the copyright office because you do it yourself? That people can go ahead and do your plays without seeking permission or paying royalties?"

"Ridiculous! No one would dare!"

"The man who's his own lawyer has a fool for a client."

Now is would be Shaw's turn to gag and bluster, challenging Fanny's professional qualifications in the most unflattering terms.

"You're wasting your voice, GBS. That's the American law."

"Then it's your job to see that it's changed!"

It was, as Fanny frequently reminded him, exactly like having an argument with Zaida —"until you came along, the most opinionated man on earth." That, she supposed, was why she put up with his niggling and his insults.

"Ha," grumbled Shaw, subsiding. "We're all alike. Father Christmas." But he came back for more: his books and plays had been plagued with overseas "pirating" problems since 1899.

After one uproarious quarrel in Shaw's drawing room, he asked Fanny where she had learned to scream like that.

"We were nine children, every one of them an archindividualist. My mother was a prima donna, too. At our table, if you didn't talk up you didn't get heard."

"You sound like an Irish family."

"We were the originals. Your people were just a lost tribe."

Shaw was a conundrum to Fanny; he fitted no familiar category. Confronted with gifted but disorganized creative personalities, she could resolve their confusions with maternal dispatch. Before a Cardozo or a Koo, a superintellect in the omniscient mold of her elder brother, she could slip without effort into girlish submissiveness.

But Shaw was neither strayed child nor robed seer; he pranced cockily through a world of his own, somewhere between Drury Lane and Downing Street.

Fanny was equally upsetting to Shaw: brainy as the bloodless heroines of his social comedies but, unlike them, violently emotional. "It takes me two days to recover from a visit by you," he complained once. "Don't come again for another year."

A head and a half are better than one.
G. B. S.

In George Bernard Shaw's cottage, 1950—one of the last pictures of him.
The erratic photographer was Blanche Patch

The following week he telephoned Blanche Patch in London: "Is Fanny still in town? Bring her down Saturday."

Fanny went, but declined to stay the night. "What makes you think I'd give up my warm suite in Claridge's for this? Listen — I like you in limited doses. I haven't recovered from my grandfather yet!"

"When will I see you again?"

"When you behave."

Sandwiched between these rows were moments of playful affection. In the spring of 1948 Shaw presented her with a snapshot inscribed "Fanny's First Fotograph of Bernard Shaw." A prize set of photographs taken together at Ayot St. Lawrence — Shaw in a series of ardent poses at the fireside with Fanny — never saw the light of day: Blanche Patch had forgotten the batteries for his Leica.

At one Saturday tea they were joined by a cousin of the playwright. After the lady left, Shaw remarked to Fanny: "She wants me to write to her — no doubt so that she can sell my letters and pick up a few bob."

"What a terrible thing to say! Why must you always take such a mercenary view?"

"I merely recognize reality. Everybody looks at me and thinks about how much can be got for my letters."

"Why do you write to *me*?"

"Because I want to enrich you." A quick, Puckish glance. "Shall I send you some love letters? They fetch a better price."

The closest he came was in the salutation "Fairest Fanny." It led into a letter that thanked her for some fountain pen refills, complained that American authors were inadequately protected, and ended on a characteristic note: "Why waste a dollar and a half on Air Mail when there is no hurry?"

In October of 1948 Shaw wrote her: "By all means send me a packet of kasha; I cannot get it here." Within weeks he was begging her to "for heaven's sake stop it; I have enough buckwheat to last my utmost lifetime." On a more somber note, he observed that it was "not worth coming to England to see the little that is left of me; but come if you will: I shall have the better of the exchange."

From that point forward, Shaw bickered less and listened more. Like a tidy housekeeper about to set out on a long journey, he wanted to leave his affairs in order. "Why should I wait for my executors and trustees to sell everything?" he demanded. "I shall attend my own liquidation." He turned over two hundred books and engravings from his Whitehall flat and the country house to Sotheby's for auction. And he began consulting Fanny with sober purpose.

In explaining this choice to a mutual friend, he invoked his longstanding feminist leanings: "I practice what I preach. Fanny Holtzmann has been special attorney to the Chinese, a civilized people who enjoyed their greatest prosperity under a woman emperor. They know whom to pick."

Quite unknown to Fanny, he sent a letter of instruction to Elizabeth Barber at the Society of Authors: "If you have any talk with Fanny Holtzmann you may treat her as *persona grata* to me. I must have a solicitor and agent in New York. My solicitor is Benjamin Stern; and everybody in America pretends to be my agent and to control all my performing rights there.

"Stern is old and will die presently. I have to consider whether I shall not in that case make Fanny double the parts of solicitor and agent.

"Be kind to her anyhow; for she has extraordinary talent as sculptress and painter, and may have to join the S. of A. in that capacity."

Two and a half weeks later, in January of 1949, Shaw sent a long letter to Fanny at Claridge's outlining his plans for disposal of his estate with the public trustee as his designated executor.

Having thus presumably settled the matter with crisp finality, Shaw promptly reopened it, by mail and later in person. In February he forwarded to Fanny in New York a synopsis of his first play, the 1892 *Widowers' Houses,* an antislum tract in theatrical form.

In March he ruminated by postcard: "The speculative element in authorship cannot be removed. A play may be either a flop or a fortune. A 20 years average is possible; but what about its incidence on Fanny's

First Play and Fanny's Fortieth? It would make the author benefit more and more for every play he wrote. This might be quite desirable, but it must be taken into account."

Meanwhile, he found time to conduct present sales: "Caesar and Cleopatra is on the market. But a revival cannot be settled by return of post. If [Richard] Aldrich has a proposal to make, let him make it. My shop is always open for business."

Soon afterward, theatrical interest in New York shifted to *Major Barbara*. Shaw was no less brisk on that score. The play was "useless without a big star like Hardwicke or Evans to play Undershaft, and a strong cast generally." Fanny should tell "all who think that contracts involving thousands of dollars and various artistic conditions can be settled at five minutes notice by cable, that I cannot negotiate with such silly people." And a week later, "Don't try to gammon me with your 'excellent cast.' If Gertrude wanted to play Ophelia, would you assure Shakespeare that the rest of the cast would be 'excellent'?"

Gertrude Lawrence figured in one of the few real battles between Fanny and Shaw. In the summer of 1949, while appearing in *September Tide* in the West End, Gertrude had been authorized by Shaw to do several scenes from *Pygmalion* over the BBC "in consideration of her knitting a pair of mittens for my personal use."

The playwright, whose hearing remained acute until his last days, monitored her broadcast himself and on July 21 wrote Gertrude a letter methodically tearing her performance apart. He attacked her reading of dialogue, her singing, and her diction, making unfavorable comparisons with Sarah Siddons, who had died well over a century earlier.

Fanny was outraged. On her next visit she confronted Shaw heatedly. How could he be so unfeeling, whatever his low opinion of modern performers? Besides, Gertrude was celebrated for the purity of her diction; like Noel Coward, she had studied with the great Italia Conti —

"Her elegant purity is just what I object to. Why couldn't she go and listen to some cockneys? Any competent actress can pick up their speech patterns."

"Listen to cockneys? Why, she was raised among them!"

"She took good care to cover *that* up. When she wasn't being American, she sounded like a duchess!"

Fanny dropped the argument. She had a feeling Gertrude would be secretly pleased to learn that she sounded to Shaw like a duchess.

The estate issue took an unexpected turn when Blanche Patch, after thirty years of loyal secretarial service, decided she would make the ninety-four-year-old widower a fine wife. After all, she pointed out to Fanny, Lloyd George had in 1943 taken as his bride Frances Louise Stevenson, who had spent an identical period with him in the same capacity. "I do everything for GBS that Charlotte ever did. Can't you get him to go through a marriage ceremony?"

Fanny hesitated. Fond as she was of Blanche, she knew that Shaw considered the lady of meager intellect.

Nonetheless, she made a friendly try. "You might want to think about fragmentizing your estate," she told Shaw. "With taxes so heavy, I hate to see so much going to escheat [the state]. Have you ever contemplated bringing Blanche into the picture?"

"Not for a moment," was the quick reply. "Blanche is a clergyman's daughter, perfectly suited to her job. I'll see that she is taken care of for the rest of her life."

With Shaw as with ordinary mortals, the process of drawing up a will evoked confidences normally reserved for psychiatrist or priest. Reflecting on his childless and apparently sexless marriage, entered upon when he was forty-two, he told Fanny: "Charlotte's supreme virtue was that she never intruded on me."

"Didn't you find that rather lonely?"

"A man who is creative is never really lonely."

He mused aloud about Nellie Harris, who had come to visit him after the war. He had expected to open the door to a pathetic creature in a shawl; instead he found a "yellow-haired, handsomely painted merry widow." Why, he wondered, had such a woman not remarried? Probably, Shaw thought, "because Frank Harris was such a miserable, self-centered husband; she would never risk another such disaster."

Shaw not only refused to be starry-eyed about marriage; he took the case a step further. What was the sense, he demanded of Fanny, in condemning homosexuals because they found comfort in other arrangements? "A gifted man like Oscar Wilde is entitled to his private life. Society has no right to persecute people for being different."

Even the well-worn topic of religion had its surprising turns. Shaw, atheist to the end (Fanny accused him of being "a practicing Christian who disavows Christianity"), scoffed at the idea of an anthropomorphic God with long flowing beard. He was willing, however, to entertain the likelihood of a Life Force, not necessarily confined to human beings, which was continually evolving toward higher forms.

"Reincarnation seems to me plausible," he told Fanny. "But if we come back, it is probably not in the same bodily manifestation."

Fanny could not pursue such metaphysical fancies without a smile. "I should hate," she offered flippantly, "to be a dog next time around."

"Why not?" She saw that he was serious. "Dogs are pampered. They often run their masters. Unlike a child, a dog isn't whipped by anybody unless he deserves it." He paused, then let out the words with unusual emphasis: "On the whole, more love is lavished on dogs than on humans."

Fanny felt uncomfortable, an accidental intruder onto Shaw's bleak boyhood in Dublin.

Meanwhile, she was moving steadily toward her own objective: to be appointed cotrustee of Shaw's estate and his literary trustee in America.

377

Shaw seemed quite content with the plan, which would not encroach on his commitment to Benjamin Stern; the only necessary alteration would be in his earlier arrangements with the public trustee.

After several trips to England by Fanny in 1949 and 1950, and much correspondence, work on a revised will for Shaw had reached the point of final phrasing. Her brother Jack was called in to review the language of the draft.

Then, with the papers virtually ready for signing, came one of the old flare-ups. While walking with Fanny in his garden on an April afternoon, Shaw observed that the postwar era was firmly under way; it was time for America to put behind it the "cynical farce" of the two-party system and "turn to Communism."

Fanny dissented. She would rather place her hopes in the people, she declared, than in an intellectual theory subject to fanatic interpretation; democracy, for all its shortcomings, held guarantees of individual freedom that should not be sacrificed to short-term advantage.

The debate mounted, and two volatile tempers with it. Suddenly Shaw banged his walking stick on the ground. "That's enough!" he cried. "I will not trust my life's labors to a woman whose politics are in the Dark Ages!" He stomped off toward the house.

Fanny took the next train back to London, crushed. She had very much wanted the crowning prestige of acting as Shaw's literary executor. And she dreaded the loss of face with her brother, who from the first had been doubtful of Shaw's intentions.

She saw GBS just once more, in the summer of 1950. His business affairs were not mentioned. No payment had ever been requested — or volunteered. The talk centered on conditions in the United States and the likelihood of Eisenhower's becoming president. Commented Shaw: "Of course he would only be a figurehead; others would make the decisions. You can put a child at the wheel of a car; with a chauffeur alongside, it will run."

On September 10, shortly after he entered his ninety-fifth year, Shaw fractured his hip while sawing logs in the garden, and a few weeks later succumbed to a kidney infection.

Left behind with Fanny were some pungent memories, a scattering of letters and photographs, and one weightier reminder of her nonagenarian friend: a volume of early folio editions, in facsimile reprint, of "Mr. William Shakespeare's Comedies, Histories and Tragedies."

For all of his ostentatious complaints about Shakespeare's political backwardness, Shaw loved and valued his "rival." The Shaw folio collection, enhanced by an extended commentary written across the blank opening pages, had been pressed upon Gertrude Lawrence by Blanche Patch during the auction of the Shaw library in 1948 as an ideal gift for Fanny. "The Master himself," Blanche told Gertrude, "wants Fanny to have it."

At a proper price, of course. Gertrude was glad to pay it, and to make

UNITED PRESS INTERNATIONAL

The twin sages in Fanny's life: GBS of Ayot St. Lawrence and Zaida of Rohatyn

Fanny a birthday gift of the plays. Thus, even from the grave, the sage would continue to dictate how he should be remembered: in association with the one writer he acknowledged as his peer.

As far as Fanny was concerned, it was a wasted effort. In her mind's eye, Shaw's partner had already been fixed for eternity, and his name was Zaida.

Chapter 16

*A*s THE TWENTIETH century rolled past its sixth decade, Fanny's achievements had created newspaper headlines from page one through the Entertainment section, Women's Features, Art, Books and International Affairs. It was only natural that the list should be rounded out with a fling at the comic strips.

"Popeye the Sailor Man" had been the subject of legal skirmishing ever since the death of his creator, Elzie Segar, in 1938. The muscular, spinach-gobbling sea dog and his friends had over the years spawned a flood of toys, clothing, novelty articles and books, as well as a hearty sixteen-bar chantey. Now his widow came to Fanny, who had aided her once before, to demand an accounting from Segar's publishers, the King Features Syndicate.

Behind the action was a wilderness of thorny legal issues. Did the Segar family, despite neglecting to renew the United States copyright in 1957 after twenty-eight years, still own the rights to Popeye? Had the cartoonist been a hired employee, as the syndicate insisted, or an independent contractor retaining subsidiary benefits? Who controlled the Popeye royalties in Great Britain, where millions had hung on the vicissitudes of his romance with Olive Oyl, and Wimpy the hamburger cadger was a household word?

Still farther back was the puzzle of the contract revision entered into by Segar on May 23, 1938, five months before his death, which astonishingly made no reference to his previously established ownership of all products based on his characters. According to Mrs. Segar, the contract had been signed at a time when the King Features representative — but not her husband — was aware of the terminal nature of his illness. The syndicate firmly denied this, and there was no documentation on the point.

Previous litigation had wound up in the appellate division of the New York State Supreme Court, where during the war Fanny had won a $90,000 judgment. The court had ruled that Mrs. Segar was entitled to continuing royalties on everything produced by her husband since the creation of Popeye in 1929. Now, in 1967, there was the issue of payments on the song "Popeye the Sailor Man," discontinued by King in 1964, as well as the dilemma posed by the expiration of the copyright in England, Canada and Australia.

As Fanny saw the situation, a protracted court battle would benefit nobody; the whole package might be thrown into the public domain. She urged a settlement. But the opposing attorneys demanded that Mrs. Segar be brought east from her California home for examination before trial. This neither Fanny nor the Segar family could countenance; the cartoonist's widow was in her seventies and infirm.

Fanny met with her adversaries to break the stalemate. What her client wanted, she knew, was not so much money as a sense of a grievance righted, of dignity restored. Suppose the syndicate were to make some goodwill gesture, some sign before the world that Elzie Segar was not forgotten?

The other side was willing. Fanny quietly dropped her lawsuit. Although formally emphasizing that there was no direct connection between the events, King Features instituted an annual Elzie Segar Award, to be administered by the National Cartoonists Society, for the best cartoon strip of the year.

With the gradual disappearance of Fanny's entertainment stars from the scene, her practice shifted during the 1960's toward the more stable if less spectacular spheres of estates, taxes and corporate structure.

Pleasant echoes of the Hollywood days came up constantly: encounters with Garbo at Fifty-seventh Street art galleries; with Fred Astaire in a Paramount Studio corridor ("We fell on each other's necks and wept"); in a Washington, D.C., lobby with former hoofer and former senator George Murphy, who reminded Fanny "how we actors used to sit in awe when you came into the commissary with L. B. Mayer, and wonder how we could get close to you!"

Less agreeable was a belated run-in with Darryl Zanuck. Fanny's friend General Sir Frederick Morgan, aging and in shaky health, had been approached by the producer for technical guidance on the Twentieth Century–Fox epic of the Normandy landings, *The Longest Day*. At a two-hour luncheon, Morgan patiently answered questions about "Overlord." A first draft of the screenplay was left with him; it was understood that revisions would follow. Nothing was said about payment, but Morgan assumed there would be some compensation for his time and trouble: "As you know, Fanny, between old-fashioned gentlemen such as Zanuck and myself, money is a dirty word!"

The general received and answered several letters requesting information, but no more scripts. And no checks. After a couple of months, he mentioned to Fanny that he thought he had been quietly "included out of the party."

Fanny telephoned Zanuck in Paris. He brushed aside any thought of payment. "We don't owe him a cent. I've got Morgan's release right here."

Fanny suggested a private screening for General Morgan. "Too busy," she was told.

Grudgingly, Zanuck offered a "gesture" that the ailing general was in no physical condition to accept: an invitation to the floodlit, hullabaloo-filled premiere of *The Longest Day* in London. Eisenhower's deputy, although listed as a "military consultant," never did see Zanuck's version of the Normandy landings.

Hedda Hopper, another of Fanny's nonfavorites, had acquired a newspaper column without benefit of newspaper training; her syndicated slingshots from Hollywood often skirted the border between reportage and fiction. On October 25, 1965, Hedda surpassed herself. Noting that the Youssoupoffs were protesting a CBS television drama about Rasputin, she recalled their much-publicized victory over MGM in 1934, and informed her readers around the country that attorney Fanny Holtzmann had "tipped the Prince off" on that occasion.

According to Hedda, Fanny had been in Hollywood for the Ina Claire–John Gilbert divorce while *Rasputin* was being filmed, and "asked if she might watch the shooting.

"Fascinated she was. She asked for a copy of the script, which they were delighted to give her. Then she contacted the Youssoupoffs and they all sat back and waited until the film was released before filing suit. It's the last time anybody at MGM ever gave a visiting lawyer the time of day."

This was a series of monstrous inaccuracies, and amounted to an accusation of barratry — the deliberate provocation of a legal action — a most serious charge against any lawyer.

But Hedda didn't stop there. She went on to assert that Fanny had tried to collect twice for her divorce services: "Incidentally, Ina told me Fanny sent Jack Gilbert a bill for the divorce after she had paid it."

Fanny was alerted to the story, which appeared in the New York *Daily News*, and understandably exploded. What she told the *News*'s managing editor was enough to send the paper's attorneys into a tailspin — accelerated when Ina Claire rejected the Hopper slur. Fanny's accounting with John Gilbert, Ina confirmed, had nothing to do with the divorce but was in connection with the settlement of his MGM contract.

The lawyers for the newspaper were very, very conciliatory. Fanny was not interested in a printed retraction: "That would only recirculate the canard!"

Would she consider a cash settlement?

In January of 1966 she was handed a check for $25,000 by the Chicago

Tribune–New York News Syndicate. Four days later Hedda Hopper, who had been discharged, died of a heart attack.

On the happier side was a rebirth of the old intimacy with Noel Coward. In the last years of his life, "Sir Noel" (he had been knighted in 1970) suddenly began showering Fanny with letters and photographs from London, his chalet in Montreux, and his hideaway in Port Maria, Jamaica. When he was granted a Doctor of Literature degree by Sussex University in the summer of 1972, Fanny received several photostatted newspaper accounts of the ceremony, proudly annotated in longhand and inscribed "For Fanny, with my love."

On December 16 — Coward's seventy-third birthday — she cabled him at Les Avants, Montreux: "Darling Noel happy birthdays for another five decades love to Graham and Colie fondly Fanny." He wrote back three days later:

Dearest Fanny,

Thank you for your dear and loving cable on my birthday. I had a very happy day. Christmas is upon us, the house is full and we are up to you know where in tinsel and holly. Thank you again, have a wonderfully happy 1973 and

my love as always,
Noel

In the winter of 1973, arrangements were in progress for Fanny and the present author to visit Coward at Blue Harbor in Jamaica when suddenly the invitation was withdrawn on grounds of health. Ten days later Coward was dead.

Panegyrics filled newspapers around the world. For Fanny, they were all summed up in a comment made to her twenty-five years earlier by George Bernard Shaw: "Your client Noel Coward will survive in history. With *Cavalcade* alone, he did more for Britain than all the generals at Waterloo."

An earlier death had struck closer to home. In 1965 Fanny's younger brother David unexpectedly succumbed to a heart attack. His passing was a jarring blow to Fanny, professionally no less than emotionally. The two had known clashes, but their storms were private and transitory; underneath they understood each other's rhythms and were a productive team. If it was Fanny whose magnetism attracted clients, it was David who with his tact and good humor had kept them. His tongue never strayed. As Eddie Goulding once remarked to his secretary, "In all my years of knowing David, I never heard him say an unkind word about anyone, never saw or heard of him doing anything out of line. I tried to find just a small hole in his armor. It was no soap. He had none."

Now suddenly Fanny was brotherless. Jack had died eighteen months before.

It was her sister Stella who leaped loyally into the breach. Despite the heavy demands of her "downtown" practice — at Jack's old Wall Street office, Stella was active in corporate finance, securities and Blue Sky Laws (state securities laws designed to protect investors) — she somehow made time to expand her duties at the Bar Building. There she not only continued her specialization in estate planning and the preparation of wills and trusts, but assumed the most important of David's responsibilities. Keenly aware of what losing David meant to Fanny, she was constantly on hand thereafter.

Fanny's bookshelves were crowded with autographed volumes and tributes, the most recent from Felix Frankfurter and Wellington Koo, but the sense of personal isolation would not go away. At a family Bar Mitzva celebration, she surveyed the quiet little house in the suburbs, one of thousands scattered along the route of the Long Island Railroad, with the inevitable swing in the garden and the Chagall prints on the living-room walls, and sighed: "This is what makes all the struggle worthwhile."

Groping for a new center of gravity, she entered a period of vacillating enthusiasms. Political leaders awakened her admiration one moment, her disgust the next, as events threw their behavior into different focus. But ultimately, as ever, Fanny sought solace in her family, reaching out to the children of her brothers and sisters. Sometimes in her anxious generosity she pressed too hard. Fundamentally indifferent to possessions, she might earmark a fur piece for one niece and then thrust it impulsively on another, with awkward consequences.

And yet her overflow of feeling was not damped. In her later years Fanny embraced friends, colleagues, even strangers in an increasing compulsion to do something useful, to justify the gift of life by lightening the burdens of others.

She had a special sensitivity to the tribulations of authors. When S. N. Behrman's autobiographical drama, *The Cold Wind and the Warm*, ran into hostile notices on Broadway, she was quick to register her praises, eliciting from the author a fervent "thank you and thank you again. . . . I know you are a tough critic and the fact that you could write me such a letter as this, believe me dear Fanny, makes up for a very great deal. I cherish it." A distant young cousin with writing ambitions found $300 in his mailbox, along with several letters of introduction ("You have absolutely changed the course of my life," he wrote, "although I have the feeling you are uncomfortable when confronted with expressions of gratitude").

And on lovers she could never turn her back. Agatha and "the Colonel" were a down-at-heel elderly couple in the neighborhood who had separately fallen from the heights to the joint refuge of a whiskey-soaked furnished room. Fanny, who knew Agatha's brother, kept them supplied with books, "resale" clothes — and an occasional ten-dollar bill for liquid refreshment.

Vincent L., a wealthy widower, wanted to marry a minxish chambermaid he had brought back to New York from his Paris hotel. But Juliette was the mother of a small boy who, under French law, could not join her in America without the permission of his father — and the father's identity was unknown; the lady had had many *petits amis*.

When the State Department said nothing could be done, Juliette tearfully packed her bags — and Vincent appealed to Fanny.

She flew with Juliette to Orly Airport, where the French representative for Paramount whisked Fanny to the police prefecture in Juliette's district. There Fanny ad-libbed a harrowing tale of an innocent waif (Juliette) being beset on her way home from church by a lascivious beast. Naturally, as Fanny explained it, the poor girl was too stunned afterward ever to identify the agent of her involuntary pregnancy.

It was a rousing adaptation of *Little Red Riding Hood*. The prefect, dabbing at his eyes, personally supervised the drafting of "emergency" papers that permitted six-year-old Philippe to depart for the United States with the two ladies that same night.

Fanny's reward came in a letter from the reunited couple two days later: "We're together, we're a family and we are so very happy. It all seems as if a Fairy Godmother waved her wand and it was done. So quickly, so cleanly and so magically. You are a wonderful person and we shall always be grateful."

Running parallel with and overshadowing all these services was Fanny's unswerving devotion, through twenty long years, to the medical innovations of Dr. Emanuel Revici.

It began in 1953, when Fanny arrived home from England to learn that her bustling little housekeeper, Jenkie, was desperately ill in St. Clare's Hospital. After copying Gertrude Lawrence's clothes, her walk and her accent, Jenkie had pursued her mimicry of the actress to its logical, ironic end, and had fallen victim to liver cancer.

Distraught, Fanny consulted Dr. John Staige Davis, who had been called in at the last stages of Gertrude's illness. Davis, then head of the arthritic clinic at St. Luke's Hospital, could not offer much consolation. It was a question of heavy sedation to ease the pain, and waiting . . .

Was there nowhere to turn, no hope from new approaches?

Davis shrugged. He had heard some talk of a refugee medical man from Rumania who was working with chemotherapy; but it was nothing he could recommend of his own knowledge, and besides he was not sure of the man's name.

Out on the street again, gloomily contemplating plans for Jenkie's funeral, Fanny saw a familiar figure approaching along Park Avenue.

She recognized the "battleship sway" of former Congressman Bruce Barton, who had recently lost his wife. Fanny offered her sympathies.

Barton shook his head. "The worst of it is, Fanny, she didn't have to die. She was making good progress before I took her up to Massachusetts. The skull tumor had disappeared. The man actually had her going to the opera —"

"What man?"

"That Rumanian doctor, Revici."

"Rumanian? Is he a refugee, with a new form of treatment?"

"That's the fellow. We were referred to him by Dr. Leonard Goldman of Queens General."

Jenkie was placed under Dr. Revici's care and transferred to St. Luke's Hospital. Her admission records described her as a terminal case with no prospects for recovery.

Three weeks later, as Fanny got off the hospital elevator she found Jenkie waiting on the landing. "I want to go home," the little housekeeper announced. "I feel fine."

Jenkie was out of bed the following month, and soon afterward resumed full-time duties at East Sixty-fourth Street. Nearly two years elapsed before, long since out of touch with Revici, she died.

Meantime, Fanny had become increasingly intrigued with Revici's work, and increasingly absorbed in his therapeutic program. The Rumanian was a controversial figure among his colleagues, sharply criticized in some quarters and praised with equal ardor in others. Over the next two decades Fanny would progress from admirer to defender to active proselytizer on his behalf, whipping up a fervor that ultimately threatened her law practice. But although everything Fanny did had emotional overtones, her dedication to Revici sprang initially from a hard-headed examination of his record and his results.

What Revici propounded was nothing less than, in the words of one of his disciples, "a whole new theory of medicine." His credentials were formidable. Trained in leading French institutions, he was an experienced medical practitioner, a highly skilled organic chemist, and an expert in theoretical physics, with six languages at his command and thirty-five years of work in clinical pathology under his belt, including laboratory experiments with hundreds of animals.

Early in his career, he had decided to focus not on the external factors causing disease — microbes, toxins, and so on — but on the role of the organism itself, what he called "the terrain." From his interlaced studies in biology, chemistry and physics he concluded that good health was characterized by a proper acid-alkaline balance within the body starting at the cellular level; and that this in turn depended on a dualistic seesaw between two opposing groups of fat-soluble substances called lipids. He offered a redefinition of lipids in terms of physics rather than chemistry, and the proposition that as a relatively separate system in the organism distinct from the water-soluble one, they held the key to the creation and machinery of life.

All disease, Revici theorized, manifested an "off-balance" in the delicate relationship between the two types of lipids; properly diagnosed, the discrepancy often could be corrected by administration of the required counteragent.

This apparently simple concept had enormously complex ramifications. It projected an Oriental-flavored dualism running throughout biology, thereby opening the door to a radical reordering of knowledge. If valid, it might have application not only to cancer but to a wide range of degenerative diseases. Over the horizon were possibilities in the fields of alcoholism and drug addiction.

Dr. Revici stressed in a talk at the New York Academy of Medicine that his method was "far from being a general panacea." Off-balances were not of equal importance in every case. And cancer treatment in particular required the most intensive and continuous individual supervision to determine what level of the organism was involved. What he was offering was an original approach, which could be used "in conjunction with other methods."

Although he cited numerous and remarkable instances of successful results, most listeners remained skeptical. Individual cases, it was argued, might be nothing more than spontaneous remission; his challengers demanded orthodox proofs of sustained testing. On the other hand, some powerful authorities rallied to Revici's support, including Dr. John Macalpine Galbraith, president of the Nassau County Medical Association, and the radiologist Dr. John J. Masterson, former president of the New York State Medical Society.

For Fanny, a fascinated layman on the sidelines, the Rumanian had earned at least a chance to expand his experiments.

In 1956, backers of Revici established a double-barreled facility for him on the upper East Side in New York City: a four-story Institute of Applied Biology on East Ninety-first Street for his research laboratories, and the Trafalgar Hospital, formerly Beth David, a block away. Beth David had been a private institution, and all efforts to acquire voluntary, nonprofit status for Trafalgar, so that Revici could treat city patients there, were fruitless. No such charter had been issued in twelve years. The situation was, in Revici's words, "not merely difficult but impossible."

Fanny charged to the rescue. She went up to Albany and spoke to the governor; Revici got his charter. Fanny's bill was the same as the sum the doctor took from his clinic patients: nothing.

She also arranged for the printing of Revici's eight-hundred-page book, *Research in Physiopathology as the Basis of Guided Chemotherapy.*

By the 1960's, Dr. Revici was gaining a modest foothold. The Society for the Promotion of International Scientific Relations awarded him a medal for his "scientific and humanitarian contributions," and his acceptance lecture at the New York Academy of Medicine was published by the American Foundation for Cancer Research.

At the end of 1962 a young physician, graduated *summa cum laude* from Harvard College and the Yale Medical School, fell victim to tumor of the brain. A craniotomy at Montefiore Hospital disclosed that the growth was too deep to be removed. Cobalt radiation produced no improvement; memory and other functions began to fail.

At twenty-nine, married and the father of two small children, Dr. F. was pronounced "in effect a dead man." With a prognosis of "a couple of months to live — if you're lucky," he was half led, half carried into Trafalgar Hospital.

Dr. Revici began tests and the lipid treatment, keeping the patient under virtual hour-by-hour check. Within two weeks there was a visible response. After four months, Dr. F. was out of bed.

In two years the last of his symptoms, a slight disability in hearing, vanished and he returned to his own practice. In 1966 an army medical examiner, unaware of Dr. F.'s history, classified him 1-A.

And there were many similar cases to buttress her enthusiasm. In 1963 Frank Scully fell victim to cancer of the bone marrow. West Coast doctors gave him a few weeks to live.

Fanny had him flown to Trafalgar Hospital on November 20. By New Year's Day he was protesting his confinement. He returned to California in a few weeks, and by spring his blood count was climbing to normal. He wrote to Fanny from Palm Springs: "My first letter in 14 weeks, and it goes to you with words so weak they hardly seem worth writing. But they are words of gratitude and love for the immeasurable devotion you have given to us and the unwavering faith you have shown in Dr. Revici. And in his case, at least, worthy of him.

"I ask God to treat all the Holtzmanns gently and little Fanny Claus most of all."

By now, Fanny was Revici's open advocate. Her partisanship, and even her very identification with the cancer issue, were not helpful either to her public image or her legal career.

She spread the Revici gospel to cancer victims among the famous, including Sir Laurence Olivier and John Foster Dulles; she dinned it into the ears of Noel Coward, who complained that he sought nothing but her legal services. Friends began tagging a request onto their dinner invitations: "Please don't talk about Dr. Revici!"

Being Fanny, of course she did talk. And she did more than that. Via the Gertrude Lawrence Foundation, she channeled substantial portions of her income into Revici's Institute for Applied Biology. She donated to Trafalgar Hospital a $15,000 portrait of Gertrude by Simon Elwes of the Royal Academy, and turned over to the institute the proceeds from sales of personal jewelry, rare books and antiques picked up on her travels.

In the early 1970's, Revici announced a significant breakthrough in the treatment of drug addicts. By the use of various sulfur, selenium, and ether-based preparations, he reported, more than twenty-four hundred addicts had been brought through withdrawal in his clinic without side effects.

Revici found a vigorous supporter in Dr. Daniel Casriel, a prominent New York psychiatrist and director of the Areba drug clinic. Casriel operated in tandem with Revici, and their results were portrayed late in 1972 on the Public Television program "The 51st State." Four ex-addicts, variously involved in the past with heroin, barbiturates and methadone, appeared on camera to testify that withdrawal à la Revici was practically painless and that they were now leading healthy lives.

The reporter-producer of the program, Ardie Ivie, made no specific endorsement of Revici's "Bionar" medication; but he did note that the Rumanian doctor had opened up a new line of inquiry, apparently the most fruitful developed to date. Ivie suggested that government agencies, instead of straining to detect technical infractions in the Revici operation, might do better to encourage the Institute for Applied Biology.

Fanny seized excitedly on this public recognition. She was working on plans to maximize its impact when she woke one morning to find herself plunged into the most crucial struggle of her life.

For almost as far back as Fanny could remember, illness had been something that happened to other people. Apart from the bad bout with measles at five, she had scarcely even seen a doctor professionally. Now, suddenly, she discovered that she was not immune.

The ailment that struck her was obscure but virulent, affecting the blood supply. Conventional medical procedures made no headway; her condition declined rapidly to critical. Fanny was rushed to Revici's Trafalgar Hospital, previously familiar to her mainly through its board room.

Ironically, Revici's passionate champion had become his helpless patient. At stake was Fanny's life and in a sense something more: the validity of her twenty years of dedication.

Revici launched a crash program of research in his laboratory. Somewhere among his vials and cultures, he assured Fanny, was the counteragent that would arrest her illness. And she believed him.

Serenely confident in his skill, Fanny carried on a brisk law practice from her hospital bed, oblivious to the surrounding nurses and medical paraphernalia. Clients had no idea where she was telephoning from, and she wasn't telling anyone. To family visitors, she quoted from Zaida's fund of amusing sickroom anecdotes; to herself, she repeated the old man's assurances that God was a "good bookkeeper."

Perhaps Zaida, sipping tea in some celestial kitchen, was listening. Maybe he was abetted by the prayers of Holtzmann supporters scattered from Brooklyn to Jerusalem, where the Israeli journalist Eliahu Amiqam made daily pilgrimages to the Western Wall.

In any event, Revici arrived one chilly dawn with a treatment he had developed in collaboration with a consultant from Mt. Sinai Hospital — and Fanny's ordeal was over. Her illness was brought completely under control. In two weeks she was home, flinging out ultimatums and proposals on everything from ecology to domestic relations: "Why not interlocutory *marriage* instead of interlocutory divorce? The states should legalize a one-year trial period of living together, with the option then of calling it off or making it permanent through a wedding ceremony. Marriage is the biggest gamble in the world. If the relationship between two people can survive the pressures of adjustment, that's time enough to formalize it."

Theoretically, Fanny was under a supervised regime of diet, rest and medication. But she was never cut out for armchair convalescence. She had the thick dark hair and flashing eye of a woman half her years — and an endless fascination with mankind.

In 1975 as in 1925 she continued to strike up impromptu conversations. "I never met a stranger" was her boast; and it was substantially true. She talked to very old people —"You learn a lot from them"— and strolled often to the nearby Central Park Zoo, not so much to see the animals as to enjoy the happy children. She could not pass a mother wheeling a baby carriage without stopping to pay her compliments to its occupant.

In moments of penitence, she turned up at Dr. Revici's institute, waiting in line with the rest of his patients. But she was, by the doctor's testimony, "a terrible patient." Moderation was not Fanny's forte. Enjoined to restrict her consumption of fruit, she seethed, balked and one day devoured half a watermelon. Told to conserve her energies, she painted all morning and then slipped downstairs to walk more than a mile to her office. Why?

"Because it was such a beautiful day."

Revici shook his head, clucked his tongue, warned Fanny that she was courting disaster — and marveled at her survival. Finally he came to accept the inescapable:

Fanny had no talent for sickness. Her talent was for life.

Acknowledgments

For PERSONAL RECOLLECTIONS of Fanny Holtzmann, I am indebted especially to her oldest and youngest sisters, Bertha and Rita Holtzmann (the late Mrs. Samuel Berkman, and the present Mrs. Arnold M. Schwartz); also to her girlhood friends Miss Sidney Ellender and the late Lucy Schneeberg, and to four former secretaries at the Bar Building office: Frances Davis Goldsmith, Lilian Birkan Cohen, Carol Tunberg, and the late Anita Gordon Newman. Valuable reminiscences were supplied as well by Mrs. Alice Scully, Anton Dolin, Gloria Swanson, Nettie King, Mrs. Samuel W. Halprin of Hadassah, former ambassador Robert D. Murphy, former New York State Attorney General Nathaniel L. Goldstein, and Kathleen McLaughlin, a staff correspondent for the New York *Times* in occupied Germany after World War II.

For factual documentation, I have drawn heavily upon the Theater Collection of the New York Public Library at Lincoln Center, where Maxwell Silverman has been a particular bulwark, and also received much help from Christine Bevan and Ann Allison at the British Information Service. Other useful public sources were the Information Branch of the New York Public Library, the United Nations History Library, the Public Affairs Office of the United States Army, and the Zionist Archives. Specialized information on events in the 1930's was provided by Robert Hertzberg of the New York *Daily News*; on the early history of Brooklyn, by Professor James F. Waters of the Local Historical Studies Institute at St. Francis College; and on the genealogy of the Russian royal family by Nikita Romanoff, grandnephew of Czar Nicholas II.

For permission and cooperation in the use of numerous letters to Miss Holtzmann from George Bernard Shaw, I am grateful to the Society of Authors in London, for and on behalf of the Bernard Shaw Estate, and also to Professor Dan H. Laurence of San Antonio, editor of the ongoing *Collected Letters of Bernard Shaw*. I thank Cole Lesley for similar privileges in connection with correspondence from Sir Noel Coward, and in the same vein, King Constantine II of Greece, nephew of King George II; Franklin D. Roosevelt, Jr.; Senator Adlai E. Stevenson III, Mrs. S. N. Behrman, Signe Toksvig Hackett, Lady Rosemary Hills, Lord Norwich, Rabbi Daniel Jeremy Silver, Donald J. Hall, Caruthers Ewing, Jr., and Mrs. Ellen Gelb, daughter of the late Louis Bromfield.

Among those who kindly authorized use of their own letters were Dr. V. R. Wellington Koo, Sir John Foster, Sir Berkeley Ormerod and James Laver.

Finally, I make bows of appreciation to Robin Straus for her editorial assistance, to Hal Lehrman for structural suggestions, and to Mrs. Edith Sobel, Fanny's friend and aide, who is the current guardian of the files in the Bar Building, for greatly facilitating my researches there.

Index

George, Prince of England. *See* Kent, Duke of

George I, King of Greece, 164

George II, King of Greece, 163–169, 231–233, 249

Gershwin, George, 351

Gershwin, Ira, 221, 351

Gest, Morris, 228

Giannini, Amadeo P., 324

Giannini, Attilio H. ("Doc"), 67, 95, 109, 195, 324

Gilbert, John, 6, 8, 9, 79, 83, 90, 96–100, 383

Gish, Dorothy, 45

Gish, Lillian, 45, 52–53, 59

Gluck, Alma, 36

Goebbels, Joseph Paul, 263

Goetz, Ben, 250, 338, 366

Golden, John, 235

Goldfeld, Angela, 184–186, 201–202

Goldfeld, Estelle, 184–186, 189

Goldfeld, Frimme Holtzmann ("Tante") (FH's aunt), 184–186, 188, 189, 201–202, 204–205

Goldfeld, Rabbi Mikhail, 184–185, 188, 204–205

Goldfeld, Moshe, 184–189, 257, 284–285

Goldfeld, Regina ("Rivka") (Mrs. Moshe), 185–186, 188–189, 257, 285

Goldfish, Sam. *See* Goldwyn, Samuel

Goldman, Dr. Leonard B., 387

Goldman, Nahum, 258, 279

Goldstein, Jonah, 235

Goldstein, Nathaniel L., 68–69

Goldwyn, Samuel, 6, 60, 87–88, 118, 337–338

Goldwyn, Mrs. Samuel. *See* Howard, Frances

Goodman, Benny, 171

Gordon, Anita, 109, 123–124

Gordon, Max, 67–68

Gordon-Howley, Pamela, 219

Göring, Hermann, 208

Gorney, Jay, 128

Gorney, Sondra (Mrs. Jay), 128

Gould, Beatrice, 350

Gould, Bruce, 350

Gould, Edwin, 211–213

Goulding, Edmund, 40–53, 55–65, 67–68, 72–73, 82–86, 89–91, 94–95, 100–103, 108, 114, 128, 165, 172, 196, 207, 218, 227, 232, 236, 256, 277, 286, 319, 333, 335–339, 384

Goulding, Lydia (Mrs. Paul Granby), 165

Graham, Sheilah, 176, 363

Grant, Cary, 91, 208, 211

Grant, Jane, 179

Greco, El, 295, 306, 355

Green, John W., 233

Green, Lorne, 116

Green, William, 224–225

Greene, Felix, 196

Gromyko, Andrei, 248, 280

Gropius, Walter, 204

Grosvenor, Lady, 213

Guggenheim, Harry Frank, 211

Guggenheim, Meyer, 7

Gwenn, Edmund, 209, 339

Gwyn, Nell, 5, 168

Hackett, Francis, 130, 132–134, 174–175, 179, 192

Hackett, Mrs. Francis, 133, 175, 179

Haile Selassie, Emperor of Ethiopia, 307

Halifax, Edward F. L. Wood, 1st Earl of, 207

Hall, Sir Edward Marshall, 71, 73, 147

Hall, J. C., 295, 297, 304–305, 355

Halperin, Leopold, 188

Halprin, Rose, 279–280

Hammerstein, Dorothy (Mrs. Oscar, II), 341, 343

Hammerstein, Oscar, II, 341–345

Hanworth, Ernest M. Pollock, 1st Viscount, 351

Hardwicke, Sir Cedric, 5, 91, 208, 376

Harriman, Margaret Case, 171

Harriman, W. Averell, 44

Harris, Frank, 358–359, 362, 377

Harris, Jed, 299

Harris, Nellie (Mrs. Frank), 358, 359, 361–362, 377

Harris, Sam, 194–195, 221

Harrison, Rex, 341

Hart, Moss, 195, 219–222, 232, 368

Hastings, Sir Patrick, 73–74, 147–148, 151–153, 155–156, 158

Hawkett, Mittie, 165, 167

Hawkins, George, 130, 132

Hayes, Helen, 60

Hayes, Irene, 42

Hayward, Leland, 120

Hearst, William Randolph, 40–41, 87–88, 98, 196, 243, 324, 369

Hecht, Ben, 128, 269

Heine, Heinrich, 11

Hemingway, Ernest, 136, 222, 294

Henderson, Archibald, 368

Henri, Robert, 303

Henry VIII, King of England, 5, 132–134, 179

Hergesheimer, Joseph, 45, 48, 50

Herzl, Theodor, 15

Hildegarde, 297

Hilton, James, 90

Hiss, Alger, 242, 245–246, 250

Hitchcock, Alfred, 211

Hitler, Adolf, 146, 173, 176, 179, 190, 191, 192, 194, 195, 197, 198, 199, 202, 206, 225, 226, 227, 228, 242, 259, 260, 268, 270, 282, 351, 352, 353

Hochman, Joseph, 33, 35–39, 40, 41, 46, 50–52, 57, 58, 61, 78, 300

Morgan, Sir Frederick Edgworth, 259–271, 285–287, 314–315, 318–319, 330, 382–383
Morgan, John Pierpont, 20
Morgenthau, Elinor (Mrs. Henry, Jr.), 283
Morris, Newbold, 234–235, 332
Morris, William, 341
Morros, Boris, 355
Moses, Anna Mary ("Grandma"), 291, 294
Moskowitz, Joseph H., 339, 341
Mosley, Sir Oswald, 353
Moss, Marjorie, 128, 172
Mowbray, Alan, 209
Murphy, George, 382
Murphy, Robert D., 198–199
Murray, Mae, 40, 43–44, 51–52, 60, 72
Murray, Philip, 224–225
Murrow, Edward R., 329
Myers, Anna (Mrs. Israel), 84
Myers, Rabbi Israel, 84

Nally, Edward J., 193
Nasser, Gamal Abdel, 328
Nathan, George Jean, 228, 292
Navarro, Ramon, 96
Nicholas II, Czar of Russia, 4–5, 137–141, 143, 149–150, 152, 164, 170, 241, 363
Nichols, Dudley, 176
Nichols, Louis B., 224
Nijinsky, Vaslav Fomich, 129
Niles, David, 190–192, 199
Niven, David, 338–339
Norr, Roy, 236
Northcliffe, Lord Alfred C. W. (Viscount Harmsworth), 8, 43
Novello, Ivor, 52, 123, 172, 362

Oberon, Merle, 211
O'Casey, Sean, 175
O'Connor, Basil ("Doc"), 251
O'Dwyer, William, 235–236, 255–256
O'Grady, Ellen, 33
Oliver, Vic, 206
Olivier, Sir Laurence, 212, 250, 297–298, 389
O'Neil, Sally, 83
Ormerod, Cyril Berkeley, 273–275
Ostermeyer, Professor, 17
Ottinger, Albert, 68

Paley, William S., 236
Pandit, Mme. Vijaya, 277
Paravicini, Nicholas, 215
Paravicini, Vincent Rudolph, 215
Parker, Dorothy, 44, 53, 131, 213
Parsons, Louella, 42, 87–88, 92, 96
Pascal, Ernest, 114
Pascal, Gabriel, 364–366
Patch, Blanche, 359–360, 362–364, 374–378
Patterson, Paul C., 247
Pavlova, Anna, 129
Payne, Graham, 298–301
Peavey, Simon F., Jr., 146–147

Pegler, Westbrook, 196
Perkins, George W., 29
Picasso, Pablo, 294
Pickford, Mary, 8, 17, 38, 72, 211, 228
Picon, Molly, 299
Pissarro, Camille, 310
Plotz, Dr. Harry, 317
Polk, Frank L., 123
Pollock, Ernest M. See Hanworth, Viscount
Poole, Sir Reginald, 144, 148
Porter, Cole, 195, 218–219, 343
Potter, E. N., IV ("Peter"), 121, 122
Potter, Eliphalet Nott ("Bo"), 120
Potter, Phyllis Livingston (Mrs. Fred Astaire), 120–123, 213
Power, Tyrone, 61, 337
Purishkevich, Vladimir, 153–155

Raizman, Ella, 185
Raizman, Isaac, 185
Rapf, Harry, 58, 83
Rasputin, Grigori Efimovich, 5, 135–137, 140–144, 148–151, 157, 336; film on, 10, 16, 142–144, 151–153, 155, 180, 189, 232, 249, 358, 363, 383; court case resulting from film, 151–160
Rathbone, Basil, 208
Reinhardt, Max, 227–230
Rennie, Michael, 339
Revici, Dr. Emanuel, 387–391
Ribbentrop, Joachim von, 76, 191
Rickett, F. W., 259
Riis, Jacob, 12–13
Rilke, Rainer Maria, 295
Rivera, Diego, 294
Robbins, Albert H. ("Bob"), 320
Robeson, Paul, 307
Rockefeller, John D., 238
Rockefeller, John D., Jr., 255–256
Rodgers, Dr. Mortimer, 342, 344
Rodgers, Richard, 341–345
Rogers, Ginger, 119, 123, 339
Romilly, Constancia, 353–354
Romilly, Esmond, 353–354
Romilly, Nellie, 353–354
Roosevelt, Curtis ("Buzzy" Roosevelt Dall), 254
Roosevelt, Eleanor (Mrs. Franklin Delano), 190, 196, 248, 251–254, 265, 283
Roosevelt, Franklin Delano, 190–192, 197, 237, 240, 251–254, 259, 269, 271
Roosevelt, James, 197
Roosevelt, Theodore, 12–14, 17–19, 23, 28–30, 72, 225
Roosevelt, Theodore, Jr., 193
Root, Elihu, 19
Rose, Billy, 129, 344
Rosen, Edward, 236, 255
Rosen, Dr. Samuel, 342
Rosenman, Samuel, 190, 192
Ross, Harold, 179
Rosten, Leo, 22n